God and History

The Dialectical Tension of Faith and History in Modern Thought

Laurence W. Wood

EMETH PRESS
www.emethpress.com

God and History, The Dialectical Tension of Faith and History in Modern Thought

Library of Congress Cataloging-in-Publication Data

God and history : the dialectical tension of faith and history in modern thought / Laurence W. Wood
        p. cm.
Includes bibliographical references (p.   ) index.
ISBN 0-9755435-4-7 (alk. paper)
1. Jesus Christ --Historicity. 2. God (Christianity). 3. History --Philosophy
BT303.2 .W66 2005
232.9/08 22
                                                    2004093651

CONTENTS

Acknowledgements

This work is a revised and updated version of my Ph. D. dissertation that was completed at Edinburgh University (Scotland) under the supervision of Professor John McIntyre. It was a honor to have studied under him and to have learned from his scholarly wisdom and his writings. My indebtedness to Professor Wolfhart Pannenberg will also be obvious throughout this work. His writings very early in my theological training helped to shape my understanding of the relation of faith and history.

The ideas in this work are often challenging to first year seminary students who come from a variety of academic backgrounds., and I would like to thank them for their helpful suggestions in my attempt to make this material more student-friendly. Special thanks go to David Brubaker, Beverly McFadden, Bethann Ayers, and David Treloar for their assistance.

Introduction

The relation of faith and history is the central issue in theology. This is why it is often said that nothing should be claimed for theology that is not also history.[1] Since the early apologists in the second century, Christian theology largely assumed the events of biblical history were to be taken at face-value. With the rise of the modern historical consciousness, theology could no longer be naïve about what counts as history. The greater challenge of history to faith however was not the application of historical criticism to the Bible, but the fact-value dichotomy that was imported into it. This dichotomy entailed a separation between the detection of facts on the one hand, and the meaning of those facts on the other hand, as if one could exist without the other. The result was that modern theology assumed a divorce between God and history and between the real Jesus of history as a man and the meaning of the Christ of faith as a symbol of humanity well-pleasing to God.

The importing of dualistic thinking into historical criticism was derived from modern philosophy, which made a radical distinction between mind and body and was variously expressed as a dualism between thought and being, necessary truths of reason and accidental truths of history, reality and appearance, and faith and history. This modern radical duality posed these critical questions—how can the historically-conditioned events in the life of Jesus serve as the point of departure for a faith that claims to have universal significance? How can the uncertain results of historical criticism guarantee the certainty of faith? Is this dialectic of faith and history reconcilable? These questions are referred to as the problem of faith and history.

Since the rise of modern thought, theology incorporated historical criticism as an integral part of its method. One of the early modern radical theologians who employed historical criticism in doing theology was David F. Strauss (1808-1874). He assumed that the rise of historical criticism meant that Christian faith was robbed of a reliable historical foundation. His theory of the origin of Christianity was developed in his groundbreaking book, *The Life of Jesus Critically Examined* (1835), and he explained away the miracles of the Gospels as a series of myths. Although his work aroused fierce opposition, causing him to be denied his teaching post at the University of Tübingen, it exerted a powerful influence on 19th-century biblical criticism.[2] As a result of his critical assessment that orthodox belief cannot be supported in the light of the rise of the modern historical consciousness, he suggested four options for the Christian minister. (1) He can try the impossible feat of persuading the church to see its historical claim is untenable. (2) He can appear to hold to the historical view of revelation though in reality he does not. (3) He can leave the pulpit and become a professor. (4) He can ignore the historical claims of Christian faith and simply expound their spiritual significance.[3] This fourth alternative with its dualistic split between the events of history and a spiritualizing interpretation became a common practice in modern theology.

Julius Wellhausen (1844-1918) was one of the influential developers of modern biblical criticism. He formulated what is known as the J E D P theory, identifying the Jahwist, Elohim, Deuteronomist, and Priestley traditions as the four main sources for the writing of the Pentateuch. In the process of critically identifying the literary sources of the biblical writings, he could see only an unbridgeable gap being created between Christian faith and historical studies. He felt the full impact what historical criticism could have for Christian faith. It was for this reason that he resigned from the theological faculty of Heidelberg in 1882, and then transferred to Halle as professor of Semitic languages.[4] He explained his resignation in a letter, saying that he had become a theologian because he was only interested in the scientific study of the Bible, but then he realized that he also had the responsibility of preparing theological students for ministry in the Lutheran Church. In spite of his caution, he admitted that his practice of historical criticism was subverting their confidence in the Scriptures and undermining their capacity to be a minister.[5] Wellhausen's retreat from theology was thus based on the notion that critical thought and faith were incompatible.

Ernst Troeltsch (1865-1923) systematically formulated the classical problem of faith and history.[6] He was professor of theology at Heidelberg for 21 years, and he later moved to Berlin where he was a professor of philosophy of religion for 15 years. His influence upon modern theology has been substantial. Troeltsch outlined three basic principles of modern historiography. First, there is the principle of criticism, which means the historian critically assesses all events of the past on the basis of sound scholarly judgment. Second, there is the principle of analogy, which means one evaluates the possibilities of the past on the analogy of what is consistent with one's own experience today. Third, there is the principle of correlation, which means that the historian sees how events are related to each other in terms of their causal connections. This third principle assumes the principle of relativity or contingency. This means that there are no gaps in history. Every event is the product of previous causal events, and there is thus no reason to believe in an absolutely unique event as the incarnation of God in Jesus of Nazareth.[7]

Troeltsch incorporated these three principles in his essay, *The Significance of the Historicity of Jesus for Faith,* in which he suggested that historical criticism had brought about the "conclusive dissolution"[8] of the traditional historical picture of Jesus. He believed that historical criticism made it impossible to speak of any temporal event as having universal significance. In a succinct and precise way, Troeltsch outlined the problem of faith and history:

> Christianity is not at all merely the production of Jesus, for Plato and the Stoics and immeasurably popular religious forces of the world of classical antiquity have had a part in it. So then the conclusion, which the Christian lay person calls the eternal, absolute center of salvation for the entire duration of humankind, appears to be impossible. One cannot say this with genuine certainty, but it is not probable. The age of humankind on the earth comes to several hundred thousand years or more. Its future may come still to more hundreds of thousands of years. It is difficult to bring out a single point of history within this long time, and specifically to think of a direct middle point of our individual religious history as the exclusive center of all humankind. It seems much too severe to absolutize our accidental individual surroundings.[9]

Troeltsch posed the following question in the very beginning of his essay: "Is it possible, then, to speak at all of an inner, substantial meaning of Jesus for faith?"[10] His answer was that the orthodox faith of the Church cannot be reconciled with historical criticism because the two views of reality are hopelessly split.

This book traces the rise of the modern historical consciousness and explores its theological implications for faith, although it does not intend to be a detailed historical account of how the modern idea of history developed. Part One highlights the emergence of historical consciousness with the Hebrews and the rise of critical thought with the Greeks.

It also explains the attempt of the Early Church Fathers to synthesize the history of salvation with the categories of Greek philosophy. Part Two shows how the fact-value dualism of modern epistemology shaped the modern historical-critical method. If the Early Church Fathers employed the Greek principle of criticism in order to synthesize faith and history, modern thought radicalized the method of criticism by driving a wedge between appearance and reality, making it virtually impossible to preserve the unity of historical fact and interpretation. Part Three shows how modern theology responded to the challenge of critical history by developing an extreme dualism of revelation and history. Modern theology developed rational criteria that replaced and seized the role of revelation, or as an over- reaction, some theologians asserted revelation alone as the method of theology and rejected the relevance of historical criticism. By modern theology, I am not referring to the post-modern trends in contemporary theology, which I will discuss in a subsequent volume. Broadly speaking, I consider classical liberal theology, along with neo-orthodox and existentialist theologies, as representative of modern theology.

This book assumes that the rise of modern criticism is not in itself antithetical to the Trinitarian faith of the Church, but this assumption entails a rejection of the epistemological split between fact and value in modern historical criticism. If theological method is the means by which doctrine is formulated, then epistemology is a more fundamental examination of the presuppositions that serve as the grounds of knowledge. Modern thought insisted that all theological beliefs, scientific notions, and historical accounts must be determined through the method of critical thought. This book maintains that the modern critical method was not critical enough because it failed to question its own epistemological presuppositions, especially its dualistic way of thinking. The fact-value dichotomy that was imported into historical criticism is the Achilles heel of modern thought.

Part Four proposes an alternative to the dualistic thinking of modern thought. Utilizing the constructive theology of Wolfhart Pannenberg, Jesus' teaching on the coming kingdom of God will be seen as offering a fundamental insight on the unity of appearance and reality in terms of the present arrival of the eschatological goal of history. It will also be argued that the Trinitarian faith of the Church is compatible with historical criticism.

A final comment. This book was written for beginning seminary students many of whom have had little exposure to critical thought in religious studies. I have tried to make these issues accessible to students without oversimplifying the material. Because so many thinkers are included within this book, I have offered a brief resume of the more significant ones as they are discussed in order for the student to see the immediate context out of which they worked.

Notes

1. Carl Michalson, *Worldly Theology* (New York: Charles Scribner's Sons, 1967), 2, 217ff.

2. Cf. Laurence W. Wood, *A Study of David Friedrich Strauss on The Problem of Faith and History*. Unpublished Masters of Theology dissertation, Christian Theological Seminary, 1969.

3. David F. Strauss, *The Life of Jesus Critically Examined*, fourth edition, trans. George Eliot (London: Swan Sonnenschein and Company, 1906), 782-784.

4. Alfred Jepsen, "The Scientific Study of the Old Testament," *Essays on Old Testament Interpretation*, ed. Claus Westermann, trans. John Bright (London: SCM Ltd., 1963), 246-247.

5. Ibid., 247.

6. Cf. Friedrich Gogarten, *Demythologizing and History*, trans. Neville H. Smith (London: SCM Press Ltd., 1955), 18-19, who says that theology must begin with Troeltsch's analysis of critical history. Cf. also Carl Michalson, *Worldly Theology*, 2, 217ff.

7. Ernst Troeltsch, "Historische und dogmatische Methode in der Theologie," *Gesammelte Schriften* (Tübingen: J. C. B. Mohr, 1913), 2:731-738; Troeltsch, "Historiography," *Encyclopedia of Religion and Ethics*, ed. James Hastings (1914), 6:718.

8. Troeltsch, *Die Bedeutung der Geschichtlichkeit Jesu für den Glauben* (Tubingen: J.C.B. Mohr, 1911), 1.

9. Ibid., 15. Translation mine.

10. Ibid., 1-2. Translation mine.

Part One

The Ancient and Pre-Modern
World Background

The rise of the modern historical consciousness cannot be truly appreciated without some awareness of the ideas and movements that lie in the ancient and pre-modern background. Part One will offer background to some of the significant developments that took place in the ancient and pre-modern world in order to highlight predisposing factors that led to the rise of the historical consciousness of the modern world.

Part One begins with the emergence of historical consciousness in the experience of the Hebrews and with the development of critical thought in Greek philosophy. The subject-object distinction, which is basic to all thinking, was an essential element in this development. By subject-object distinction I mean the fundamental difference between spirit and nature, which was fused and confused in the mythical literature of the Ancient Near East. Part One explores the earliest development of this subject–object distinction, showing how the idea of the self-revelation of God to the Hebrews opened up a new understanding of reality as history. This historical consciousness was joined with the critical thinking of Greek philosophy in the Patristic period, producing a synthesis of salvation history and rational clarity.

Part One concludes with an examination of the emergence of critical history in ancient Greece with Herodotus, noting its compatibility and difference from the Hebrew understanding. In particular, the substantialism of classical Greek philosophy is inherently anti-historical, and it will be noted that Christian theology was able to break out of this substantialism with its relational and historical understanding of reality.

1

The Emergence of
Historical Consciousness and
Critical Thinking

The human capacity to distinguish between oneself as knowing *subject* and nature as the *object* of what-is-known led to the historical consciousness of the Hebrews and to the critical thinking of the Greeks. This chapter examines this *subject-object distinction* that first took shape in embryonic form in the Hebrew religion (beginning with Abraham, ca. 2000–1500 B.C.) and was made explicit in the rise of Greek philosophy in the 7th century B. C. As Hegel pointed out in his *History of Philosophy*, it is this subject-object distinction that has been the primary theme in the history of thought.[1] More recently, Richard J. Bernstein has shown that the dichotomy of subjectivism and objectivism has led to "the primary cultural conflicts of contemporary life."[2]

In a classical work on speculative thought in Mesopotamia and Egypt, four Near Eastern scholars (Henri Frankfort, Mrs. H. A. Frankfort, John A. Wilson, and Thorkild Jacobsen) have demonstrated that this subject-object distinction was absent in the mythical thought of ancient peoples. They further pointed out the necessity of a critical awareness of this subject-object distinction before philosophy and science could emerge. A summary of their findings will show that this subject-object distinction first began with the historical consciousness of the Hebrews and was made explicit in Greek philosophy.

Mythical Thinking in The Ancient Near East

Myth and reality were often fused together in the literature of the Ancient Near East, the cradle of civilization. The written records that have survived are largely ensconced in imagination. Natural phenomena were imagined to be an extension of human experience, and human experience was considered to be cosmic in proportion because the distinction between *physical nature* and the *human spirit* was not explicit. If we perceive the natural world as largely an "it," the ancient world perceived the phenomena of nature as a personal "you." The subject-object distinction that emerged in the history of Israel with Abraham and also in the history of philosophy beginning with Thales and the Ionian philosophers at the end the 7th Century B. C. was foreign to the mythical thinking of the ancient world. Rather, human beings were considered part of society, and society was embedded in physical nature. The idea of an inanimate world was completely foreign to them. Primal people considered everything alive and endowed with individuality, including humans, beasts, plants, the thunderclap, or a stone. [3]

Because of their animistic way of imagining reality, the ancient world told myths and were unable to appreciate the uniqueness of human existence over against physical nature, between thought and being, between subject and object. For example, their mythical mindset conceived of the creation of the world as a birth. All forms of life were generated out of a primeval couple who were the parents of everything that existed. "It seems that for the Egyptians, as for the Greeks and the Maoris, Earth and Sky were the primeval pair."[4] The gods were personified as natural powers and humanity was personified as depending upon its ability to maintain harmony with the gods and nature. This bond between the gods, nature, and humanity was mythically expressed in their many rituals. In Babylon, the New Year's Festival that celebrated the renewal of the generative forces of nature was the high point of their year. In all of the Mesopotamian cities celebrations interrupted the daily routines of the people several times each month as the moon completed one of its phases or other changes occurred in other natural phenomena. The people in Mesopotamia worshiped the Great Mother because her fertility was responsible for the produce on the earth, and the earth was seen as the complement (=spouse) of heaven, Anu. The Frankfurts further show that this same feeling of involvement in nature was expressed in festivals at Thebes, Memphis, and other Egyptian cities as celebrations were held to mark the rise of the Nile, the end of the inundation, or the completion of harvest.[5] This inseparable unity of everything (monism) is represented in the literature of the Ancient Near East from the middle of the fourth millennia until the middle of the first millennia B.C. An internationally known Oxford professor and historian, R. G. Collingwood (1889-1943), noted in his classic work, *The Idea of History*, that the ancient Sumerians showed no signs of a historical consciousness because of their animistic view of nature. He observed that it is difficult for modern people to understand how anyone could lack a sense of history.[6]

Nature-Spirit Distinction in Hebrew Thought

Henri and H. A. Frankfort show how two radically new developments came on the scene in the Ancient Near East and in the West that broke with this comprehensive monism. One was the Hebrew religion and the other was the rise of Greek philosophy. First, the Old Testament brought about "the emancipation of thought from myth"[7] because the Hebrews understood the difference between God as Creator and God's creation. The idea of God's transcendence over nature led to an understanding of the difference between the human spirit and physical nature, between subject and object, between thought and being.

Henri and H. A. Frankfort noted the sharp contrast between the worldview of the Old Testament expressed in Psalm 19, "the heavens declare the glory of God; and the firmament shows his handiwork," and the beliefs of the Egyptians and Babylonians. For the Mesopotomians, the heavens were identified with the gods, with Anu being the highest ruler. For the Egyptians, the heavens were identified with the divine mother who gave birth to humanity. For the Egyptians and the Mesopotomians, the gods were immanent in nature. For the psalmist, God is one who made nature and transcended it. The God of the psalmists and prophets also transcended the realm of mythopoeic ways of thinking.[8] The psalmist says: "I lift up my eyes to the hills. From whence does my help come? My help comes from the Lord, who made heaven and earth?" (Psalm 121:1). Here the psalmist "mocks" the views of their polytheistic neighbors who looked up to the hills for their help because they believed the gods were in the hills. The Hebrews looked up to God who made the hills. God is transcendent, not immanent in nature. The Hebrews did not conceive of God in mythical imagery because God transcended nature.

In mythopoeic thought, individuals were part of society, and society was embedded in nature, with nature being the manifestation of the divine. This monistic worldview was universally accepted in the ancient world with "the single exception of the Hebrews."[9] The Hebrews came late on the scene into a land that was permeated with the culture of two countries far superior to them. It would have been customary for these latecomers to borrow the way of thinking from these prestigious cultures. But that did not happen. The Hebrews were not prone to assimilate the cultural attitudes of other nations. Rather with a remarkable degree of stubbornness the Hebrews maintained a view of God's transcendence. From all the available evidence, the Hebrews' concept of the divine was original with them. The consequence was that the Hebrews came to understand the difference between the human spirit (subject) and physical nature (object) because they came to understand they had been made in the image of God who created the world. They perceived themselves to be in relationship with this God who transcended nature. They stood before God in an "I-Thou" relationship, and their relationship to nature was in terms of an "I-it."

The Frankfurts show that this subject-object distinction is fundamental to their way of thinking, and it arose out of their experiences in history. The Hebrew God was one God—infinite and yet a personal reality. This God was known as the God of Abraham, Isaac, and Jacob. He was the God of the Exodus who was revealed through "many signs and wonders." He was the God of the Conquest who brought the Israelites into "a land that flowed with milk and honey." The land of Palestine was a "holy land" because it was the "abode of Jahweh" (Exodus 15:17) and everyone who lived within its boundaries was required to be holy because a proper relationship with this one God must be maintained. When the Israelites compromised their relationship to God by worshiping the nature deities of their neighbors, God sent prophets to warn them. When they resisted the message of the prophets, their God sent them into captivity as a lesson that what they believed about God should shape their relationship with Him accordingly and give them sense of their personal identity. God's self- revelation to the Israelites was a heavy responsibility placed upon them to be faithful to their calling, but it also brought a sense of freedom liberating them from the bondage of fear to the gods of nature whose tyrannical, vindictive powers controlled everything.

The God of Israel was revealed as the Lord of history who entered into relationship with them. It was this relationship that constituted their true identity as a people. God was thus first and foremost a God of love who wills to know everyone, and by knowing God they achieve a sense of their own true humanness and identity as persons (Genesis 12:2; Hosea 1:9-11). God's purpose in electing Israel was not simply for their own sakes, but for the sake of the whole world (Galatians 3:8).

This self-revealing God confronts the Hebrews in a personal manner. God is revealed as radically different from creation, and all human beings have a personal value that transcends the world of nature. The world is finite; God is infinite. Human beings are a composite of the finite and the infinite, sharing in both the world of nature and in a spiritual likeness of God. To confuse God as the infinite *subject* with finite *objects* in the world was blasphemy (Exodus 20:4-5). God's cosmological transcendence explains why the "Old Testament is remarkably poor in mythology of the type we have encountered in Egypt and Mesopotamia."[10] Instead of the mythopoeic way of thinking with its fusion of nature and spirit, the Hebrews experienced the world in terms of the meaningfulness of historical events. This understanding of history depended on the recognition of the radical difference between God and the world and a corresponding distinction between physical nature and the human spirit, although nature and spirit formed a composite unit in individuals.[11]

Though the early Greeks wrote history for its social value, deriving inspiration from the examples of their ancestors, they did not understand history as a basis for their faith in God.[12] Hence "no Greek ever heard his gods ordering him to 'remember'" the past as a decisive moment of revelation, as Arnaldo Momigliano put it.[13] The understanding of reality as history is thus unique to the biblical revelation of God.

While the ancient Oriental world recognized the importance of historical events and even developed a historiography, they could not find any eternal meaning in history because it was constantly changing. People in the ancient world believed that ultimate meaning could be experienced through participation in non-temporal divine events, which were reported in myths. Only Israel understood the centrality of history for experiencing true and ultimate meaning in the world. Not in a timeless realm of myth, but in the changing events of world history did Israel come to learn about the reality of God.[14]

Significantly enough, the Hebrews' experience of reality as history was a prominent factor in the emergence of the modern notion of personhood. It is generally recognized that the story of Abraham's encounter with God as a transcendent reality was the first step toward understanding the uniqueness of human life.[15] Gerhard von Rad has also pointed out that the biblical God is revealed in history as personal and is the original source of the concept of person. "Here alone, in his encounter with God, does mankind become great and interesting, breaking through the enigma of his humanity to discover all the inherent potentialities of his self-conscious existence."[16] The late neo-Marxist Czech philosopher, Vitézslav Gardavsky, has also argued that the Old Testament revelation of God to Abraham as a self-conscious, transcendent being who stands outside of nature is the original source for the emergence of the concept of person in the modern world.[17]

The concept of God as a personal reality over against nature and as standing over against individual human beings led to the idea of an "I-Thou" relationship with God, an "I-thou" relationship with other individuals, and an "I-It" relationship with physical nature. These implicit distinctions were the epistemological presuppositions for the Hebrew understanding of history. God was revealed to Abraham as the Lord of history who called him to leave his native home in the land of Ur of the Chaldees and migrate to a new country. Abraham's pilgrimage with his family to the land of Canaan was marked with further personal disclosures of the being of God in the events of their history, thus showing God to be the Lord of history. What became evident to the Hebrews was that the fundamental nature of reality is history, and history means the engagement of persons in relationship to one another ("I-thou") and with God ("I-Thou").[18]

This implicit subject-object distinction was also significant in terms of the development of modern science. It led to the view that there is an "order of nature" distinct from God who created it, as A. N. Whitehead has pointed out. Until physical nature had been stripped of the divine attributes ascribed to it in a polytheistic culture and had been thus downgraded to an "order of things" governed by contingency, the possibility of experimental science was virtually impossible.[19]

The Emergence of Critical Thinking in Greek Philosophy

A further stage in transcending the mythical worldview of the Ancient Near East came with Greek philosophy in the 7th century B. C. when the Ionian philosophers (the Ionic coast is now part of Turkey) began to ask critical questions about the nature of reality as they experienced it. Prior to the rise of philosophical thought, the ancient Greeks borrowed from the Oriental mythical worldview with its monistic view of reality;[20] but beginning with Thales (ca. 624-547 B.C.), an engineer and statesman instead of a priest, there was a decisive turn away from nature religions to find a philosophical explanation of why things were the way they are. His concern was not with spiritual matters, but with a general understanding about the basic elements of nature. The issue for these Ionian philosophers was the question, what is the stuff that reality is made of? Thales believed it was "water"; Anaximander (611 BC - 546 B.C.) believed that is was "the Boundless"; Anaximenes (6th Century B. C.) believed it was "air"; Heraclitus (c 544-483 B.C.) believed that it was "fire."

These philosophical reflections led to the later theory of materialism developed by Democritus—that atoms constitute the basic element of everything. Democritus interpreted these earliest philosophers as "scientists" because they seemed to equate reality with the physical world. The Frankfurts, however, point out that this overlooks the real achievement of these quasi-materialist philosophers—making "the distinction between the objective and the subjective. And only on the basis of this distinction is scientific thought possible."[21] Likewise A. N. Whitehead has noted that the critical rationality of Greek philosophy was also a decisive factor in the emergence of modern science, along with the Hebrew concept of Yahweh who created the world.[22]

An intellectual explanation for what is real earned these early Greek thinkers the right to be called the first philosophers ("lovers of wisdom"). The Frankfurts noted: "This change is breath-taking. It transfers the problems of man in nature from the realm of faith and poetic intuition to the intellectual sphere."[23]

The Socratic Method

The greatest of the early Greek philosophers were of course Socrates (470?-399), Plato (429-347 B.C.), and Aristotle (384-322 B. C.). Socrates imagined himself to be like a "gadfly" because he considered his calling in life to irritate people with disturbing questions even as a gadfly provokes horses with its annoying stings.[24] He spent his life as a wandering philosopher ("lover of wisdom"), engaging leaders in Athenian society with questions about the meaning of life. He acknowledged he did not have answers, but he believed through a dialogical method of conversing with others in probing the meaning of words used in ordinary discourse that a critical understanding of human life could be reasonably determined. He did not please most people with his haggling over the dialectical meaning of words, but this did not deter him from his belief that "the unexamined life is not worth living."[25] His critical questioning of ideas and the meaning of words marked a new phase in the history of philosophy, and came to be known as the Socratic method.

Socrates in particular criticized the quasi-materialism of the earliest philosophers because they failed to see beyond the material (sensuous) world to the spiritual (supersensuous) world. That is, they failed to appreciate the basic *subject-object distinction* between the intellectual and the bodily dimensions.[26] This radical contrast between the intellectual and the physical was linked to his distinction between a supersensible world of Forms (or Ideas) and the fleeting world of sense-perception. The supersensuous world is independent of the physical world, although it serves as a model of truth and is the basis of reality for the changing world of sense experience. To put it simplistically, Socrates (as reported and interpreted by Plato) believed that ideas such as temperance, courage, wisdom, and justice suggested that there was a supersensuous world beyond the world of physical nature. Ideas are not mere ideas, but they are the real things, while the physical world of actual things are less than real. For example, we talk about "a person of wisdom," but wisdom has an existence of its own independent of a person. Ultimate reality was thus assumed to be a world of ideas independent of the physical world.

A knowledge of the supersensuous world of Forms is achieved through a rational recollection of what one knew before one was born into this world, a theory based on his idea of reincarnation. The soul was an entity in itself and had its origin in the realm of eternal Forms before it was incarcerated in a physical body. To rely on sense-perception leads to confused opinions about the nature of reality and hinders the release of one's soul at death into the realm of the gods and heroes who conquered the desires of the sensuous world.

However, Socrates was not a traditionalist in his religious views. He also criticized the irrational behavior of the gods contained in the writings of Homer and Hesiod.[27] His critics accused of him being an "atheist"[28] because he rejected traditional nature religion. Though Socrates was a devoutly religious man, he developed a full-blown dualistic worldview as if physical nature and the human intellect were totally different realities. Socrates and Plato of course did not have a view of God's transcendence over nature, but the early Christian apologists believed that they came as close as possible without the benefit of special revelation to a right view of God, serving as a kind of preparatory stage to Christian faith.[29]

Socrates Identified the Soul (Subject) with Reason

If the first decisive step toward the concept of *personhood* emerged out of the Old Testament *history of salvation*, then a second decisive step came from the philosophy of Socrates. As Platonic scholar, A. E. Taylor, has shown, no previous thinker had ever defined the human "soul" as "rational." Rather the concept of the soul (as, for example, in the ancient Pythagorians) assumed that the soul was the vital aspect of life, but it was not linked as such to the concept of reason.[30] Of course Socrates never wrote down his philosophy, but his student, Plato (428-348 B. C.), recorded the oral tradition of his teacher and presented Socrates as the formal spokesman for his point of view. Plato was thus the *first writer* to define a human being as a thinking, rational, intelligent soul whose personal existence survived beyond the death of the body.[31] Plato was the first writer to make an explicit philosophical distinction between the material world and the immaterial "world beyond."[32]

For Socrates and Plato, the decisive characteristic of human life was the rational soul as distinct from the physical body. The purpose of the Platonic *Dialogues* was to cultivate the soul and prepare it for life after death. Plato maintained that human life is distinct from physical nature because human beings possess critical intelligence and can make themselves an object of their own reflections. This capacity for *self*-consciousness is different from simple consciousness. An animal is conscious of its external environment, but is it really aware of this awareness? An animal has brain power, but does it think? Thinking is the reasoning ability to construct ideas and to understand their larger implications. Thinking leads to verbal communication and makes possible community, civilization, and religion. There has been considerable debate about the ability of animals to think and have self-consciousness in recent literature,[33] but the capacity to think in a human way is surely unique. Human beings are conscious of their environment, but they are also *conscious of their consciousness* of their environment and hence are *self*-conscious. As a subject, one can make oneself an object to oneself and to think impartially about oneself. One is able through thinking to transcend the past and present, anticipate the future, and to organize all of one's knowledge around what is called the "self." Without the self-transcending quality of human life, one would be immersed in the relativities of nature and would be governed solely by instinct and thus would not be a free self. To possess intelligence (as distinct from mere brain power) is to be free to choose one's course of actions and to understand its possible implications. The greater the degree of intelligence the greater is one's degree of freedom and moral accountability. *Self*-awareness and *self*-reflection mean the *self* is morally responsible for its own behavior because one knows right from wrong. The human capacity for freedom thus indicates one lives one's life on a higher level than physical instinct.

The human capacity for self-reflection led Socrates to posit the concept of the immortality of the soul, which he believed was imprisoned in a body. He assumed a radical dualism of the body and soul as opposed to the Hebrew understanding of the psychophysical unity of human life. After Socrates, the notion that human beings are more than their bodies and possess an independent soul came to be redefined in a semi-Greek way in Judaism and in Christian theology.[34] Although the Jewish idea of the resurrection developed only gradually out of its own history, a corollary idea of disembodied souls arose in Judaism through reflecting on the status of persons existing between death and resurrection. A modified Greek idea of the soul thus offered Judaism a way to explain this belief without falling into a body/soul dualism.[35]

The idea of an innate, rational, immortal soul as opposed to an evil body has had enormous influence throughout the history of Western thought, but it was fundamentally contrary to the Hebrew belief in the goodness of creation and the unity of human life. Having said this, the Hebrews understood God to be an intelligent being without a physical body. So it is not unreasonable to assume that a mind or rational soul could exist without a body, at least in the case of God. It is also not necessarily unbiblical to believe that a particular view of immortality of the soul and resurrection of the body can be connected. The Pharisees in Jesus' day believed there was an intermediate state between death and resurrection, and the dead preserved their sense of personal identity in a disembodied state like the angels until their bodies were raised at some future time.[36] This shows that the Platonic notion was not the only way to define immortality.[37]

The biblical source for belief in the resurrection is Daniel 12:2-3, which affirmed embodied existence, not the concept of a ghost.[38] This idea of resurrection reaches back into the writings of Isaiah and Hosea, and it is based on the belief in God as Creator.[39] To be sure, the use of the term, immortality, in the New Testament lacks the Greek notion of a soul existing as an independent entity that permanently survives the body. As a term, immortality simply means unending life, and resurrection is a type of immortality, as seen in 1 Cor. 15:53, where immortality entails the notion of embodied existence.[40] Other New Testament references (2 Cor. 5:8; Phil.1:23) assume the widely-held Jewish idea of an intermediate state between death and the resurrection of the body. The body sleeps during this intermediate state, but the soul enjoys the conscious presence of Christ.[41]

The Platonic idea of rational soul figured prominently in the writings of the early Christian Apologists like Justin Martyr who believed that the seeds of the Logos were found in those who "lived with reason" before the coming of Christ. Such people were considered Christians in a qualified sense before Christ had come to be the incarnate Logos, and now that Christ had come in the history of salvation he incorporated the entire divine Logos within himself as the Father's intelligence or rational thought.[42]

Aristotle's Concept of God as Self-Knowing Mind

Plato's pupil was Aristotle who extended and modified the philosophy of Plato. In his *Metaphysics,* Aristotle defines God as a self-knowing mind which is unmoved by anything since God is the Prime Mover of everything that exists.[43] This does not mean that Aristotle thought of God as cosmologically transcendent in the sense of God creating the world *ex nihilo*. Rather God is like the outer realm of a group of concentric circles that make up reality. God thus exists at the top of things and is totally self-sufficient. God is without the slightest awareness of anything else that is below, and this means God is merely self-aware. To know what is below would be a deficiency because it would involve God being conditioned by something else. In other words, God would no longer be an Unmoved Mover, for God's knowledge would be indebted to other lesser beings.

God's rationality is the capacity to be absolutely independent and totally self-conscious without any awareness of lesser beings, all of which are dependent upon God as the Prime Mover. And the philosopher is likewise one who rises above the limitations of the world through one's own self-knowing mind and enjoys the contemplation of the divine mind. Hence, for Aristotle, the defining characteristic of human life is one's capacity for rational comprehension of one's true self in relation to divine truth.[44]

Some Differences between Plato and Aristotle

A difference emerged between Plato and Aristotle, however, over the link between one's mind and one's bodily existence. Whereas Plato was a thoroughgoing dualist, Aristotle insisted on their essential connectedness, although he allowed for a distinction between them. Instead of the soul existing in a supersensuous world of Forms, it was a composite unity. The body is the matter of the soul, and the soul is the form of the body. Without the body there is no soul, according to Aristotle. Hence Aristotle did not allow for the immortality of the soul.

Etienne Gilson, who was director of studies of the Pontifical Institute of Medieval Studies in Toronto before his death in 1978, pointed out another difference between Plato and Aristotle. Plato allowed for the existence of the gods side by side with philosophical principles and he made no attempt to relate them. However, with Aristotle, the divine realm was converted into a realm of metaphysical principles (or eternal substances), which in effect disallowed the personality of the gods. To be sure, Greek philosophy after Aristotle continued to speak of the gods, but as Gilson pointed out, "the rationalized gods of the philosophers no longer had any religious function to perform."[45] In this respect, abstract metaphysical principles were deified. Gilson observed: "With Aristotle, the Greeks had gained an indisputably rational theology, but they had lost their religion" because there were no longer any gods to be worshiped. That is, divine worship was transformed into the intellectual contemplation of abstract divine principles.

The Contrasting Views of the Hebrews and the Greeks

Aristotle's philosophy had a powerful influence on the development of Christian theology as his categories were used to give theological precision to biblical teaching. However, there is a striking contrast between Greek philosophy and the Hebrew experience of reality as history. Etienne Gilson noted that while the Greek philosophers were trying to figure out a place for their gods, the Hebrews had already found a solution, not through the imagination of its poets nor through the discoveries of its thinkers, but through the self-revelation of God in the events of their history. [46] Their God had been first revealed to Abraham as One who had called him to leave his homeland and go to a place where God would lead him. It was to be a holy place because God lived there in a unique sense. In this place, God would bestow upon Abraham and his descendents a personal identity through a special relationship that they would enjoy with God. That promise led to a long and difficult journey in their quest to be a holy people and well-pleasing to God. Their circumstances often presented them with what seemed insurmountable obstacles, but in the midst of their severest trial as slaves in Egypt, God was revealed as their deliverer from oppression. In this context of their history, God's *personal* name was revealed to Moses in a burning bush—traditionally translated as "I Am Who I Am" (Exodus 3:14).[47]

Gilson further pointed out that the fundamental difference between Greek\Roman philosophy and Christian faith is that the ultimate principle is not simply "that which is" but "He Who Is." In this respect, "He Who Is" is also "that which is," since "somebody" is also "something," but the reverse is not necessarily true. For "something" is not necessarily "somebody." Gilson points out that this is the dividing line between philosophy and Christian theology.[48] In the strict sense of the term,

Christian faith is not philosophy, but it is history because God is "somebody" who is revealed and is not a mere principle. The self-revelation of God made known in the history of Israel, culminating in the history of Jesus, represents a significant contrast from Greek philosophy.

Further, not only is this ultimate reality a personal God, but God is the Creator of the world. The idea of a divine creator is something that was foreign to the Greek mind. In the *Timaeus,* Plato spoke of the creator of the world as a demiurge whose task was to shape the world into some semblance of order and truth, but otherwise the Greeks assumed that the world was eternal. The distinctive implication of the Hebrew understanding of God is that God created the world out of nothing (*ex nihilo).* God was not a dimurge who shaped previously existing matter, but rather God transcends everything in nature as its Creator.[49] Hence God transcends the world and exists independently of the world, although God created the world and its existence depends upon God. This idea of God who created the world out of sheer nothing underlies the Hebrew understanding of reality as history as opposed to the mythical thinking of the ancient world in which no distinction was made between the divine and the world. This idea of "creation out of nothing" has its sole origin in Hebrew thinking. No other religion ever came up with this idea of God as Creator *ex nihilo* because only the biblical religion arrived at this idea through its belief in the God of history.

Notes

1. Hegel, *Science of Logic,* trans. W. H. Johnston and L. G. Struthers, with an introductory preface by Vicount Haldane (London: George Allen and Unwin Ltd., 1929), 1:59-60, 65; Hegel, *History of Philosophy,* trans. T. M. Knox and A. V. Miller (Oxford: Clarendon Press, 1985), 3:409, 545.

2. Richard J. Bernstein, *Beyond Objectivism and Relativism: Science, Hermeneutics, and Praxis* (Oxford, England: Basic Blackwell, 1983), xiv.

3. Henri Frankfort, Mrs. H. A. Frankfort, John A. Wilson, and Thorkild Jacobsen, *Before Philosophy* (Baltimore, MD: Penguin Books, 1964), 14.

4. Ibid., 17.

5. Ibid., 238.

6. R. G. Collingwood, *The Idea of History* (New York: Oxford University Press, 1976), 12.

7. Ibid., 237.

8. Frankfort, *Before Philosophy,* 139.

9. Ibid., 241.

10. Ibid., 244.

11. Pannenberg notes that the basis of the historical consciousness of Israel

was due to its view of God as transcendent. "Redemptive Event and History," *Basic Questions in Theology* (London: SCM Press, 1970), 1:18.

12. Arnaldo Momigliano, "Time in Ancient Historiography," *History and the Concept of Time* (Middletown, CT: Wesleyan University Press, 1966), 19-20.

13. Ibid.

14. Pannenberg, "Redemptive Event and History, *Basic Questions in Theology,* 1:16-17.

15. Erich Fromm, *The Art of Loving* (New York: Harper, 1963), 53-63.

16. Gerhard von Rad, *The Problem of the Hexateuch,* trans. E. Dickens (New York: McGraw Hill, 1966), 153.

17. Vitezslav Gardavsky, *God is Not Yet Dead,* trans. Vivenne Menkes (Baltimore: Penguin, 1973), 28. He wrote: "Not merely the Book of Genesis but the Old Testament as a whole contains something which is exceedingly important for the whole of European thought in particular: this is the first appearance of the idea of transcendence, of a step beyond all that has so far been achieved–although it is revealed here in a pre-scientific and mythological form, it is nonetheless perfectly clear; the dream of a personal identity in the midst of Time begins to show itself here for the first time" (ibid., 28). Cf. W. Pannenberg, *What is Man?* Trans Duane A. Priebe (Philadelphia: Fortress Press, 1970), 11-13, 90, 137-149; Pannenberg, *Anthopology in Theological Perspective,* trans. Matthew J. O'Connell (Philadelphia: Westminster, 1985), 45, 487, 525. Reinhold Niebuhr offered a careful and thorough discussion of the biblical concept of personal individuality and concluded: "Thus only Christianity (and Judaism . . .) sees and establishes the human spirit in its total depth and uniqueness," *The Nature and Destiny of Man* (New York: Charles Scribner's Sons), 1:58

18. Cf. Martin Buber, *I and Thou,* trans. Ronald Gregor Smith (Edinburgh : T. & T. Clark, 1937).

19. A. N. Whitehead, *Science and the Modern World* (New York: The Macmillan Company, 1954), 5., 18-19.

20. *Before Philosophy,* 248.

21. Ibid., 252.

22. A. N. Whitehead, *Science and the Modern World,* 18-19.

23. Ibid., 251.

24. *Apology* 30e.

25. *Apology* 38a.

26. *Phaedo* 96-98.

27. *Republic,* 2:377d; *Euthrphro,* 6, 8.

28. *Apology* 24-29.

29. J. N. D. Kelly, *Early Christian Doctrines,* Second Edition. (New York: Harper & Row, Publishers, 1960) 84, 96; Collingwood, *The Idea of History,* 50-51.

30. A. E. Taylor, *Socrates* (New York: Doubleday, 1953), 13ff.

31. *Timaeus* 30b.

32. *Republic* X.614b,c.

33. There has been a considerable tightening of the link between the mind and brain in recent neurophysiology, and yet at the same time there has been a growing consensus that there is also an important distinction between them. In the 1960's, Roger Sperry of the California Institute of Technology and his associates, Ronald Myers, Michael Gazzaniga, Jerre Levy, Joseph Bogen, and Phillip Vogel, reported history-making neurological research. Their work suggested that the hemispheres of the brain perform distinct functions of consciousness. These research reports came from tests done with patients who had their corpus callosum severed (commissurotomy) because they were suffering from intractable epilepsy. The results of these studies have reinstated the importance of consciousness as a valid concept. Cf. Michael S. Gazzaniga, "The Split Brain in Man," *The Nature of Human Consciousness,* ed. Robert E. Ornstein (San Francisco: W. H. Freeman and Company, 1973), 87-100; Roger Sperry, "Some Effects of Disconnecting the Central Hemispheres," *Science* 217:24 (September, 1982), p1223-1226; Sally Springer and George Deutsch, *Left Brain, Right Brain,* revised edition (New York: W. H. Freeman and Co., 1985). Malcolm Jeeves, a neuroscientist of St. Andrews University (Scotland) and a member of the Church of England, warns against making too much of this new appreciation of consciousness. Although he thinks it is helpful that this new research restores the distinction between consciousness (mind) and brain, he believes it would be unwise to assume a dualism between mind and brain, as if the mind could exist independently of the body. He emphasizes the psychophysical unity of personhood. Cf. *Mind Fields, Reflections on the Science of Mind and Brain* (Grand Rapids, MI: Baker Books. 1993), 105ff. An important question that has emerged in the tightening of the link between the mind and brain in recent neuroscience is whether or not animals have consciousness. Surely they do have consciousness in the sense that they are aware of their surroundings, but are they aware of their awareness of the outside world? That is, do they have *self*-consciousness? Are they aware of a self? Perhaps this is a question that cannot be answered, but at least human self-awareness involves the awareness that one is responsible for one's actions and hence humans are moral beings. Further, human self-awareness entails a sense of self-transcendence in the sense that we know that we are more than mere physical beings and thus we possess the capacity for spiritual reality. In a conference held at Asbury Theological Seminary during the Fall Semester of 2002 on "Body and Mind," Jeeves suggested that terms such as monism and dualism are not helpful. He proposed the phrase, "duality without dualism," as perhaps an alternative way of describing the relation of mind and brain. Cf. Laurence W. Wood, "Recent Brain Research and the Mind-Body Dilemma," *The Best in Theology,* ed. James I. Packer and Paul Fromer (Carol Stream, Illinois: Christianity Today, Inc, 1987), 2:199-239..

34. Cf. N. T. Wright, *The Resurrection of the Son of God* (Minneapolis: Fortress Press, 2003), 142; Reinhold Niebuhr, *The Nature and Destiny of Man,* 1:54ff

35. Ibid., 174-175.

36. Ibid., 133.

37. Ibid., 162-175.

38. Ibid., 130.

39. N. T.Wright argues that it is very doubtful that Daniel borrowed this concept from Zoroastrianism. For one thing scholars do not know for sure what constituted the beliefs of ancient Zoroastrianism. Wright writes: "There is no evidence of Persian motifs in such crucial Jewish passages as Daniel 12 and *1 Enoch* 22." Ibid., 125.

40. Ibid., 164.

41. Ibid., 216.

42. Kelly, *Early Christian Doctrines*, 96.

43. Cf. W. T. Jones, *The Classical Mind* (New York: Harcourt, Brace, & World, Inc., 1969) for a concise discussion on Aristotle's theological views. Cf. also Frederick Copleston, *A History of Philosophy, Greece and Rome* (Garden City, NJ: Doubleday, 1962): 1.2.57ff.

44. Cf. Etienne Gilson, *God and Philosophy* (New Haven: Yale University Press, 1941), 33.

45. Ibid., 35

46. Ibid., 39-40.

47. Contemporary exegesis translates this as "I shall be whom I shall be." The emphasis is upon the idea that God's identity is determined by a freedom to act in the future. The name JHWH is thus not to be interpreted as if God is a timeless and abstract being.

48. Ibid., 42.

49. Gerhard May, *Creatio Ex Nihilo, The Doctrine of "Creation out of Nothing" in Early Christian Thought* (T. T. Clark, 1994) is a definitive study on this topic. He argues that there was no reflection on the creation process until the second century (ibid., 1ff.). May writes: "The statements on the creation of the world which we still possess from the time before Justin Martyr by authors who are not declared gnostics, only serve to make it clear that the question of the origin of the cosmos had not yet become a problem" (ibid. 35). Much like the Trinitarian and Christological doctrines which were not systematically formulated until the 3rd and 4th centuries, so other doctrines as well, including *creatio ex nihilo*, were only developed later as Christianity was forced to defend itself against "heresies" and it necessarily employed philosophical categories to clarify what it believed. Earlier Biblical scholars like Philo do not take a position on the eternity of matter, because that was not an issue they reflected on theologically. May shows that for Philo the idea of preexistent matter was "nothing more than a conventional thought-form" and carried no suggestion that matter "is an ontologically equal principle alongside God" (ibid., 15). Likewise, Clement of Alexandria emphatically asserted the will of God alone is the ground of creation (ibid., 178), and his view was close to Irenaeus (ibid., 178). Justin Martyr also emphasized that sin is the product of human choice alone, not matter. May explains: "What the New Testament statements about the creation intend is quite legitimately interchangeable with the idea of *creatio ex nihilo*" (ibid. 26).

Origen also affirmed *creatio ex nihilo* (ibid., 178). *Creatio ex nihilo* first became an issue with the Gnostics who argued that matter had a beginning and was not made by God but by demiurgical powers. Hence the Gnostic explanation for the origin of evil. The first and second century Gnostics were philosophically more educated and hence their views were first developed along the lines of their gnostic beliefs, but this occasioned the need for the "orthodox" theologians in the 3rd century to challenge and refute gnosticism, arguing that the Gnostics had falsified the biblical view of *creatio ex nihilo*. May shows that with Ireneaus the doctrine of *creatio ex nihilo* took on a settled and fixed position for subsequent orthodox thinking about creation. His view of creation was linked to his view of salvation history, that the purpose of creation out of nothing was the framework for the history of salvation (ibid., 176). Since the time the doctrine of *creatio ex nihilo* was formally developed and affirmed by Ireneaus. As May puts it, "as early as the beginning of the third century [*creatio ex nihilo*] is regarded as a fundamental tenet of Christian theology" (ibid., 179). May argues that *creatio ex nihilo* was only making explicit what was assumed in earlier Jewish and Christian authors for whom the implications of the doctrine of creation had not yet become an issue. Here is what May says about Origen: "Origen, who made the first great attempt to expound systematically the Christian doctrine of creation and to show that it was reasonable and meaningful even from Platonist presuppositions, makes it clear that he cannot understand how so many eminent men had been of the opinion that matter was unoriginate and not created by God. For him, *creatio ex nihilo* is a necessary fundamental proposition, without which the idea of providence is impossible" (ibid., 178).

2

Stoicism and Neo-Platonism: The Fusion of Subject and Object

Stoicism and neo-Platonism were two philosophies that exerted great influence upon the development of Christian theology. One of their primary goals was to explain how "the one and the many" could be synthesized into a unity. Both movements posed a serious challenge to Christianity because of their intellectual and non-mythical way of interpreting reality. Christianity ultimately won out over both of them because of its understanding of reality as history. Stoicism and neo-Platonism merged the subject-object distinction into a pantheistic monism. On the other hand, Christian theology held this distinction in dialectical tension, which enabled it to affirm the real difference between God and the world while preserving their inseparable relationship.

The Monism of Stoicism

The most influential philosophy after Plato and Aristotle was Stoicism. It originated with Zeno of Citium (ca. 300 B.C.) and was a carefully constructed system of thought integrating logic, metaphysics, and ethics.[1] It vigorously opposed the Platonic notion of a supersensuous, invisible realm of Ideas as existing independently of physical nature. Whatever existed must be bodily and the universe as a whole was material. It distinguished between passive and active principles. The passive principle is unformed matter that has no quality or value in itself. The active principle is linked to reason, or logos, which pervades everything and organized a plan (logos) for the unformed, passive aspects of reality. This active principle is called "spirit," and it was described as a fiery mist. Stoicism was a pantheistic materialism. God is conceived of as the active principle, or Mind, but God is nonetheless materialistic. God inheres in reality as consciousness inheres in the body. God, the Soul of the universe, Nature, and Divine Providence are used interchangeably.

If the Ancient Near Eastern literature identified everything in nature (including heavenly bodies such as the sun, moon, and stars) mythically as living organisms, then Stoicism was just as monistic and materialistic, except that it viewed the divinity of the world as the impersonal, intellectual principle inherent in everything. If the earliest Greek philosophers defined reality in terms of water, air, fire, or the boundless, they did not deny the existence of the realm of personal gods. On the other hand, Stoicism denied the existence of personal gods, as well as the Platonic world of Ideas. God was the pervasive impersonal, rational, and fiery substance within nature. Because reason is the inherent quality of matter, divine Providence has arranged what is best for human beings. This highest ethical good is defined as the soul's resignation to the will of God.

In the final analysis, the subject-object distinction is obliterated in Stoicism. First, it is obliterated because the highest ethical goal is attaining mystical union with the divine Fire of the universe through intellectual contemplation, thus transcending the disturbances associated with the particularity of one's bodily existence. As a drop of water is merged into the sea of ocean water and thus loses its individuality, so one's individual self is merged into the larger sea of being of the universe. Self-negation is the goal, and even suicide is applauded for those who have transcended the sense of fear and anxiety associated with human existence. Second, the subject-object distinction is obliterated because the end of the world will result in a great conflagration. The soul of every individual is an emanation from the divine Fire (Logos); the soul is a spirit penetrating the body, forming its character and giving it a sense of organization and purpose. At death the individual's soul ceases to be, though one's material being continues to exist until the final obliteration of all matter in a cosmic inferno.

During the first two centuries of Christianity, Stoicism was widely embraced among intellectual people, and though it still retained the original features of Stoicism along with pantheistic materialism, there were elements introduced into it that came close to affirming the idea of God as transcending the natural order. This is seen particularly in the Stoicism of Seneca (ca. 4 B.C- 65 A.D.), Epictetus (ca. 55-138), and Marcus Aurelius (121-180). For example, Marcus Aurelius viewed one's intelligence as an offshoot of God, who is a spiritual substance and is greater than matter. Nevertheless, God was not a personal reality, and one's highest goal was a fateful resignation to the will of God.[2] For example, Gilson quotes from Marcus Aurelius: "A little while and thou wilt have forgotten everything, a little while and everything will have forgotten thee." Gilson then notes: "These words of the great Stoic also are the last words of Greek wisdom, and they clearly mark the failure of the Greeks to build up an all-comprehensive philosophical explanation of the world without at the same time losing their religion."[3] One might refer to this rationalized, pantheistic view of the gods as a demythologized polytheism. Gilson noted that "men can be preached into worshiping any living being, from a wholly imaginary one like Zeus to a wholly ridiculous one like the Golden Calf. Provided only it be somebody or something which they can mistake for somebody, they may eventually worship it. What men cannot possibly bring themselves to do is to worship a thing."[4] The demythologizing of polytheism in Stoicism was intellectually superior to any religious point of view in the ancient world, but its weakness was that its god was turned into a thing. However, the Early Church Fathers were able to make progress along these lines in the 4th century because they were able to incorporate the metaphysical principles of Greek philosophy into their theology of the self-revealing God in history, showing how ultimate principles and ultimate personhood could be united.[5]

Paul Tillich (1886-1965) noted that the real threat to Christianity in its earliest days of expansion was not religious syncretism such as Gnosticism. These syncretistic religious movements had one thing in common with Christian faith—the idea of a descent of a divine being for the salvation of the world, but they lacked intellectual credibility because their beliefs were mythical rather than historical. Tillich noted that "Christianity, although adhering to a similar faith, was superior to syncretism in the individual character of the Savior Jesus Christ and in its concrete-historical basis."[6] In other words, the intellectually superior aspect of Christian faith over religious syncretism was that its beliefs were rooted in the facts of history, not in mythopoeic thought.

On the other hand, Tillich noted that a serious threat to Christian faith was Stoicism. Why? Because the basic Stoic attitude was a courageous self-acceptance of one's fate based on the idea of participation in the divine reason, salvation did not depend upon fables and myths. The Stoic sense of unity with God also did not depend upon the events of history, and some of the most notable people in later antiquity espoused it as their worldview. Tillich pointed out that Christian faith with its universal offer of salvation eventually "pushed Stoicism into an obscurity from which it emerged only in the beginning of the modern period."[7]

However, it would be wrong to conclude that the early Christian Apologists withdrew from dialog with Stoicism. In fact, Justin Martyr incorporated some of his theological categories from "the Platonizing Stoicism of his day," even arguing that many of its ideas, especially the idea of God's oneness, was something that it had apparently learned from the works of Moses in the Pentateuch.[8] Aristides of Athens introduces himself in his *Apology* to the Roman emperor as a "Christian philosopher,"[9] and he offered a proof for God's existence based on Aristotle's argument from motion. He argued that order and beauty requires one to believe in a supreme Being who is the prime Mover and who is invisible, incorruptible, unchanging, and uncreated.[10] In this way, Christian philosophy and theology "truly begin with the generation of the Apologists."[11]

However, the ideas of these earliest Christian theologians were derived primarily from the history of salvation contained in the Bible and Judaism, not from Stoicism.[12] As a result, the theology of the Apostolic Fathers[13] and the Apologists in the second century A.D. lacked a technical vocabulary for explaining the eternal distinctions within the One God, and thus they did not try to explain philosophically how Jesus was both divine and human. Yet, patristic scholars have shown that their ideas were in essential agreement with the later Nicene and Chalcedonian creeds, which borrowed from contemporary philosophy and Stoicism in particular.[14]

Noteworthy about these second century apologists was their reliance upon the history of salvation as the method for doing theology, although their view of history was naïve according to modern standards. Irenaeus represented the orthodox way of thinking for the second century, and he basically conceived of God in terms of God's revelation in history. He spoke of the way that God is intrinsically, on the one hand, and the way God is revealed in "the economy," on the other hand. By economy, he means the manner in which God has been revealed in history as Father, Son, and Holy Spirit. This Economic Trinitarianism means that God was revealed in history as Father, Son, and Holy Spirit and this implies that history is a reflex of what God is in God's eternal being.[15]

Economic Trinitarianism continued to have influence in the third century A.D. However, some in the Western Church began to fear that the divine unity was being threatened by the triplicity manifested in the history of salvation. Tertullian of North Africa referred to these critics as embracing "the monarchy" because they "took fright at the economy."[16]

This monarchian tendency was to influence the Western view of the Trinity throughout its entire history. A different trend was evident in the Eastern Church; it wanted to highlight the notion of God in terms of three Persons, intending at the same time to preserve the divine oneness.[17] To this very day, the Western Church emphasizes the oneness of God over the threeness of God, while the Eastern Church emphasizes the threeness of God over the oneness of God.

Plotinus—Divine Oneness and Mystical Pantheism

Another philosophical movement that thrived around the middle of the third century A.D was neo-Platonism.[18] It too made a significant attempt to reconcile the subject-object distinction. It is called neo-Platonism primarily because it was inspired largely by Platonic thought, but it also integrated aspects of Aristotelian, Stoic, and Oriental thinking. Plotinus (205-270) is its best spokesman, and he is recognized as one of the best thinkers of the ancient world. He developed the religious implications of Plato's philosophy. Plato had largely laid out his philosophical ideas somewhat independent of his religious views. Plotinus brought them together.

While Aristotle synthesized Plato's philosophy and religious ideas into abstract philosophical principles, Plotinus synthesized Plato's philosophy and religious ideas into a comprehensive pantheistic mysticism. With Aristotle the subject-object distinction was transcended in terms of the self-knowing mind that was engaged in an act of contemplating divine truth. For all practical purposes this meant that the subject-object distinction was dissolved into an abstract unity of thought, and likewise with Plotinus the subject-object distinction was merged into an undifferentiated oneness of the divine.

A primary motivation of both thinkers was to overcome the comprehensive dualism of Plato's philosophy in which the ultimate principles of reality (the Forms) and the concrete physical world (the realm of shadows and copies) were polarized. Aristotle had integrated the supersensuous realm of Forms and the sensuous realm of the physical world with his theory of a hierarchical reality that was pictured as a series of concentric circles with the earth as its stationary center. Outermost was the sphere of the fixed stars. An unmoved Mover (God) insured an eternal and absolutely regular motion that was passed on successively to each of the inner spheres. God was the Unmoved Mover who existed on the outer sphere. Each sphere had its own lesser unmoved movers. The ultimate good was for human thought to contemplate the Mind of God. What possessed priority for Aristotle was the realism of physical things (known as philosophical realism), from which ultimate truth could be inferred. Aristotle denied the objective existence of Platonic ideas, but rather re- interpreted these ideas as the intellectual basis for categorizing our experiences of the concrete world. Plato's philosophy is known as *idealism* because it affirmed the objective reality of eternal ideas existing beyond the realm of our senses, whereas Aristotle's philosophy is known as *realism* because it affirmed the priority of what is known through our senses.

The subsequent history of philosophy and Christian theology is riddled with controversy over the epistemological soundness of these conflicting views, but what is clear is that Stoicism, drawing heavily from the monistic tendencies in Aristotle's metaphysical principles in which the ultimate goal is union with the self-knowing God through intellectual contemplation, developed a materialistic pantheism, while Plotinus, drawing heavily from Plato's idealistic philosophy, developed a monistic view of reality in which God is ultimately an undifferentiated unity of everything. For Plotinus, God is an undifferentiated One, but emanating from this Oneness is Mind, which accounts for the multiplicity of things in the world. Mind contemplates the realm of Forms and seeks to be reunited with Oneness. Emanating from Mind is the World-Soul which shapes and gives a degree of meaning to the multiplicity of things in the world. At the lowest level of this very complex hierarchical structure is the material body which is non-being and is an evil. In spite of the elements of despair present in the descending order of reality, Plotinus highlights a strong spirit of optimism. The world is the result of the overflowing nature of God and thus God suffuses everything. This means that there is a longing of the human soul for union with God as the ultimate One. This longing can be transformed into actual stages leading up the ladder of reality to the Oneness of God. It begins with purification, thus enabling one to be set free from entanglements associated with the body and sense-perceptions. At the next stage of the mind, the soul focuses self-consciously on philosophy and science. The final ascending stage is mystical union with divine Oneness in which the subject-object distinction is transcended.[19]

What has emerged in this discussion is that Plato and Aristotle spent their philosophical careers trying to come to terms with the subject-object distinction, but in the final analysis their solutions led to either materialistic pantheism (Stoicism) or an immaterial pantheistic mysticism (Plotinus). And in both cases the subject-object distinction was effectively obliterated through a monistic system in which the individual's identity is lost through absorption into an ultimate, impersonal principle. If the mythopoeic thinking of the Ancient Near East confused nature and spirit as if everything was sensuously alive with no subject-object distinction, the rise of philosophy with the Greeks developed an explicit awareness of this distinction, but then it was intellectually and spiritually dissolved into an abstract monism. A useful oversimplification would be: myth personified everything; Greek philosophy intellectualized everything; Greek religious philosophy spiritualized everything. In all cases, the multiplicity of things remained inscrutable and insoluble.

Origen—A Synthesis of Christian Revelation and Greek Philosophy

If the task of theology is to explain rationally the doctrines of Christian faith, it is a self-conscious attempt of the Church to understand itself and to explain its beliefs in a thoughtful way based on the history of salvation. Consequently, Christian theology and Christian philosophy in the second through the fourth centuries produced a synthesis between Greco-Roman philosophy and the Christian revelation. Greco-Roman philosophy provided *rational categories* for explaining the nature of reality, while Christian faith provided the *revelational content*. In this way, Christian theologians using the categories of Greco-Roman philosophy were able to say things of great philosophical and theological import because of the revelation of God in Jesus Christ, but these things were not capable of being said in Greco-Roman philosophy because it lacked any knowledge of the history of salvation. Thus, in a sense the categories of Greek philosophy prepared the way for the development of Christian theology with its task of explaining clearly and precisely the meaning of its religious beliefs implicit in the history of salvation. Clement of Alexandria (ca. 150 to ca. 215) has noted in this regard: "Hellenic philosophy has torn off a fragment of eternal truth, not from the mythology of Dionysus, but from the theology of the ever-living Word."[20] He means some degree of truth has "fallen on foreign soil" that Christians can appreciate and use for explaining more fully the knowledge of God.

This synthesis between Greek philosophy and the Bible can be especially seen in the theology of Origen (ca.185- ca. 254) whose ideas became so decisive for the thinking of the Eastern Church. The center

of the Eastern Church was at Alexandria, Egypt. Origen's theological suc-
cessors were the famous Greek Fathers of the Church who formulated
for us the orthodox doctrines of the Incarnation and the Trinity. These
Early Church Fathers were Athanasius (296–373 A. D.) and the
Cappadocian Fathers—Basil of Caesarea (329-379 A. D.), Gregory
Nazianzus (330–389 A. D.), and Gregory of Nyssa (330-395 A. D.).[21] If
these Early Church Fathers were able to define so precisely the theological understanding of Christ and the Trinity, it was because they followed
the lead of Origen in using Greek philosophy to make explicit the meaning of biblical faith.

Origen was a contemporary of Plotinus, and both were influenced by
the Middle Platonism popular at Alexandria through the teaching of
Ammonius Saccas. Origen particularly explained the triadic nature of
God in terms of Middle Platonism. He stated that the Father, Son, and
Holy Spirit are "three Persons" and they, as distinct hypostases (subsistences), have existed from all eternity. This is linked to his notion of the
eternal generation of the Son from the Father. His affirmation of the
eternity of three Persons as distinct from "the economy" (that is, the way
in which God is revealed in history) is considered by patristic scholars to
be his chief contribution to the theology of the Church. He used both
the Stoic word, *hypostasis,* and the Platonic word, *ousia,* which were used
interchangeably, but Origen gives *hypostasis* a specific connotation of
individual subsistence. He criticized modalism (a Trinitarian heresy that
held the idea that God is One Being revealed in three *temporal* modes,
first as Father, then as Son, and finally as Spirit) because it made the three
Persons numerically indistinguishable as if they were distinct in thought
only. Origen insisted that God is one in essence but exists as three individual subsistences. Origen's theology contributed to the subsequent
development of the Trinitarian faith of classic Christianity; it was in effect
a synthesis of Stoic categories with the biblical history of salvation.

A distinctive mark of Origen's theology upon Christian theology was
his identification of the Spirit *(pneuma)* of God with Reason *(nous).*
Wolfhart Pannenberg, Emeritus Professor of Systematic Theology, at the
Faculty of Protestant Theology, at the University of Munich, has shown
this was an innovation that had far-reaching consequences for the way
that theology began to think of God's nature. Since Plato, the trend in
philosophy was to locate ultimate truth in a timeless realm of abstract
reason. This concept made its way into Christian theology through
Origen, under the influence of Platonism in the Third Century, [22] and
the consequence was that the biblical definition of God as Spirit (I Cor.

2:11; II Cor. 3:17; John 4:24) was linked to *nous* (mind).[23] This innovation implied that God was primarily a supreme, rational subject in spite of Origen's insistence upon the Trinitarian Persons. The biblical idea of God as *pneuma* (a mysteriously natural force like wind) was substituted with the philosophical idea of God as reason (*nous*) who transcended the physical world. Part of the purpose of equating God with reason was to show that God was not bodily. Linking God's Spirit with reason was explicitly developed by Augustine, and the idea of God as a divine monarch who stands above the world in a timeless realm of eternity has prevailed in Western Christianity.[24] The consequence has been to make the Trinitarian relationship difficult to understand because God came to be understood primarily as a rational Subject instead of three Persons.

In pointing out this basic incompatible notion of God as Subject and God as Trinitarian Persons, Pannenberg is not arguing against the Early Church Father's project of integrating philosophical categories and the history of salvation. Indeed it can be said that his own theology is intended in some measure to be an updated version of the theology of the Cappadocian Fathers. Pannenberg's point is that theologians must be careful to insist that the starting point of theology is the history of salvation and that philosophy is primarily a useful tool for clarifying its meaning. In this respect, the subject-object partition in which one makes a self-conscious distinction between oneself (what-is-thought) and what one knows as different from oneself (what-is-being) is a necessary assumption in theologizing the history of salvation. But it is contradictory to Trinitarian doctrine to turn God into a single divine subject whose primary essence is that of a thinking subject (monarchianism). Rather, God is Spirit whose essence is love and thus God has the capacity for fellowship because God is Three Persons, which of course Origen and Augustine affirmed in spite of their contradictory tendency to highlight that God is primarily Reason instead of Spirit.[25]

As we have seen in this chapter, this subject-object distinction first came to light in the historical consciousness of the Hebrews. With the Greeks, this subject-object distinction led to a critical analysis of the meaning of ideas, resulting in the rational attempt to construct a view of reality consistent with human experience. The synthesis of Christian revelation and Greek philosophy created the need for theology to maintain a balance between faith and reason. In the next chapter, we will examine how Christian orthodoxy emerged out of the need for the Church to clarify what it believed about the history of Jesus Christ through using Greek categories. Even before the rise of the modern historical consciousness, the Early Church Fathers were asking what enduring meaning did Jesus have for faith in God.

Notes

1. Cf. Kelly, *Early Christian Doctrines*, 12-15 for a concise explanation of Stoicism. Cf. W. T. Jones, *The Classical Mind*, 326-347.

2. Gilson, *God and Philosophy*, 36.

3. Ibid., 37.

4. Ibid.

5. Ibid.

6. Paul Tillich, *Courage to Be* (New Haven: Yale University Press, 1952), 10.

7. Ibid.

8. *I Apology*, xliv, 8. Cf. J.N.D. Kelly, *Early Christian Doctrines*, 84. Cf. Etienne Gilson, *History of Christian Philosophy in the Middle Ages* (New York: Random House, 1955), 13.

9. Etienne Gilson, *History of Christian Philosophy in the Middle Ages*, 10.

10. Kelly, *Early Christian Doctrines*, 84.

11. Gilson, *History of Christian Philosophy in the Middle Ages*, 9.

12. Kelly, *Early Christian Doctrines*, 83.

13. The "Apostolic Fathers" refers to those writers who were disciples of one of the Apostles or of someone who was an immediate disciple of an Apostle. Their writing style, like that of Ignatius of Antioch, was similar to the canonical writings of Paul. It was with the Apologists that Christian theology and Christian philosophy was begun. Cf. Gilson, *A History of Christian Philosophy in the Middle Ages*, 9.

14. Kelly, *Early Christian Doctrines*, 101, 103,

15. Ibid., 104-105, 109.

16. Ibid., 109.

17. Ibid., 110.

18. Ibid, 15-17. Cf. Thomas Whittaker, *The Neo-Platonists, A Study in the History of Hellenism*, second edition (Freeport, NY: Books for Libraries Press,1970), 40-106.

19. Cf. Kelly, *Early Christian Doctrines*, 15-17.

20. Clement of Alexandria, "The Stromata, or Miscellanies," in *Ante-Nicene Fathers*, ed. Alexander Roberts and James Donaldson (Hendrickson Publishers), 2:313.

21. Cf. Kelly, *Early Christian Doctrines*, 128-136.

22. Gilson, *History of Christian Philosophy in the Middle Ages*, 38-39.

23. Pannenberg, *Systematic Theology*, trans. Geoffrey W. Bromiley (Grand Rapids: Eerdmans, 1991): 1:382.

24. Ibid., 401-410.

25. Ibid., 422-448.

3

Athens or Jerusalem?
The Academy or the Church?

In the previous chapters, we pointed out the significance of the distinction between a knowing mind (a rational *subject*) and the *object* of what one knows. We are able to comprehend our environment and to explain it in terms of an "I-it" relationship. This subject-object distinction seems so commonsensical to us that we are puzzled that it was not so obvious to ancient peoples, and yet it arose out of two independent traditions— the Hebrew experience of history and Greek philosophical speculation.

Because Socrates defined a human as a subject with critical rationality, it is understandable that his philosophy (as expanded by Plato and Aristotle) would become a decisive moment in the history of thought, ultimately influencing the way Christian faith was to be explained in a Greco-Roman culture. Theology has always had an uneasy alliance with philosophy since the 2nd century. We noted that the early Christian Apologists were the first to use Greek philosophy in defending the articles of Christian belief, and they of course had no intention of allowing its message to be altered. However, some modifications were inevitable. We have already observed that Origen Hellenized the Christian idea of God in terms of the category of *nous*, resulting in a tendency to misconstrue the unity of the Trinity.[1] This possibility of mistranslating the biblical message serves as a constant reminder that theology is a fallible undertaking, and that is why each generation of believers must reconsider its language about the self-revelation of God to be sure that its speech is a responsible representation of the original witness of Scripture.

The uneasiness of this theological task of explaining faith in the terms of contemporary philosophy was expressed by Tertullian (ca. 160–ca. 220) with his famous question, "What indeed has Athens to do with Jerusalem? What concord is there between the Academy and the Church? what between heretics and Christians?"[2] He said: "Away with all attempts to produce a mottled Christianity of Stoic, Platonic, and dialectic composition! We want no curious disputation after possessing Christ Jesus, no inquisition after enjoying the gospel! With our faith, we desire no further belief. For this is our palmary faith, that there is nothing which we ought to believe besides."[3] Tertullian made it clear that the standard of truth is the history of Jesus, not the metaphysical speculations of Aristotle and his Academy in Athens. He particularly attacked Stoicism, noting that "heresies are themselves instigated by philosophy."[4]

It would be a mistake to think that Tertullian was simply jettisoning Greek philosophical categories. His comments in *The Prescription Against Heretics* were directed against eclecticism and syncretism. Although he strongly warned against heretical distortions being superimposed on the original Christian message, his writings show that he possessed an extensive knowledge of Greek and Latin literature. Before becoming a Christian, he was trained in law and was a practicing lawyer in Rome. He was thus a scholar well versed in the thought of his day. He earned the reputation of being the first writer in Latin to formulate Christian theological concepts, and he coined the term *trinitas* in *Adversus Praxean (Against Praxeas)* even before the systematic development of the Trinity had taken shape.[5] He used Greek categories, as well as the legal terms of Rome, to explain theological implications of the gospel.[6] The need to translate the history of Jesus in the thought-forms of the contemporary period is an unavoidable responsibility for theology, including Tertullian who was keenly aware of the pitfalls of philosophy.

As an example of this unavoidable need to relate contemporary thought and Christian faith, this chapter will show that substantialist philosophy played a decisive role in Christological and Trinitarian thinking. Substantialism means that there is an unchanging core to things, that true being is a fixed metaphysical entity representing "that which is eternal and unchanging," as Plato defined it in the Republic.[7]

Substantialism is especially evident in the way that it was used in Christological orthodoxy to explain how Jesus could be one person with a human and divine nature on one hand, and the way that it was used in Trinitarian orthodoxy to explain how God could be one nature with three persons on the other hand. For all his appropriate reservations about the intrusions of philosophy, Tertullian was "the first theologian frankly to tackle this issue" concerning the relationship between the two natures of Christ.[8] In this respect, Tertullian used the concept of "substance" to explain that the human and divine substances co-existed in Jesus as an indivisible person.[9] His views on this subject predated the formulation of orthodox thinking contained in the Creed (325 A.D.), but

Tertullian anticipated its results. Next we will see how classic orthodox theology synthesized Greek substantialism and the history of Jesus.

The Nicene Creed—Did Jesus Possess the Same Substance as the Father?

The most dramatic moments in Christian tradition occurred in the bitter political conflict and theological debate that began with Alexander, bishop of Alexandria, and Arius, a presbyter of Alexandria, over the question of Jesus' oneness with God. The main point of Arianism was that Christ as the Word was less than God, who united himself to a human body but lacked a rational soul. If this is so, was Jesus really God in his very essence (*homoousia*), or was he like God (*homoiousia*)? This debate took place within the Greek speaking division of the Church, while Western theologians were not actively involved.[10] This debate shows how decisive the categories of Greek philosophy were in defining what Christians believed about the history of Jesus.

This conflict was initially resolved at the Council of Nicea (325 A.D) where it was decided that Jesus was "of one substance with the Father." In a paradoxical way, the person of Jesus was defined in both historical and philosophical categories. While the Economic Trinity is assumed in the creed, the primary attention focuses on Christology.

> We believe in one God, the Father almighty, maker of all things, visible and invisible;

> And in one Lord Jesus Christ, the Son of God, begotten from the Father, only-begotten, that is, from the substance of the Father, God from God, light from light, true God from true God, begotten not made, of one substance with the Father, through Whom all things came into being, things in heaven and things on earth, Who because of us men and because of our salvation came down and became incarnate, becoming man, suffered and rose again on the third day, ascended to the heavens, and will come to judge the living and the dead;

> And in the Holy Spirit.

> But as for those who say, There was when He was not, and, Before being born He was not, and that He came into existence out of nothing, or who assert that the Son of God is from a different hypostasis or substance, or is created, or is subject to alteration or change—these the Catholic Church anathematizes.[11]

The Nicene Creed did not end the conflict and confusion over the meaning of Jesus' unity with God. Athanasius, the patriarch of Alexandria, became its greatest defender, and his pioneering contributions to the doctrine of the Trinity were significant.[12] The Nicene Creed only mentioned the Holy Spirit as the third article of belief about God, but Athanasius showed that the Spirit is fully divine and is consubstantial with the Father and Son. In this way, Athanasius prepared the way for the development of the orthodox Trinitarian doctrine that was formulated in the writings of the Cappadocian fathers.[13]

Athanasius also contributed to an understanding of the unity of Jesus with God, but he left one unresolved problem. On the one hand, he insisted (based on John 1:14) that the Word became a man, not that it simply entered into him as the inspired word had done with the Old Testament prophets. As the Word of God, he defined Jesus as one Person who combined the actions of God and God-made-man. The unresolved problem was whether or not Athanasius considered Jesus' humanity as including a human rational soul. Since his anthropology was Platonic in the sense that he considered the soul to be independent of the body, it was consistent with the view that the divine Logos replaced Jesus' need for a human rational soul.[14]

What was needed was a further clarification of this issue. Many views were developed to address this unresolved question. Some of the views developed an inadequate interpretation of his divinity or humanity. For example, Apollinarianism held that the person of Jesus excluded the spirit of man, while he assumed the mind and flesh of a man. This made Jesus into a kind of divinized man.[15] Eutychianism held that Jesus' humanity was completely absorbed by his divinity. Some views failed to develop a sense of Jesus' personal unity like Nestorianism, which interpreted Jesus as being two distinct persons as well as two distinct natures. This troubling period of time set the stage for an imperial call for a council to resolve the issue. The Emperor Marcian was sympathetic to the orthodox view of Jesus as one person with two natures, and his intent was to bring about a single faith throughout the Roman empire. Hence a Church council was called to meet at Chalcedon, October 8, 451, to formulate a new Christological statement.

The Chalcedonian Settlement and the Subject-Predicate Distinction in Aristotelian Logic

The majority of the bishops objected to the formulation of a new creed, insisting that the Nicene Creed (325 A.D.) and the Constantinopolitan Creed (381 A.D.), along with Cyril's two Letters and Leo's Tome, were adequate. The Nicene Creed had established that Jesus was fully God and fully human, and the Constantinopolitan Creed ratified the Trinitarian doctrine of one God existing in three co-equal Persons. Cyril, the patriarch of Alexandria, composed two letters that refuted Nestorianism and Pope Leo's Tome refuted Eutychianism. The commissioners acting on behalf of the emperor satisfied the bishops that the new confession must be one that everyone could sign, and hence the first order of business was to affirm these earlier creeds and documents as constituting the standards of orthodoxy.[16]

The next order of business was to establish confessional clarity regarding the true humanity and divinity of the one person of Jesus of Nazareth. To resolve the issue, they declared:

> In agreement, therefore, with the holy fathers, we all unanimously teach that we should confess that our Lord Jesus Christ is one and the same Son, the same perfect in Godhead and the same perfect in manhood, truly God and truly man, the same of a rational soul and body, consubstantial with the Father in Godhead, and the same consubstantial with us in manhood, like us in all things except sin; begotten from the Father before the ages as regards His Godhead, and in the last days, the same, because of us and because of our salvation begotten from the Virgin Mary, the *Theotokos*, as regards His manhood; one and the same Christ, Son, Lord, only-begotten, made known in two natures without confusion, without change, without division, without separation, the difference of the natures being by no means removed because of the union, but the property of each nature being preserved and coalescing in one *prosopon* and one *hypostasis*—not parted or divided into two *prosopa*, but one and the same Son, only-begotten, divine Word, the Lord Jesus Christ, as the prophets of old and Jesus Christ Himself have taught us about Him and the creed of our fathers has handed down.[17]

The creed's use of "rational soul and body" shows the extent of the influence of Greek philosophy upon its Christology, and if the term, person, was used primarily to denote the way that Jesus is related to God and to us as one being with two natures, its intent was to show that there are not two persons being affirmed here as if God had two sons. Jesus is "one person," but he possesses "two natures."

Aristotelian Categories as an Explanation of Jesus' Unity with God and Man

John McIntrye, Professor Emeritus of Divinity, University of Edinburgh, has demonstrated how this concept of two natures is derived from the Aristotelian categories of "primary substance" and "secondary substance".[18] A primary substance is something that actually exists in the real world, whereas a secondary substance is a quality that inheres in a primary substance. Thus something is true or false based on the subject-predicate relationship of a particular thing and its universal quality. Consider for example the statement: "Socrates is a man." Socrates is the "primary substance" because Socrates is the subject who stands concretely in the real world. However, the concept of "man" is a quality (a species, a predicate) that inheres in Socrates. The concept of manhood is not something concrete as such. You cannot see, smell, touch, taste, or hear manhood, but rather you see real men, such as Socrates. Yet the concept of manhood is a universal concept that is used as a predicate to describe objectively who Socrates is. Without the actually existing subject (the primary substance) there could be no secondary substances (predicate). We noted earlier that Plato believed that universal ideas (which he called Forms) existed in a realm of perfection whether their copies in this world actually existed or not. So manhood existed universally in the realm of perfection even if there were no men. This is why Plato's philosophy is known as "idealism" because it insists that "ideas" really exist in a realm of perfection even if they do not exist in the physical realm. On the other hand, Aristotle insisted that "ideas" (or thought forms) have existence only in "real" things that we can see, feel, smell, touch, taste, or hear. That is why Aristotle's philosophy is known as "realism." In this sense, there can be no secondary substance without a primary substance.

This realist premise is foundational to the two-nature model of the one person of Jesus with the difference that *hypostasis* (person) and *physis* (nature) were substituted for primary substance and secondary substance. Just as in Aristotelian realism where universal categories can only exist in the things themselves, so in Christian theology there can be no *physis* (nature) without an *hypostasis* (a real person). This is known in theology as the "no *physis anhypostatos*" principle. In reference to Jesus, if he possesses a human nature and a divine nature there must be a real person in whom these natures exist. This means there is no such thing as human nature except as it is reflected as a universal quality typical of particular and individual people. In this way, the particular person is the actual reality (primary substance), whereas human nature is the universal, abstract concept (secondary substance). This principle is the meaning of the statement in the Chalcedonian Creed: "The property of each nature being preserved and concurring in one person."

In the Chalcedonian Creed, the fullness of human nature and divine nature exist in the person of Jesus. However, if there is only a divine person in whom the two natures exist, in what sense can it really be said that Jesus is also human? According to the basic Aristotelian premise that the Chalcedonian Creed assumed, Jesus is only one person, and it is clear that the person is a divine person, not a human person. There is no attempt in the Chalcedonian statement to correct this apparent oversight and make the Christological confession conform to the basic philosophical principle, and that is why subsequent theologies (including the present day) have accused the creed of holding to an impersonal view of Jesus' human nature. The most serious implication of this apparent inconsistency is that it calls into question the entire salvation and redemption of the human race—because, as Gregory of Nazianzus (one of the theologians responsible for formulating the orthodox Trinitarian faith) put it: "What has not been assumed [by Christ] cannot be restored."[19] That is, unless Jesus was really human, he could not redeem humanity.

Two solutions were proposed in subsequent Church history. One was by Leontius of Byzantium (ca. 485-543). He suggested that the real intent of the Chalcedonian creed was to say that the human nature of Jesus has its person (*hypostasis*) in (*en*) the divine Logos (*enhypostasis*). In other words, the integrity of the human nature of Jesus was preserved in the divine person. This means that Jesus' human nature was not absorbed into the divine Logos, although his human nature had no corresponding human person in which it inhered. Thus it supposedly corresponded to the premise of no *physis anhypostatos*, an enhypostatic nature.

This view has had considerable influence in Christian theology to this very day, and it has been subject to serious criticism. Basically, the issue is still whether or not it preserves the personal character of Jesus' human nature. E. L. Mascall has noted that the concept of *enhypostasis* makes Jesus' human nature a mere abstraction.[20] Its most notable defender in modern theology was Karl Barth, but his defense has not been effective in silencing its critics.[21]

A second solution to the problem was suggested by Ephraim of

Antioch (d. 545) although it has received inadequate attention, but is one which John McIntyre thinks goes a long way toward solving the problem of no *physis anhypostasis*. Ephraim of Antioch affirmed the Chalcedonian view that the two natures of Jesus are not to be divorced from each other since they share the same person, but his original contribution to the problem was his view that the two persons were fused together to form a composite person. McIntyre recommends this view: "It secures the wholeness of the humanity which Jesus Christ took, and firmly avoids the docetic and Apollinarian tendencies of the enhypostatic theory."[22] In this way, the full atonement of Jesus Christ can be affirmed since he fully assumed the meaning of human existence.

Instead of resolving the logical problem of the principle, no *physis anhypostasis*, I believe this notion sidesteps the problem since it does not explain how a composite person is an intelligible concept within the Aristotelian framework. Perhaps the more basic problem is the Aristotelian concept of substance that lies at the basis of the distinction between a substratum (*hypostasis*) and *physis* (nature). For its fundamental meaning is the idea that a subject has permanent, static existence and thus every subject has a specific unchanging, ontological status. This notion treats human life and human values as if they are metaphysical things with a fixed nature.

Of course, the New Testament does not make this explicit distinction between the divine and human natures in Jesus. It does not use philosophically precise language to say that Jesus does one thing as divine and another thing as human. Rather, the categories of the gospels are historical, functional, and confessional. Luke says that "Jesus increased in wisdom and stature, and in favor with God and man" (Luke 2:52), but he does not qualify this by saying that Jesus was thus acting out his human nature. In his highly priestly prayer, Jesus spoke of his oneness with the Father (John 17:5), but there is nothing in the text that says Jesus was speaking of his divinity. There are numerous statements in the New Testament that reflect both divine and human elements in Jesus' personhood, but it did not occur to the Palestinian followers of Jesus that is was important to write like Greek logicians. Take the example of Jesus' disclosure of himself to the disciples at Caesarea Phillippi. He asked his disciples: "Whom do people say that I the Son of Man am?" Peter specifically did not say: "Some say that you are two persons and two natures [Nesotorianism]; some say that you are a mixture of the divine and human natures [Eutychianism]; some say that you were adopted as the son of God without being really divine [adoptionism]; some say that you are lower than God but higher than men [Arianism]; but I say you are one person inseparably linking the divine and human natures in their fullest sense of the words [Athanasius and the Nicene Creed]." Instead, Peter simply said: "You are the Christ, the Son of the living God."

The Jews thought primarily in relational and functional ways, not explicitly in terms of precise logical distinctions. What the christological formulation of the Nicene Creed was thus attempting to make explicit was implicit in the relational categories of New Testament so that Greeks too could understand the New Testament kerygma. After all, by 60 A.D, there were "a hundred thousand Greeks in the Church for every Jew who was a Christian," and "Jewish ideas were completely strange to the Greeks."[23] If the Christian message was to be understood, the necessity for contextualizing it in terms of Greek categories was obvious.

The Concept of Personhood in Trinitarian Theology

An example of this synthesis between Greek-Roman philosophy and Christian faith can be seen in the writings of Augustine who was influenced as a young Christian convert by Neo-Platonism, especially the writings of Plotinus.[24] Reading the *Enneads*, Augustine saw in Plotinus' triad—the One, the Nous, and the World Soul—a philosophical insight which he believed was a vestige of the Trinity. The One of Plotinus is reinterpreted as God the Father, the ultimate source of everything that is; *Nous* is reinterpreted as the God the Son in whom the Mind of God is expressed; the World Soul is reinterpreted as God the Holy Spirit who is God's agent in creation and redemption. For Plotinus, the dividing line is between the One and the *Nous*, which emanates from the One. Augustine showed that the dividing line is not between God as Father and the Word of God (Logos); rather the Oneness of God is seen in that the Father eternally begets the Son in the power of the Holy Spirit, and the dividing line is between the three Persons of God on the one hand, and creation on the other hand. The material creation itself is not evil, but rather evil is the deprivation of what is good; in this sense sin is always a parasite living off what once was good but has become distorted through its estranged relationship with God.[25]

Augustine's theological writings made him the most significant theologian of the Western church, even as his older contemporaries, the Cappadocian fathers (Gregory of Nazianzus, Basil of Caesarea, and Gregory of Nyssa), were the most significant theologians of the Eastern church, especially in formulating the doctrine of the Trinity. One point of difference between Augustine (the Western, Latin Church) and the

Cappadocian Fathers (the Eastern, Greek Church) is the emphasis that each gave to the *oneness* of God as opposed to the *threeness* of God. While both views are considered orthodox in the sense that they represent the New Testament witness, Augustine's emphasized primarily the *oneness* of God, in part stemming from the influence of neo-Platonism with its emphasis upon the divine oneness. On the other hand, the Cappadocian fathers emphasized primarily the Trinitarian Persons of God, in part stemming from their emphasis upon the economy of salvation, that is, the history of salvation in which God is revealed progressively as Father, Son, and Holy Spirit.[26] This difference between the Western and Eastern Churches stems largely from the fact the Eastern Orthodox Church has historically had a stronger emphasis upon the personhood of the Holy Spirit than the Western Church, as J. N. D. Kelly has shown.[27] This difference has also occasioned the charge sometimes made against the Western church—that it tends toward a monarchical view of God (that is, God is really only one person with three different temporal manifestations). On the other hand, the Eastern Church has been said to tend toward tritheism because it inadequately explained the divine unity.[28]

Here again the subject-object distinction is a basic presupposition of Trinitarian thinking. In what sense is God as a subject also an object to God's very self? Plotinus postulated the idea that Oneness emanates out of itself into Nous who emanates out of itself into the World-Soul without any return. On the other hand, Trinitarian thinking assumes that there is a return (a relationship) of the Father back to the Father through the Son and the power of the Spirit. He begets the Son and through the power of the Spirit God enjoys the fellowship of the Son.

Trinitarian theology says that God is three Persons and each confronts ("faces towards") the other two Persons. Yet Trinitarian theology also says God is one essence so that the Father, the Son, and Holy Spirit mutually work together. This means that God does not have three independent centers of consciousness, but as the Cappadocian Fathers insisted, the Father, the Son, and the Holy Spirit function together in unity in their respective tasks as distinctive Persons.[29]

The Formulation of the Concept of Personhood

The significance of the synthesis between Christian revelation and Greek philosophy is seen in the way that it led to a matured concept of personhood. E. L. Mascall, an Anglican and Benedictine philosopher-theologian, shows in his work, *The Importance of Being Human*, that the

Christological and Trinitarian controversies of the 4ᵗʰ and 5ᵗʰ centuries were the decisive factors in the formulation of the concept of personhood. He noted that "the idea of personality was present in Greek thought only in embryo, and to this day it is practically absent from Hinduism and Buddhism."[30]

We noted in the first chapter that the beginning of the concept of personhood emerged from the historical consciousness of the Hebrews, and that this historical consciousness was rooted in the self-revelation of God to Abraham in terms of an "I-thou" relationship. Now we have seen that an explicit concept of personhood emerged from the attempt of the early Church Fathers to define the meaning of Jesus as he appeared in the history of salvation by using the substantialist categories of Greek philosophy.

Notes

1. Cf. Kelly, Early Christian Doctrines, 131.
2. Tertullian, "On Prescription Against Heretics," *The Ante-Nicene Fathers*, ed. Alexander Roberts and James Donaldson (Grand Rapids: Wm. B. Eerdmans, Reprinted 1980), 3:246.
3. Ibid.
4. Ibid.
5. Cf. Kelly, *Early Christian Doctrines*, 113.
6. In *The Influence of Philosophy on The Mind of Tertullian* (London: Elliot Stock Publisher, 1933?), C. De Lisle Shortt says: "Although the opposition of Tertullian to philosophy is evident, yet it is no less apparent that there is another aspect to be carefully considered. His inconsistency appears when he does not hesitate to claim the support of the philosophers when it suits his purpose. He emphasizes his belief that Zeno confirms the Christian view that the Logos is the Creator of the universe, and that Cleanthes maintains that the Spirit is the Creator of the universe. Again, in another passage he asserts that Christians believe in demons and angels, but so also do Socrates and Plato. In another passage, he is not backward in saying: 'I call on the Stoics also to help me, who, while declaring almost in our very terms that the soul is a spiritual essence, will yet have no difficulty in persuading us that the soul is a corporeal substance'" (15).
7. *Republic*, Book VI.b.
8. Kelly, *Early Christian Doctrines*, 151.
9. Ibid., 151.
10. Ibid., 223.
11. Cited by Kelly, *Early Christian Doctrines*, 232.
12. Kelly, *Early Christian Doctrines*, 238.
13. Ibid., 257.

14. Ibid., 286-287.

15. Ibid., 289-295.

16. Ibid., 339.

17. Cited by Kelly, *Early Christian Doctrines,* 339-340.

18. John McIntyre, *The Shape of Christology* (Philadelphia: Westminster Press, 1966, 1998), 86-91.

19. Cf. Kelly, *Early Christian Doctrines,* 297.

20. Cf. McIntyre, *The Shape of Christology,* 97.

21. Ibid., 99ff.

22. Ibid., 102.

23. Cf. William Barclay, *The Gospel of John* (Philadelphia: Westminster Press, 1956), 1: 2.

24. Gilson, *God and Philosophy,* 44ff.; cf. Kelly, *Early Christian Doctrines,* 270ff.

25. Gilson, *God and Philosophy,* 48-73.

26. Cf. Kelly, *Early Christian Doctrines,* 271-279.

27. Ibid., 275ff.

28. Ibid., 268.

29. Ibid., 267.

30. E. L. Mascall, *The Importance of Being Human* (New York : Columbia University Press, 1958), 39.

4

The Invention of Scientific History

In Chapter 1, we discussed the importance of the subject-object distinction for the emergence of historical consciousness and critical thought. In Chapters 2 and 3, we pointed out that as different and independent of each other as they were, the biblical history of salvation and Greek thought were fairly successfully synthesized by the early Apologists and Fathers of the Church. We now turn to another dimension of history, which first emerged with the Greeks. It is what R. G. Collingwood has called "scientific history." Here he is not defining history as a new way of understanding reality, for it was the Hebrews who first understood reality as history. Rather, Collingwood is speaking of the Greeks' discovery of a new method of reporting history.

In his widely acclaimed book, *The Idea of History*, Collingwood defines "scientific history" as doing four things: (1) it asks critical questions; (2) it documents human actions performed in the datable past, not divine actions that happened indefinitely "once upon a time"; (3) it is rational in that its facts are based on evidence; and (4) it is self-explanatory in that it explains what human beings are as a result of what they have done.[1]

Collingwood showed that the discipline of critical history began with the Greeks. He writes: "The fact that history as a science was a Greek invention is recorded to this day by its very name. History is a Greek word, meaning simply an investigation or inquiry."[2] Given these criteria of "scientific history," he credits Herodotus (484-432 B. C.) as being "the father of history" who along with Thucydides (460/55-400 B.C.) created "a literary revolution"[3] in developing an explicit understanding of what constitutes history. Collingwood writes: "It is the use of this word [*historein*], and its implications, that make Herodotus the father of history. The conversion of legend-writing into the science of history was not native to the Greek mind, it was a fifth-century invention, and

Herodotus was the man who invented it."[4] Herodotus is thus called the "father of history" because he critically examined eyewitness testimony regarding the military activities of his day.[5]

Collingwood classified the writings of the Old Testament as "providential history" as opposed to scientific history since they intend to report information to others about what has happened in their religious history concerning divine revelation.[6] In this respect, Pannenberg has questioned Collingwood's unqualified portrayal of Herodotus as the originator of history,[7] for the Old Testament was deeply concerned about the truthfulness of what it reported as a happening or an event in their datable past. More specifically, the Hebrews assumed that history is the very meaning of reality itself in contrast to the Greeks who looked for meaning outside of history in a metahistorical realm of impersonal principles and abstractions. For the Greeks, history was "not a consciousness of agelong tradition moulding the life of one generation after another into a uniform pattern." Rather, history was a consciousness of "catastrophic changes…from pride to abasement, from happiness to misery."[8]

To be sure, the Greeks did not think that history was deterministic, but rather they believed their history was open to change through responsible actions of well-meaning persons. If one were overcome by fate, it was because one was too blind to the implicit dangers lurking about one.[9] In particular, Herodotus viewed the gods as largely responsible for their misery because they delighted in "upsetting and disturbing things."[10] The lessons of history had their limitations because there was no inherent meaning in history. History's "value is limited by the unintelligibility of its subject-matter."[11] It was the realm of the changing world, and for this reason Aristotle said that history was only a collection of empirical facts without any ultimate significance.[12] So if meaning was to be obtained for the educated Greeks it was to be through philosophy.

Herodotus as the father of scientific history was quickly upstaged by the anti-historical tendency in Greek philosophy. Collingwood noted that the critical historical consciousness that was begun with Herodotus was soon eclipsed. Although Herodotus was a contemporary of Socrates, he was not in the main stream of the Greek intellectual tradition.[13] Socrates had refocused the subject matter of philosophy away from the gods and the natural makeup of the physical world toward the meaning of human existence through dialectical reasoning about the basic questions of everyday life. In this respect, Socrates was not interested in the questions of the first Ionian philosophers who asked *what* is the stuff of which the world is made. Instead he asked the question, *what is human life?* Socrates' purpose was to discover the substantial principles that ought to govern human behavior. In this respect, Socrates was in the mainstream of Greek thinking, and his ideas were further developed by Plato and Aristotle. But Herodotus had no worthy successor to pursue his research project of uncovering the basic events of Greek history. Even "Plato writes as if Herodotus had never lived." Collingwood noted that "the Greek mind tended to harden and narrow itself in its anti-historical tendency. The genius of Herodotus triumphed over that tendency, but after him the search for unchangeable and eternal objects of knowledge gradually stifled the historical consciousness"[14]

Greek Substantialism as Anti-Historical

Collingwood believed the Greek idea of substantialism was the greatest defect of Greek historiography because it contained an "anti-historical tendency" within it.[15] Substance did not mean physical substance. In fact, many Greek philosophers thought that substance could not be material at all. This is particularly true of Plato's philosophical idealism. For him, anything that was material or existed in the finite world was in the process of becoming and hence it had not yet attained reality. For Aristotle, the ultimately real substance is the self-knowing mind of God. Of course, as we have already noted, Aristotle's concept of God as the Unmoved Mover did not mean that God was discontinuous with the rest of the universe. God was so self-sufficient that God did not need to know anything below; otherwise, God would be a dependent being inasmuch as God's knowledge would be conditioned by what existed on the outside.[16] As already noted, it should be remembered that Aristotle's reference to God as a self-knowing mind does not carry with it the notion of personality as assumed in the Scriptures or in Christian theology.

According to substantialistic philosophy, one can only know what is unchanging. If something is changing, it cannot be known because it changes the instant after one knows it and thus it no longer exists. This means that history cannot really be known because history is the realm of changing. Hence substantialistic thinking is incompatible with historical thinking.

The Contribution of Early Christian Theology to Scientific History

Collingwood identified three great crises in the rise of "scientific history." The first one occurred in the fifth century B. C. when the idea of history as a form of research first emerged with Herodotus. The second crisis came with the "revolutionary effect of Christian thought" when the "substantialist idea of eternal entities underlying the process of historical change" was rejected.[17] It was rejected because it conflicted with the Christian doctrine of creation. God alone is eternal, and everything else is created by God. Peoples and nations are not eternal substances, nor is the human soul. There are no eternal forms as such, and history itself is under the governance of God. History can be altered and is open to new things. Although Christian theology continued to use the concept of substance, it was altered so that its original Greek meaning was dropped. The human soul is still called a substance, but it is a substance that is created by God. The natural world is also called a substance, but it is not an eternal substance. It too is a creation of God. God alone is an eternal substance, but the divine substance is unknowable.

The Christian view is that God cannot be discovered by human thinking, and God's reality as an eternal substance cannot be comprehended. The only knowledge that one can have of God is from God's activities based on divine self-revelation. Collingwood noted that "by degrees, as the leaven of Christianity worked, even these quasi-substances disappeared. It was in the thirteenth century that Thomas Aquinas threw overboard the conception of divine substance and defined God in terms of activity, as *actus purus*."[18]

The Christian influence had a "threefold effect on the way in which history was conceived." First, it introduced a new attitude towards history, emphasizing that God's will was to be accomplished through human agents. Second, it assumed that history was important for human beings as well as for groups of people as a means of accomplishing the will of God. As such, the human soul appears in the world to perform a specific responsibility and then disappears from the scene. Likewise a thing like Rome is not eternal but is a temporary entity that came into existence at a certain time to fulfill a specific function and then it too passes away. A third effect was universalism. All people are equal before God. There are no chosen people, but rather all people are the object of God's concern. Thus a Christian is not interested just in Roman history or Jewish history, but in universal history. The Christian attitude thus overcame the substantialism and particularism of Greco-Roman history.[19]

Irenaeus is an example of this way of thinking who interpreted God's self-revelation in terms of the history of salvation, which has universal significance. Although by the 3rd century, Origen, Athanasius, the Cappadocian Fathers, and Augustine used the categories of Greek philosophy to explain the history of salvation, the idea of substance was used differently because the history of salvation was the norm, not philosophy. Eusebius of Caesarea, who overlapped the 3rd and 4th centuries A. D., composed a universal history in his *Chronicles.* He arranged within a single chronological framework the events in the Old Testament history of Israel, as well as the events in the history of Greece and Rome, showing them to be preparatory to the birth of Jesus. In another work, *Praeparatio Evangelica,* he presented the history of the pre-Christian world as a process that culminated in the Incarnation.[20] Collingwood's point is that Christian theology broke through the substantialist thinking of Greek philosophy, which had prevented history from being seen as the realm of real change with an openness toward the future.

The Universal Concept of History in the Medieval Period

History written by premodern Christian authors was an uncritical reconstruction of the past, naïvely assuming what counts as real history.[21] However, the contribution of medieval historiography was its universalistic point of view, recognizing that history has a larger significance than the nationalistic interests of any particular country. This was connected with its view of God's providential governance over the affairs of human life. Collingwood pointed out that this view of history was not based on Greek substantialism, but based on the concept of divine transcendence.[22] This means that God, not people, is in control of the events of history. An example of this theocratic view of history is seen in Joachim of Fiore (a 12th Century Cistercian abbot) who proclaimed that the "age of the Spirit" had already begun.[23] He distinguished among the reign of the Father (the pre-Christian age), the reign of the Son (the Christian age), and the reign of the Holy Spirit (the future age).[24]

This idea of divisions of history and series of historical ages was typical of medieval historiography and it represented "advanced and mature historical thought" that was "not afraid to interpret facts instead of merely ascertaining them."[25] However, the primary weakness of medieval historians was their failure to incorporate "critical method." This was partly due to the theological interests of interpreting history according to their understanding of the implications of the biblical revelation. However, a main reason for this deficiency in critical scholarship was that "no one had yet discovered how to criticize sources and to ascertain facts in a scholarly manner, for this was the work of historical thought in the centuries that followed the close of the Middle Ages."[26]

Humanistic Historiography of the Renaissance

The Renaissance period refocused theological and philosophical view of history into a humanistic one. Collingwood says: "The positive fruits of this new movement were found first of all in a great clearing away of what had been fanciful and ill-founded medieval historiography."[27] He particularly noted the work of Francis Bacon with his division of knowledge into three categories—poetry, history, and philosophy governed by the three faculties of imagination, memory, and understanding.[28] The purpose of history, Bacon insisted, should be a focus on the past for its own sake.

Bacon thus properly understood that the subject matter of history was the past as it really happened, but he had not yet conceived of the right methodology for doing so. In this respect, "Bacon's definition of history as the realm of memory was wrong, because the past only requires historical investigation so far as it is not and cannot be remembered."[29] Collingwood believed the Renaissance view of historiography "had freed itself from the errors of medieval thought, but it had still to find its own proper function. It had a definite programme, the rediscovery of the past, but it had no methods or principles by which this programme could be carried out."[30] That development was to take shape in the modern period, especially during the period of Romanticism in 19th century Germany.

Notes

1. Collingwood, *The Idea of History*, 18.
2. Ibid., 18.
3. Ibid., 19.
4. Ibid., 19.
5. Pannenberg points out that Collingwood failed to appreciate the unique understanding of history in the Old Testament and that he too easily classified it in the same category of ancient Oriental literature. Pannenberg, "Redemptive Event and History, *Basic Questions in Theology*, 1:21.
6. Collingwood, *The Idea of History*, 14, 50.

7. Pannenberg, "Redemptive Event and History," *Basic Questions in Theology*, 1:21.

8. Collingwood, *The Idea of History*, 22.

9. Ibid., 24.

10. Ibid., 22.

11. Ibid., 24.

12. Ibid., 24.

13. Ibid., 28.

14. Ibid., 29.

15. Ibid., 20.

16. Cf. Gilson, *God and Philosophy*, 54.

17. Collingwood, *The Idea of History*, 42-47. Cf. below, pp. 82, 110 for the third great crisis moment in the development of scientific history.

18. Ibid., 47.

19. Ibid., 48-49.

20. Ibid., 50-51.

21. Ibid., 52.

22. Ibid., 55.

23. Jürgen Moltmann, *The Spirit of Life*, tran. Margaret Kohl (Minneapolis: Fortress Press, 1992), 2, 203-209.

24. Collingwood, *The Idea of History*, 54.

25. Ibid., 53.

26. Ibid., 56.

27. Ibid., 57.

28. Ibid., 58.

29. Ibid., 58.

30. Ibid., 58.

Part Two

Modern Philosophy and the Rise of Critical History

The debate in theology over the meaning of history for Christian faith is rooted in the rise of modern thought, which produced a decisive change in the mode of thinking about the universe.[1] The experimental method of the natural sciences introduced a radical change in the thinking process itself. Previously science had consisted largely in accumulating knowledge rather than engaging in a critical process of questioning one's observations about nature based on experimental evidence.[2] The new method of modern science sought to discover universal laws derived from experimentation with the particular and the concrete data of empirical observation, assisted by understanding their mathematical and quantitative relationships. Herbert Butterfield pointed out that Galileo believed "that the book of the universe was written in mathematical language, and its alphabet consisted of triangles, circles, and geometrical figures."[3] This search for universal laws influenced the rise of modern philosophy and contributed to the idea of a radical distinction between sensibility and intellect, between experience and thought.[4] This change meant the rejection of the medieval distinction between reason and revelation. Nature was no longer seen as the creation of a transcendent God; rather God was redefined as immanent in the workings of nature. Nature was no longer something that was moved from without, but something that moved from within according to the universal principle of natural law.

The Roman Catholic Church burned Giordano Bruno at the stake in 1600 because of his pantheistic interpretation of natural law. Whitehead dates the beginning of the modern period and the rise of modern science with this event. He thus represented Bruno as a martyr of modernity and as a symbol of the decisive shift that was taking place in thinking about the world away from traditional Christian faith.[5]

The pre-modern worldview was dominated by the Aristotelian theory that the terrestrial bodies moved toward the center of the universe, which for the medievals was at or near the center of the earth. This motion of the terrestrial bodies required an explanation, which Aristotle ascribed to the Prime Mover and the medievals, to the supernatural interference of God. With the rise of the modern law of inertia, natural science ruled out the Aristotelian theory.[6] Herbert Butterfield put it this way: "The modern law of inertia, the modern theory of motion, is the great factor which in the seventeenth century helped to drive the spirits out of the world and opened the way to a universe that ran like a piece of clockwork."[7]

This mechanistic working of nature was interpreted to mean that nature possesses its own inner principle of motion. As Giordano Bruno said: "God is not an external intelligence rolling around and leading around; it is more worthy for him to be the internal principle of motion, which is his own nature, his own appearance, his own soul than that as many entities as live in his bosom should have motion."[8] This meant that natural law replaced the supernatural law of medieval theology, in which *lex naturalis* had never been more than a point of departure for *lex divina*.[9]

In 1600 William Gilbert published a work in which he described gravity as a form of magnetic attraction and pointed out that the principle of the magnet explained the workings of the Copernican system. Galileo and Kepler, influenced by Gilbert's work, further expanded the idea of natural law by demonstrating how it worked in individual cases, as in the phenomena of freely falling bodies and planetary motion. By 1678, Newton had established the principle of gravitation as a universal law.[10] Thus the method of natural science was no longer based on the understanding of nature through the Church's doctrine of creation and Aristotelian philosophy of nature. In this respect, the substantialism of Aristotle was replaced with the natural law relationship of cause and effect, and the methodological point of departure for knowledge was to make an exact analysis of things instead of appealing to ecclesiastical authority and the scientific tradition of Aristotle.

Philosophically, the rise of modern science led to what is called "the modern scientific worldview." This is the view that the world of nature and history is governed by mechanical causality. Whitehead has called this modern scientific worldview "scientific materialism." He meant by this term "the naïve faith" that nature simply does what it is going to do in a predictable way without any need for explanation or philosophical justification, thus blindly assuming that there is an inherent order of things in nature.[11]

Connected to this mechanistic idea of nature is that the world is made up of simple facts. This idea of irreducible brute facts replaced the medieval belief in metaphysical truth. Whitehead writes:

> There persists, however, throughout the whole period of the fixed scientific cosmology which presupposes the ultimate fact of an irreducible brute matter, or material, spread throughout space in a flux of configurations. In itself such a material is senseless, valueless, purposeless. It just does what it does do, following a fixed routine imposed by external relations which do not spring from the nature of its being. It is this assumption that I call 'scientific materialism.'[12]

Just as the new method of natural science freed itself from the influence of medieval theology, so did the rise of modern philosophy. In medieval theology, philosophy had been the servant of theology. Now philosophy in the modern period stood on its own feet and forged ahead with the critical questions of the validity and objectivity of human knowledge that was independent of the Church. Following the lead of natural science in setting itself up as an independent discipline of study, its task was to discover the truth of reality through clear and distinct ideas discovered by reason.

The decisive feature of modernism is a comprehensive dualism. If the pre-modern world held to an hierarchical view of reality consisting largely of an architectonics of being with everything arranged ontologically in an orderly fashion with God as the First Cause, the modern world turned away from ontological speculations to epistemological concerns, focusing not on reality itself but on the subjectivity of the knower. The consequence was a divorce between the idea of a real world beyond our senses that allegedly is unknowable and the knowable world of human experience.

If the pre-modern age assumed that the intellect through sense perceptions could receive an objective knowledge of the way that the world really is, we will see in Part Two that modernism at its very core in Enlightenment philosophy insisted that the mind actively creates its own world. Any law or order found in nature is there because the autonomous rational will put it there. If the pre-modern world was focused on a theological explanation of the will of God based on divine revelation, modernism was focused on ethical choices arising out of the subjective decisions of the human will. In effect, if there is moral law it is because human rationality is its legislator. If there are universal principles governing the world, it is because human reason has ordained it. If the pre-modern age believed there was objective truth, the modern world affirmed subjective truth universally established by reason.

If the modern age believed that its subjectivity was not anarchy, it was because it assumed that human rationality retained a memory of divine goodness and being, enabling it to exercise its reasoning process in a responsible and reliable way. Hence, all human knowledge is subjective in the sense that truth is an assertion of the will, but it has objective validity because reason is generally common to all human beings. Even the idea of God depended upon the subjective inferences of the rational will. Natural theology in the pre-modern age was closely aligned with, though distinct from, biblical revelation, but in the modern age natural theology and divine revelation were completely severed.

Finally, modernism carefully crafted a concept of the contingency of history that it used to separate faith and reason. History is the realm of causal connection among all events, allowing for no miracles and no gaps between events. Faith belongs to the realm of freedom and values, based on a responsible use of inferential reasoning. The peaceful coexistence of faith and history meant that faith in God and belief in the eternal human soul could be affirmed as logical inferences, not as a result of the self-revealing history of God. As Kant put it, he abolished knowledge in order to make room for faith (in the sense that we are entitled to believe certain ideas out of practical considerations of reason). We are entitled to believe that God exists, but faith is not real knowledge; it is only a supposition. It will be seen in this section that a pervasive epistemological dualism of fact and value, of reason and faith, was the decisive feature of modernism.

Notes

1. A. N. Whitehead, *Science and the Modern World* (New York: Macmillan Company, 1954), 5.

2. Ernst Cassirer, *The Philosophy of the Enlightenment*, trans. Fritz C. A. Koelin and James Pettegrove (Princeton University Press, 1951), 39.

3. Herbert Butterfield, *The Origins of Modern Science* (New York: Macmillan Company, 1959), 90.

4. Ibid., 38.

5. A. N. Whitehead, *Science and the Modern World*, 5.

6. Herbert Butterfield, *The Origins of Modern Science*, 3.

7. Ibid., 7

8. Cited by Cassirer, *The Philosophy of the Enlightenment*, 41.

9. Ibid., 40.

10. Ibid., 43.
11. A. N. Whitehead, *Science and the Modern World*, 5, 25, 74.
12. Ibid., 25.

5

Cartesian Historiography

Descartes: Methodological Skepticism

René Descartes in his essay, "Discourse on Method" (1637), initiated what became a long series of attempts in modern philosophy to provide a foundation for irrefutable knowledge of God, the self, and the world. Descartes' system of thought is called Cartesian, which is the Latinized form of his French name. Because he replaced the authoritarianism of the Medieval Church with a rational method to seek no other knowledge than that which he might find "within myself," this essay earned Descartes the right to be known as the father of modern philosophy. His autobiographical method ("to study my own self") represented a revolution in philosophy. It was revolutionary because he believed in the unique ability of each individual to discover the final and universal truth about the world within one's own reason.[1]

It was also revolutionary because epistemology replaced the medieval focus on ontology.[2] The premodern period was primarily concerned with describing the essential nature (ontology) of God, the world and human life, whereas Descartes focused attention on epistemology and methodology. Epistemology has to do with a critical analysis of the conditions of knowing, whereas method has to do with the organized way that one uses specific categories and principles for reaching conclusions and constructing a system of thought. Epistemology and methodology became the primary focus of the modern world, replacing the commonsense and intuitive assumption of the premodern world that things could be known as they really are in their very essence. Beginning with Descartes, the modern world virtually suspended the questions of what-is (ontology) by putting everything in doubt.

In the early part of his educational training as a young man under the Jesuits in La Flèche, France, Descartes complained of an overwhelming sense of religious doubt. While he greatly respected and accepted the beliefs of the Church, he found them to be far above the powers of human reason to prove. He sought to establish an alternative system that would lead to absolute certainty within the limitations of human reason.[3] Although his anthropocentric method intended to construct a rational foundation for universal truth independent of Christian revelation, he believed that it would assist theology by helping to convince unbelievers of the truths of Christian faith.[4]

Unlike medieval philosophers such as Thomas Aquinas who distinguished between natural theology and revealed theology in order to integrate them, Descartes divided them in order to make them entirely separate ways of thinking.[5] Whereas the philosophers of the medieval age were largely monks and clerics, the philosophers of the modern period beginning with Descartes were primarily layman. According to neo-Thomist philosopher Etienne Gilson, the result has been that "modern philosophy has been created by laymen, not by churchmen, and to the ends of the natural cities of men, not the end of the supernatural city of God."[6] Gilson has noted that throughout the modern period beginning in the 17th Century until the present day "very few churchmen have exhibited real creative genius in the field of philosophy."[7] The consequence of the divorce between theology and philosophy has been enormous, especially in terms of human reason and revelation as competing methods of knowing God. Prior to Descartes, theologians like Thomas Aquinas believed *in principle* that reason could demonstrate the existence of God, but as neo-Thomist philosopher, E. L. Mascall, has shown, Thomas Aquinas recognized that no natural theology could be successful without revelation because sin had blighted the moral ability to see what ought to be the most obvious reality in the world—namely, the existence of God. Hence natural theology must depend upon the facts of God's revelation in history in order to make its case for theism.[8] Descartes turned this distinction between natural and revealed theology into a divorce. Although Descartes assumed that the results of his philosophy of rationalism would reinforce the beliefs of the church, the actual course of modern thinking has shown otherwise. More specifically, Descartes' method of rationalism and his anti-historical attitude unwittingly destabilized the historical claims of Christian revelation.[9]

Since Descartes believed that Christian revelation was not the method for convincing modern skeptics, he turned to an examination of his own personal history and inner experience in order to set out rationally what epistemological principles could serve as a foundation for a new method that would lead to the discovery of absolute certainty. He believed that the method of geometry was the model to follow. If the ideal of certainty was to be reached, this required the consistent application of reason as practiced in geometry. This meant discovering the axiomatic and *foundational* premises of philosophy, which were as self-evident and universal as geometric axioms. Nothing should be accepted as true unless it could be proven as being rationally "clear and distinct." This foundationalist theory of truth was to become the hallmark of modern thought.

In order to establish the axiomatic truths of philosophy, Descartes employed the use of methodological skepticism (as distinguished from actual skepticism). His method was to doubt everything that could be doubted until some irrefutable and self-evident principle imposed itself on his reason as being beyond doubt and absolutely certain. This entailed four general principles. (1) Never accept anything as true which is not self-evident. This means the philosopher must renounce as false anything that is merely plausible. One must avoid bias and one must not include anything in one's judgments which does not present itself clearly and distinctly to his mind. (2) Divide each philosophical difficulty into as many parts as possible in order to reach a satisfactory solution. (3) Conduct one's thoughts in an orderly manner. Begin with those objects that are simplest and easiest to know, and then rise little by little to knowledge of the most complex events. (4) One must be careful not to omit any of the facts, carefully scrutinizing every event and making a complete enumeration and comprehensive review in order that nothing will be overlooked.[10]

These four principles helped to lay down a basis for critical historical methodology. In terms of philosophical truth, Descartes' methodological skepticism led him to the following conclusions. First, there is the *a priori* (that is, deductive and self-evident) knowledge of the self. We could doubt the existence of everything around us, but we could not doubt the fact of our doubting. This could only point to the undeniable certainty that each person is a thinking self. "I think, therefore, I am." Descartes believed one could have no misgivings about this self-evident truth.[11] Here Descartes was making the "self" the basis of all that can be known.

In premodern thought, the soul was like an entity that existed alongside everything else, but it did not make the self the basis of what is real. Now with the emergence of modern thought in Descartes' philosophy, the unity of self-consciousness became the basis of everything, although Descartes continued to interpret God as the foundation of reality.

Pannenberg has noted that "we do not find anything like this conception of the subjectivity of the human ego" in the previous history of
thought.[12] Subsequent modern thought, especially in Kant, radicalized
this concept of human subjectivity, altogether eliminating the necessity
of God's existence as the basis of our experience of reality. Certainly,
Kant believed in God, but he believed that God's existence was a postulate of human moral reasoning. So Descartes introduced this radical
concept of human subjectivity and self-consciousness, but Kant subsequently made the divorce between God and the world complete by
making human subjectivity the basis of everything.

A second distinct idea that Descartes' rationalistic method allegedly
was able to prove is the existence of God. Because Descartes could
think of a more perfect Being than himself, it was evident to him that
this idea must have come from a Being who is more perfect than he is.
Descartes believed this argument could not be used in regard to the
sense-world. The stars, the sun, and the moon stand in a different relation to him, and he can see nothing in them which could cause him to
think that they were superior to him. In fact, it could be deduced that
their existence really depends upon his own imagination. On the other
hand, the conception of a Being more perfect than himself could not
have come from nothing, for it would be contradictory to believe that
the more perfect would follow and be dependent upon the less perfect.[13] This distinct idea of a Being greater than himself can only be the
result of it coming from beyond himself. Descartes writes: "From the fact
that I exist and have in me the idea of a supremely perfect being, that is,
of God, it must be concluded that the existence of God is demonstrated in the most evident manner."[14]

Gilson pointed out that the God whom Descartes assumed to have
proven by his philosophical method was actually an unrecognized result
"of what he had learned in church when he was a little boy."[15] Even
though Descartes had the idea of a Supreme Being, this idea did not
mean that he had proven the existence of a personal God. The idea of
a perfect island does not mean that one actually existed.[16] The reality of
anything (including God) cannot be proven by asserting that an idea of
something is equivalent to proving that it exists. Wolfhart Pannenberg
has pointed out that a proof of perfection does not prove the reality of
the God of Christian faith. The idea of will and personality are more
basic to the notion of God than maximal perfection,[17] and the proof of
God has to be more than a philosophical argument. It must entail a personal disclosure in history.

If Descartes too easily linked his proof of perfection with the idea of God, similarly he mistakenly assumed that he had proven the existence of the immortal self. If Descartes believed in the immortal self, it was the result of his having learned it from his Christian tradition and not from his rationalistic philosophy. "I think; therefore I am" is thus not a demonstrative proof of one's immortal, spiritual existence. Such reasoning at best only proved that Descartes had the mental ability to think.

Descartes' third axiomatic truth is that the soul is entirely distinct from the body. In fact, he believed the soul is easier to know than the body and would be known if there were no body.[18] This is so because he maintained it was an axiomatic truth that "intellectual nature is distinct from corporeal nature."[19] The justification for this argument is also found in his method of skepticism concerning the empirical world. Anything that is based on sense perception does not qualify as genuine knowledge, though of course it may possess a strong degree of credibility.[20] "We ought never to let ourselves be convinced of anything except by the evidence of our reason," and not by our imagination or our senses.[21] Irrefutable knowledge is thus deduced from *a priori* concepts. Our ability to reason is totally capable of mapping out the nature of reality simply by thinking coherently about axiomatic ideas (concerning God, the immortal self, and the world), which were present in our minds at birth. There is thus a bifurcation between body and mind, the intellectual and the empirical. Descartes believed innate ideas do not need any corresponding reality in the empirical world as proof of their reality.[22] For these innate ideas are embedded within the mind from birth. They are just as axiomatic and clear as any mathematical demonstration.

If there is such a radical distinction between mind and body, between self-evident concepts and sense perceptions, then methodological skepticism becomes actual skepticism in regard to historical knowledge, for empirical perceptions cannot be compared with the clear and self-evident knowledge of the mind. This is why Gustave Lanson says that the Cartesian method is radically hostile to history; history as a science is in fact abolished and becomes nothing more than a curiosity and a series of confused representations, capable only of amusing the imagination.[23] The implications of this historical skepticism are obviously negative for Christian theology with its belief in the historic character of revelation.

This historical skepticism marked the beginning, in a paradoxical way, of the modern historical movement.[24] It served as a challenge to historians to establish a solid and sure foundation for historical knowledge. Collingwood called this constructive response, "Cartesian historiogra-

phy," since it was based on the critical principles of Cartesian methodological skepticism.[25]

Pierre Bayle: Historical Positivism

Pierre Bayle (1647-1706) was one historian who responded to the challenge of the Cartesian methodological skepticism. He adopted the
Cartesian criterion of the clear and distinct idea, thus seeking to establish *certain* (absolute) knowledge of historical facts. His concern was not
with any teleological or theological interpretation of history, but with
establishing the bare facts of history using critical methodology. His
General Dictionary, Historical and Critical "proposes only to collect errors
with regard to fact."[26] It intends to be of "the most minute detail."[27] With
this ideal of ascertaining bare historical facts uninfluenced by personal
judgments as if facts are independent of interpretation, he became the
first historical "positivist."[28]

His method was to examine all phenomena and to distinguish
between the certain and the uncertain, the probable and the erroneous.
He writes: "Errors are the only thing that can be of any service to me,
provided I am able to correct them."[29] He thus did not use his Cartesian
methodological doubt against historical knowledge, but rather used it to
examine critically what can be certain historically. In each of the articles
of his dictionary, he restricted his primary remarks to correcting historical errors about the subject in question.[30] This idea of uninterpreted,
bare facts is what positivistic historiography entails.

Bayle imagined he overcame the Cartesian anti-historical influence
with his belief that historical study can lead to a greater type of certainty than mathematical study.[31] Geometric truths may not exist outside the
mind, while historical facts offer a greater kind of reality and certainty
because they exist both in the mind and they exist externally to what the
mind merely thinks. He says: "Thus it is more certain metaphysically,
that Cicero has existed out of the understanding of any other man, than
it is certain that the object of the Mathematics exists out of our understanding."[32]

Bayle's critical approach to history illustrates how Descartes' negative
view of historical truth helped to provoke the rise of historical criticism.
Descartes elevated the axiomatic truths of reason, but Bayle elevated
historical facts. Bayle's goal was to release history from all authoritarianism and to put historical studies on an entirely independent basis, which
would be free from other disciplines of thought. [33] In this respect, Ernst

Cassirer points out: "Bayle accomplished scarcely less for history than Galileo did for natural science....It is he who carries out the 'Copernican revolution' in the realm of historical science."[34]

Spinoza: Reason and History

Another Cartesian thinker, Baruch Spinoza (1632-1677), became the founder of modern biblical criticism with his publication of *Theologico-Political Treatise* in 1670.[35] For Spinoza, pure being is the source of absolute certainty, while temporal things exist in becoming and thus are relative, uncertain and virtually unreal. Spinoza believed the philosopher is able to rise above the temporal world through thinking about truth and hence is able to ascertain what is truth with absolute certainty. This rationalist view had negative consequences for the Bible as a medium of truth because it is a book that relied upon history.[36]

Spinoza made a sharp differentiation between what is self-evident knowledge (reason) and what is experiential knowledge (history). [37] Conclusions reached through the rational deductions of general truths entail extensive arguments, and consequently the intellectual effort required for such deductions causes most people to prefer to learn through personal experience "rather than deduce their conclusion from a few axioms, and set them out in logical order."[38] Religion is thus for the majority of people, while philosophy is for the learned.[39] Eternal truths of reason known through philosophical deduction are allegedly far superior to truths learned through experience. Spinoza did not believe this means that the Scriptures are irrelevant to most people. Quite the contrary, the Scriptures teach what can be otherwise known through the light of reason.[40] The Scriptures infer eternal truths through allegories, legends, and parables.[41] The chief speculative doctrine of the Bible is the existence of God and that God directs and governs the world. Although experience cannot "explain the nature of God, nor how He directs and sustains all things, it can nevertheless teach and enlighten men sufficiently to impress obedience and devotion on their minds."[42] A philosopher may thus allow limited validity to the teachings of the Bible, but at the same time Spinoza argued that it had a subordinate position to philosophy.

Spinoza believed that the historical trustworthiness of the Bible was of no consequence to knowledge of God. "The truth of a historical narrative, however assured, cannot give us the knowledge nor consequently the love of God, for love of God springs from knowledge of Him, and knowledge of Him should be derived from general ideas, in themselves certain and known, so that the truth of a historical narrative is very far from being a necessary requisite for our attaining our highest good."[43] What Spinoza contended was that philosophy and theology are entirely separate in their approach to knowledge.[44] In this connection, he identified the "Word of God," not with the books of the Bible, but with the idea of God that was impressed upon the prophets and the apostles, who in turn urged obedience to God.[45] It is this obedience to God that constitutes faith and piety, and it is not contrary to reason.[46] This means theology is not doctrine, but precepts and rules of life.[47] Theology exercises a necessary and practical task for the majority of people, but it is restricted in that it does not teach philosophy, i.e., its teaching comes from experience rather than the self-evident and distinct ideas of reason. Nevertheless, if one will strip away the historical framework of the Bible, Spinoza thinks that theology and philosophy will agree.[48] This divorce of revelation and philosophy, historical knowledge and philosophical knowledge, means that the Scriptures only have a practical value. Spinoza writes: "The sphere of reason is, as we have said, truth and wisdom; the sphere of theology is piety and obedience."[49]

Spinoza as the Founder of Biblical Criticism

Spinoza was the first person to provide a foundation for biblical criticism[50] (whose method is not dissimilar to our own procedure today),[51] and he assumed a radical epistemological dualism, thus using the Cartesian dualism to weaken the historical character of revelation. Spinoza became the founder of modern biblical criticism with his publication of the *Theologico-Political Treatise*.[52] The immediate occasion for his interest in the Bible was that the ultimate authority ascribed to it by the Church was in direct conflict with his own metaphysical presupposition that the basis of absolute certainty was rational, not empirical. We noted earlier that Spinoza located the source of certainty in pure being, not in becoming. This means that temporal elements have no significance for philosophical knowledge because history and reason lie on different levels. If the Bible should be accorded primary authority for religious belief, this would mean that reason is sacrificed, for how can the absolute certainty of metaphysical truth in any way depend on the historically-conditioned elements of the Bible? Cassirer explained: "And yet Spinoza was the originator of the idea of the historicity of the Bible, and the first to develop it with sober precision and clarity. If we pursue this idea to its place in Spinoza's system as a whole, we find that it arose from no immediate historical tendency, from no interest in historical method as such, but that it represents an indirect conclusion from the logical premises of the system."[53] Why then did Spinoza express an intense interest in the historicity of the Bible? Cassirer answered: "Spinoza's [pantheistic] monism is offended by the special position of the Bible" because he believed pure thought was the surest way to find truth.[54] His interest in historical criticism thus arose out of his desire to show that historically conditioned events cannot have any real significance for truth. This was the logical conclusion that he drew from Cartesian rationalism with its sharp distinction between the intellectual and sensuous aspects of reality. Because historical knowledge is a form of sensuous knowledge, it is impure and unreliable.

Spinoza's Philosophy of Identity

Spinoza's philosophy presupposed the principle of identity.[55] This principle assumes that reality is larger than the accumulation of individual objects or things because there is an underlying identity or sameness in reality. It entails the view that everything is unified and ultimately grounded in the nature of God. This means the essence of reality is greater than the mere existence of individual things because reality is bounded together in the creativity and unity of God. However, Spinoza ignored the corollary principle of distance, which assumes there is also a basic difference between subject and object, between the essence and individual existence of things. Spinoza's one-sided emphasis on identity is why he was a pantheist because he included nature within God's essence.

Related to these two principles of identity and distance is the ancient problem of the one and the many.[56] This was Plato's big issue—how can reality be one when there is such diversity in the world. His answer was that the power of being-itself is present in everything. True being is immaterial and is the unifying principle of the many. As we noted earlier, Plotinus in the 3rd century A.D. gave Plato's philosophy a pantheistic interpretation, while the early Church Fathers also used Plato's philosophy of identity but adjusted it to include the principle of difference between God and the world. Because the principle of distance was integrated within the principle of identity, Christian theology was able to affirm God's relationship to the world without falling into pantheism. Hence God existed before there was a world, but the world cannot exist without God. God as its creator is also related to it as its sustainer and redeemer. However, Spinoza developed an extreme philosophy of identity that dissolved the multiple aspects of reality into a monism. This in effect denied the real existence of the world because the world lacked any true substance and was downgraded to a minor attribute of God's larger being.[57] This denial eliminated any possibility that God could be made known in the history of salvation because events in the world lacked true substance. Spinoza believed that access to God was through participation in mystical oneness with God through philosophy. All pantheistic systems entail a basic distrust of the history of salvation as a means of knowing God.

Richard Simon: Faith vs. Historical Uncertainty

Cartesian philosopher Nicole Malebranche inspired Richard Simon, a French priest, to conduct a critical study of the development of the books of the Bible.[58] This was the first time that a comprehensive critical study of the books of the Bible had ever been conducted.[59] In his work, *A Critical History of the Old Testament* (1678), he set forth a critical study of the original texts along with the various translations. Simon's indirect purpose for this analysis of the biblical books was to enhance the authority of the Roman Catholic Church that had been challenged by the Protestant Reformation. He attempted to argue that the Bible alone is no sure protection against doubt, but needs to be supported by the tradition and the authority of the Church.[60] Thus, the Protestant reliance upon the Bible was thought to be inadequate.

Some of the presuppositions of this critical study are: (1) The original texts of the Bible were fully and equally inspired. Simon objected to a certain "Divine" who believed the Bible was inspired only in matters of faith.[61] (2) The original authors abbreviated and edited those larger acts of the people that were the most instructive.[62] (3) The original authors did not always intend to give an exact chronological order of things, for they were not merely writing factual and chronological history. Rather, they were writing theological history, though the matters of detail were likewise accurate.[63] (4) Biblical books were sometimes written by authors of a later age who compiled the book from the public records. Nevertheless, these authors were inspired by the Holy Spirit.[64] (5) Moses was not the author of the Pentateuch as we have it, though the original composition was extracted from Moses' public records.[65] (6) The original texts have undergone serious changes with the result that our present texts are replete with errors.[66] (7) Consequently, the authority of the Roman Catholic Church is needed to provide faith with its foundation.

Simon concluded: "Instead of believing with the Protestants that the shortest and most certain way of deciding the questions of Faith is to consult the Holy Scriptures, we shall on the contrary find in this Work that if we join not Tradition with the Scripture, we can hardly affirm any thing for certain in Religion."[67]

Simon believed that the certainty of faith must be independent of the results of historical research. This means that the Scriptures cannot serve as the foundation of certainty because they contain information that is subject to historical development and thus uncertain. Nothing "certain in Religion" can be established from historical study. Rather, the certainty of faith finds its support in the authority of the Church. The Cartesian methodological doubt was thus used to argue for the authority of the Roman Catholic Church.[68]

Notes

1. Rene Descartes, "Discourse on Method," *Essential Works of Descartes*, trans. Lowell Blair with an intro. By Daniel J. Bronstein (New York: Bantam Books, 1966), 4-6.

2. Ernst Cassirer, *The Philosophy of the Enlightenment*, 93-133; Cf. Richard Rorty, *Philosophy and the Mirror of Nature* (Princeton: Princeton University Press, 1979), 132ff.

3. Rene Descartes, "Discourse on Method," *Essential Works of Descartes*, 4-6.

4. Descartes, "Meditations on First Philosophy," *Essential Works of Descartes*, 48.

5. Cf. Etienne Gilson, *God and Philosophy*, 77.

6. Ibid., 74.

7. Ibid.

8. E. L. Mascall, *He Who Is* (Archon Books, 1970), 14, 25.

9. Gilson, *God and Philosophy*, 82.

10. "Discourse on Method," *Essential Works of Descartes*, 12.

11. Ibid., 20.

12. Pannenberg, *Metaphysics and The Idea of God* (Grand Rapids: Wm. B. Eerdmans, 1990) 44.

13. Ibid., 21.

14. "Meditations of First Philosophy," *Essential Works of Descartes*, 81.

15. Gilson, *God and Philosophy*, 83.

16. Anselm, *Proslogium: Monologium ; An Appendix in Behalf of the Fool, by Gaunilon ; and Cur Deus homo*, ed. Deane, Sidney Norton (Chicago: Open Court, 1935).

17. Wolfhart Pannenberg, *Metaphysics and the Idea of God* (Grand Rapids: Wm. B. Eerdmans, 1990), 28.

18. "Discourse on Method," *Essential Works of Descartes*, 20.

19. Ibid., 22.

20. Ibid., 24.

21. Ibid.

22. "Meditations on First Philosophy," *Essential Works of Descartes*, 99.

23. Gustave Lanson, "L'Influence De La Philosophie Cartésienne Sue La Littérature Francaise," *Revue de Métaphysique et de Morale*, (1896), 4:533.

24. Cassirer, *The Philosophy of the Enlightenment*, 201.

25. Collingwood, *The Idea of History*, 60.

26. Pierre Bayle, "A Proposal for a Critical Dictionary," *A General Dictionary, Historical and Critical*, trans. J. Bernard, et al. (London: James Bettenheim, 1741), 10:388.

27. Ibid., 383.

28. Cassirer, *The Philosophy of the Enlightenment*, 202.

29. Ibid., 378.

30. Ibid., 379.

31. Ibid., 386.

32. Ibid., 387.

33. Bayle, *A General Dictionary, Historical and Critical*, 10:69. Cf. Cassirer, *The Philosophy of the Enlightenment*, 208-209.

34. Cassirer, *The Philosophy of the Enlightenment*, 207.

35. Ibid., 185-186.

36. Ibid., 185.

37. "A Theologico-Political Treatise", *The Chief Works of Benedict de Spinoza*, translated with an introduction by R. H. M. Elwes (London: George Bell and Sons, 1883), 1:76-77.

38. Ibid., 77.

39. Ibid.

40. Ibid., 14.

41. Ibid., 25.

42. Ibid., 78.

43. Ibid., 61.

44. Ibid., 10.

45. Ibid., 9.

46. Ibid., 195.

47. Ibid.

48. Ibid., 9.

49. Ibid., 194.

50. Cassirer, *The Philosophy of the Enlightenment*, 184.

51. Robert M. Grant, *A Short History of the Interpretation of the Bible* (New York: The Macmillan Company, 1963), 149. That Spinoza's method is similar to our today can be seen with the following four principles: (1) the original language should be known; (2) an analysis of each book should be thoroughly made according to its content, with special attention being given to obscure or contradictory passages; (3) a thorough historical background study of each author

and book should be made—who wrote it, how did it become a part of the canon, etc.; (4) the interpretation must take into full account the intention of the author, so that our study will be objective and without the interference of our opinions. *The Chief Works of Benedict de Spinoza,* 1: 100-103..

52. Cassirer, *The Philosophy of the Enlightenment,* 184-185.

53. Ibid, 185.

54. Ibid, 185.

55. Tillich, *A History of Christian Thought,* ed. Carl E. Braaten (New York: Harper and Row, 1967), 440.

56. Ibid.

57. Hegel, *The Encyclopaedia Logic,* trans. T. F. Garets, W. A. Suchting, and H. S. Harris (Indianapolis: Hackett Publishing Company, 1991), 226-227

58. Ibid, 184.

59. Ibid.

60. Ibid.

61. Richard Simon, *A Critical History of the Old Testament,* translator unknown (London: Walter David, 1682), iv.

62. Ibid., vii

63. Ibid.

64. Ibid., iv.

65. Ibid.

66. Ibid., viii.

67. Ibid., ix.

68. Cassirer, *The Philosophy of the Enlightenment,* 184.

6

The Logic of Historical Probability, Individuality, and Relativity

In the previous chapter, we considered the anti-historical implications of Cartesian rationalism in the 17th century and its claims that the surest way to know God was through reason alone. We noted some of the theological implications of modern dualistic thinking. We will see in this chapter how the problem of faith and history was more definitively formulated in the late 17th and 18th centuries.

Leibniz: The Concept of Historical Probability

G.W. Leibniz (1646-1716) was a German philosopher, mathematical genius, and Christian apologist. He traveled extensively and corresponded with all the major thinkers of his time, including Locke, Spinoza, Huygens, and Newton. His significance for understanding the relation of faith and history is that he reformulated the Cartesian body-mind dualism into a distinction between the facts of experience and reason.[1] As opposed to Descartes who defined reason as a faculty of inborn ideas, Leibniz defined reason as an activity enabling the mind to reach conclusions.[2] Leibniz does not speak of reason in the classical Greek sense of *nous* as if the mind were a faculty of inborn ideas and principles; rather, reason is *logos*, the power to connect truths and draw conclusions.[3]

Leibniz made a distinction between *necessary truths of reason* and *contingent truths of fact*, but he was an exception in modern philosophy because he did not turn the subject-object distinction into a divorce. Truths of fact are interpretations of data derived from our five senses. Reason recognizes that sense-data have objective existence so that what we perceive as external objects are not dreams.[4] Reason analyzes and interprets sense-data, but its conclusions are contingent. If I see a rock sink to the bottom of a tub of water, my knowledge of this sinking rock is contingent because it is based on what I observe happening in the outside world. On the other hand, necessary truths of reason are not contingent because they are always the same and are independent of what I actually sense in the outside world, as in geometry.[5] For example, a triangle always and necessarily has 180°, even if there is no actual triangle existing in the outside world.

Leibniz believed that this distinction between necessary truths and contingent truths shows that the laws of nature are not absolute and necessary. This is because the laws of nature are contingent truths. They are contingent because they are subject to the creative act of God: "It is therefore true that God gave such laws not without reason, for he chooses nothing from caprice and as though by chance or in pure indifference; but the general reasons of good and of order, which have prompted him to the choice, may be overcome in some cases by stronger reasons of a superior order."[6] Simply stated, if God chooses to suspend this law, God is free to do so. In such cases, Leibniz referred to unusual happenings as miracles. A miracle does not mean the laws of nature have broken down, but rather God has chosen to suspend them for a higher purpose.

Whatever is believed to be true should be shown to be so, whether it is a truth of reason or a truth of fact. All knowing involves a careful reasoning process of perceiving the connection of things and making inferences.[7] The truths of fact rely upon the law of sufficient reason,[8] while the necessary truths of reason rely upon the principles of formal logic and mathematics.[9] However, necessary truths of reason would not even enter our minds if it were not for our senses; for reasoning would not occur without a mind and a mind could not think without a brain. The necessary truths of reasons are thus abstractions, whereas truths of fact have a foundation in the outside world.

Leibniz made the distinction between necessary and contingent truths of reason to bridge the difference between the philosophy of Descartes (known as Continental rationalism) and the philosophy of John Locke (known as British empiricism). Continental rationalism and British empiricism were developed in the 17th century as alternate ways of explaining how knowledge is attained. Continental rationalism assumed innate ideas were the basis of what one knows about the ultimate nature of reality; British empiricism assumed sense experience is the source of all that is known. British empiricism denied that we are born with "innate ideas," insisting instead that the mind is like a blank sheet of paper at birth. It maintained that our knowledge of the self, the world, and God is derived through a reasoning process based on what the five senses furnish to the mind. It is as if "sense data" is like a pencil which writes ideas on the mind.

British empiricism was systematically developed in John Locke's *Essays on Human Understanding,* but Leibniz was not satisfied with many of its premises and arguments. He particularly argued against the idea of the mind being like a "blank tablet." Rather, he argued that the mind contains fundamental powers to know and that it is suited to make judgments about the very nature of reality itself. Although we do not have innate knowledge, we do have an innate capacity to know.

Leibniz was not satisfied with the rationalism of Descartes either. In his work, *New Essays on Human Understanding,* he sought a mediating position between Locke and Descartes. Although this work was first published in 1690 and being the gentleman that he was, Leibniz suppressed it because Locke died at the age of 72 and was unable to respond to its criticism. Leibniz believed the rationalist notion that necessary truths of reason were superior to actual experience of the world was a mere abstraction because they do not really exist as such. He also rejected the rationalist notion that one must doubt the facts of experience simply because they cannot be proved with absolute, geometric certainty. Leibniz explained: "For I do not believe that any one can seriously be so skeptical as to be uncertain of the existence of things which he sees and feels. At least, he who can carry his doubts so far will never have any controversy with me, since he can never be certain that I say anything contrary to his opinion."[10]

Leibniz was the first modern scholar to propose the need for a *"new kind of logic"*[11] regarding the probabilities of historical knowledge. He showed that knowing entails varying degrees of probability.[12] He called probable knowledge "opinion" in the best sense of the word.[13] Such knowledge is also called truths of experience because those truths are derived from a study of history. The truths of experience can also be called contingent truths of reason, since the truths of experience are a reasoned understanding of the connection that exists among empirical facts.[14] The concern of Leibniz with epistemology was to provide a valid basis for the historical claims of Christian faith, and this is why he wanted to restore a sense of confidence in the truths of experience. Because conclusions concerning facts of nature are contingent and not necessary, one cannot "disprove" the truths of faith, such as the resurrection of Jesus. Just because the miracles of Christian revelation go against the usual laws of nature, this is not a proof against them because they are not necessary truths of reason. If one objects to the miracles of the Bible because they violate the laws of nature, this is not a rationally compelling argument either because this is a misunderstanding of the laws of nature. This is only "a probable argument, which has no force against faith, since it is agreed that the Mysteries of religion are contrary to appearance."[15] Leibniz was an exception among modern philosophers because he did not accept that the law of cause and effect was mechanistic, but rather they had their basis in the will of God.

To say historical events are contingent is not to say one must therefore doubt them. To doubt something simply because it does not bear the necessary demonstration of mathematical proof is "madness."[16] What is important for contingent truths is that they be established with sufficient reason,[17] and they can be considered sufficiently based when they stand in a positive relationship to what is practical to believe. Leibniz argued that "*to doubt seriously* is to doubt" something that is practical to doubt. To doubt for the sake of doubting is irrational. Further, one ought not to doubt something unless "we could not doubt without deserving to be severely blamed." On the other hand, we judge the evidence for accepting some historical facts very strong "because of the connection we see between ideas. According to this definition of certainty, we are certain that Constantinople is in the world, that Constantine, Alexander the Great, and Julius Caesar lived. It is true that some peasant of Ardennes might justly doubt about these, for lack of information; but a man of letters and of the world could not do so without great derangement of mind."[18]

Leibniz argued that the truths of fact are conditioned by degrees of probability.[19] (1) When a particular fact conforms with what we repeatedly and constantly observe, and it concurs likewise with the testimony of others, then this particular fact may be considered certain knowledge. This is a reasoned knowledge of the highest degree of probability; e.g., that fire warms, that a rock sinks in water. This level of probability prompts *assurance*. (2) When historians report than an individual preferred his or her own selfish interests to that of the public interests, then these histories are met with *confidence*, because we observe this to be the custom of the majority of men. (3) If a fact is reported by those of highest integrity whom we have no reason to suspect and if this fact does not contradict our experience, then it may be received with a *firm belief*. For example, that Julius Caesar lived can be firmly believed. (4) If a reported fact is contrary to what we usually experience, or if the fact is reported with conflicting testimonies among historians, then the degrees of probability will vary, ranging from belief, conjecture, doubt, uncertainty, to distrust. In this case, we must "proportion our assent to the degrees of probability."[20]

Leibniz illustrated the problem of the varying degrees of probable knowledge in connection with the judicial process of law.[21] There is "notoriety," which demands no proof. There are "complete" proofs upon which sentences of conviction are based, and the degrees of "complete" proof will be demanded in severe cases of criminal trials. There are also "presumptions" which may serve as sufficient ground for a conviction. Thus, the legal scholar will show that proofs may vary from notoriety, to more than half complete proofs, to less than half complete, presumptions which hold good unless the contrary is proved, finally down to varying degrees of conjectures.

As opposed to the anti-historical implications of Cartesian philosophy, Leibniz defended the possibility of historical knowledge and the importance of historical criticism. Not only is historical criticism a legitimate study for Leibniz, but it is a necessary study for lending support to the foundation of revelation.[22] He says that faith finds its justification "upon the experience of those who have seen the miracles whereon revelation is founded, and upon the trustworthy tradition which has handed them down to us, whether through the Scriptures or by the account of those who have preserved them."[23] Just as reliable and responsible testimony is necessary for the credibility of a witness,[24] even so faith "is a firm assent, and assent, regulated as it should be, can only be given upon good reasons."[25] Leibniz said: "He who believes without any reason for believing may be in love with his fancies."[26] Leibniz also took into account "the inward motion of the Holy Spirit" that inspires one with a sense of confidence in the truth of Holy Scripture.[27]

Leibniz did not bifurcate the necessary truths of reason and the probable truths of reason in order to make a place for the truths of faith. He was quite emphatic that faith is not contrary to the truths of reason. He said the proper use of reason does not deceive, i.e., reason defined in terms of linking facts and ideas together. On the other hand, our senses and understanding may be misled, but not reason. Whatever is seen to be contrary to reason *must* be acknowledged as false.[28] Leibniz complained that many are willing "to grant that the Holy Trinity is contrary to that great principle which states that two things which are the same as a third are also the same as each other: that is to say, if A is the same as B, and if C is the same as B, then A and C must also be the same as each other."[29] If this basic principle of logic is rejected allegedly in favor of faith, then the basis for reasoning is destroyed. Leibniz argued: "Thus when one says that the Father is God, that the Son is God and that the Holy Spirit is God, and that nevertheless there is only one God, although these three Persons differ from one another, one must consider that this word *God* has not the same sense at the beginning as at the end of this statement. Indeed it signifies now the Divine Substance and now a Person of the Godhead."[30]

Leibniz brings Pierre Bayle into sharp criticism for confusing the relationship of faith and reason. Under the influence of the Cartesian dualism of the distinct ideas of reason and the empirical facts of the world, Bayle failed to correlate adequately the relationship of faith and reason. Austin Farrer has shown: "So far as he [Bayle] had a philosophical opinion, he was a Cartesian; in theology he was an orthodox Calvinist. He could not reconcile his theology with his Cartesianism and he did not try to. He made a merit of the oppositions of faith to reason and reason to itself, so that he could throw himself upon a meritorious and voluntary faith."[31]

Leibniz would not allow this opposition of faith and reason. Leibniz noted: "M. Bayle…declares himself against reason, when he might have been content to censure its abuse. He quotes the words of Cotta in Cicero, where he goes so far as to say that if reason were a gift of the gods providence would be to blame for having given it, since it tends to our harm."[32] Leibniz further remarked: "M. Bayle also thinks that human reason is a source of destruction and not of edification…that it is a runner who knows not where to stop, and who, like another Penelope, herself destroys her own work."[33]

Instead of opposing faith and reason, Leibniz distinguished between what is above reason and what is contrary to reason. "What is contrary to reason is contrary to the absolutely certain and inevitable truths; and what is above reason is in opposition only to what one is wont to experience or understand."[34] The distinction between truths of reason and truths of faith served the purpose of pointing out that faith is in harmony with the truths of reason. The contingent truths of fact have "no force against faith," for they are inconclusive and probable.[35] The truths of fact illustrate the orderly working of nature, yet these laws "may be overcome in some cases by stronger reasons of a superior order."[36] Leibniz also contended that the necessary truths of reason are not contrary to the truths of faith; rather, they illustrate the coherence of belief.

The truths of faith stand on a higher level than the truths of facts because faith sees what is contrary to appearance. Although faith cannot be fully explained, it can be sufficiently understood so that one may give assent to its truth. Leibniz explained: "Thus we agreed that Mysteries should receive an explanation, but this explanation is imperfect. It suffices for us to have some analogical understanding of a Mystery such as the Trinity and the Incarnation, to the end that in accepting them we pronounce not words altogether devoid of meaning: but it is not necessary that the explanation go as far as we would wish, that is, to the extent of comprehension and to the how."[37] The presupposition of faith is thus not the *how it is*, but *what it is*.

Leibniz argued that faith is substantiated by the following: (1) the credibility of the Scriptures can be established through the logic of historical probability;[38] (2) the truths of faiths can be shown to be in harmony with the necessary truths of reason and that the articles of faith are as exact and coherent as the proofs of mathematics;[39] and finally (3) the internal testimony of the Holy Spirit persuades and prompts one to faith and love.[40] Leibniz argued that the faculty of reason is not to be disparaged, especially because it, like faith, is a gift of God.[41] He finds the harmony of faith and reason to be one of "the motives of credibility" for believing in the Christian faith.[42]

The clarity of the thinking of Leibniz on the relationship among the necessary truths of reason, the contingent truths of reason, and the truths of faith was short-lived. Subsequent philosophers often borrowed Leibnizian categories, but failed to integrate faith and history, faith and reason, perpetuating instead the radical dualistic thinking initiated by Descartes.

Lessing: The Fallacy of Misplaced Necessity

Ephraim Lessing (1729-1781) was influenced largely through the philosophy of Spinoza and Leibniz. He transposed the philosophical distinctions between the truths of reason and the truths of facts into theology.[43] The critical question that Cartesian rationalism had posed for theology is—how can religious certainty be attained for Christian faith if history is an unreliable means of knowing? We observed in the previous chapter that Spinoza did not hesitate to draw the conclusion that biblical history is an inferior form of knowing compared to the truths achieved by reason alone. Lessing agreed with Spinoza that history can have no decisive significance for salvation, for historical events are merely probable and uncertain: "We all believe that an Alexander lived who in a short time conquered almost all Asia. But who, on the basis of this belief, would risk anything of great, permanent worth, the loss of which would be irreparable?" Lessing answered: "Certainly not I." [44] Revealing an attitude of extreme skepticism, Lessing confessed: "Now I have no objection to raise against Alexander and his victory: but it might still be possible that the story was founded on a mere poem of Choerilus just as the ten-year siege of Troy depends on no better authority than Homer's poetry."[45]

We noted above that Leibniz had said "a man of letters and of the world could not [seriously doubt the existence of Alexander the Great] ...without great derangement of mind." Lessing held to an extreme historical skepticism, not because he was mentally unstable, but because he wanted to make a philosophical point—why rely on history as a means of knowing God when reason can offer unquestionable truth? Hence he said: "*Accidental truths of history can never become the proof of necessary truths of reason.*"[46] He confessed that he would refuse to believe the most reliable witnesses of a historical event if it contradicted what he thought was possible. Even though historical evidence may support the belief that Jesus was raised from the dead, he still could not believe it because reason says this simply cannot happen.[47] "To jump with that historical truth to a quite different class of truths, and to demand of me that I should form all my metaphysical and moral ideas accordingly; to expect me to alter all my fundamental ideas of the nature of the Godhead because I cannot set any credible testimony against the resurrection of Christ: if that is no *metabasis eis allo genos* [changing into another category], then I do not know what Aristotle meant by this phrase."

Lessing called this difference between history and reason "the ugly, broad ditch which I cannot get across, however often and however earnestly I have tried to make the leap."[49] He then said: "If anyone can help me over it, let him do it, I beg him, I adjure him. He will deserve a divine reward from me."[50] Cassirer showed how Lessing developed his own answer to the problem of faith and history: "Neither the theology nor the systematic metaphysics of the eighteenth century contained a principle by virtue of which Lessing's question could really be answered and his demand truly satisfied...In his *Education of Humanity* Lessing created a new synthesis of the historical and the rational. The historical is no longer opposed to the rational"[51] Rather, history is the place where reason comes into its own through a process of education. Lessing defined revelation in terms of the growth of moral perfection in the stages of history. He said: "Education is revelation coming to the individual man; and revelation is education which has come, and is still coming, to the human race."[52] This education entails the idea of moral perfection and is universally available to everyone because it is contained implicitly within the mind of everyone. He explained: "Revelation gives nothing to the human race which human reason could not arrive at on its own."[53]

The progressive development of this moral education in history is traced from early polytheism, through the Hebrews and the Greeks, up to the Christian religion. This development is defined as the movement from revealed truths to truths of reason. He put it this way: "The development of revealed truths into truths of reason, is absolutely necessary, if the human race is to be assisted by them. When they were revealed they were certainly not truths of reason, but they were revealed in order to become such."[54] Only through the progressive education of the human race did the idea of God and morality become recognized as universal truths of reason. In essence, Lessing de-historicized the biblical idea of revelation by stripping it of miraculous events and turning it into a natural religion of reason.[55]

His essay on the *Education of the Human Race* had certain similarities to Spinoza and Leibniz. Spinoza maintained: (1) "that the truth of a historical narrative is very far from being a necessary requisite for our attaining our highest good,"[56] even as Lessing says that historical facts, no matter how certain, cannot serve as the basis for belief, for no one "would risk anything of great, permanent worth, the loss of which would be irreparable," upon historical facts.[57] (2) Spinoza maintained that the essential teachings of Scripture are in virtual harmony with the eternal truths of reason,[58] even as Lessing maintains that revealed truths must be turned into truths of reason to form natural religion.[59] (3) Spinoza maintained that theology teaches eternal truth "in the style . . . which would most deeply move the mind of the masses to devotion to God,"[60] which teaching is easy to comprehend, while philosophy reaches its conclusions through the deductions of general truths *a priori.*[61] Lessing maintained that natural religion clothed abstract truths in historical allegories, for this made it possible for the religious education of the human race to take place sooner, which he believed had reached its high point in his day.[62]

Lessing's main theological points are essentially derived from Spinoza's philosophy.[63] On the other hand, Leibniz's philosophical categories served as Lessing's point of departure.[64] Lessing adapted Leibniz's work, *Theodicy,* as a model for showing that humanity is progressing toward spiritual maturity in history.[65] Theodicy means a defense of the ways of God in the world, and Lessing intended his philosophy to show

how God provided for moral perfection through the progress of history.

The Leibnizian influence is further seen in the way that Lessing made a distinction between the truths of reason and the truths of history.[66] However, there is a profound difference between them. Lessing failed to draw the proper distinctions between the two kinds of reason. Lessing's distinction between "the accidental truths of history" and "the necessary truths of reason" was not in line with Leibniz. This can be seen when Lessing suggested that he cannot believe in miracles because "I live in the eighteenth century, in which miracles no longer happen."[67] Lessing confused his own private views with "necessary truths." For example, he believed that it was a necessary truth of reason that miracles such as Jesus' resurrection cannot happen. When Lessing said "accidental truths of history can never become the proof of necessary truths of reason," Leibniz would argue otherwise. Leibniz would show: (1) that necessary truths of reason cannot disprove the truths of faith; (2) that pure reason is in perfect harmony with faith, though faith stands above reason, but not against reason; (3) that Lessing's argument against the factual resurrection of Jesus on the basis that reason will not permit him to alter his fundamental ideas of the laws of nature is a misunderstanding of the laws of nature and is an example of a wrong judgment and yields no force against faith; and (4) that "the truths of history" are not necessarily "accidental," if they are divine acts.

Lessing's misunderstanding of the relation between faith and history was based on a fallacy of misplaced necessity. He argued that the laws of nature are absolutely necessary and cannot be superseded by a higher law of divine providence. In order to protect faith from uncertainty, Lessing classified faith as a necessary truth of reason and independent of historical criticism.[68] He assumed that the substance of faith is the moral teachings of Jesus, which are established by reason as well.[69] History thus had no decisive significance for faith except to exemplify the moral maxims of reason and to educate humanity to understand these necessary truths of natural religion.

Lessing's formulation of the problem of faith and history has been highly influential in modern theology. His reinterpretation of the essence of faith as denoting the moral teachings of Jesus instead of the Incarnation of God came to be widely accepted in modern theology. As opposed to Leibniz, Lessing assumed that historical criticism disproved the idea of miracles, although it could not affect the moral insights of reason because these are universal truths. Cassirer believed that "theology had recognized an ally [in historical criticism] which was to prove stronger than itself, and which in the end was to challenge it on its own ground."[70] I would qualify this observation by saying historical criticism only seemed to be "stronger" than traditional theology because Lessing assumed that historical criticism entailed a split between the truths of reason and the facts of history, which Leibniz avoided but which Lessing embraced.

Herder: The Historical Categories of Individuality and Relativity

Johann Gottfried Herder (1744-1803) was a German philosopher, literary critic, and Lutheran pastor whose father was a Pietist schoolmaster. He was a student of Immanuel Kant at the University of Königsberg, but he rejected the rationalistic principles of the Enlightenment because it failed to see the historical and cultural conditioning of truth. His writings were highly influential in his day, and he helped to introduce German romanticism, which was a protest movement against Enlightenment thought.[71]

He gave theology a new direction (already initiated by Lessing) by emphasizing the moral and human element in religious experience. Herder spoke of the study of theology as a focus on "the most sublime truths for the human race" that constitute "the most beautiful, significant, and true philosophy."[72] He minimized the importance of doctrinal speculation and insisted that the language of the Bible "speaks *humanly* to human beings."[73] He rejected the Christology of the Early Church Fathers,[74] emphasizing instead the history of Jesus as a man whose life we are to imitate and whose teachings we are to receive as ethical instructions. He presented an aesthetic interpretation of Jesus, describing him as the most beautiful picture of God in human history. Herder put it this way: "The Christ is not a picture in the clouds to be wondered at, but a type on earth for imitation and instruction."[75] He called the traditional view of Jesus as God and man a "monkish delusion."[76]

Herder held the Bible in high esteem, but Barth showed that he redefined the idea of biblical inspiration by emphasizing the naturalness of "the spirit of these writings."[77] To theologize the idea of inspiration into a systematic doctrine was to superimpose upon the Bible an unnatural explanation derived from Greek philosophy. In his *Letters Concerning the Study of Theology*, he said: "The best way to study theology is to study the Bible, and the best way to read this divine book is *in a human way*."[78] Herder gave a new direction to theology with an emphasis upon the *human* history of Jesus without theologizing it in classical Christological categories.[79] To be sure, Herder's new method contained its own set of philosophical presuppositions. In particular, he appropriated the liberal categories of Enlightenment thought for re-interpreting the "character of Jesus" who is seen as "the imitation of God as the original image of right-eousness and justice, of universal goodness and generosity."[80] Jesus' unique mission was that he "awakened the divine in human beings as children of God."[81] His basic message was "simple and intelligible to all: *God is your Father; you are all brothers.*"[82]

Herder's concept of history became especially significant for the development of what Collingwood called "scientific history."[83] There are two significant features of Herder's concept of history. (1) There is the principle of unique individuality.[84] Herder sought to understand every development and phase of history as possessing its own unique signifi-cance.[85] Herder condemned the Enlightenment for dismissing the European Middle Ages as an era of darkness and barbarity.[86] He argued that historiography should try to understand each era within its own context and social location.[87] (2) Herder's second concept is the princi-ple of historical relativity.[88] For Herder, history is a continuous tradition. This means that historical beings are "but links in a chain, drops of water in a stream, the living cells of a growing organism."[89] As Lessing had sought for the reconciliation of "the accidental truths of history" with "the necessary truths of reason," so Herder sought to develop a reconcil-iation between God and the world, reason and history. This reconcilia-tion required no miraculous intervention of God in the events of the world.[90] Herder maintained that the history of the world forms a contin-uous and dynamic unfolding plan of God. This means history shows no breaks in the unbroken cause-effect link of events, but rather there is a steady movement upward in history toward the moral perfection of humanity.[91]

Herder acknowledged his dependence on Lessing,[92] affirming that "*revelation* is the *education of the human race.*"[93] Barth also pointed this out: "In what concerns history, too, Herder shouted what Lessing had whispered. History, for him, is nothing else but living experience under-stood in the macrocosmic and universal sense."[94] Following the lead of Lessing, Herder minimized the historical events of the Bible as possess-ing decisive significance for faith. What is important for theology is not isolated facts because there is "no gap, no leap, no island" in history or the world[95] Rather, what is important for theology is the history of the world seen in its *necessary* and inter-connecting phases, which exempli-fy morality.[96] Herder rejected Leibniz's view that the laws of nature operated only out of a "moral necessity" based on God's will.[97] He believed instead that the laws of nature are mechanistically necessary and immutable and hence cannot be suspended.[98]

Herder played down the significance of traditional doctrines. All metaphysical speculation, such as the Chalcedonian notion of Jesus as one Person with two natures and two wills, was said to be irrelevant. What one knows is always derived from personal experience, and he believed that personal experiences cannot be transplanted "to the province of demonstration."[99] To demand such demonstration would be to engage in "metaphysical hair-splitting"[100] and "hypercriticism."[101] Barth believed that Herder is largely responsible for the trend in modern theology to minimize doctrinal standards: "We must get used to the idea that with Herder and with the whole line of theological development which began with him there is not that burning interest in the question of truth." [102] Barth believed this was because Herder located revelation "in feeling or practical knowledge" and considered doctrinal interpretation relatively unimportant.[103]

Herder believed these two principles of historiography—individuality and relativity—set aside the relevance of the traditional concept of special divine revelation. He proposed that theology must be reconstructed with the awareness that each event is unique within its own social context and that each event is connected to, and a natural development out of, all previous events. Together these events form a continuous whole and reflect the larger moral meaning of the universe. The significance of Jesus is not that he is truly God and truly man. Rather, the significance of Jesus was his sense of moral responsibility to God and others. As with Lessing, Herder attempted to construct a moral theology, and this anticipated subsequent liberal theology with its denial of miracles in favor of a moralistic reinterpretation of the gospels.[104]

Herder represented a break with the Early Church Fathers who sought to integrate Greek philosophy and salvation history because he believed the categories of individuality and historical relativity would not permit it. His insights into the nature of history were a significant contribution to theology and helped to usher in the era of "scientific history." However, his emphasis upon the personal dimension of knowing and the cultural influences that shape the way we think surely can be appreciated without having to draw the negative conclusion that all doctrinal speculation is bad. His moral reinterpretation of the Gospel was indeed an instance of doctrinal thinking, and it possessed an important meaning for faith. Yet the primary meaning of faith is not derived from the human history of Jesus alone, but rather the human history of Jesus is linked to, and is the culmination of, the decisive acts of God in salvation history. It is necessary for each generation to theologize this history in terms which can best explain it. The Early Church Fathers are not to be condemned for doing this, as though they produced a "monkish delusion." Rather, they are to be congratulated for helping to bring clarity to the meaning of salvation history for all subsequent generations. Herder's skeptical attitude toward traditional metaphysics and traditional theology was a reflection of the spirit of his times as the modern historical consciousness was taking shape.

David Hume: From Probability to Skepticism

The development of rationalism from Descartes through Spinoza and Leibniz to Lessing and Herder was a European Continental movement. The alternative to Continental rationalism was British empiricism. John Locke (1632-1704) is regarded as the actual founder of British empiricism, although it was first advocated by the English philosopher and statesman Francis Bacon (1551-1626). Bacon is regarded as having inaugurated the new era of modern science because he criticized the medieval reliance on tradition and authority. He also established new principles of scientific method, being the first person to lay out a set of rules of inductive logic.[105] Locke subsequently gave systematic formulation to empiricism in his *Essay Concerning Human Understanding* (1690). As noted above, Leibniz produced a response to Locke's empiricism, which he called *New Essays Concerning Human Understanding* (1704). He explained his philosophy in constructive dialog with Locke's philosophy, seeking to bridge the gap between British empiricism and Continental rationalism. In particular, Leibniz sought to integrate faith and the probabilities of history. Unfortunately, Leibniz's real success in bridging these two movements was ignored in Britain and superficially popularized in Germany in the philosophy of Christian Wolff (1679-1754).[106]

David Hume (1711-1776), the leading figure of the Scottish Enlightenment, brought the development of British empiricism to its logical conclusion with his philosophical and religious skepticism. He ignored the synthesis of rationalism and empiricism in Leibniz's philosophy.

If absolute knowledge for the rationalists could only be derived from the innate ideas of reason, British empiricism believed knowledge was derived from sense experience alone. Locke distinguished between primary qualities and secondary qualities. Primary qualities referred to objects themselves in their actual shapes and being, whereas secondary qualities referred to our five senses which mediated these objects to our minds. Locke concluded that the "substance" underlying primary qualities was "Something-I-Know-Not-What" because it was impossible to get outside of one's five senses in order to examine it. In spite of this limitation, Locke believed that one could reasonably infer the existence of God, the world, and the immortality of the human soul.

Hume developed the logical implications of Locke's notion of an unknowable substance into a full-blown metaphysical agnosticism. If the only way to know the real world was through the five senses and if the real world could not be really known because the senses filter out reality, then Hume's skeptical conclusion is persuasive. Hume denied that our ideas derived from experience can be trusted to *re-present* reality. Locke's epistemology is called a representative theory of knowledge because of his belief that ideas re-present reality to the mind. Hume rejected the substantialism of the pre-modern world, as well as the idea of an unknowable substance in Locke's philosophy. He further rejected the concept of salvation history. If one cannot trust the five senses to provide an understanding of what lies outside oneself, then one has no basis to believe that God is revealed in the events of history.

Hume's Radical Historical Method and Skepticism

It is generally assumed that the question of critical history and its relation to Christian faith was given its classic formulation in the nineteenth century writings of Ernst Troeltsch, as noted in the introduction. However, we showed above that Leibniz was the first to call for a logic of historical probability, but his proposal was ignored probably because it did not embrace the radical criticism of modern thought and its split between faith and history. Although anticipated in Lessing, radical historical criticism was systematically formulated by David Hume during the Scottish Enlightenment. In *An Inquiry Concerning Human Understanding,* Hume claimed he discovered a unique argument which will forever make it impossible for any thoughtful person to believe in miracles occurring in history.[107]

His argument goes like this. Our own personal experience is our only guide in determining what is a true happening in the world. What is normal and customary according to our own experience is the foundation for making judgments concerning past events. Second, a thoughtful person will proportion their faith to the evidence. There are degrees of probability concerning what is to be believed, and we must critically assess all the known facts in establishing what is to be believed based on our own experience. In applying these principles, Hume explained that it is common and natural for us to accept what someone else tells us about a past experience. We are by nature inclined to tell the truth and our capacity to remember is tenacious. Of course, a person who is delirious or noted for telling falsehoods is easily discredited. But, generally speaking, we assume that people speak the truth.[108] What then would cause us not to accept the testimony of someone? Only if we are convinced, based on our own experience and observation, that the person is mistaken in believing unnatural and unlikely events, such as miracles.

Hume defined a miracle as "a violation of the laws of nature." It is contrary to the "uniform experience" of all people.[109] Otherwise, it would not be called a miracle. It is no miracle that a person should die suddenly, but it is a miracle that a dead man should come back to life, if he really had died. Can such a report of a dead man being brought back to life be accepted as a reliable testimony? To answer this question, Hume said we must consider which alternative is the more probable. Is the testimony of someone with moral integrity more likely to be true than the likelihood of the event being false? In other words, which would be the greater miracle—that the witness is mistaken, or that the event really happened? "If the falsehood of his testimony would be more miraculous than the event which he relates, then, and not till then, can he pretend to command my belief or opinion."[110] This is his main argument against miracles and against the probability that a historical revelation of God could have occurred. Hume said he "flatters" himself to have "discovered" this argument.[111]

Hume said the laws of nature are based on the principle of cause and effect. This principle is uniformly established according to our experience and observation. It would be a miracle if this law were violated. At the same time, if the report of a highly credible witness is most unlikely to be false so that if the witness were mistaken it would constitute a miracle, then we have reached an impasse. At best "there exists a mutual destruction of arguments," so that one miracle cancels out the other.[112] This impasse leaves us with no basis for believing that a dead man can come back to life. Hume allowed that one could be expected to believe in miracles if discrediting a particular witness would be a greater miracle than the alleged physical miracle; but he offers other supportive reasons why miracles are impossible. Taken together, they create a cumulative effect which makes it fairly certain that a rejection of a witness would not be a greater miracle than the alleged miracle itself.[113] Hence Paul and his list of eyewitness testimony (1 Cor. 15) should be rejected because it would be a greater   miracle to go against our experience that miracles cannot happen than to discount Paul's witness. Hume thus concluded that we cannot accept the testimony of the apostles because the evidence for "the truth of the Christian religion is less than the evidence for the truth of our senses,"[114] which provide no basis for believing in miracles.

Hume's argument was seriously flawed because, on the one hand, he argued that the law of cause and effect made the idea of the resurrection impossible, but, on the other hand, he inconsistently argued that the law of cause and effect could not be used to prove God as the cause of the world because the notion of causality is only a mere idea and not an objective reality.[115] Hume further denied the possibility of God being revealed in history because we are imprisoned in a world of mere physical sensations. We cannot trust our five senses to give us information about the world and cannot trust the testimony of salvation history that God is the cause of the world and the cause of human redemption.

Here is how he argued for sensationalism and against the law of cause-effect.. He began with a divorce between "matters of fact" and "relation of ideas."[116] "Matters of fact" entail information derived from the five senses. "Relation of ideas" entails logical inferences that are derived from our empirical sensations. For example, when one plays a game of pool, the cue stick strikes a billiard ball which moves against another ball. We can observe this action of the balls and we form ideas of what we see. Ideas are formed by the mind to help us remember our physical sensations, and hence ideas are merely copies of sensations. We relate one idea, namely that a ball strikes another ball, to another idea, namely that the ball that is struck moves with the force with which it is struck and is replaced by the first ball. We infer that there is a cause and effect relation by connecting these two ideas, but we do not know if there is really a law of cause and effect because we cannot sense it with our five senses.[117] Hume emphasized that the only thing one knows is an immediate sensation. Whatever cannot be sensed is not knowledge. Because cause-effect is a mere inference and cannot be sensed with the five senses, it is only a notion of the mind and not a verifiable reality. Consequently, we are locked into a world of five senses (sensationalism) beyond which we can know nothing. The only valid ideas are the ones that are copies of isolated sensations, and hence God cannot be known because God is not a physical sensation. Any book, such as the Bible, that contains beliefs not based on immediate sensory experience can be set aside as false. Hume argued: "If we take in our hand any volume; of divinity or school metaphysics, for instance; let us ask, *Does it contain any abstract reasoning concerning quantity or number?* No. *Does it contain any experimental reasoning concerning matter of fact and existence?* No. Commit it then to the flames: for it can contain nothing but sophistry and illusion."[118]

If taken seriously, Hume's critique would eliminate his own philosophy considering that there is no way to sense his theory of sensationalism—that nothing exists if it cannot be sensed with the five senses. In fairness to Hume, he admitted that in everyday life he ignored his philosophy because commonsense dictated that he must behave as if there is causality and that his senses are reliable.[119] This contradiction between everyday living and his philosophy should have indicated to him that something was fundamentally flawed about his skepticism. In essence, Hume reduced all knowing to the facts of one's immediate sensation and denied the possibility of knowing anything else. This is in effect a philosophy of solipsism—that nothing really exists except the content of one's own immediate consciousness. Only the individual subject remains. There is nothing but "me" is the essence of solipsism. One can argue that modern dualistic thinking leads to this extreme subjectivism if the world as it objectively is cannot be known. Only commonsense kept Hume from falling into this extremism.

Notes

1. Cf. Niels Thulstrup, "Commentator's Introduction" in Kierkegaard, *Philosophical Fragments*, trans. David F. Swenson and Niels Thustrup (Princeton: Princeton University Press, 1962), xlvi-xlvii. Cited hereafter as *Fragments*. Cf. Cassirer, *The Philosophy of the Enlightenment*, 192f.

2. Leibniz, *Theodicy*, ed. with an introduction by Austin Farrer, trans. E. M. Huggard (London: Routledge & Kegan, Ltd., 1951), 73f. Cited hereafter as *Theodicy*.

3. Langley's editorial note in Leibniz, *New Essays Concerning Human Understanding*, trans. Alfred Gideon Langley (New York: The Macmillan Company, 1896), 555n. Cited hereafter as *New Essays*.

4. *New Essays*, 421.

5. *Theodicy*, 74.

6. Ibid.

7. Ibid., 556.

8. *The Philosophical Works of Leibniz*, trans. George Martin Duncan (New Haven: Tuttle, Morehouse, and Taylor, Publishers, 1890), 222.

9. *New Essays*, 404f.

10 Ibid., 511.

11 Ibid, 541. In 1699, John Craig argued for the historical probability of the gospels based on algebraic equations. He was a mathematician, not a historian or philosopher, and he calculated that the probability of an event diminishes over a period of time. He estimated the probability of the "written History of Christ" being perceived as true will continue to diminish until it vanishes in the year 3150 A.D. Hence he argued that Jesus Christ will return to earth before then, and so he believed it was not necessary to anticipate Jesus returning soon. Cf. "Craig's Rules of Historical Evidence," *History and Theory*, 4 (1964): 4.27. Craig's method of argument was Newtonian, and he personally knew Newton. Ibid., editor's note, 1. He was also the first scholar to use Leibniz's calculus notations in Britain. However, his method of probability was more mathematical and statistical than historical and critical and hence less philosophical and theological. Cf. "John Craig" *Wikipedia Encyclopedia*, http://www.fact-index. com/j/jo/john_craig.html (31 March 2004). Cf. the website maintained by the School of Mathematics and Statistics of the University of St. Andrews (Scotland)on "John Craig,"http://www-history.mcs.st-an-drews.ac.uk/Mathematicians/Craig.html (31 March 2004).

12. *New Essays*, 420.

13. Ibid., 417.

14. *Theodicy*, 74.

15. Ibid., 75.

16. *The Philosophical Works of Leibniz*, 222.

17. *The Philosophical Works of Leibniz*, 222.

18. *New Essays*, 513.

19. Ibid., 537-538.

20. Ibid., 538. Cf. N. T. Wright, *The Resurrection of the Son of God* (Minneapolis: Fortress Press, 2003), 687.

21. *New Essays*, 538f.

22. Ibid., 547.

23. *Theodicy*, 74.

24. Ibid.

25. *New Essays*, 580.

26. Ibid.

27. *Theodicy*, 74.

28. Ibid., 89, 110.

29. Ibid., 87.

30. Ibid., 87-88.

31. "Editor's Introduction," *Theodicy*, 35.

32. Ibid., 99.

33. Ibid., 99.

34. Ibid., 88.

35. Ibid., 75.

36. Ibid., 74.

37. Ibid., 103.

38. Ibid., 74; *New Essays*, 547.

39 *Theodicy*, 87.

40. Ibid., 74.

41. Ibid., 91.

42 Ibid., 76, 91; *New Essays*, 579.

43. Cassirer, *Philosophy of the Enlightenment*, 190-194.

44. *Lessing's Theological Writings*, translated with an introductory essay by Henry Chadwick (London: Adam and Charles Black, 1956), 54.

45. Ibid.

46. Ibid., 53.

47. Ibid., 51, 53.

48. Ibid., 54.

49. Ibid., 55.

50. Ibid.

51. Cassirer, *Philosophy of the Enlightenment*, 194.

52. *Lessing's Theological Writings*, 83, 96.

53. Ibid., 83.

54. Ibid., 95.

55. Lessing says that all revealed (or, positive) religions are equally true and equally false. They are "equally true: insofar as it had everywhere been necessary to come to an agreement over various things in order to get uniformity and unity in public religion." They are "equally false: in that the matters on which agreement is reached not only stand beside what is essential but also weaken and supplant it." This leads him to say: "The best revealed or positive religion is that which contains the fewest conventional additions to natural religion, and least hinders the good effects of natural religion," Ibid., 105.

56. "A Theologico-Political Treatise," *The Chief Works of Benedict de Spinoza*, 61.

57. *Lessings' Theological Writings*, 54.

58. "A Theologico-Political Treatise," *The Chief Works of Benedict de Spinoza*, 9.

59. *Lessings' Theological Writings*, 105.

60. "A Theologico-Political Treatise," *The Chief Works of Benedict de Spinoza*, 9.

61. Ibid._

62. *Lessing's Theological Writings*, 83, 91.

63. Cassirer, *The Philosophy of the Enlightenment*, 190. Cf. William Walker, *Prolegomena to the Study of Hegel's Philosophy* (Oxford: Clarendon Press, 1894), 43, 144.

64. Cassirer, *The Philosophy of the Enlightenment*, 192.

65. Ibid,.

66. Ibid.

67. *Lessing's Theological Writings*, 52.

68. Ibid.

69. Ibid., 55.

70. Cassirer, *The Philosophy of the Enlightenment*, 201.

71. Johann Gottfried Herder, *Against Pure Reason, Writings on Religion, Language, and History*, trans, ed. with an introduction by Marcia Bunge (Minneapolis: Fortress Press, 1993), 1-37.

72. Herder, *Briefe, das Studium der Theologie betreffend*, ed. B. Suphan (Berlin, 1780), 10:355; cited by Karl Barth, *Protestant Thought: From Rousseau to Ritschl*, trans. Rian Cozens (New York: Harper and Row, Publishers, 1959), 222.

73 Herder, *Against Pure Reason*, 238.

74. Cf. Barth's detailed analysis of Herder's theology in *Protestant Thought: From Rousseau to Ritschl*, 220.

75. Herder, *Briefe, das Studium der Theologie betreffend*, ed B. Suphan (Berlin, 1780), 10:238f; cited by Karl Barth, *Church Dogmatics*, eds. G. W. Bromiley and T. F. Torrance (Edinburgh: T. & T. Clark, 1956), 1.2.126.

76. *Briefe, das Studium der Theologie betreffend*, 10:338f; cited by Barth, *Church Dogmatics*, 1.2.126.

77. *Briefe, das Studium der Theologie betreffend*, 10:145f; cited by Barth, *Protestant Thought: From Rousseau to Ritschl*, 218.

78. Herder, *Against Pure Reason*, 218.

79. Ibid. 176ff.

80 Ibid., 188.

81 Ibid., 188.

82 Ibid., 187.

83. Collingwood, 86-93, 113. Cf. Rudolf Bultmann, *History and Eschatology* (Edinburgh: The University Press, 1957), 9f., 78, 84. Friedrich Gogarten, *Demythologizing and History*, trans. Neville Horton Smith (New York: Scribner, 1955), 27-28. Cassirer, *The Philosophy of the Enlightenment*, 195, 230-233.

84. While the idea of individuality is clearly formulated by Herder, Troeltsch pointed out that it was Schleiermacher who actually "coined the catchword 'individual.'" (Ernst Troeltsch, *The Absoluteness of Christianity*, trans. David Reid (London: SCM Press Ltd., 1972), 76.

85. Cassirer, *The Philosophy of the Enlightenment*, 231. Cf. Herder, "Human Nature, Language, and History," *Against Pure Reason*, 38-77.

86. Herder, "Auch eine Philosophie der Geschichte zue Bildung der Menschheit," *Werke*, ed Suphan, 5:93f., cited by Barth, *Protestant Thought*, 209.

87. "Auch eine Philosophie der Geschichte zue Bildung der Menschheit," *Werke*, 5:489f., 501f., cited by Cassirer, *The Philosophy of the Enlightenment*, 231.

88. The principle of historical relativity was to become the dominant motif in Troelsch's philosophy of history. For him, "the historical and the relative are identical" (*The Absoluteness of Christianity*, 85). He offers this concise definition of historical relativity: "Relativity simply means that all historical phenomena are unique, individual configurations acted on by influences from a universal context that comes to bear on them in varying degrees of immediacy. It means, therefore, that every independent structure leads one to a perspective that embraces broader and still broader horizons till finally it opens out onto the

whole" (Ibid., 89.)

89. *Briefe d. Stu. Theol. Betr. Werke,* ed. B. Suphan, Berlin, 1877ff, 10:290, cited by Barth, *Protestant Thought,* 210.

90. Herder, *God, Some Conversations,* trans. with a critical introduction and notes by Frederick H. Burkhardt (New York: Hafner Publishing Company, 1949), 101-113.

91. Ibid., 137.

92. Ibid., 134-161. Cf. Cassirer, *The Philosophy of the Enlightenment,* 190ff. Cf. Herder, *Against Pure Reason,* 120-125.

93 Herder, *Against Pure Reason,* 225.

94. Barth, *Protestant Thought,* 211.

95. *God, Some Conversations,* 174.

96. Ibid., 152.

97. *Theodicy,* 74; *God, Some Conversations,* 142.

98. *God, Some Conversations,* 150-152, 173.

99. Ibid., 153.

100. Ibid., 146.

101. Ibid., 153.

102. Barth, *Protestant Thought,* 216.

103. Ibid., 216.

104. Ibid., 200.

105. Herbert Butterfield, *The Origins of Moderns Science,* 113-124.

106. Theodore M. Green, "The Historical Context and Religious Significance of Kant's Religion," in Kant, *Religion within the Limits of Reason Alone,* trans Theodore M. Greene and Hoyt H. Hudson (New York: Harper Torchbooks, 1960), xv-xviii.

107. David Hume, *An Inquiry Concerning Human Understanding,* edited with an introduction by Charles W.Hendel (Indianapolis: Bobbs-Merrill, Inc., 1955), 118.

108. Ibid., 118-120.

109. Ibid., 122.

110. Ibid., 124.

111. Ibid., 118.

112. Ibid., 123.

113. Ibid., 124-137. This argumentation continues to serve as the basis for contemporary arguments against theism. Cf. J. L. Mackie, *The Miracle of Theism* (New York: Oxford University Press, 1982). Hume is the mentor of many contemporary analytical philosophers.

114. *An Inquiry Concerning Human Understanding,* 118.

115. Ibid., 91.

116. Ibid., 46.

117. Ibid., 28-34, 91.

118. Ibid., 167.

119. Ibid., 161-163.

7

Kant: The Comprehensive Dualism of Modernism

If David Hume believed he destroyed the foundation for religious knowledge, Immanuel Kant intended to restore a basis for faith in God that was protected from historical criticism and philosophical refutation. Kant's understanding of the relation between faith and reason formed the background of modern theology. Kant (1724-1804) taught at the University of Königsberg, Germany. He lectured first on science and mathematics, and then in 1770 he was made professor of logic and metaphysics. His parents were Lutheran Pietists, but he abandoned his childhood faith in favor of the new rationalism that was sweeping the German universities during the Enlightenment period, although he retained a respect for Pietism and believed it was the authentic interpretation of Christianity.[1] His book, *Religion Within The Limits of Reason Alone*, was a secularized version of Lutheran Pietism.[2]

The Enlightenment Project

Kant's philosophy represented the high point of the German Enlightenment. In an essay entitled, "What is Enlightenment?" Kant considered autonomous reason the decisive method for determining the nature of reality. He wrote: "Enlightenment is man's release from his self-incurred tutelage. Tutelage is man's inability to make use of his understanding without direction from another. Self-incurred is this tutelage when its cause lies not in lack of reason but in lack of resolution and courage to use it without direction from another. *Sapere aude!* [Dare to know!] 'Have courage to use your own reason!'—that is the motto of enlightenment."[3] Kant's belief in the power of reason to determine the nature of universal truth is the touchstone of modern thought.

Kant's influence upon the development of modern theology can hardly be exaggerated. His distinction between reality-in-itself (noumenon) and reality-as it-appears (phenomenon) serves as the basis of his understanding of the relationship between faith and history. This distinction is known as a fact-value dichotomy and profoundly shaped and revolutionized Christian theology in the modern world. Kant's intention was to bring about the synthesis of Continental rationalism and British empiricism. Kant at first accepted the rationalism of Christian Wolff (1679-1754) who had popularized the philosophy of Leibniz. This was the prevailing philosophy of Germany at that time.[4] However, after he read Hume's skeptical philosophy, Kant realized that he had too easily assumed that the mind could know reality. Hume awakened him from his "dogmatic slumbers."[5] Although he did not accept Hume's skeptical philosophy, he believed it exposed the weaknesses of both empiricism and rationalism.

Kant formulated what he called "critical philosophy." He developed two basic convictions concerning the nature of knowledge. First, knowledge of objective reality cannot be deduced from certain innate ideas of reason (rationalism). Second, British empiricism was correct in emphasizing the priority of sense experience over self-evident notions, but it was wrong in saying that sensuous contact with reality in itself is equivalent to knowledge.[6]

The Knowledge Box

Kant distinguished between what may be called a "knowledge box" and a "faith box." The "knowledge box" contains the things that we know from two sources—(1) data derived from our five senses and (2) our capacity for understanding this data through built-in concepts in our minds. The first source of what we know is thus our *senses*, and the second source is the faculty of *understanding*, which contains the inborn power of reasoning.[7] When we *synthesize* sense data and the concepts of understanding, the result is knowledge. However, sense data are not to be confused with the world that lies beyond our five senses. Here Kant agreed with Hume that the mind is incapable of knowing things as they really are; we only know things as they appear to our senses. Kant maintained: "What objects may be in themselves . . . remains completely unknown to us."[8]

The five senses are conditioned by space and time, which are mere forms of sensing the world. As such, Kant did not believe that space and time are objective realities. The *pre-modern* Christian world assumed that time and space are aspects of the real world and created by God, and hence creation is the framework for the history of salvation in which God is revealed.[9] However, Kant believed space and time are *forms* through which our senses intuit the world, and not real properties of the world. This means the world we know is one of our own creation (phenomena). Hence the idea of salvation history is impossible within the context of Kant's critical philosophy because history is only about finite, human happenings. The idea of salvation history in which God is revealed in an objective world of space and time is impossible if we are confined to a world of appearance and are barred from knowing the real world beyond us that God created. Hence Kant was a deist, i.e., one who affirms the existence of God but who is beyond the world and is uninvolved in the affairs of our world.

The second source of knowing is called the faculty of *understanding*. It contains the built-in concepts of the mind. If space and time are considered *forms* which condition the way the five senses intuit the world, *concepts* of the understanding condition the way the mind interprets the data provided by the senses. These concepts are not innate ideas, but rather arise out of the built-in capacity of the mind to generate them as the mind receives raw data from the five senses. Concepts would be mere abstractions without the concrete data of the five senses; empirical data would be meaningless without the built-in concepts of the understanding to interpret them. Kant writes: "Thoughts without [physical] content are empty," while "intuitions [of sense data] without concepts are blind."[10]

Concepts are universal terms used to speak of the world. Aristotle in *Categories* and *Topics* first organized them into ten different categories: (1) substance or essence (what-is, such as: a person), (2) quantity (how much, such as: hundred pounds), (3) quality (what sort of thing: educated), (4) relation (related to what, such as: twice as tall as Plato), (5) place (where, such as: in the marketplace), (6) time (when, such as: yesterday), (7) position (being situated somewhere, such as: sitting down), (8) habit or state (possessing, such as: having a coat on), (9) activity (doing, such as: teaching), and (10) passivity (undergoing something, such as: being insulted). These ten concepts cover everything we need for explaining our experiences of the world. Kant reorganized these ten categories into four broader concepts – quantity, quality, relation, and modality.[11]

To understand the implications of Kant's epistemology for theology, it is necessary to emphasize that the senses perceive only appearance (phenomenon), not reality as it is in itself (noumenon). Kant writes: "The only manner in which objects can be given to us is by modification of our sensibility."[12] Kant even goes so far as to say that "the order and regularity in the appearances, which we entitle *nature*, we ourselves introduce. We could never find them in appearances, had not we ourselves, or the nature of our mind, originally set them there."[13] Quite literally, the things we know are created by our mind, which is why Kant also called his philosophy a "critical idealism." Philosophical idealism might be called idea-ism because ideas shape the structure of the world. To be sure, he allowed that the world beyond our senses might still exist and probably does but that world is not the world we know.[14] The world we know is the world of our senses and the mind creates and shapes the structure of that world through its built-in ideas. Pannenberg points out that Kant was "the first thinker" to interpret the human self as the basis of what-is and what is known, and in this sense he refers to Kant as the real founder of modern subjectivism instead of Descartes; for Descartes inconsistently retained the premodern view that God was the basis of reality and of human consciousness.[15]

History Excludes Divine Revelation By Definition

This dualism of appearance and reality, noumenon and phenomenon, had far-reaching influence in the epistemology of history. Maurice Mandelbaum showed that Kant's theory of knowledge became the presupposition of subsequent philosophies of history—that whatever meaning and value lie in the objects of our knowledge are the result of the activity of the mind and not the inherent characteristics of reality itself.[16] This aspect of historical relativism is to be found in Kant's philosophy of history, *Idee zu einer allgemeinen Geschichte in weltbürgelicher Absicht* (*Idea for a Universal History from a Cosmopolitan Point of View*). Kant says that human deeds are the results of moral laws, i.e., they stem from freedom of the will (which has its spiritual basis in noumenon), but these deeds as seen from the perspective of the historian are considered phenomena and are subject to natural laws. Thus, one can only know history as it appears according to the mechanistic law of cause-effect.[17]

Kant's philosophy represented the ultimate optimism of the Enlightenment with its beliefs in human reason and the eventual perfectibility of society as it progressively unfolds in history. Kant believed that history is the rational expression of human freedom (noumena) as it evolves in the phenomena of the world. Paradoxically, these phenomena are explained according to the mechanistic laws of natural happenings. Here freedom (noumena) and historical causation (phenomena) are divorced, although Kant allowed for the idea of something more beyond the world of our five senses. Yet history as such excludes the revelation of God *by definition* since history is the realm of phenomena and not noumena.

The Faith Box

Kant affirmed belief in the reality of God, but he based that belief on a dualism of theoretical reason and practical reason. This dualism corresponds to the distinction between the *knowledge box* and the *faith box*. I use the metaphor of boxes because Kant carefully circumscribed the nature of reality in fairly rigid terms. Within the *knowledge box* is a theoretical (i.e., critical and precise) awareness of what we know of phenomena. Within the *faith box* are the "practical ideas" of reason—(1) that there is a real world beyond our senses, (2) that there is an eternal self beyond our empirical self-consciousness, and (3) that there is the ideal of all ideas who is God. These faith-ideas are derived from the ability of reason to make responsible inferences. We do not know these "ideas" as realities, but we only know them as logical inferences based on our reasoning ability. In this sense, faith is a practical inference. Faith is the reasoning process that logically infers that there are ideas of the objective world, the immortal self, and God. Although he of course did not claim to know for sure that these ideas actually existed, he believed it was intellectually responsible to think that they did.

The task of Kant's *Critique of Pure Reason* was thus to determine the boundary lines of human knowledge and to show that reason could speak of a transcendental world, a transcendental self, and the transcendental idea of God without resorting to doctrinaire views derived from alleged claims of divine revelation. Kant explains: "It is a call to reason to undertake anew the most difficult of all its tasks, namely, that of self-knowledge, and to institute a tribunal which will assure to reason its lawful claims, and dismiss all groundless pretensions, not by despotic decrees, but in accordance with its own eternal and unalterable laws."[18] What resulted from this critique is that "reason by all its *a priori* principles never teaches us anything more than objects of possible experience, and even of these nothing more than can be known in experience."[19] On the other hand, there is nothing to "prevent reason from leading us to the objective boundary of experience, namely, to the relation to something which is not itself an object of experience but is the ground of all experience."[20] This boundary line beyond which experience cannot go is called "transcendental" instead of "transcendent." If we could go beyond this boundary line, then our knowledge of what lies beyond human experience would be genuinely "transcendent." Since we cannot go beyond this boundary line and yet we are still aware that there is a boundary line shows that we really do come against this boundary and consequently we infer that something must exist beyond it. Otherwise, we would not be aware of any boundary line at all. Here then is the practical use of pure reason—to move beyond the limits of the five senses.[21] This distinction between practical and theoretical reason corresponds to his distinction between noumenon and phenomenon and between transcendent and transcendental.

We normally think of speculation as making guesses about the nature of something, but that is not how Kant defined this term. Speculative reason is "knowledge" of phenomena, while practical reason is having "faith" in the existence of another world (the noumenal world). To speculate is to theorize and that means to actually know it. In this sense, speculative knowledge is what we know, whereas faith is like a guessing game in which we logically infer the existence of something that we cannot know because it transcends our sense experience. Practical reason thus must "surrender the language of *knowledge*" and employ "the quite legitimate language of a firm *faith.*"[22] Hence the well-known comment of Kant: "I have therefore found it necessary to deny *knowledge*, in order to make room for *faith.*"[23]

The Refutation of Natural Theology

Kant's philosophy was a deistic religion designed to replace traditional Christian faith. Kant also rejected natural theology associated with earlier modern thinkers, like Descartes, Locke, and Leibniz who believed that the existence of God could be proven from reason alone. He also rejected premodern natural theology, which was largely associated with Thomas Aquinas who believed that the arguments of reason for God's existence supplemented the claims of revelation. Kant rejected the three traditional proofs (ontological, cosmological, and teleological arguments) for the existence of God because of their over-stepping the boundary of pure reason. The *ontological argument* sought to prove God's existence through analyzing the idea of a supreme being which everyone seems to have. All people know that they are imperfect, and yet everyone has the idea of perfection. Where did this idea come from—except from God? Kant says the ontological argument is faulty because reality cannot be postulated on the basis of mere thinking. Whether or not something exists must be proven by experience and not by mere thinking.[24] The *cosmological argument* assumes the absolutely necessity of a Supreme Being as a sufficient cause for all effects. The law of cause-effect is observed on the phenomenal level of reality, but there is no proof that such a law reaches back to an ultimate ground.[25] Kant believed the *teleological argument* deserves respect, for the idea of a universally-recognized order in the world and its complex designs would seem to suggest the idea of a divine designer. Kant recognized it is the oldest philosophical argument and the most adequate to common sense.[26] However, it cannot claim to be successful, for there is no way we can experiment with the noumenal level of reality.[27]

The Moral Argument for God's Existence

What, then, is the basis for postulating the existence of God? Is there no intellectual basis? Having rejected the idea of finite reason reaching into the infinite, Kant believed there was a moral basis rooted in intuitive awareness.[28] A sense of freedom means we know that we transcend the boundary of the finite world and stand above it. If we were not free, we would be totally immersed in the relativities of the finite, natural world and would not even know it. Without freedom there could be no moral law and without the moral law we would not know freedom.[29] Because we know we are free and feel obligated to obey the moral law that is built within our own conscience, this leads to the idea of God as the moral legislator and rewarder of our good actions, thus guaranteeing to us the immortality of life, if we are dutiful in obeying the moral law.

Kant was not appealing to God as the foundation of our knowledge of morality. The ideas of God and immortality are not conditions of the moral law, but rather the moral law is the condition for believing in God and immortality. The moral law is a sense of "ought" which is built right into the fabric of our conscience. It is a law within itself.[30] Religious ideas can only be *assumed* from a practical and moral standpoint, but they are not proven from any necessary or theoretical reason.[31] Theoretical reason sees these transcendental ideas only in terms of "a merely *subjective* principle of assent," while practical reason sees them as "objectively valid...by means of the concept of freedom." Freedom is the sense of ought within each individual, showing that everyone has a moral obligation to live a life well-pleasing to the divine legislator. A sense of inner freedom inducing a feeling of personal responsibility is thus the rational foundation of faith and "assures objective reality and authority to the ideas of God and Immortality."[32]

God's existence is thus postulated on the basis of a moral certainty. It is not a theoretical certainty and is not derived from the history of salvation. The obvious consequence of Kant's divorce between faith and knowledge means that one can never claim knowledge of the object of one's worship. Kant said Hume's devastating criticism of natural theology[33] really affects theism more so than deism.[34] In the final analysis, God is only a regulative idea. Although we cannot really know that God exists, we are entitled to believe "as if" (*als ob*) God does exist. One cannot say that "*it is* morally certain that there is a God," but only, "*I am* morally certain."[35] This "as if" concept of God's existence means "there remains a concept of the Supreme Being sufficiently determined *for us*, though we have left out everything that could determine it absolutely or *in itself*."[36]

Faith in God thus serves no constitutive purpose especially since the categorical imperative (the built-in sense that we ought and must do what is right and good) is sufficient in itself for morality. Kant believed the only significance of Jesus Christ is that he served as a moral example of humanity well-pleasing to God.[37] The divorce of reason and faith, noumenon and phenomenon, the Supreme Being "in itself" and the Supreme Being "for us," became a basic presupposition of modern theology. This is why Kant has been called the philosopher of modern, liberal Protestantism,[38] similar to the way that Thomas Aquinas is considered the philosopher of Roman Catholicism.

Notes

1. Cf. Theodore Greene, "Introduction," in Kant, *Religion with the Limits of Reason Alone,* trans. with an introduction and notes by Theodore M. Greene and Hoyt H. Hudson (London: The Open Court Publishing Company, 1934), pp. xxx.

2. Ibid., pp. xiv, xxx.

3. Cf. Kant, "What is Enlightenment?" *The Enlightenment, A Comprehensive Anthology,* ed. Peter Gay (New York: Simon and Schuster, 1973), pp. 384-389.

4. Green, "The Historical Context and Religious Significance of Kant's *Religion*," in *Religion Within The Limits of Reason Alone,* pp. xxii-xxvii.

5. *Prolegomena to any Future Metaphysics,* with an introduction by Lewis White Black (Indianapolis: The Bobbs-Merrill Company, Inc., 1950), p. 8. Cited hereafter as *Prolegomena.*

6. Kant, *Critique of Pure Reason,* trans. Norman Kemp Smith (London: Macmillan and Co., Ltd., 1929), p. 32.

7. Ibid., p. 105.

8. Ibid., p. 82.

9. Basil of Caesarea, "The Hexaemeron," *Nicene and Post-Nicene Fathers*, ed. Philip Schaff and Henry Wace (Peabody, Mass: Hendrickson, 1994), 8:54-5. Gregory of Nyssa, "Against Eunomius, Book I," *Nicene and Post-Nicene Fathers*, ed. Philip Schaff and Henry Wace (Peabody, Mass: Hendrickson, 1994), 5:69. Postmodern science has shown through the general and special relativity theories of Einstein that time and space are two dimensions of the same reality and that the real world is the space-time continuum. Thus postmodern science is compatible with the idea of salvation history. On the other hand, the modern, Kantian idea of space and time has been contradicted by postmodern science. This new development in science has led largely to the rejection of Kantian epistemology and the overthrow of Newtonian physics. However, the scope of the modern scientific worldview had far-reaching influence in Christian theology and continues to play a role to this very day in spite of the newer developments in science.

10. *Critique of Pure Reason*, p. 93.

11. *Prolegomena*, p. 51.

12. *Critique of Pure Reason*, p. 182.

13. Ibid., p. 147.

14. Cf. H. W. Cassirer, *Kant's First Critique* (London: George Allen and Unwin Ltd., 1954), pp. 75-76.

15. Wolfhart Pannenberg, *Metaphysics and The Idea of God*, trans. Philip Clayton (Grand Rapids: Wm. B. Eerdmans, 1990), p. 44

16. *The Problem of Historical Knowledge* (New York: Liveright Publishing Corporation, 1938), p. 203.

17. Kant, "Iden zu einer allgemeinen Geschichte in weltbürgerlicher Absicht," *Sämmtliche Werke*, IV, 143. Cf. Collingwood, pp. 83ff.

18. *Critique of Pure Reason*, p. 9.

19. *Prolegomena*, p. 110.

20. Ibid.

21. *Critique of Pure Reason*, p. 27.

22. *Critique of Pure Reason*, p. 597.

23. Ibid., p. 29.

24. Ibid., 500-507.

25. Ibid., p. 511.

26. Ibid., p. 520.

27. Ibid., 522-523.

28. *Critique of Practical Reason and other works on the theory of Ethics*, trans. T. K. Abbott (London: Longmans, Green, and Co., Ltd., 1927), p. 88. Cited hereafter as *Critique of Practical Reason*.

29. Ibid., p. 117.

30. Kant, *Religion with the Limits of Reason Alone*, p. 3.

31. *Critique of Practical Reason*, 88-89.

32. Ibid., 89.

33. Cf. Hume's classical refutation of natural theology in his book, *Dialogues Concerning Natural Religion*, edited with an introduction by Henry D. Aiken. New York : Hafner Pub. Co., 1948).

34. *Prolegomena*, 104.

35. *Critique of Pure Reason*, 650.

36. Ibid.

37. This is the main thesis of his book, *Religion Within The Limits of Reason Alone.*.

38. Tillich, *A History of Christian Thought*, 65-66.

8

Hegel: Absolute Knowledge and World History

In the previous chapter, we noted that Kant was an important turning point in modern thought and that his critical philosophy was the basis of doing theology in the modern world. The first significant response to Kant came from Hegel, whose philosophy is scarcely less influential. Hegel was born in Stuttgart on August 27, 1770. He was brought up in an atmosphere of Protestant Pietism.[1] Encouraged by his father to become a clergyman, Hegel entered the seminary at the University of Tübingen in 1788.[2] After completing a course of study in philosophy and theology, he decided not to enter the ministry. In 1793 Hegel became a private tutor in Berne, Switzerland.[3] Around 1794, he began a serious study of the writings of Immanuel Kant.[4] Hegel's first writings were *The Life of Jesus* and *The Positivity of Christian Religion*, neither of which he published. They were published posthumously in 1907, although Hegel probably never intended them to be. These writings represented a period in his life (shortly after his studies in seminary) when he was flirting with the religious skepticism of Enlightenment thought.[5] He taught for a while at the Universities of Frankfurt and Jena,[6] and in 1816 he became professor of philosophy at the University of Heidelberg. In 1818, he was invited to teach at the new University of Berlin where he remained until he died from a cholera epidemic in Berlin in 1831.

Hegel proposed a new way of doing theology in the modern world, developing the most daring philosophical account of the historical process that probably has ever been written. He introduced the idea that all reality is historical. His intent was to provide a philosophical translation of the Christian faith in modern terms that would not surrender its historical meaning as the Enlightenment had done. His key idea was that history is the actualization (incarnation) of absolute truth in time through a dialectical process of unifying contradictions. It has been said that the categories of Hegel significantly contributed to the rise of historical science even as the categories of Kant had contributed to the rise of modern science.⁷

Hegel's Critique of Kant's Skepticism

Hegel's starting point was to critique Kant's Enlightenment philosophy.⁸ He rejected Kant's basic premise, "that reason can cognize no valid content, and with regard to absolute truths must be referred to faith."⁹ Hegel believed this skepticism had become "a pillow for intellectual sloth, which soothes itself with the idea that everything has been already proved and done with. Those who look for knowledge and a definite content of thought, [it is] not to be found in this dry and sterile acquiescence."¹⁰ Hegel embraced and modified some of the basic ideas of Kant, even as Aristotle did the same with Plato's philosophy. Just as Aristotle rejected Plato's notion of a realm of ideas as actually existing beyond the real world, so Hegel rejected Kant's idea of a transcendental realm that was beyond the knowable confines of finite reason.

His key category was that "Reason" governs world history. He said that the justification for this presupposition is to be found in his *Science of Logic*.¹¹ By logic, Hegel did not mean traditional Aristotelian logic, which entailed the formal rules of thinking, but rather he believed the logic of reality (metaphysics) was embedded in the very nature of human language. Hence the study of logic provided access to the nature of reality as it actually is.

Because Kant was Hegel's precursor, it will be helpful to explain Hegel's philosophy by offering a comparison between them, which will help to lessen some of the complexities of Hegel's thought. The preceding chapter pointed out that Kant divided the cognitive faculties into (1) sense, (2) understanding, and (3) reason.¹² The function of the *senses* is to perceive phenomena (appearances) and the function of the *understanding* is to take these facts derived from our senses and to link them with the built-in concepts of the mind, resulting in knowledge. *Reason* uses these built-in concepts as sources for making faith-inferences about what might lie beyond sense experience.¹³ Based on these faith-inferences, reason is able to develop three transcendental ideas according to Kant—(1) the idea of the immortal self beyond the immediate awareness of the empirical self, (2) the idea of the world beyond our senses, and (3) the idea of God, who is the ideal and unifying reality of all things.¹⁴ Because our knowledge is limited to the finite world of our five sense, these transcendental ideas about the infinite world, including the very idea that something really exists beyond our senses at all, are mere suppositions, and not real knowledge.

Because of Kant's skepticism, Hegel complained that Kant merely replaced the *objective dogmatism* of rationalism with *subjective dogmatism*. This is because he denied knowledge of what is objectively true about the real world beyond our senses and dogmatically asserted what is subjectively true about our sense experiences.[15] Hegel rejected this skepticism. He tried to demonstrate that human beings could have knowledge of the infinite world. That is, it is possible to know the real world, the real self, and God.[16] If Kant was skeptical of knowing reality in itself, it could be said that Hegel abandoned epistemological humility by claiming to have developed an epistemology of absolute truth.[17]

Hegel's Critique of Kant's Logical Categories

Although Kant affirmed that the mind possesses universal categories, reason could not use these categories to speak of transcendent realities. The built-in categories of the mind had validity only if human beings existed. If human beings did not exist, these concepts would be nonexistent.[18] This was a fundamental implication of German idealism—without a subject there is no object. This is why philosophical idealism might be better called idea-ism. There would be no appearances of things without minds to formulate ideas of them.[19] Kant reached this negative conclusion through his critique of reason, but Hegel believed Kant should have made a critique of the traditional categories of logic instead of a critique of reason. He provided such a critique in his *Science of Logic*. He said to criticize the knowing faculties before exercising the power of reason is like trying to learn to swim before getting into water.[20]

Hegel commended Kant for re-classifying the ten traditional categories of formal logic into four larger divisions. In our earlier discussion of Socrates, we noted how he spent his life walking about in the marketplace in Athens, trying to engage others in examining the meaning of life. He did this by asking others to help him define the meaning of words, such as goodness, soul, body, courage, justice. This conversational style of trying to explain life by unpacking the meaning of ideas is known as "the Socratic method," which Plato effectively used in his famous *Dialogues*. After Plato, Aristotle formally classified all the possible ways of thinking into ten categories. Kant subdivided these ten categories into four triadic divisions with each division being further subdivided into a thesis, antithesis, and synthesis: (1) as to Quantity: Unity

(Measure), Plurality (Magnitude), Totality (Whole); (2) as to Quality: Reality, Negation, and Limitation; (3) as to Relation: Substance, Cause, Community; and (4) as to Modality: Possibility, Existence, and Necessity.[21] Hegel believed classifying the categories into four triadic divisions was moving in the right direction of seeing that one universal reality is the larger whole of all the various categories.[22]

The concept of one universal entails the idea that the whole is greater than merely the sum of its parts. For example, each of us is a centered self who is able to organize everything we experience into a coherent whole in our minds. A distinction (though not a divorce) can thus be made between what one thinks and who-one-is. Who-one-is is thus a larger whole than merely the sum of what one thinks here and there. God as the infinite Idea is the absolutely centered personal reality. God is distinct from the world, and yet God is manifested in the world as its creator. Because a human being is a created reflection of God, one is also a centered self and able to understand the very nature of reality itself. The categories of logic thus indicate that we were made to know the world, to know ourselves, and to know God.

Hegel's Dialectic

Kant subdivided the ten logical categories into four general concepts only as a convenient way of organizing them, but Hegel suggested this re-organization implies the development of the categories into one universal.[23] Kant subdivided these categories into an arrangement of thesis-antithesis-synthesis, but Hegel argued that this arrangement pointed to the idea of one larger Idea of God. He thus maintained the categories of logic reflect a development in reality itself toward the unity of everything in God. "It betrays a great instinct for the Notion [Idea] when Kant says that the first category is positive, the second the negative of the first, the third the synthesis of the two. The triplicity . . . conceals within itself the absolute form, the Notion [the Idea of the triune God]."[24]

Hegel complained that Kant merely accepted the traditional categories and put them in the form of a stilted triplicity. Kant failed to appreciate the "rhythm of knowledge" that followed from one concept to its opposite which was then united into a larger whole. Take, for example, the first triplicity of the ten categories—unity (thesis), plurality (antithesis), and totality (synthesis). [25] Commenting on this triplicity, Hegel said: "Kant has thus made an historical statement of the moments of the whole, and has correctly determined and distinguished them."[26]

However, Kant did not recognize the dialectical process of movement from one category to its opposite, which becomes synthesized in a third unifying contradiction. Because Kant did not follow through with a dynamic interpretation of his triplicity, he ended up with a divorce between the subjective and objective aspects of reality, unable to see that the categories of thought show that the two realms are related dialectically.[27]

Hegel rearranged the categories of logic into three main divisions in his *Science of Logic*. These were: (1) the doctrine of being, (2) the doctrine of essence, and (3) the doctrine of the absolute idea. *Being* relates to what is immediately given (thesis); *essence* relates to what is mediated as the deeper understanding of being, suggesting that what merely appears is contrary to what really is (antithesis); *absolute idea* is *self*-conscious ego (synthesis), i.e., the synthetic unity of objective reality (being) and subjective reality (essence).[28] In *Philosophy of the Christian Religion*, Hegel explains this triplicity in terms of the Christian doctrine of the Trinity. God the Father is the source of everything (being); God the Son is the essence and deeper reflection of who God is (essence); God the Holy Spirit is the presence (the self-consciousness) of God in history. This means all knowing is patterned after the Trinity.[29] Just as the Father knows the Son through the power of the Holy Spirit, so our knowledge is a dialectical synthesis of subject and object. Whether it is knowledge of God or ourselves, or anything in the world, knowledge is a relational unity of subject and object. So truth is not merely having knowledge of some *object* (such as the ontological emphasis of the premodern world); truth is not merely identified with ideas created by a knowing *subject* (such as in Kant's epistemology); rather, truth is relational and dialectical. This means reality is accessible through dialectical thinking. Truth occurs in the synthetic moment when object and subject are dialectically reconciled in thought. Hegel noted that Kant and the Enlightenment failed to understand that the doctrine of the Trinity was the center of faith because it failed to appreciate dialectical thinking.[30]

At the risk of oversimplifying Hegel's epistemology, I offer this analogy. Just as the truth of God is the togetherness of the Father and the Son through their relationship in the Spirit, so the dialectical nature of all truth is patterned after this inter-trinitarian relationship.[31] For example, if I hold a pencil in my hand, the truth is not in the pencil as an object; the truth is not in me as the subject; rather, the truth is the dialectical *relationship* of my subjective idea and the object itself. Truth is always relational; it is the dialectical synthesis of object and subject and not simply the object or the subject alone. This is why Hegel often emphasized that truth is concrete and reflects the larger whole of reality. [32]

Hegel believed his dialectic method was based on the doctrine of the Trinity and was unique in the history of thought, representing the highest point of philosophy that would never be superceded.[33] For Socrates, dialectic was a haggling game of confusing disputants with the meaning of words in attempt to get them to reflect more deeply on the meaning of life.[34] Kant used the term, dialectic, to speak of the insoluble contradictions of reason when philosophy tries to speak of transcendent reality.[35] For example, Kant said it is reasonable to affirm that the world had a finite beginning in time and also to affirm that the world is infinite and did not have a beginning in time. Both statements are rational, but equally contradictory. Hence Kant believed reason could not resolve these antinomies. Hegel agreed that reason confronts equally contradicting notions, but he believed contradictions can be resolved dialectically because reality contains opposing tendencies, not absolute differences.[36] Hence the categories of logic have multiple nuances, but there are no irreconcilable contradictions in reality itself.[37] For example, God and the world are contradicting categories, but these are reconciled through a dialectical synthesis of unifying opposites.[38] For example, the reconciliation of God and the world takes place in the progressive realization of freedom in world history.[39] Freedom is derived from the personal nature of God, and its actualization in history is through the world being reconciled to God.[40] The supreme example and basis of this reconciliation of God and the world occurred in "the historical, sensible presence of Christ."[41]

Hegel's dialectic is often explained as involving a thesis-antithesis-synthesis pattern of thought as reality moves upward in unending progress. However, this was more typical of his older contemporary, Johann Fichte.[42] If Hegel believed that Kant's division of the categories into a triplicity was too rigid, as noted above, Hegel believed Fichte was too open-ended in his use of dialectic as if the future was unbounded in its openness for change.[43] The point of Hegel's dialectic was to highlight that reality is composed of opposing elements which negate each other, such as the tension between being and nonbeing, the finite and the infinite, the individual and the universal, and which are united into a larger synthesis.[44] The goal of the dialectical movement in history is personal and social freedom, which Hegel believed was being actualized in his day.[45]

Karl Marx's Use of Hegel's Dialectic

One reason why Hegel is misinterpreted today as proposing a rigid three step process in history as thesis-antithesis-synthesis is partly due to Karl Marx (1818-1883). Marx studied at the University of Berlin during the heyday of Hegel's popularity, but he significantly re-adjusted Hegel's dialectic by "turning it on its head." In The Communist Manifesto (1848), Marx applied Hegel's dialectic in a concrete way to conflicting economic forces in society. Marx charged that Hegel's dialectic was merely abstract and unrelated to the real world. Marx proposed a theory of dialectical materialism in which the dialectic movement occurs in the economic-material structure of society. The history of the world is a dialectic of class warfare between those-who-have and those-who-have-not. Dialectical materialism means that "the seeds of destruction" are implicit in each epoch of history. For example, the feudal system of the medieval world involved class conflicts among feudal lords, vassals, guild-masters, and serfs. The modern middle class (the bourgeois society) emerged out of the class conflicts of the feudal society. The middle class in turn created a new class, the workers (the proletariat), who have to sell their labor to support the lifestyle of the middle class by the profits which can be made from their work. Modern society is thus made up of the conflict between the middle class (thesis) and the working class (antithesis). Marx believed the next stage was to be a classless society (synthesis) when the workers of the world would unite against their oppressors, the middle class. His dialectical opposition between the middle class (thesis) and the working class (antithesis), leading to a classless, utopian society (synthesis), is an atheistic version of Marx's earlier Christian belief in the coming kingdom of God in history.

Marx's dialectical materialism is not without some merit, although it is certainly reductionistic and utopian in the worst senses of those terms. His insight that history is composed of conflicting economic forces is surely one of the practical applications of Hegel's dialectic, although Marx's rigid three step process of thesis, antithesis, and synthesis was greatly overdone. Hegel did not apply the dialectic in a rigid three-step manner. He used the dialectic method primarily as a theodicy of history.[46]

Hegel's Dialectic as a Theodicy

As a theodicy, Hegel's dialectic method intended to demonstrate that "Reason" governs world history and that history "is the exhibition of

Spirit striving to attain knowledge of its own nature."[47] "World history in general is the development of Spirit in *Time*."[48] Stated concretely, Hegel believed divine self-consciousness was being achieved in history among all people and as a result freedom will emerge for all people.[49] Without a conscious awareness of the divine Being and reverence for God he believed there can be no freedom.[50] When Hegel said that history is "Spirit striving to attain knowledge of its own nature," Hegel was saying that God can be known because God is the origin of all truth, and the very act of thinking is thinking God's thoughts. What we know of God is derived from the knowledge of God's very self. God's Spirit shares this knowledge with us in the context of our consciousness. So quite literally, knowing God is through God's self-knowledge. This is not altogether unlike what Paul said: "For the Spirit searches everything, even the depths of God. For what person knows a man's thoughts except the spirit of the man which is in him?   So also no one comprehends the thoughts of God except the Spirit of God Now we have received not the spirit of the world, but the Spirit which is from God, that we might understand" (1 Cor. 2:10-12).

Hegel interpreted each thinker in the history of philosophy as leading to a higher understanding by resolving opposing self-contradictions of previous thought. This was a long and arduous process, leading finally to his own dialectic method.[51] Hegel also interpreted the history of religions as a long and arduous process, leading finally to the absolute religion, which is Christian faith. He particularly referenced the doctrine of the Trinity as "the main content of the faith itself," along with the resurrection of Jesus.[52] Hegel claimed that his lectures on *Philosophy of History*[53] and *History of Philosophy*[54] and his philosophy in general can be viewed as a "justification" and "true affirmation"[55] of the Trinitarian revelation of God in history. Reason (God) governs history, he maintained, and God's purposes will be achieved, not by human initiative, but by the outworking of the divine Spirit. Hegel believed his philosophy was the dialectical fulfillment of all previous thought and that his philosophy confirmed and superceded traditional theology by offering a clear and coherent vindication of the doctrine of the knowledge of God.

The Reconciliation of Reason and History, God and the World

Collingwood pointed out that "the culmination of the historical movement which began in 1784 with Herder came with Hegel" in his lectures on the Philosophy of History.[56] Hegel's interest in the philosophy of history, as well as in the history of philosophy, was motivated by his desire to reconcile subject and object, thought and being, reason and history.[57] It was at this point that Hegel criticized the weakness of Locke's philosophy, which he said was not adequately aware of the difficulties of the problem of objective knowledge because it did not understand the dialectic between the outer and inner worlds. Hegel wrote: "Before the need for reconciliation can be satisfied, the pain of disunion must be excited."[58] It is this "pain of disunion" between thought and being, reason and history that prompted all of Hegel's writings.[59]

In depicting "this strife"[60] between reason and history, thought and being, absolute Spirit and finite self-consciousness, Hegel enunciated his own means of effecting a reconciliation. In the closing lecture of his *History of Philosophy*, which parallels the intention of his *Philosophy of History*,[61] he laid out principles for interpreting history. [62] (1) Reason governs the movements and progress of history.[63] (2) Each stage in history is a necessary movement of the whole development of history. (3) Each successive stage includes all the previous stages of truth. (4) History is the growth of the self-conscious spirit toward freedom, which is the ultimate goal of world history.[64] (5) History is a movement toward human perfectibility.[65] (6) History means both *Geschehen* and *Geschichte*; it is both events and the narration of events.[66] History is not merely ascertaining what happened, but apprehending why the event happened.[67] History can be known, for being and thought, history and reason are not irreconcilable opposites. Being is what it is because of thought; history is what it is because of reason.

Hegel systematically developed the relativity of history, which means that events are interrelated and must be explained in reference to the rhythm of thought coming to expression in history. Truth (or, Reason) is progressively actualizing itself in each stage of history. Each subsequent generation more fully embraces the various aspects of truth that have existed in the previous stages. Hegel said that his method was the only true and absolute method for reconciling thought and being (history and reason),[68] but he did not claim that philosophy nor history would make no further progress beyond his own system or the present day. He insisted that he could only write from "the standpoint of the present day."[69]

Reason vs. Feeling—Hegel or Schleiermacher?

Schleiermacher, one of Hegel's bitter opponents, preferred the concept of feeling over reason. Schleiermacher taught in the department of theology at the University of Berlin when Hegel taught in the department of philosophy.[70] Schleiermacher is known today as the father of modern theology because of the new methodological direction he gave to theology. He was brought up in a Pietist home, but with his very sensitive and probing intellect in his youthful days, he turned to Kant's philosophy for answers to his questions. However, he could not accept Kant's extreme supernaturalism with its deistic view that God permanently transcended the natural world, as if God were "wholly other" from the world. This made God unavailable for the religious needs of human beings. Schleiermacher thus turned away from Enlightenment rationalism and replaced it with what can be called a new version of Pietism. In place of the Bible as the authoritative source of doctrine, he substituted individual religious consciousness. The methodologically decisive element in his theology was that all statements about God were to be derived from religious experience.[71] The Bible was thus largely a commentary on religious experience, while religious feeling was the primary source of one's knowledge of God. Two of his main works were *On Religion: Speeches to Its Cultured Despisers*[72] and *The Christian Faith,*[73] which have had far-reaching influence in modern theology.

Hegel energetically repudiated Schleiermacher's method of feeling as the main source of faith. To be sure, Schleiermacher introduced cognitive elements into his concept of feeling. He defined feeling as a sense of absolute dependence upon God, and in this feeling-relationship with God one comes to know God intuitively in one's own self-consciousness. Paul Tillich has suggested that Schleiermacher made a terminological mistake in identifying religious consciousness as feeling because of its misleading psychological implications. In many ways a contemporary spokesman of Schleiermacher's views, Tillich preferred the term, "ultimate concern."[74]

Hegel ridiculed the idea that feeling is the method of determining the truth of faith. "If what is in feeling is true just for that reason, then everything would have to be true: Egyptian veneration of [the sacred bull] Apis, Hindu veneration of the cow, and so on."[75] He noted that animals also have feeling, but they do not have religion.[76] To be sure, Hegel affirmed the importance of feeling in religion, emphasizing "the fire and heat of devotion,"[77] but because the method of feeling had been made the decisive element in the theological faculty at Berlin, it had become incumbent upon him as one who taught in the department of philosophy to defend orthodox teaching. Hegel argued that his philosophy of religion was closer to authentic Christian doctrines and the Early Church fathers than modern theologians.[78] Over against Schleiermacher's psychological reinterpretation of faith,[79] Hegel insisted that the story of Jesus was real history as opposed to myth.[80] He further criticized modern theology because it reduced faith to ethics and morality and rejected orthodox doctrines.[81]

Hegel criticized Enlightenment thought because its rational theology had turned God into an empty abstraction. He complained that "all definitions of God—and belief—are reduced" in modern theology to hollow abstractions.[82] This is because the Bible as the rule of faith has been "degraded"[83] in Enlightenment-Pietistic theology and replaced with "the modern religion of the understanding."[84] Hegel believed that the proper reply to Kant should not have been made by moving away from an intellectualized faith to the feeling end of the pendulum, as Schleiermacher did.

Hegel insisted that "the Christian religion, the true religion" had been defended in his lectures on the philosophy of religion.[85] In contrast to Kant and Schleiermacher for whom the doctrine of Trinity was set aside, Hegel believed the doctrine of the Trinity was central to the Christian faith and was central to philosophy as well. His intent was to defend "the idea that God as triune is not a dead abstraction."[86] He also insisted that Jesus Christ is more than a good teacher like Socrates; rather, he is "the God-man."[87] On the other hand, he believed the Pietist tradition (especially as represented in Schleiermacher) "restricts itself" to "the pious life of feeling" which "acknowledges no objective truth and opposes itself to dogmas and the content of religion." The Pietistic version of Enlightenment thought insisted on a relationship to Christ, but it was supposedly "one of mere feeling and inner sensibility," based on "privatism in which everyone has his own individual religion" as opposed to the community.[88]

The idea that history is the framework in which the divine being is brought into full view is a very optimistic view. Hegel noted that modern theology (Schleiermacher) had abandoned this emphasis upon "the revelation of the divine essence"[89] in history and it had become incumbent upon philosophy to pick up the slack and correct the neglect of theologians to speak about the divine, historical revelation in Jesus Christ.[90] Hegel explained:

> Basic doctrines of Christianity have been partly set aside and partly explained in quite lukewarm fashion [today]. Dogmas such as those of the Trinity and the miracles have been put in the shadows by theology itself. Their justification and true affirmation can occur only by means of

the cognizing spirit, and for this reason much more of dogmatics has been preserved in philosophy [i.e., Hegel's philosophy] than dogmatics or in theology itself [i.e. Schleiermacher's theology].[91]

Is Hegel's Philosophy A Pantheism, An Atheism or Christian Theism?

Hegel's concept of the Absolute Idea could be interpreted as not referring to the God of the Christian religion. Viscount Haldane argued this point in an introductory preface to Hegel's *Science of Logic*: "He [Hegel] had, notwithstanding what has been said by people who have not mastered his system, nothing of the mystic in his composition."[92] Haldane believed that Hegel's notion of absolute knowledge and his use of God-language allegedly was only employing the language of theology for the purpose of explaining a humanistic philosophy. J. N. Findlay argued that Hegel's philosophy has no place for "faith," and in this sense it is quite anti-metaphysical as well as wholly non-religious. [93] Findlay explained that "Hegel often speaks the language of a metaphysical theology, but such language, it is plain, is a mere concession to the pictorial mode of religious expression."[94]

Haldane's and Findlay's interpretation of Hegel's religious ideas represent what is known as the view of "left-wing Hegelians." This is a view first introduced by David Friedrich Strauss[95] and further promoted by Ludwig Feuerbach, Bruno Bauer, Friedrich Engels, and Karl Marx. These younger students of Hegel believed that he was "a subtle subverter of Christian faith," as one contemporary left-wing Hegelian, Robert Solomon, has put it.[96] These "left wing Hegelians" were pantheists or atheists, but there were also the "right-wing Hegelians" who were the older students of Hegel, and they "took Hegel at his word as a Lutheran and as a defender of the faith"[97]

There are plenty of conservative interpreters of Hegel today, including scholars as diverse as Emil Fackenheim and Quentin Lauer. Fackenheim (a Jewish scholar) believed that Hegel's intent was to give a philosophical demonstration of the proof of traditional Lutheran Christianity: "There is no greater attempt than the Hegelian to unite the God of the philosophers with the God of Abraham, Isaac, and Jacob. The 'result' of its failure is that the two fall radically and finally apart." [98] Quentin Lauer (a Jesuit scholar), on the other hand, believes that Hegel was fairly successful in philosophically defending orthodox, Trinitarian theology.[99] Lauer acknowledged that Hegel was not merely a traditionalist in theology, but rather he sought to defend Christian theism "in a new sort of way."[100]

One of the first to charge Hegel with pantheism was Friedrich-August G. Tholuck (1799-1877), a revivalist theologian, in 1823. Hegel responded in 1827 in the second edition of his *Philosophy of Mind*.[101] In spite of Hegel's defense, Pannenberg notes that "this did not prevent the obstinate persistence of the prejudice against Hegel's philosophy on the grounds that it was pantheist."[102] Pannenberg further notes: "It is difficult to understand how anyone could overlook the idea of the personality of God in Hegel."[103]

Hegel was critical of the deism of Enlightenment thought and the pantheism of Spinoza's philosophy. Hegel criticized Spinoza because he failed to see that God was more than a divine substance. Spinoza interpreted God as possessing the attributes of thought (the universal and all inclusive category) and bodily extension (the particular aspects), but he failed to see the "return" (the dialectical unity) of the particular to the universal.[104] As distinct from the pantheism of Spinoza, Hegel said that God is not only the substantial basis of all reality, but, in Hegel's words, "at the same time he is the absolute *Person*, too. This is the point that Spinoza never reached, and it must be admitted that in this respect his philosophy fell short of the true concept of God which forms the content of the Christian religious consciousness."[105] Hegel defended Spinoza against the charge of being an atheist, suggesting instead that Spinoza's system was an "acosmism" because it effectively eliminated the actuality of the finite world because of his monism in which nothing really is—except God.[106] On the other hand, Hegel says that Spinoza's "philosophy is certainly pantheistic, precisely because of its acosmism."[107]

Pannenberg has also refuted "the misinterpretation of Hegel's philosophy of the Absolute as pantheism, and a denial of the personality of God, neither of which can be verified in the text of his writings."[108] Pannenberg notes that Hegel included personality as an important definition of God. Hegel wrote: "One may define believing in God how one will, but if personality is not there, the definition is inadequate."[109] Pannenberg also defends Hegel against the charge that he identified God with the world. He writes: "It is impossible to deny that Hegel distinguished between the movement of God within the Trinity and the world process."[110] To be sure, the "left-wing Hegelians" admitted that Hegel's language, literally interpreted, supports the conservative view. As Solomon sarcastically put it: "Using Hegel's own public declarations, his explicit celebration of 'revealed religion,' and his consistently religious vocabulary, any theologian with a first degree in pedantry can prove that Hegel was a Christian."[111]

In his book, *Hegel's Concept of God,* Lauer has argued vigorously against the left-wing interpretation of Hegel, showing him to be a defender of Trinitarian theology against Enlightenment critics. In the following manner, Lauer responded to those who think that Hegel cloaked his atheism in Christian categories as a judicious way of deceiving the Prussian state censors: "It might make sense for a philosopher to say that philosophers should not talk about God, because it is beyond philosophy's competence to do so—Kant and Fichte, after all, were not nonsensical. It might even make sense to say that philosophy should not talk about God, because there is no God to talk about—Feuerbach and Marx were not *purely* nonsensical either!" Lauer then comments: "It is difficult, however, to make sense out of the contention that a philosopher of Hegel's competence would choose to employ a highly elaborate 'God-language' as a smoke screen for something else he wanted to say."[112]

Was Hegel's philosophy really Christian? If Lauer believed Hegel had successfully defended the Christian faith, Fackenheim believed that Hegel's project was a dismal failure. [113] He appeared to believe that Hegel's failure was due in large part to the philosophical inadequacy of Christian faith itself. Fackenheim believed that Hegel's philosophy of religion was a fairly accurate representation of Christian belief: "Christian theologians have never taken the *Philosophy of Religion* seriously. Falling into the virtually universal error of mistaking Hegel's speculative transfiguration of Christianity for an armchair speculation with no serious resemblance to their historical faith. But . . . the Christianity presupposed and transfigured by the *Philosophy of Religion* is astonishingly close to the Christianity of history.[114]

If Hegel and Christian faith are essentially one in content, Fackenheim believed they are equally mistaken. Fackenheim argued: "First, the Hegelian peace between Christian faith and philosophy is unsurpassable, and marks the end of an era: if it fails, no similar effort can hope to succeed. Secondly, if the Hegelian enterprise does fail, it is significant in its very failure. Much, if not most, important religious thought until today is post-Hegelian in essence as well as in time."[115] Perhaps Fackenheim too easily assumed their identity.

Pannenberg likewise considers Hegel's project unsuccessful, but he believes that Hegel's goal of reconciling Christianity with modern thought "must be thought out much more deeply than it has been in Hegel."[116] To be sure, one may certainly appreciate many aspects of

Hegel's philosophy, especially his historical and relational understanding of reality and his emphasis upon the doctrine of Trinity. Like no one before, Hegel made the doctrine of the Trinity the central focus of his thought, and the emphasis in contemporary theology upon the doctrine of the Trinity is indebted to him, primarily through the theology of Karl Barth, Jürgen Moltmann, and Wolfhart Pannenberg, although none of these theologians can be called Hegelian in the strict sense of the term. Hegel's attempt to reconcile history and faith in a manner consistent with Christian orthodoxy was commendable. His criticism of Enlightenment rationalism as transforming the personal reality of God into an empty abstraction was a powerful critique, but the question must be asked whether or not Hegel himself succumbed to a similar kind of abstraction in his defense of the biblical and orthodox view of the triune God.

The debate over Hegel's alleged atheism, pantheism, or Christian theism may never be universally agreed upon,[117] but there is no debate over his intent to argue that ultimate reality can be known and that he believed that reality was historical in its very core. And there can be no doubt that Hegel wrote with the apparent conviction that he was defending orthodoxy. This can be seen repeatedly throughout his published writings, as, for example, when he said: "The consummate, absolute religion in which it is manifest what spirit is, what God is; and this religion is the Christian religion."[118] It is also clear that when Hegel argued that all reality is history he is not saying all reality is finite. History entails reason, meaning, purpose, choice, events, and actions which are the properties of human beings and God. Hegel thus proposed a historical and relational understanding of reality.

Did Hegel Turn The Concept of God into An Abstraction?

Like the attempt of the early Church Fathers to synthesize Greek philosophy and the history of salvation, Hegel tried to synthesize Enlightenment categories and Trinitarian faith with the intent of making Christian faith comprehensible in modern terms. Did Hegel succeed? Not everyone agrees, but it is worth quoting from Hegel's *Faith and Knowledge* (first published in 1802) to show how he believed Enlightenment thought had failed in this task because it turned faith and reason into a mere abstraction. He wrote: "Enlightened Reason won a glorious victory over what it believed . . . to be faith as opposed to Reason. Yet seen in a clear light the victory comes to no more than this:

the positive [i.e., the historical] element with which Reason busied itself to do battle, is no longer religion, and victorious reason is no longer Reason. The new born peace that hovers triumphantly over the corpse of Reason and faith, uniting them as the child of both, has as little of Reason in it as it has of authentic faith."[119] Hegel opposed the Enlightenment disconnection of faith and reason, faith and history, God and the world, thought and being, subject and object because he believed these opposing categories could be united dialectically in human self-consciousness because the pattern of synthesis is the self-consciousness of the divine Trinity.

Despite his apparent intentions, did Hegel's dialectical synthesis dissolve the subject-object distinction into a pantheistic monism or into an atheistic humanism? Or did he clarify and make Trinitarian thinking comprehensible? I believe that if he did not succeed in his purpose to defend historic Christianity, it was because his system was methodologically flawed by thinking that the self-revelation of God could be distinctly and clearly translated into the secular language of philosophy.

The irony is that Hegel wanted to show that reality is relational and historical because God is triune, but his concept of the absolute subverted this intent. The word *absolute* (Latin, *absolutus*) essentially means unrelated in the sense that something stands alone and is independently free from everything else. Kant had the deistic idea of God as the Infinite who existed wholly separate from the finite world. Hegel believed that this dualism of God and the world in effect transformed God into another finite being because it entails the notion that two independent worlds existed alongside each other. Hegel believed this was an implicit denial of divine absoluteness because this meant God is just one more being alongside other beings. God and the world were thus on a par with each other.[120] In order to preserve the absoluteness of God, Hegel used the concept of the absolute to argue that God is the all-inclusive reality who holds everything together in a dialectical, synthetical whole. However, Hegel's concept of the absolute as the synthetic whole comes dangerously close to pantheism because the whole is predetermined from the beginning and the individual components within the absolute pale into insignificance.

Paul Ricoeur argues that Hegel unintentionally undermined the mystery of faith because he diminished the personal, devotional, affective and poetic dimensions of religious language and substituted it with the idea of absolute knowledge.[121] Ricoeur argues that Hegel, despite his intentions, turned God into a logical abstraction by insisting that God could be comprehended in terms of absolute knowledge. For all practical purposes the concept of absolute knowledge eliminated divine transcendence by placing God in a closed system.[122] To put it concisely, if God is triune, God is not a philosophical absolute. If everything is relationally based in God's permission that things exist freely and contingently, even this statement denying there is any such thing as a philosophical absolute is not an absolute statement. Rather, it is a confessional statement, and it is relationally based in the self-revealing history of the triune God who is the relational paradigm of all things. The idea of absolute truth is a modernist notion based on the Cartesian principle that for something to be true it must be self-evident, self-contained, and irrefutable. The God of history is not a self-contained deity unrelated to the world, but is the Father of Jesus Christ.

Finally, Hegel's concept of the absolute in effect reduced the eschatological future to the present moment. Hegel's philosophy of history was more like a modernized reworking of Aristotelian teleology than Christian eschatology. This is because Hegel defined the goal of history in terms of a logically-fixed concept which predetermines the future. Like Aristotle's notion of teleology, each historical epoch represents the development of the rational potentialities of reality implicit and present from the very beginning. Pannenberg shows that historical contingency and openness to new things in history were thus eliminated in Hegel's notion of the absolute.[123] The result is that the historical present is converted into an abstract concept of the absolute rather than being providentially guided by the triune God who permits finite things to exist freely and who speaks and acts and makes all things new.

Notes

1. Cf. H. S. Harris, *Hegel's Development, Toward the Sunlight 1770-1801* (Oxford: Clarendon Press, 1972), 94. Cited hereafter as *Hegel's Development.*

2. Harris, *Hegel's Development,* 56-57

3. Harris, *Hegel's Development,* 155

4. Harris, *Hegel's Development,* 195ff.

5. Emil Fackenheim, The Religious Dimension in Hegel's Thought (Bloomington: Indiana University Press, 1967), 53, 128, 231. Cf. Quentin Lauer, *Hegel's Concept of God* (Albany: State University of New York Press, 1982), 20.

6. Harris, *Hegel's Development,* 258-477.

7. *Theories of History*, ed. with an introduction by Patrick Gardiner (New York: The Fress Press, 1960), 6.

8. Hegel, *Science of Logic,* trans. W. H. Johnston and L. G. Struthers, with an introductory preface by Vicount Haldane (London: George Allen and Unwin

Ltd., 1929), 1: 73n. Cited hereafter as *Logic.* Cf. H. S. Harris, "Introduction" in Hegel, *Faith and Know-ledge,* ed. Walter Cerf and H. S. Harris (Albany: State University of New York Press, 1977), 17..

    9. *Logic,* 1:73.

    10. Ibid.

    11. Hegel, *Reason in History,* trans. with an intro. Robert S. Hartman (Indianapolis: The Bobbs-Merrill Company, 1953), p11, 22, 31.

    12. *Critique of Pure Reason,* p300-301.

    13. Ibid., 300-301, 318, 386-389, 533, 557, 569.

    14. Ibid., 323.

    15. Hegel, *Lectures on the History of Philosophy,* trans. E. S. Haldane (London: Kegan Paul, Trench, Trubner and Co., 1892), 3: 427.

    16. *Critique of Pure Reason,* 308.

    17. *Lectures on the History of Philosophy,* 3: 551

    18. Kant, *Prolegomena to Any Future Metaphysics,* 37f.

    19. This view is classical developed by Arthur Schopenhauer (1788-1860), *The World As Will and Idea,* trans. R. B. Haldane and J. Kemp, 2nd ed. (London : Routledge & K. Paul, 1957). Cf. Paul Tillich, *A History of Christian Thought,* 488-493.

    20. *Lectures on the History of Philosophy,* 3: 428-429.

    21. *Prolegomena to Any Future Metaphysics,* 51

    22. *Logic,* 1: 91.

    23. Ibid.

    24. *Lectures on the History of Philosophy,* 3: 439.

    25. Ibid., 477. Walter Kaufmann pointed out that Hegel did not make use of any rigorous three-step dialectic—"Fichte introduced into German philosophy the three-step of thesis, antithesis, and synthesis, using these three terms. Schelling took up this terminology; Hegel did not." Walter Kaufmann, *Hegel: A Reinterpretation* (Notre Dame, Indiana: University of Notre Dame Press, 1978, 168.

    26. *Lectures on the History of Philosophy,* 3:478.

    27. Ibid., 3:476.

    28. Cf. Logic, 1:71; 2:217, especially 479-480.

    29. *Hegel's Lectures on the Philosophy of Religion,* one volume edition, ed. Peter C. Hodgson, trans. R. F. Brown, C. Hodgson, and J. M. Stewart (Berkeley: University of California Press, 1988), 426 n.93., 473 et al.

    30. Hegel, *The Encyclopaedia Logic,* 217.

    31. *Hegel's Lectures on the Philosophy of Religion,* p63, 425 n. 93.

    32. *Logic,* 2:466.

    33. *Logic,* 1: 65.

    34. *Logic,* 1: 67.

    35. *Logic,* 1: 67.

    36. J. N. Findlay, *Hegel: A Re-Examination* (London: George Allen & Unwin Ltd., 1958), 193.

37. *Lectures on the History of Philosophy*, 3:450-451.
38. *Logic*, 2:468.
39. *Reason in History*, 24-25.
40. *Lectures on the Philosophy of Religion*, 482.
41. Ibid., 458.
42. Walter Kaufmann, *Hegel: A Reinterpretation*, 168; Arthur O. Lovejoy, *Essays in the History of Ideas* (New York: George Braziller, Inc., 1955), 211.
43. *Lectures on the History of Philosophy*, 3:478, 481, 486, 504.
44. *Logic*, 2: 475.
45. *Reason in History*, p. 22ff.
46. Ibid., 18.
47. Ibid., 23.
48. Ibid., 87.
49. Ibid., 23, 74.
50. Ibid., 64.
51. Logic, 1: 65.
52. Hegel, *The Encyclopaedia Logic*, 13
53. *Lectures on the Philosophy of History*, 3: 546.
54. *Reason in History*, 18.
55. *Lectures on the Philosophy of Religion*, 94.
56. Collingwood, *The Idea of History*, 113.
57. *Reason in History*, 11-67; *Lectures on the History of Philosophy*, 3: 545.
58. *Lectures on the History of Philosophy*, 3: 312.
59. *Reason in History*, 11-67; Lectures on the History of Philosophy, 3: 545.
60. *Lectures on the History of Philosophy*, 3: 552.
61. *Reason in History*, 68-95.
62. *Lectures on the History of Philosophy*, 3: 552-553.
63. Cf. *Reason in History*, 11.
64. Ibid., 70.
65. Ibid., 68.
66. Ibid., 75.
67. Collingwood, *The Idea of History*, 113.
68. Logic, 1: 65.
69. *Lectures on the History of Philosophy*, 3: 552. Cf. Walter Kaufmann, *Hegel: A Reinterpretation*, 70.
70. Cf .H. R. Mackintosh, *Types of Modern Theology* (London: Collins, 1964), Chapters 2-3, 36-101, for an excellent summary of Schleiermacher's life and thought
71. Cf. Paul, *A History of Christian Thought*, p391-398 for a lucid discussion.
72. Friedrich Schleiermacher, *On religion: Speeches to its Cultured Despisers*, translated by John Oman, introduction by Rudolf Otto (New York : Harper, c1958).
73. Friedrich Schleiermacher, *The Christian Faith*, ed. H.R. Mackintosh and J.S. Stewart (New York : Harper & Row, 1963).

74. Tillich, *A History of Christian Thought,* 391-398

75. Hegel's *Lectures on the Philosophy of Religion,* 151.

76. Ibid., 121.

77. Ibid., 193.

78. Ibid., 79, 85.

79 .Ibid., 82.

80. Ibid., 147.

81. Ibid., 92-93.

82. Ibid., 206-207.

83. Ibid., 94.

84. Ibid., 207.

85. Ibid., 487.

86. Ibid., 485.

87. Ibid., 458.

88. Ibid., 486.

89. Ibid., p16-17.

90. Ibid., 85.

91. Ibid., 94.

92. Logic, 1: 8.

93. Findlay, *Hegel: A Re-Examination,* 348. Cf. W. Kaufmann, *Hegel: A Reinterpretation,* p273-278.

94. Findlay, *Hegel: A Re-Examination,* 348.

95.Cf. John Edward Toews, *Hegelianism, The Path Toward Dialectical Humanism 1805-1841* (New York: Cambridge University Press, 1980), 167. Cf. Wolfhart Pannenberg, *The Idea of God and Human Freedom,* trans. R. A. Wilson (Philadelphia: The Westminster Press, 1973), 160ff.

96. Robert Solomon, *In the Spirit of Hegel* (New York: Oxford University Press, 1983), 583.

97. Ibid.

98. Fackenheim *The Religious Dimension in Hegel's Thought,* 240.

99. Lauer, *Hegel's Concept of God,* 283- 324.

100. Ibid., 5.

101. *Philosophy of Mind* (Part 3 of *The Encyclopaedia of Philosophical Sciences*), trans. A. V. Miller, 1971), 282f., 290, cited by Pannenberg, *The Idea of God and Human Freedom,* 160.

102. Pannenberg, *The Idea of God and Human Freedom,* 161.

103. Ibid., 165.

104. Hegel, *The Encyclopaedia Logic,* p226-227.

105. Ibid., 226. Italics Hegel's.

106. Ibid., 226.

107. Ibid., 227.

108. Pannenberg, *The Idea of God and Human Freedom,* 168.

109. *Grundlinien der Philosophie des Rechts,* ed. J. Hoffmeister (Werke 6, PhB 124a), 4th ed., 1955), 234, cited by Pannenberg, *The Idea of God and Human*

Freedom, 167.

110. Pannenberg, *The Idea of God and Human Freedom,* 164.

111. Solomon, *In the Spirit of Hegel,* 583.

112. Lauer, *Hegel's Idea of God,* 45.

113. Fackenheim *The Religious Dimension in Hegel's Thought,* 240.

114. Ibid., 119.

115. Ibid., 224.

116. Pannenberg, *The Idea of God and Human Freedom,* 177.

117. Cf. Bernard M. G. Reardon, *Hegel's Philosophy of Religion* (London: The MacMillan Press, Ltd., 1977) for a helpful discussion.

118. Hegel, *Lectures on the Philosophy of Religion,* 1:183.

119. Hegel, *Faith and Knowledge,* 55.

120. Logic, I, 150-153.

121. Paul Ricoeur, *De L 'interprétation* (Paris: Seuil, 1965), p505-506, cited by Lauer, *Hegel's Concept of God,* 4.

122. Paul Ricoeur, *Essays on Biblical Interpretation* (Philadelphia: Fortress Press, 1980), 152.

123. Pannenberg, *The Idea of God and Human Freedom,* 174ff.

9

Kierkegaard's Dualistic Philosophy and The Schizoid Position of Modern Thought

The philosophy of Søren Kierkegaard (1813-1855) was autobiographical because so much of his life was deeply embedded in it. He was brought up in Copenhagen, Denmark, rarely going beyond its borders. He embraced his father's religious views, which were shaped by the Pietism of the Moravian Brethren.[1] He was educated at Copenhagen University, majoring in philosophy and theology. He lived during the "Golden Age" of Danish intellectual and artistic life. His writings were prolific and inter-disciplinary, spanning philosophy, theology, psychology, literary criticism, religious educational instruction, and art. He spent his recreational time attending theatres, often showing up only during intermission so that people would not be suspicious that he was the busy author of the many pseudonymous works that were appearing under the name of Johannes Climacus. Another one of his favorite pastimes was walking the streets of Copenhagen talking to ordinary people. He occasionally took a carriage ride in the surrounding areas of the city, but in spite of these restricted activities, his life was spent with lots of intrigue.[2]

His failed romance with Regina Olsen was like a parable of his philosophy, which focused on the relational problems of existence. Suffering from commitment-anxiety, he loved her so much but could not trust himself to marry her. Ostensibly, he decided not to marry her because he felt a divine call to remain unmarried so that he could carry on his work as an author with a purpose of trying "to restore Christianity to Christendom" in Denmark. He also believed his melancholy was incompatible with her happy and pleasant temperament.[3]

After his broken engagement with her, he fled to Berlin for the first of three brief visits.[4] There he attended the lectures of the philosopher Schelling, which were openly and defiantly directed against Hegel. Schelling especially criticized Hegel for failing to address the uncon-scious and irrational elements of human existence.[5] Kierkegaard was confirmed in his negative attitude about Hegelianism after hearing Schelling's severe critique of Hegel's objectivism, which included Schelling's charge that Hegel was only a "sophisticated Spinozist" (a pantheist).[6] Although Kierkegaard came away from Schelling's lectures disappointed because Schelling failed to resolve the problem of subjectivity and objectivity, the lectures served partly as the basis of Kierkegaard's attack on complacent Lutheran orthodoxy associated primarily with right-wing Hegelianism in Denmark.[7]

The Subject-Object Reality Split and The Schizoid Position

We have observed throughout this work how the subject-object distinction has influenced the development of philosophical and theological thought. We noted how modern thought radicalized this distinction into a dualism between faith and history. For the sake of putting Christianity back into Christendom,[8] Kierkegaard further radicalized this dualism in order to show that truth is beyond the pale of human attainment and only in faith as a gift of God can one achieve eternal happiness. Inwardness or subjectivity is the prevailing theme throughout his writings.

If Kierkegaard's philosophy assumed a radical split between fact and value, he acted out a similar split in his own personal life. For example, his second flight to Berlin was partly occasioned by seeing Regina Olsen nod to him in Church.[9] Unable to deal with his emotions, Kierkegaard protected himself through an intellectualist absorption in academic study in Berlin. This was not an isolated event but typical of the way Kierkegaard dealt with his emotions by retreating into his intellect. He left behind lots of evidence in his writings and diaries about his personal life, showing that he was an extremely melancholy person who suppressed his emotions through exercising intellectual control over them. Kierkegaard kept a diary, which he believed would be published after his death. He said: "After my death not only my works but my life will be studied and studied."[10]

One of the most sympathetic and penetrating psychological studies into the life of Kierkegaard was performed by psychiatrist and Anglican pastoral theologian, Frank Lake, who may be the most significant pastoral theologian in the 20th century. He showed how the existentialist philosophy of Kierkegaard is grounded in the schizoid position,[11] which is a psychological category listed in The *Diagnostic and Statistical Manual of Mental Disorders* (4th edition) of the American Psychiatric Association.[12] This is a personality disorder that afflicts people with commitment-anxiety who deal defensively with crippling insecurities and dread through emotional detachment and introversion. They retreat into an intellectualistic world where they feel insulated against emotional pain brought on by a general but pervasive fear of the loss of personal relationships.

This defensive reaction is not to be confused with schizophrenia, which entails severe personality disintegration and inability to function in the real world. Rather, schizoid persons have a split almost down to the roots of their personality and are unable to connect their emotional and intellectual spheres appropriately, but in spite of this they are often able to compensate for their fractured self-image with a great deal of creativity.[13] On the other hand, schizophrenia entails a split off from reality as if one's personality were like a tree trunk split from top to bottom, whereas the schizoid split is not so total. Clinical studies show that rarely does the schizoid position result in schizophrenia.[14]

Kierkegaard described this condition as "the sickness unto death" and an "incurable melancholy."[15] He said this sickness unto death is not the last phase of physical life, but the continual feeling of death. It is a sense of despair.[16] The basic defensive pattern of the schizoid position is flight from social involvement, resulting in a feeling of depersonalization. Karen Horney described it in terms of "moving away from people."[17] The direction of the flight might be flight into spirituality and virtue or flight into sensuality and vice. The flight is not motivated by genuine freedom of choice, but rather the afflicted person's behavior is compulsively driven.[18]

Kierkegaard believed that the spiritual resources of Christian faith provide one with an advantage over non-believers in dealing with this sickness.[19] If the cause of this sickness is the overwhelming feeling of the loss of meaningful relationship with others, the cure is the "God-relationship."[20] Hence, "to be healed of this sickness is the Christian's bliss" as opposed to the "natural man" who has little hope.[21]

Ironically, non-Christian philosophers have drawn extensively from the existentialist categories of Kierkegaard while ignoring his Christian perspective. The connection between the schizoid position and existentialist philosophy can be seen in the way that they struggle with the same categories of dread, ambiguity, alienation, finitude, guilt, passion, pessimism, despair, doubt, and death. If the schizoid position is unable to appropriately connect the subjective and objective poles of reality because one's personality is split almost to the bottom of existence, existentialist philosophy also portrays reality as split between rationality and irrationality, subjectivity and objectivity, meaning and absurdity, with priority being given to the irrational and meaningless aspects of life.

Lake noted that one of the implications of the schizoid position is a Gnostic view of life in which the concrete and historical elements of life are largely disregarded.[22] This is because of the basic split between the inside (subjectivity) and the outside (objectivity). Existentialist philosophy is also obsessed with the inner meaning of life, which is set off against the objective and historical interpretation of the world. The panic need to create meaning in a subjective world of the mind is part and parcel of the schizoid position and existentialist philosophy. Both the schizoid position and existentialist philosophy assume a high degree of intellectual self-sufficiency for attaining a superior view of life than can be obtained through being dependent upon others (or even upon a personal God) for one's source of truth and reality. A religious characteristic of some who suffer from the schizoid position is to scorn those who embrace a personal view of God as Father as if it is emotionally immature.[23] However, it can also be argued that pantheism and atheism are equally anxiety-based interpretations of the world as a theistic one, for pantheism or atheism can be used as an irrational device to protect one from the panic need to feel dependent upon Another or being interfered with. C. S. Lewis said that one of the reasons why he cherished his youthful atheism was because it liberated him from the Divine Interferer, which meant there was a secret part of his life which he did not have to share with anyone.[24] Atheism and pantheism are safe havens from having to trust and interact in a meaningful relationship with the divine other, although Lewis found out that atheism was not really a safe haven. Intellectual people and scholars are particularly susceptible to this schizoid position and to a feeling of intellectual self-sufficiency and seem to be more prone toward an impersonal worldview, such as pantheism and atheism, than the average person.

If Kierkegaard wrote so vigorously against pantheism and Gnosticism,[25] it was in spite of being predisposed in their favor because of his psychological propensity to retreat inwardly and away from history. He noted that the Gnostic flight away from historical reality entailed "acosmism," which means a basic denial of the outside world.[26] If Kierkegaard highlighted the decisiveness of history for faith, it was in spite of his embedded schizoid distrust of objectivity. If Kierkegaard could write so convincingly about the uniqueness of Jesus as God's historical revelation, it was because he experienced the gift of faith, which allowed him to transcend his intellectual predisposition to be self-sufficient. Lake said that Kierkegaard was "the most perceptive diagnostician of the tortuous paradoxes of the schizoid person" of all writers in the past and present.[27] His works on this sickness appears primarily in *Fear And Trembling, The Concept of Dread, and The Sickness Unto Death.*[28] Lake believed "it would not have been possible for him to write with such insight into the schizoid position as he does …unless, at the same time, he had been sustained by a life of entire devotion to God and fellowship with Christ in the power of the Holy Spirit."[29]

Lake did extensive clinical work with schizoid persons, and he traced its source back to a felt loss of relationship in early childhood. He noted that the bitter memories of unloving faces and stern voices from the moment of birth "are the beginnings of man's distortion of the truth about the ultimate personal reality, God Himself." With rare insight, Lake showed that this buried infant memory of unloving and non-welcoming faces "is where the lie is first told about God, the lie which bedevils humanity, which determines our solidarity with the race in ignorance, pride, fear, anxiety, despair, idolatry and lust, unbelief and murderous hatred of God Himself."[30] If relationships at home during infancy have been developed in an appropriate fashion, the foundation for the mature development of one's own ideas and beliefs has been laid. But when this foundation has been cracked by poor relationships, the child learns to relate to the outside world either by anxiously clinging to others or by nervously detaching oneself from others. Many people have a hysterical, clinging and panic-driven relationship to God, and they often speak of their relationship to God in highly emotional and affective terms. They may even give the appearance of being super-spiritual, which is usually compensation for feelings of deep insecurity.

On the other hand, detaching oneself from others reflects a commitment-anxiety disorder. This is the attempt to protect oneself from being hurt by creating distance from others. The affliction of dread is seen particularly in the intellectualist type of personality, and these people are especially resourceful in creating a world of ideas which "promises protection from experience" and requires no obligations to others.[31] The special problem of someone suffering from anxiety-commitment is the inability to feel the presence and love of God as a caring heavenly Father. This person finds it difficult to *feel* because he or she is locked into a world of protective *reason*. Kierkegaard understood in his mind so insightfully and wrote so persuasively about the importance of relationships and intimacy with God, and yet he suffered emotional isolation and separation and was largely unable to feel in the depth of his being what he saw so clearly with his mind.

Lake shows that the hysterical-clinging person desires a person-centered universe which will guarantee security and safety, but the schizoid position has no need for such a personal universe. As Lake put it: "The craving is for an order based on *anything but* dependence on others. Since all that has been offered by available persons amounts, not to an ordered world, but to chaos, the ego takes refuge in a order based on its own cogitations."[32] Lake identified the existentialist theologians, Rudolf Bultmann and Paul Tillich, as representative of the schizoid position because of their attitude of distrust toward the historical foundation of Christian faith and their impersonal view of God.[33] Lake shows that Paul's warnings against inflated intellectualism and Gnostic speculation, in the first letter to the Corinthians and the Colossian letters, are directed at the kinds of defenses typical of the schizoid position. Lake wrote: "The gnostic's view of ordinary Christians and indeed of the Biblical record itself is that of the superior person. He assumes he knows better than the record of the witnesses."[34] This is because Gnostics believe that they are better equipped intellectually without having to trust the objective evidence provided by the testimony of witnesses. Lake showed that "Gnostics show disdain, and not a little bitterness," toward witnesses. Lake maintained: "This reveals something of the secret scorn of themselves in which they were driven. It conceals and denies their deep envy of warm human ties."[35]

If Kierkegaard distinguished so sharply between the subjective decision of faith and the objective facts of history, it was not because he wanted to dehistoricize the basis of Christian faith, as later existentialist theologians did. If his intent was to make the foundation of faith as intellectually uncertain as possible, it was because he believed that the leap of faith was just that—a leap made possible by God and not the works-righteousness attempt of self-sufficient reason to provide a basis for knowledge of God.

Kierkegaard's Pietistic Over-Correction of Modernist Thought

Kierkegaard's influence was restricted in his own day because his thought was not in step with the Hegelian philosophy on the one hand and complacent Lutheran orthodoxy on the other,[36] and also because his writings were not in one of the major world languages. After World War I, his writings shaped modern existentialist philosophy and neo-orthodox theology.[37] Paul Tillich spoke of Kierkegaard's influence upon his own thought during his days as a student in theology at the University of Halle. He happened across Kierkegaard's writings through a translation made by an isolated individual in Württemberg. Tillich found in Kierkegaard important suggestions for a constructive alternative to modern attempts to rehabilitate orthodox theology (such as Kähler's and Barth's). Tillich believed the conservative option failed to incorporate historical criticism into its thinking. On the other hand, Tillich said he could not be satisfied with liberal theology because of its non-mystical theology and empty moralism.[38] "So we were extremely happy when we encountered Kierkegaard," Tillich said. Kierkegaard's "combination of intense piety which went into the depths of human existence and the philosophical greatness which he had received from Hegel…made him so important for us."[39] Tillich was impressed with the way that Kierkegaard was able to use Hegel's philosophy constructively, even using it against Hegel's own system of thought.[40]

Kierkegaard said he felt his mission in life was to preserve the meaning of authentic faith against both the left-wing Hegelians and right-wing Hegelians.[41] The left-wing Hegelians were the radical critics of Christianity like David Strauss, Feuerbach, and Marx, and the right-wing Hegelians were the older students of Hegel who took him at his word that he was defending Lutheran orthodoxy. Kierkegaard offered a third alternative by integrating modernist thought with Pietistic themes. Pietism was originally a Lutheran movement that arose in the 17th century as a protest against the formality of Lutheran orthodoxy. It emphasized heart-felt religious experience, sanctification, works of charity, and devotional theology as opposed to sacramental emphases and doctrinal precision. Kierkegaard's epistemology intensified the subjectivism of Pietism, making personal experience and the decision of faith more crucial than intellectual insight and right understanding.

Karl Barth has shown that modern thought was highly indebted to the rise of Pietism.[42] If Pietism focused on the inner certainty of the Holy Spirit as the means of knowing God, modern thought focused on the inner certainty of the human spirit to rationally grasp the idea of God and universal truth. Barth has shown that modernism is in many respects a secular version of the Pietistic doctrine of the Holy Spirit. Kant, Herder, and Schleiermacher were brought up in Pietistic homes, and their modernist views were profoundly shaped by Pietism. Kant recognized this explicitly in his book, *Religion Within the Limits of Reason Alone,* noting that he was giving a rational and secular restatement of Pietistic methodology. Kant allowed that theology begins with the Bible as its method, whereas philosophy begins with reason. He asserted that the confirmation of the truth of the Bible is the subjective testimony of the Holy Spirit, whereas the confirmation of the truth of philosophy is the subjective certainty of the reasoning process.[43] Kant of course rejected Pietism in favor of his religion of reason.

Kierkegaard borrowed the categories of Kant and Hegel, and then he used these against them. He radicalized the Kantian fact-value dichotomy, and he transposed it into theological usage in order to defend the subjectivity of faith. He used Hegel's dialectical method to show that reason cannot attain absolute knowledge of reality because it is paradoxical and irreconcilable in the human mind. The only way to bridge the distance between subject and object, between faith and knowledge, between the infinite and the finite, is by a dialectical leap of the will to affirm what cannot be objectively known. Kierkegaard struck out new ground in his thinking, and this earned him the title of "father of modern existentialism."

His views on the relationship between faith and history underlie much of modern theology. In fact, no other previous author understood so profoundly the decisive significance of history for Christian faith like Kierkegaard. His contrast between philosophy and revelation, between Socrates and Jesus, and between reason and history in his short treatise, *Philosophical Fragments*, is one of the most brilliant presentation of the uniqueness of Christianity ever written, and yet his epistemology veered toward subjectivism because of his broadside attack on reason. However, this attack was motivated by the desire to make room for authentic faith. His intent was to restore "New Testament Christianity"[44] and bring it back into "Christendom."[45] He had no intention of trying to destroy the established Church of Denmark, but "to infuse inwardness into it."[46] He blamed Hegel primarily for producing a sense of spiritual complacency in the Church because his categories were used to prove doctrinal orthodoxy, which was equated with salvation. This objectivist and complacent orthodoxy required no suffering, no regeneration, and no personal devotion. This is why Kierkegaard complained that "there is no philosophy so harmful to Christianity as the Hegelian."[47] He noted: "If it is really God's view that Christianity is only doctrine, a collection of doctrinal propositions, then the New Testament is a ridiculous book—to set everything in motion, to have Christ suffer thus, in order to produce a collection of propositions!"[48]

Kierkegaard was keenly aware that his attack was one-sided, but he believed it was necessary to over-correct in order to bring about a proper correction. He noted: "The person who is to provide the 'corrective' must study the weak sides of the established scrupulously and penetratingly and then one-sidedly present the opposite—with expert one sidedness. Precisely in this consists the corrective."[49] He called his approach a "pinch of spice" because he acknowledged that it served as a corrective to the abuses of theology in modern philosophy, which tried to equate truth with rational proof.[50] He frankly said that his approach could not be turned into a system of thought because it was a protest against the over-confidence of reason in modern thought.[51] One cannot make an exclusive diet out of sheer spice without serious health problems, and neither can one turn Kierkeggard's protest into a normative statement of truth without serious theological abnormalities. This is why he warned against trying to make his corrective spice the normative truth.

The atheistic, existentialist systems of Jean-Paul Sartre and Martin Heidegger are examples of what happens when Kierkegaard's "pinch of spice" is taken as the philosophical norm. The humanistic reinterpretation of faith in the existentialist theology of Rudolf Bultmann is an illustration of what happens when Kierkegaard's attack on objectivity is made the theological norm. Understanding the problem of faith and history is not enhanced when Kierkegaard's dualisms are taken as normative. I believe Kierkegaard would have agreed with this assessment, and yet he must assume responsibility for the negative fallout in subsequent theological developments because he did not offer a balanced way of relating faith and history. His extremely dualistic way of contrasting subjectivity and objectivity, although it was intended primarily to be a correction to the overly confident unifying function of reason, inadvertently moved faith away from its basis in history despite Kierkegaard's best intentions.

The following dualisms illustrate why Kierkegaard insisted that faith and history stand in paradoxical relationship to each other. These dualisms also show the schizoid tendency of his philosophy and modern thought, but more importantly these dualisms have the pedagogical value of carefully scrutinizing and putting into full view the two sides of reality by exaggerating the subject-object distinction.

Thought and Being

Kierkegaard argued that subjective *thought* and objective *being* cannot be brought together into a self-identity except in an abstract way. Being is based in existence, and whatever exists is in the process of becoming.

Hence truth itself is a process of becoming. This means that truth—the conformity of what is *thought* with what actually has *being*—is only realized for God.[52] In order to achieve truth as an objective certainty, one would have to be capable of standing outside time completely. But, because a human being is a synthesis of finite and infinite elements, it is impossible for one to completely transcend the temporal order.[53] What kind of truth then is accessible to humans? Kierkegaard answered: "*An objective uncertainty held fast in an appropriation-process of the most passionate inwardness is the truth.*"[54] This means truth is not intellectual insight, but it is a decision of the will to believe what is objectively uncertain and intellectually ambiguous.

Kierkegaard's dialectic of thought and being stands in sharp contrast to Hegel's dialectic of unifying opposites. Hegel believed that the human mind was capable of synthesizing the contradiction of thought and being into absolute, irrefutable knowledge. Kierkegaard believed the synthesis was only an existential one—a choice of the will to affirm as true what reason cannot prove. Kierkegaard rejected the idea that skepticism and uncertainty could simply be brushed aside in Hegel's dialectic method with such an easy intellectual victory. Kierkegaard repudiated this intellectualist approach as a mere abstraction. "[For Hegel] to answer Kant within the fantastic shadow-place of pure thought is precisely not to answer him."[55] Kierkegaard said the only way to overcome skepticism is simply to break with it by risking a decision and postulating what you *believe* the truth is.[56] Kierkegaard believed that Hegel's attempt to turn subjective certainty into objective truth is impossible for finite human beings, and Hegel's claim that there is real movement from possibility to actuality dialectically is merely contrived. Rather, Kierkegaard believed that movement always takes place in the realm of existence, not the in realm of logic and abstract thought. He described this movement as a leap, an act of the will.[57] Kierkegaard concluded that Hegel's "pure thought is a phantom"[58]

Kierkegaard also criticized Kant for confusing reality with thought. Kierkegaard insists that being has priority over abstract thought, maintaining that *what one thinks* is merely abstract (it does not relate to existence); *what one is* is existence. At this point Kierkegaard further radicalized Kant's dualism of thought and being. Kant said that the concepts of the understanding provided an objective basis for knowing things-as-they-appear, although he maintained that one must be skeptical about knowing things-as-they-really-are. Hegel wanted to establish irrefutable knowledge of both appearances and things-in-themselves, disallowing any agnosticism of reality. Kierkegaard disallowed irrefutable knowledge either for appearances (noumena) or things-in-themselves (phenomena), and he believed the mistake of both Kant and Hegel was to assume that truth is something that could be determined in the realm of logic.

Kierkegaard argued that to assert the priority of thought over being is Gnosticism.[59] Reality for human beings is subjective; it is existence; it is action. Thought only deals with possibility, whereas reality is "an internal decision in which the individual puts an end to the mere possibility and identifies himself with the content of his thought in order to exist in it."[60] When an individual thinks, one does not think existence: "The only thing-in-itself which cannot be thought is existence, and this does not come within the province of thought to think."[61] What does an individual think, then, when one thinks? One thinks abstractly, i.e., one abstracts from existence. "It signifies that he thinks intermittently, that he thinks before and after. His thought cannot attain to absolute continuity. It is only in a fantastic sense that existing individual can be constantly *sub specie aeterni*."[62] Because we are not able to think outside of time, we always think from the standpoint of our existence, and to exist is to become and to develop. This is why God does not exist; God simply is. To exist is to be caught between the finite and infinite elements of human life. Hence there can be no synthesis between thought and being because everything is in process of becoming for human beings. Kierkegaard maintained: "God does not think, he creates; God does not exist, He is eternal. Man thinks and exists, and existence separates thought and being, holding them apart from one another in succession."[63]

Kierkegaard introduced the *will* as the category through which one achieves the unity of the infinite and the finite as opposed to Hegel's dialectic method of unifying *thought*. This unity is the moment of passion, the leap of faith.[64] The unity of thought and being is the passionate appropriation of the will to believe what reason cannot prove. In summary, Kierkegaard revived the Kantian dualism of thing-as-it-appears (phenomenon) and the thing-as-it-is (noumenon) in terms of a radical distinction between existence and abstract thought, between *what is believed in existence and what is ambiguously known through thought*. The intellect is helpless to know reality because everything is ambiguous, but the will is capable of making a decision concerning the nature of truth by affirming its belief in what might be true.

Paragraph-Material and Existential Communication

Kierkegaard observed that Christianity is a historical religion from an objective viewpoint. As such, it comes under the investigation of critical study.[65] But, to view Christianity objectively as doctrine (paragraph-material) or a historical religion is to eliminate the true meaning of Christianity. Kierkegaard says that Christianity is not a doctrine (a series of propositions to be understood), but is an existential communication. Christianity is not primarily a historical religion which can be objectively studied from a critical, academic standpoint. To be sure, Christianity entails historical events, particularly the incarnation and Jesus' resurrection, but these events are accepted in faith and not on the basis of critical study. This does not mean that Christianity is without content. "When the believer exists in faith his existence acquires tremendous content, but not in the sense of paragraph-material."[66] He further said that Christianity understood as a doctrine of the Incarnation or of the Atonement is a misunderstanding, for this would reduce Christianity to the level of speculative philosophy.[67] Christianity may be defined as a doctrine only in the restricted sense that it is intended to be practiced in real existence.[68] This means the question of the truth of Christianity can be raised only as an existential problem, not as an objective problem that the intellect is able to resolve.[69]

This distinction between paragraph-material and existential communication assumes that the idea of objective truth has very limited value. For example, that "Christ died for our sins" can be considered either as paragraph-material or as existential communication, but Christianity is not concerned with this truth as paragraph-material because Kierkegaard would not allow that Christianity has any interest in speculative epistemology. The question of the Bible as a *historical document* also cannot be the basis of religious authority because this is a speculative question of epistemology.[70] Christianity is *not* to be discussed; it is *not* to be intellectually grasped; it is to be received; it is to be believed. The only presupposition allowed for a "Christian philosophy" is, "that Christianity is the precise opposite of speculation, that it is the miraculous, the absurd, a challenge to the individual to exist in it, and not to waste his time by trying to understand it speculatively."[71]

At this point Kierkegaard invites a misunderstanding. He restricted the validity of trying to understand objectively the truth of Christianity and he denied that the Bible intends to be an objective standard of religious authority. He said that one must believe against the understanding.[72] What is important is to believe, to take the leap of faith. The only objective content necessary is "the historical fact that the God has been in human form"[73] He further said: "If the contemporary generation had left nothing behind them but these words: 'We have believed that in such and such a year the God appeared among us in the humble figure of a servant, that he lived and taught in our community, and finally died,' it would be more than enough. The contemporary generation would have done all that was necessary...to afford an occasion for a successor."[74]

The question arises whether this is enough paragraph-material for one to take a leap of faith. Tillich pointed out that faith needs more content than the mere fact that Christ came. "Can we solve the problem which historical criticism has opened up by a theology of the leap? I do not believe it is possible. Philosophically the question is this: In which direction am I to leap?"[75] Unless one has some idea what he or she wills to be true, one falls into arbitrariness. One must always have a reason for willing the leap of faith because "the mere name alone does not say anything,"[76] Tillich maintained.

Quantitative Approximation and Qualitative Dialectic

The distinction between paragraph-material and existential communication parallels yet another distinction—quantitative approximation and qualitative dialectic. A qualitative dialectic is a decision of the will to overcome the disjunction between subject and object, thought and being. It presupposes the impossibility of direct communication because direct communication implies certainty, and certainty is impossible for one who is in process of becoming.[77] Thus, an existential system cannot be formulated. Reality is a system only for God; it cannot be a system for an existing person.[78]

Dialectic is the place "where the resistance of an objective uncertainty tortures forth the passionate certainty of faith."[79] Dialectics leads one to take the leap of faith—to make a decision concerning the truth of what is objectively uncertain. It is this decision that the ancient Greek skeptics refused to make. Thus, by abstaining from judgment on issues they sought to avoid mental insecurity,[80] but a qualitative dialectics assumes the courage of the will to make a decision in spite of intellectual uncertainty. Skepticism is thus overcome through a passionate choice of the will to affirm what one believes in spite of intellectual uncertainty. Subjective truth is the certainty of faith in which skepticism is rejected, while objective knowledge is only a quantitative approximation. The pursuit of objective knowledge leads to skepticism because it is an impossible goal for existing individuals. On the other hand, faith (subjective truth) is a venture, an uncertainty of knowledge. This venture is "madness" (passion). It is a risk. "To ask for [objective] certainty is . . . an excuse to evade the venture and its strenuosity, and to transfer the problem into the realm of knowledge and of prattle."[81]

In contrast to dialectics which leads to faith, critical study leads to quantitative approximation and uncertainty. This uncertainty points to the inadequacy of any objective scientific investigation of the Bible when such an attempts intends to provide faith with an objective basis and wants to secure faith against the doubt that it may not have a basis beyond itself. The certainty of faith does not rely upon the dependability of the Bible as a historical document.[82] Kierkegaard said faith is independent of the incertitudes of historical research. He rejected the idea of the Bible as the final authority of Christian truth when it is turned into an epistemological theory. He said that all philological and critical scholarship is of no concern for faith.[83] All that scientific inquiry can produce is an approximation, which is insufficient as a basis for faith. Whenever faith seeks a demonstration, it ceases to be faith.[84] "Anyone who posits inspiration, as a believer does, must consistently consider every critical deliberation, whether for or against, as a misdirection, a temptation for the spirit."[85]

The question arises whether or not Kierkegaard's disjunction between qualitative dialectics and the quantitative approximation-process does justice to the historical frame of reference of Christian faith. He does not draw a proper distinction between the certainty of faith and the certainty of historical knowledge. The two certainties lie on different levels, but are not antithetical. It is impossible to escape the conclusion that if historical study could historically demonstrate that revelation had not taken place in the world (a fact which Christian faith must at least in principle allow), then one would be compelled to accept this fact. Further, if faith does not have some assurance that its basis in history is reasonable, then faith could hardly survive skepticism.

Faith and Knowledge

The dualisms of Kierkegaard can further be seen in the sharp distinction that he drew between faith and knowledge. He defined reality in terms of truth as *known* and truth as *believed*. Faith and doubt are passions and have nothing to do with objective certainty. Certainty relates to knowledge (metaphysical truth); faith relates to passion.[86] One does not believe what one knows. To relate critical inquiry to faith, Kierkegaard said, is to confuse knowledge with faith.[87] It is this separation of faith and the certainty of objective knowledge that intensifies the passion of faith. The less objective knowledge is seen to be, the greater the passion of faith. The more objective knowledge one has, the less is the passion of faith. [88]

Kierkegaard differentiated between two levels of faith—faith in the general sense and Faith in the eminent sense. Faith in the general sense is not a form of knowledge, but a free act of the will. Faith is daring to overcome uncertainty. Belief is thus without error, for belief does not draw logical conclusions, but makes resolutions. "The conclusion of belief [about anything] is not so much a conclusion as a resolution, and it is for this reason that belief excludes doubt."[89] When an event takes place before the eyes of a contemporary, its actual perception is immediate and can be said to be non-deceiving.[90] But after this event has happened, then it becomes history and its truth becomes uncertain even for the contemporary who witnessed the actual event. The contemporary witness to the event does not *know* the past that he once witnessed, but he himself only *believes* it.[91]

So far we have examined Kierkegaard's definition of faith in the general sense, but now we turn to his definition of Faith in the eminent sense, which will be spelled with a capital F(aith). This Faith is eminent because it entails the belief that God came into existence. Faith is a paradox, that the eternal and the historical were united at a definite point of time. However, this Faith is not objective knowledge. It does not raise the question of objective content, but rather raises the question of assent—will one believe? Yet this faith has a historical frame of reference. One can speak of Faith in God only from a historical perspective. Thus, to say that Socrates had Faith in God is a misunderstanding: "Socrates did not have faith that the God existed. What he knew about the God he arrived at by way of Recollection; the God's existence was for him by no means historical existence...; for Faith does not have to do with essence, but with being, and the assumption that the God is determines him eternally and not historically."[92] In other words, Socrates maintained a knowledge of God based on rational considerations, whereas Christian faith is based on the belief that God came into existence.

Kierkegaard does not suggest that Faith is a mere act of the will (as with faith in the general sense). Rather, Faith receives its sole condition from God alone. Although Faith has a historical point of departure, Faith is not based on historical knowledge, but rather it is based on the condition created by God alone in the Moment when God confronts us. Kierkegaard argued: "How does the learner then become a believer or disciple? When the Reason is set aside and he receives the condition. When does he receive the condition? In the Moment. What does this condition? The understanding of the Eternal." Faith is thus received "in the Moment" and it is received "from the Teacher himself," who came into existence.[93]

This disjunction between faith and knowledge corresponds to the disjunction between certainty and passion. If knowledge is objective and certain, it is because it is abstract and relates to the realm of mere ideas and essences. On the other hand, Faith is subjective and passionate and relates to the realm of existence. Christian faith is existential truth, a truth which is objectively uncertain, but believed through a passionate intensity of the will. Faith is a risk. Kierkegaard wrote: "Without risk there is no faith. Faith is precisely the contradiction between the infinite passion of the individual's inwardness and the objective uncertainty. If I am capable of grasping God objectively, I do not believe, but precisely because I cannot do this I must believe."[94] With dramatic imagery, Kierkegaard said: "If I wish to preserve myself in Faith I must constantly be intent upon holding fast the objective uncertainty, so as to remain out upon the deep, over seventy thousand fathoms of water, still preserving my Faith."[95] The belief that God became man exists for Faith as color exists for sight and sound for hearing.[96] It was necessary that the first disciples really saw the historical Jesus if Faith is to exist just as it is imperative that this belief be preached today if people are to have Faith. "The successor believes *by means of* (this expresses the occasional) the testimony of the contemporary, and *in virtue of* the condition he himself receives from the God."[97] Yet it is through Faith and Faith alone that this historical reality can be believed, not through critical and objective thought.

Eternity and Time, the Moment and the Historical

Kierkegaard further distinguished between the Moment and the historical. The Moment is decisive; it is filled with the eternal; it is the "fulness of time"; it is brief; it passes away.[98] The Moment is immediate perception and immediate cognition. The Moment comes into existence, then is ceases to be the Moment and becomes historical.[99] The Moment is known so long as it is *this* Moment, but when it is a past Moment it becomes uncertain. Immediate sensation and immediate cognition cannot deceive, for it is this moment. Immediacy does not have the suspicion of uncertainty which attaches to each following moment.[100] Whatever has come into existence is historical. "But the historical is past (for the present pressing upon the confines of the future has not yet become historical)."[101] On the other hand, Kierkegaard said the eternal has no history because it is timeless.[102] Time is characterized by a duality, for what is present becomes past.[103] Faith is thus the divine Moment when God is revealed within one's personal history. Here time and eternity come together through God's initiative.

This distinction between the Moment and the historical, between time and eternity, is Kierkegaard's answer to Lessing's problem when he said that the accidental truths of history cannot serve as the necessary truths of reason.[104] For Kierkegaard, it is this breach between the historical and the eternal that is united paradoxically through the leap of faith in the Moment. This decision of Faith happens in the Moment and is not historical. Thus, one can speak of the certainty of Faith, for it is the Moment and what is present as *this* Moment is immediate and thus certain. This means that Faith happens now, but whenever Faith is made dependent upon historical research it ceases to be Faith and becomes speculative doctrine.

The Moment is similar to the eternal in that the Moment and the eternal are without any history and thus are certain. The difference between the Moment and the eternal is that the moment takes place in time and thus passes away, whereas, the eternal is timeless and never passes away.[105] Yet, the absolute paradox is that the eternal did enter time and became historical.

It was this paradoxical relationship of eternal happiness and its historical point of departure that Kierkegaard intended to show was incompatible not only with Hegelianism, but with all idealistic philosophy. Kierkegaard argued this by going back to the beginnings of idealistic philosophy with Socrates.[106] It is a presupposition of Socratic thought that truth inheres in humanity. One cannot be taught truth, but can only be reminded of what one already knows. This is the doctrine of recollection, that one existed prior to birth and thus has the truth within oneself. Socrates, as a dialectical teacher, only serves as the *accidental* (incidental) occasion whereby the learner can come to an understanding of one's own self, and this provides Socrates himself with an *accidental* occasion for coming to an understanding of himself. From this one sees that truth is eternal and has nothing to do with the accidental truths of experience. Reconciliation for Socrates is a matter of being reconciled with the truth which already inheres in the mind.

The historical cannot have any decisive significance for the existing individual in Socrates, for truth is already immanent in one's mind. It is this Socratic doctrine of recollection and idealism that most characteristically differentiates Christianity from philosophy and paganism. The teacher and the pupil in Socratic thought exist in a state of error, and the teacher can only serve as an accidental occasion for both the teacher and the learner to remember what one already knows. For Christianity, however, the historical takes on *decisive* significance, for one is not in a mere state of error, but exists in a state of sin. Truth does not inhere in the individual, but the Teacher brings the learner to the Truth. But this is no mere teacher; the Teacher is God. The Teacher prompts the learner to recall that he or she is in error, due to their own guilt, which is sin. Thus, the doctrine of recollection does not bring pleasure but anguish. One becomes aware of the break that separates God and humanity. But, God is not responsible for this breach, nor is it due to an accident. Rather, it is due to sin. This Teacher, through a self-imposed bondage, becomes Saviour, Redeemer, Reconciler, Judge. This means that the Teacher brings to the learner not only truth (which the learner does not already possess), but also makes the learner aware of his or her own sin. In this respect, Socrates did not have the consciousness of sin.[107]

With a clarity rarely expressed, Kierkegaard argued: "It is well known that Christianity is the only historical phenomenon which in spite of the historical, nay precisely by means of the historical, has intended itself to be for the single individual the point of departure for his eternal consciousness, has intended to interest him otherwise than merely historically, has intended to base his eternal happiness on his relation to something historical.[108] Kierkegaard further argued that this decisive historical nature of Christian faith is unique in the history of the world: "No system of philosophy addressing itself only to thought, no mythology, addressing itself to the imagination, no historical knowledge, addressing itself to the memory, has ever had this idea; of which it may be said with all possible ambiguity in this connection, that it did not arise in the heart of any man."[109]

Kierkegaard maintained that the historical nature of Christianity cannot be eliminated without resorting back to the pagan identification of God with nature.[110] When modern philosophy believed it had moved beyond the claim of Christianity that God became historical in favor of symbolic ideas it has in fact only moved back to paganism and to

Socratic thought.[111] If one rejects the historical point of departure of faith by rejecting the Incarnation he or she is denying that which make Christianity Christian. It is this paradoxical relationship of Faith to something which is at the same time eternal and historically conditioned that distinguishes Christianity from all philosophy and primal religions.

This is the point where the absolute paradox can be seen. For Socratic thought, the historical can have only an *accidental* significance.[112] For Christianity, the historical takes on decisive significance for truth. The absolute paradox is the moment when the eternal and the historical are united. It is the supreme paradox because faith is the moment when something happens, which thought cannot think. Kierkegaard argued that paradox is characteristic of thought. One cannot think without it. It is this paradoxical passion of reason—for thought to reach out beyond itself to the Unknown—that unsettles one's knowledge of oneself. How is one to know this Unknown? Socrates believed one could have onto-logical truth through recollection. For Christianity, this truth can be known only through the absolute paradox—that God entered time and that Faith has its condition in God's initiative.[113] It is an absolute para-dox, for it cannot be thought, only encountered in the moment of Faith.

God and Humanity

The bifurcation between eternity and time is further worked out in terms of an absolute difference between God and humanity. This absolute difference is that human finitude, temporality, and creature-hood stand opposed to God who is eternal.

> But the absolute difference between God and man consists precisely in this, that man is a particular existing being (which is just as much true of the most gifted human being as it is of the most stupid), whose essential task cannot be to think *sub specie aeterni*, since as long as he exists he is, though eternal, essentially an existing individual, whose essential task it is to concentrate upon inwardness in existing; while God is infinite and eternal.[114]

He also described this absolute difference as an "infinite qualitative difference" between "God and man."[115] It is this infinite difference between God and humanity that leads Kierkegaard to call the Incarnation an absolute paradox: "That God has existed in human form has been born, grown up, and so forth, is . . . the absolute paradox." [116] It is an absolute paradox because it is impossible for anyone, no matter how brilliant they might be, to explain it. Nor is it something that could have ever been imagined by the world religions. "In paganism man made God a man (the Man-God); in Christianity God makes Himself man (the God-Man)."[117] Religions are human attempts to find God; Christianity is the attempt of God to find humans out of "the infinite love of His compassionate grace."[118] The unthinkable nature of the incarnation thus requires one to think paradoxically.

To explain the paradox would be to explain it away. That one's understanding cannot grasp the paradox is to say that it is "the absurd," to believe what one cannot think. Yet, Kierkegaard was careful to point out that this absurdity is not nonsense. He recognized the awkwardness of this term "absurd."[119] He spoke of the absurd as a higher understanding, but this does not mean that one can "defend oneself against every accusation by remarking that it is a higher understanding."[120] He also pointed out that reason is not sacrificed, but that reason itself becomes the principle for understanding that the historical revelation of God in Jesus cannot be fully understood. Kierkegaard also used philosophy to show that philosophy cannot think up this paradox. One "believes against the understanding," but one does not believe irrational statements or stupid things. "Nonsense therefore he cannot believe against the understanding, for precisely the understanding will discern that it is nonsense and will prevent him from believing it; but he makes so much use of the understanding that he becomes aware of the incomprehensible, and then he holds to this, believing against the understanding."[121] Kierkegaard is thus providing a critique of reason—reason coming to an understanding of its limitation—in an analogous way to the Kantian philosophical critique of reason. By limiting the scope of reason's possibilities, Kierkegaard is making room for revelation.

However, there are problems with Kierkegaard's terminology. While it is to be admitted that a "thinker without paradox is like a lover without feeling,"[122] it does not necessarily follow that one needs to speak of the Incarnation as the absurd or as an absolute paradox when such terms are used to stress the absolute difference between God and humanity. Is it justifiable to speak of an absolute difference between God and humanity? To be sure, there is a qualitative difference in so far as God is holy and human beings are sinful and God is infinite and human beings are finite. In *Philosophical Fragments*, Kierkegaard more appropriately speaks of the absolute difference between God and humanity in terms of sin.[123] But, even human beings can hardly be absolutely sinful, for if such were the case there would not be any good in the world and the human race would hardly have survived to this date. Thus, the doctrine of prevenient grace (Wesley) or common grace (Calvin) means that there is not an absolute difference between God and humanity even in a qualitative sense, for humanity was created in the image of God and there is a measure of grace inherent in human beings as an unconditional benefit of the Atonement.

Kierkegaard thus radicalized the Kantian dualism of reality. With his focus on radical subjectivity, does this leave Faith open to the charge that it is mere arbitrariness and that the will merely compels belief in spite of what reason says the facts really are. Kierkegaard made it quite clear that any existential system is impossible and that all critical inquiry is of no concern to Faith. Faith is a risk. It takes its point of departure from an "if."[124] Existentialist theologians (like Bultmann) drew the conclusion that if historical events surrounding the life of Jesus (including his resurrection) are so opaque, then why should historical events be considered an integral part of it? The irony is that Kierkegaard was dead set against Gnosticism and rationalism, insisting that history is the decisive element of Christian Faith, and yet the subjectivism of his philosophy was used by theologians like Paul Tillich to deny the realism of salvation history.

Modern Thought as Schizoid

The philosophy of Kierkegaard illustrates the abnormality of modern thought because of its schizoid split between the subjective and objective dimensions of reality. Those individuals who suffer from "the sickness unto death" are forced to compensate in a psychological way in order to deal creatively with their transmarginal stress. Those like Kierkegaard have been able to develop unusual insights by bringing into forefront aspects about the nature of reality, which otherwise would not have been recognized.

The same can be said about modern philosophy. Its one-sided focus on the importance and necessity of critical thought has contributed significantly to a greater understanding of the world. The technological advancements of the modern world and the growing scientific knowledge of the universe have been phenomenal. In terms of historical criticism, our knowledge of the world of the Bible has been much enlarged as we are able to appreciate its historical development and are better able to understand the problem of trying to bridge the distance between now and when the Bible was written. On the other hand, the divorce between the subjective and objective aspects of reality have led to a spiritual vacuum in our culture because it has led to a split between scientific facts and ethical values, between science and religion, between the secular and the sacred, with the result that values and religion have been downgraded to the subjective status of emotional feeling as opposed to objective truths discovered by empirical experience and reason.

Technologically, we are able to conquer outer space, but the modern world suffers from an emotionally diminished inner world because it is locked into a split between the objective and the subjective. Theologically, the schizoid thinking of modern thought made it virtually impossible to speak of the real history of salvation. Kierkegaard certainly did not intend to dismiss religion as his existentialist descendants have done, and he did not intend to undermine the decisive meaning of history for faith as existential theology has done. However, his divorce between thought and being nonetheless contributed to this state of affairs in the modern world.

The existentialism of Heidegger, which we will consider in the next chapter, will show how Kierkegaard's descendants took his thought in the opposite direction of his emphasis upon the historical nature of faith. Kierkegaard assumed that the decision of the will is the dialectical synthesis between objective uncertainty and faith, but existentialist philosophy was unconcerned with the need for a synthesis. His descendants postulated an unbridgeable gap between objective knowledge and personal values.

Notes

1. Walter Lowrie, *A Short Life of Søren Kierkegaard* (New Jersey: Princeton University Press, 1942), 25.

2. For an excellent but brief account of the life of Kierkegaard, cf. Walter Lowrie, *A Short Life of Søren Kierkegaard.*

3. Walter Lowrie, *Kierkegaard* (New York: Harper & Bros, 1962), 1:192-199.

4. Ibid., 1:192, 224, 233.

5. For a discussion of Schelling's philosophy and his influence on Kierkegaard, cf. Paul Tillich, *A History of Christian Thought*, 437, 442, 446, 458. Tillich's doctoral dissertation was on the philosophy of Schelling. Ibid., 371. Schelling's lectures were on the distinction between negative and positive philosophies, and Tillich showed that the negative philosophy assumed the principle of identity-that ideas are reality. Positive philosophy emphasized concrete existence in time and space. Tillich explained: "The term 'positive philosophy' expresses the same thing that we call existentialist today. It deals with the positive, the actual situation in time and space. This is not possible without the negative side, the essential structure of reality." Ibid., 446-447. For an extended explanation of Schelling's lectures, cf. Niels Thulstrup, *Kierkegaard's Relation to*

Hegel, trans. George L. Stengren (New Jersey: Princeton University Press, 1980), p267-274.

6. Thulstrup, *Kierkegaard's Relation to Hegel*, p264, 271.

7. Ibid., 370-372.

8. This is a theme in his book, *Training in Christianity*, trans. Walter Lowrie (New York: Oxford University Press, 1941). Cf. Lowrie, *Kierkegaard*, 1:430.

9. Walter Lowrie, *Kierkegaard*, 1:192.

10. Lowrie, *A Short Life of Søren Kierkegaard*, 62.

11. Frank Lake, *Clinical Theology*, 581.

12. *Diagnostic and Statistical Manual of Mental Disorders: DSM-IV.* (Washington, DC : American Psychiatric Association, 2000), 694-696.

13. Frank Lake, *Clinical Theology: A Theological and Psychiatric Basis to Clinical Pastoral Care* (London : Darton, Longman & Todd, 1966.), 559.

14. Ibid. p.557. Cf. *Diagnostic and Statistical Manual of Mental Disorders*, 695.

15. Cf. Kierkegaard, *Sickness Unto Death*, trans. Walter Lowrie (Princeton: Princeton University, 1941), 24; Frank Lake, *Clinical Theology*, 558.

16. *The Sickness Unto Death*, 30.

17. Karen Horney, *Our Inner Conflicts, A Constructive Theory of Neurosis*, in *The Collected Works of Karen Horney* (New York: W. W. Norton & Co., Inc. 1945), 1:73. Frank Lake, *Clinical Theology*, 570.

18. Lake, *Clinical Theology*, 563, 570.

19. *The Sickness Unto Death*, p14, 20. Lake, *Clinical Theology*, 560.

20. *The Sickness Unto Death*, p21, 73.

21. Ibid., 20.

22. Lake, *Clinical Theology*, 555. For a helpful explanation of Gnosticism in relation to Christianity, cf. Hans Jonas, *The Gnostic Religion* (Boston: Beacon Press, second edition, revised, 1958.

23. Cf. Mackie, *The Miracle of Theism. Arguments For And Against The Existence of God* (New York: Oxford University Press, 1982), 196, who argues for atheism along this line. Karl Jung interpreted Freud's atheism and his concept of the Oedipus Complex as a rationalization for Freud's own neurotic fears. C. G. Young, *Memories, Dreams, Reflections*, recorded and edited by Aniela Jaffé, trans. Richard and Clara Winstand (New York: Pantheon Books, 1961), p150-153, 167. Cf. Paul Vitz who argues that atheism is an emotional response to the fear associated with the loss of meaningful relationship early in life. *Sigmund Freud's Christian Unconscious* (New York: Guilford Press, 1988), p.221,

24. C. S. Lewis, *Surprised by Joy, The Shape of My Early Life* (New York: Harcourt, Brace, and World, Inc., 1955), 228. Lewis experienced a severe blow to his religious faith as a child when his mother died, leaving him with his father who was a difficult person to relate to. He wrote: "With my mother's death all settled happiness, all that was tranquil and reliable, disappeared from my life." Ibid., 21. His search in life was for joy and happiness, which eluded him since his mother's death, leaving with a sense of being alone in the world. Only with his reconciliation with God did he experience the joy that he had been look-

ing for. If Lewis was successful as a Christian apologist who defended the faith with intellectual rigor, it was in spite of his tendency to be aloof and to retreat inwardly away from the world. Like Kierkegaard, Lewis transcended his natural propensity for pantheism and atheism in favor of the biblical witnesses who invited him to trust the reliability of their testimony that God had become a man in Jesus Christ. Trust did not come easy for Lewis.

25. Kierkegaard, *A Concluding Unscientific Postscript*, trans. David F. Swenson and Walter Lowrie (Princeton: Princeton University Press, 1941), 111, 203, 210-216, 305. cited hereafter as *Postscript.*

26. Ibid., 305.

27. Frank Lake, *Clinical Theology*, 595.

28. Ibid.

29. Ibid.

30. Ibid., 180

31. Jung, *Memories, Dreams, and Reflections*, 144.

32. Lake, *Clinical Theology*, 606.

33. Ibid., 599.

34. Ibid., 590-591.

35. Ibid., 590-591.

36. Niels Thulstrup, "Commentator's Introduction" to *Fragments*, xcv.

37. Tillich, *History of Christian Thought*, 164.

38. Ibid., p162-163.

39. Ibid., 163.

40. Ibid., 163.

41. *Postscript*, 210-216. Cf. Niels Thulstrup, "Commentator's Introduction," *Fragments*, lvi-lx.

42. Karl Barth, *The Theology of Schleiermacher*, ed. Dietrich Ritschl, trans. Geoffrey W. Bromiley (Grand Rapids: Wm. B. Eerdmans, 1982), 276-279.

43. Kant, Immanuel, "Der Streit der Facultaten in drei Abschnitten," ed. G. Hartenstein (Leipzig: Leopold Voss, 1868), 7:339-340. Kant, *Religion within the Limits of Reason Alone*, 8. Cf. Karl Barth, *Protestant Thought*, 191-196.

44. Søren Kierkegaard, *The Last Years, Journals 1853-1855*, ed and trans Ronald Gregor Smith (New York: Harper and Row, 1965), 276.

45. Ibid.,

46. *Søren Kierkegaard's Journals and Papers, Autobiographical Part Two 1848-1855*, ed. and trans. Howard V. Hong and Edna H. Hong (Bloomington: Indiana University Press, 1978), 6:250.

47. Søren Kierkegaard, *The Last Years, Journals 1853-1855*, ed. and trans. Ronald Gregor Smith, 30.

48. Ibid., 275.

49. *Søren Kierkegaard's Journals and Papers, Autobiographical Part Two 1848-1855*, 6:188-189.

50. Cf. Walter Lowrie, *A Short Life of Kierkegaard*, 259-260. Karl Barth, "A Thank You and a Bow: Kierkegaard's Reveille," *Christian Journal of Theology*,

trans. H. Martin Rumscheidt, XI, (January, 1965): 7.
51. *Postscript*, 107
52. Ibid., 169-170.
53 Ibid.
54. Ibid., 182. Italics Kierkegaard's.
55. Ibid.
56. Ibid.
57. Ibid., 306.
58. Ibid., 279.
59. Ibid., 305.
60. Ibid., 302.
61. Ibid., 292.
62. Ibid., 293.
63. Ibid., 296.
64. Ibid., 176.
65. Ibid., 23.
66. Ibid., 339-340.
67. Ibid., 340.
68. Ibid., 339n.
69. Ibid., 331.
70. Ibid., 4, 38.
71. Ibid., 338.
72. Ibid., 504.
73. *Fragments*, 130.
74. Ibid., p130-131.
75. Tillich, *A History of Christian Thought*, 175.
76. Ibid..
77. *Postscript*, 68n.
78. Ibid., 107.
79. Ibid., 438.
80. Cf. Thulstrup, "Commentary," *Fragments*, 249.
81. *Postscript*, 381.
82. Ibid., p25-26.
83. Ibid., 29.
84. Ibid., 31.
85. Ibid., 27.
86. Ibid., 30.
87. Ibid.
88. Ibid., 182.
89. *Fragments*, p104-105.
90. Ibid., 100.
91. Ibid., 106.
92. Ibid., 108.
93. Ibid., 79.

94. *Postscript,* 182.

95. Ibid., 182.

96. *Fragments,* 128.

97. Ibid., 131.

98. Ibid., 22.

99. Ibid., 100.

100. Ibid., 101.

101. Ibid., 94.

102. Ibid.

103. Ibid., 97.

104. *Postscript,* 86.

105. *Fragments,* 97.

106. Ibid., 11-45.

107. Ibid., 58.

108. Ibid., 137-138.

109. Ibid., 137-138.

110. *Postscript,* 330.

111. Ibid., 323.

112. *Fragments,* 13.

113. Ibid., 18.

114. *Postscript,* 195.

115. *Sickness Unto Death,* 207.

116. *Postscript,* 194-195.

117. *Sickness Unto Death,* 207.

118. Ibid..

119. Ibid., 504n.

120. Ibid., 504.

121. Ibid.

122. *Fragments,* 46.

123. Ibid., 58.

124. *Journals of Søren Kierkegaard,* edited and translated by Alexander Dru (London: Oxford University Press, 1938), 368.

10

Heidegger: Truth as
the Self-Disclosure of Being[1]

If Kant and Hegel were the preeminent developers of modern religious thought, Kierkegaard radicalized their views by downgrading the role of reason in favor of the will as the source of truth. Kierkegaard argued that truth is not an irrefutable conclusion based on sound reasoning, but is a leap of the will to affirm what is intellectually ambiguous. His attack on reason and his focus on uncertainty, paradox, dread, subjectivity, death, alienation, and finite existence as the decisive characteristics of human existence influenced a whole generation of philosophers in the 20th century, known as existentialists. One of these key existentialists was Martin Heidegger (1889-1976).

Heidegger was brought up in the Roman Catholic Church, was educated in Jesuit secondary schools, and began to prepare for the priesthood at the Albert-Ludwig University in Freiburg in 1909. In 1911 he dropped out of seminary and began studying philosophy at the university. During his university days as a student, he became an atheist. He was professor of philosophy at Marburg from 1923 to 1928, and then went back to the University of Freiburg in 1928 where he taught until 1944. He was made rector in 1933 during the Nazi regime, but he resigned after one year as rector because of conflict between the university faculty and the regime of Hitler.[2] His suspected complicity with Hitler and the Nazi party was a serious dark spot in his life and continues to be a heated moral controversy among philosophers.[3] His support of Nazism was ambiguous in that he was not directly involved with implementing the policies of Nazism. Yet he did not renounce his earlier allegiance to Hitler even after he realized he had made a mistake. A well-known American philosopher from New York once said to me that he would never read anything that Heidegger wrote because of his association with Nazism. Although his politics were despicable, one cannot afford to ignore his philosophy because his writings have profoundly influenced contemporary theology and philosophy, and he marked a transitional period between modern and postmodern thinking. Some consider him to have been the most original philosopher in the 20th century, and because his ideas drew heavily from his Christian heritage, theology cannot bypass his influence.

Overcoming the Subject-Object Split

Heidegger's central concern as a philosopher was to resolve the subject-object split in modern epistemology. He believed this could be done in terms of what he called *primordial thinking*, that is, he wanted to reclaim an understanding of reality comparable to the primitive thinking of the ancient world before the subject-object distinction was ever developed. This goal was not a naïve belief that one can simply turn the philosophical clock back to the Ancient Near East and think again in mythical terms. However, Heidegger believed that Western metaphysics represented a breakdown in thought because it focused attention on *factual* knowledge of what-is and technology instead of focusing on the *values* associated with human existence. He said the ontological difference between Being and beings[4] had been obscured in modern philosophy from Descartes to Hegel.

Heidegger complained that modern metaphysics focused on the categories of the natural sciences, while at the same time ignoring the meaning of human existence. We noted earlier that Socrates spent his time in the marketplace of Athens discussing concepts that defined the meaning of human existence and that Aristotle formally and systematically developed these basic concepts of reality into ten categories. Kant in the modern period further subdivided these categories into four classification, giving them primarily a reference to the world of nature. Hegel further subdivided these categories into three main divisions—being, essence, and the Absolute Idea that synthesized all of reality into one larger whole. Heidegger believed the focus of modern epistemology upon the categories of nature and objective knowledge brought the larger meaning of Being under scientific control, which emphasized that truth is a *known* conformity of subject and object. This focus on objective, factual knowledge and technology degraded Being as beings. Heidegger called for "destroying of the history of ontology" and backtracking to the primeval foundation of metaphysics.[5] One might interpret this as a philosophical version of the Protestant Reformation because Heidegger insisted that philosophy must return to its primitive roots. If the Protestant Reformation rediscovered the authentic roots of Christian faith in primitive Christianity, Heidegger wanted to go back and rediscover the unity of subject and object before it was split in two at the beginning of Western metaphysics with the early Greek philosophers. If modern philosophy replaced the Bible with reason as the source of knowledge, Heidegger replaced the modernist notion of reason with an existentialist analysis of what it means to be a human being.

If the subject-object split was to be transcended, this required going behind the modern conception of truth as a *known* conformity of subject-object to the existential significance of truth as un-concealment (*a-lētheia*), as a letting-be. This "letting-be" of truth entails the idea that what is true will manifest itself in self-reflection, leading to the subject's awareness of the inner meaning of human existence. Heidegger was thus not interested in the outside world of objects, but the inner world of true being. He was not interested in a grandiose knowledge of everything, but only the values that belong to human existence. Although Heidegger recognized the need to overcome the split between subject and object, I will point out that his epistemology did not overcome this split, but rather it fell into a fact-value dualism of its own which is expressed as, things-present-at-hand (*Vorhandenheit*) as opposed to existence (*Existenz*), nature as opposed to history, language as a "statement" of fact as opposed to language as "unconcealment" (intuitive, non-rational insight).

Heidegger's philosophy is difficult to read largely because he created a lot of new words and phrases to express the many nuances of reality which he believed could not be grasped in a literal way as demanded by scientific precision. Because of the complexity of his terms and phrases, it is difficult to translate Heidegger's German into English. The literature often will not translate those German words, which he used as technical terms. This can be challenging to the reader. I will explain these technical terms in order to lessen some of the difficulties, but one cannot simply substitute his categories with easier categories if one is going to understand how subsequent theologians used his terms to reshape the way theology is done.

Being and Human Existence (Dasein)

Heidegger maintained that the question of Being is the fundamental question of human existence. This may seem like he is talking about God, but do not be misled by his concept of Being. He transformed the concept of God into a philosophical notion of abstract Being. He made similar statements about Being that theology makes about God. He said that Being is the Being of beings, it is not a Being among beings. It is not one category among other categories. It is not that of a class or a genus.[6] Just what Being is, however, is the question which he believed philosophy must once again raise. It is a question that cannot be assumed to be unimportant or self-evident, as if it refers to God. It is not a new question, but one that extends back to the very beginning of Western metaphysics. It is a question that Heidegger believed had become muddled in the course of the history of philosophy, beginning with Plato's reduction of Being to the distinction between *idea* as what really is and *sensibility* as a mere copy of an idea. Heidegger said this distinction was then intensified with Descartes' dualism of thought (*res cogitans*) and nature (*res extensa*), and it finally culminated in Hegel's theory of absolute knowledge—that truth is the absolute unity of subject and object, thought and being.

Heidegger believed what was required of philosophy was a "backtracking" to the primordial origins of thinking. One must go behind beings to Being as it is manifested in the most basic self-awareness of human subjects.[7] The earlier Heidegger sought to get at the truth of Being through an interrogation of beings, but this interrogation was not just any being. Rather, it is the interrogation of *human beings* as they stand related to Being. Thus, the German word *Dasein* is translated *human* existence. *Dasein* literally translated is "there-Being," that is, "there" in human beings is an instance of true being. This means that a human being "exists," whereas objects such as a piece of wood have being but no existence because it does not stand in relationship to Being.[8] To stand in relationship to Being means to be self-aware that one has choices about the possibilities of existence. Obviously a piece of wood does not have self-awareness and hence it lacks a relationship to Being. Heidegger says that *Dasein* in its forgetfulness of Being is inauthentic existence, while *Dasein* reconciled with Being means that one experiences authentic existence.[9]

Because it is the nature of *Dasein* to ask the question of Being, this means that human beings are ontic-ontological beings. One is an *ontical* being because one is a being (an object) as such. One is an *ontological* being because one stands in a relationship to Being (a subject). Heidegger further clarifies the terminological distinction between ontic and ontological by his use of the terms, *existenzial* and *existenziell*.[10] *Existenzial* refers to the philosophical analysis of *Dasein's* existence.

Existenziell refers to the actual existence itself of *Dasein*. Thus, ontic and *existenziell*, on the one hand, and ontological and *existenzial*, on the other hand, closely correspond.[11] In essence, the subject-object distinction is explained as a difference between the ontological (*existenzial*) and the ontic (*existenziell*).

Heidegger said what he was really concerned with was not *Dasein*, but *Sein* (Being). Not the "there" of Being (*ontic-existenziell*), but the Being which effects the "there." The distinction between the ontic and the ontological was intended by Heidegger to point out the inadequacy of the traditional categories, especially as they were formalized in Kant's *Critique of Pure Reason*. Kant's categories were used to label natural objects. Kant pursued an ontical inquiry rather than an ontological one. Kant (following Aristotle) established a foundation for the natural sciences which investigates beings. On the other hand, Heidegger called for an "ontological inquiry" that "is indeed more primordial, as over against the ontical inquiry of the positive sciences."[12] The ontical sciences are severely restricted until they have become ontological. It is not enough to interrogate scientifically beings as such, but one must "back track" to the primordial investigation of Being. "The domineering nature of modern technology" must give way to a "back track" to the essence of metaphysics if the nature of Being is to be unfolded.[13] This backtracking to Being makes it understandable why Heidegger claimed he was an ontologist rather than an existentialist.[14] However, because he inquired after Being through an *existenzial* analysis of *Dasein*, this justifies classifying him also as an existentialist, as is done by all philosophers. This is particularly pronounced in *Being and Time*. It is in this work that he seeks to clarify *Dasein*, which in turn would open up the meaning of Being.

A Hermeneutic of Dasein

Heidegger believed the method for discovering the essence of true Being is phenomenology.[15] This is the method which he learned from his teacher, Edmund Husserl.[16] The basic idea of the phenomenological method is that the essence of reality can be discovered through bracketing out everything on the outside world and focusing exclusively on the immediate contents of self-consciousness. The phenomenological method supposedly allowed the philosopher to go directly to the things themselves in self-consciousness. Heidegger believed this is how the Being of beings can be discovered. The task of encountering Being through *Dasein* by the means of the phenomenological method is not "the *naiveté* of a haphazard, 'immediate', and unreflective 'beholding'."[17] Rather, it is a method in which Being must "be *wrested* from the objects of phenomenology."[18] Heidegger called this phenomenological method a "hermeneutic of *Dasein*."[19]

Hermeneutics is a term which Heidegger learned during his days in training as a Jesuit priest in seminary. Theological hermeneutics is the task of analyzing the meaning of the biblical text, but Heidegger used the concept of hermeneutics to refer to the philosophical task of providing "an analytic of the existentiality [possibilities] of existence."[20] Hermeneutics refers to the task of unfolding the meaning of the historicity (*Geschichtlichkeit*) of human existence.[21] Historicity, existence, ontology, meaningfulness are parallel terms. The scientific study of history (*Historie*), *existenziell*, ontic, positive sciences, factuality are also parallel terms and are only secondarily derived from the more basic idea of historicity, *existenzial*, and ontology. Thus hermeneutics is an exposition of the inner meaning of human existence as opposed to the scientific treatment of the facts of the objective world.

Heidegger used three existentialist terms to explain the meaning of *Dasein*. He called these terms "existentials (*Existenzialien*)" as distinct from "concepts," which are labels used in the natural sciences to objectify beings.[22] A general sense of anxiety that underlies human existence leads to an awareness of these "existentials.". As a result of feeling that one is a "Being-unto-death," one becomes ontologically anxious, not about the physical demise of one's body, but about the meaning of one's existence. The phenomena of death and anxiety lead to the development of these three basic existentials: (1) existentiality, (2) facticity, and (3) Being-fallen.[23]

Existentiality refers to the potentialities of human existence.[24] These possibilities do not refer to objective things such as the hope of the resurrection of the body. Existentiality refers to *Dasein's* "ownmost potentiality-for-Being."[25] It refers to one's inner possibility for developing a personal sense of one's own well being and self-actualization. Because this potentiality of true being is built into the very fabric of human existence, Heidegger says: "Become what you are."[26]

The second "existential" that surfaces in human consciousness is *facticity*. Facticity means that Being is not a world-less and thus indeterminate subject. Being is Being-in-the-world. "To Being-in-the-world, however, belongs the fact that it has been delivered over to itself—that it has in each case already been thrown *into a world*."[27] The "world" that we have been thrown into, however, is not a reference to the physical world of mere things (a *factum brutum*). It is not a world of objects "welded together with a subject."[28] Rather to be thrown into the world is a feeling of sheer meaninglessness, that one exists here and now with no ultimate explanation for the feeling of futility and nothingness.[29] The world that one is thrown into is not the cosmos; it is not the world of cause-effect mechanism; it is rather like a state-of mind or a disposition.[30]

The third existential term that characterizes *Dasein* is *"Being-fallen"* (*Verfallensein*). The fallenness of *Dasein* is further described as "everydayness," "publicness of the 'they'," and "inauthenticity." This fallenness means that *Dasein* is a "not-Being-its-self."[31] Being-fallen means that one's life is dominated by facticity in the sense of thrownness into the world. What awakens one out of the everydayness of Being-fallen is the feeling of anxiety that provokes one to consider the future with its possibilities of authentic existence. This phenomenon of anxiety is an indefinable threat.[32] It is the feeling of nothingness which one gets from simply Being-in-the-world. It is a sense of dread because one knows that one is a Being-unto-death. It is this sense of existential anxiety and despair that jars one loose from one's self-forgetfulness. It offers one hope for release from a feeling of everydayness and provokes one to decide for authentic being.

The potentiality for authentic existence is further attested through the voice of conscience. Conscience is not understood here in a theological sense, or as a proof of God. Rather, conscience is the call of Being. This call of conscience "asserts nothing, gives no information about world-events, has nothing to tell."[33] "'Nothing' gets called *to* this Self, but it has been *summoned* to itself—that is, to its ownmost potentiality-for-Being."[34] The authentic answer to conscience is "resoluteness," a decision to become what one already is.[35]

Stated succinctly, authentic existence is a decision to appropriate one's true potentialities in spite of the absence of any specific objective information based on divine revelation or rational conclusions about the nature of an objective world. The basic call of conscience is the moment of decision to live courageously and meaningfully in a world where there is no objective meaning.

Being, Historicity, and Temporality

The comprehensive term Heidegger used for expressing the meaning of existence is "care" (*Sorge*).[36] The idea of care designates one's existence as it stands inauthentically towards Being.[37] Care is also defined as temporality (*Zeitlichkeit*) in the sense that one exists as time, not "in time" like a thing. Temporality is an attitude of the mind and does not refer to clock time. It is existentialist time, not factual time.[38] It is ontological (a condition of Being), not ontical (something actual and factual).

Existenzial time, as a state of mind, points in three directions.[39] First, it points to the future, which refers to one's existentiality, i.e., the possibilities of existence.[40] Heidegger also called this direction "ahead-of-itself."[41] Second, *existenzial* time points to the past through one's facticity, i.e., one's thrownness into the world, one's "had-beenness."[42] Third, *existenzial* time points to the present. The present is defined as fallenness, i.e., one's lostness in everydayness.[43]

The existentialist idea of time as a state of mind is thus more basic than the idea of clock time. Heidegger assumed that clock time is a mechanistic, cause-effect flow of the present moment passing into the past with the future simply being the unrealized development of the present, which then fades into the past.[44] Existentialist time and clock time are thus entirely divorced from each other. Meaningfulness entails existentialist time as opposed to the factuality of clock time. One attains authentic existence if one lives from the standpoint of the future with its possibilities of being. One falls into inauthentic existence (Being-fallen) if one lives in the present, which is dominated by the existentialist past with its sense of "facticity" and "everydayness." Authentic existence is thus eschatological existence, i.e., living from the standpoint of the future.

The idea of existentialist time is further explained as the meaning of historicity (*Geschichtlichkeit*). Just as human existence does not mean that one exists "in time" neither does one exist "in history." Rather, *Dasein* is history as temporality.[45] In contrast to Hegel who said that all reality is history and is knowable, Heidegger said human existence is history although not history in the sense of bits and pieces of information. History is the "happening" (*Geschehen*) of a human being; it is the essence of one's existence. It is a feeling of the "connectedness of life" and "the movement of existence."[46] Here again the idea of movement does not mean real motion as if something is literally moving. Heidegger writes: "The movement of existence is not the motion of something present-at-hand (*eines Vorhandenen*)."[47] The movement of existence is rather a feeling or a state of mind, and an existentialist sense of "happening" (*Geschehen*).[48] A happening is not making something to be present-at-hand in the sense of an objective happening. Rather, it is a feeling of "happening," a sense of making history, a connectedness of life. This means, in an existentialist sense, one's life is "connected" ontologically from birth to death. The existentialist feeling of happening includes the "end" and the "between" of human existence (*Dasein*). This happening is not like the happening of salvation history in which God is revealed through specific events of history. The existentialist idea of happening has nothing to do with real events in world history.

Another term that Heidegger used to express the idea of happening is care. Care is what constitutes the feeling of what is "between" the beginning of existence and its end. Heidegger says the "ends" and their "between" simply *are*, in the sense that he is not talking about the actual succession of time in the objective world[49] This existentialist idea of happening (*Geschehen*) as temporality (*Zeitlichkeit*) is what Heidegger meant by the historicity (*Geschichtlichkeit*)[50] of human existence. Simply put, historicity means a feeling of meaningfulness without reference to objective events. It is as though one can have meaning without the need of actual events in life to give meaning

The "connectedness of life," or the sense of historicity, means that the future, past, and present (in that order) are united into a whole. *Dasein* does not live in history, which has a real past, present, and future. Rather, historicity means that one lives in such a way that the past, present, and future *are* simultaneously the very structure of *Dasein*. When this ontological unity "happens" in the "moments of vision," then one's "fate" is achieved. Fate, or destiny, thus is authentic historicity.[51]

Heidegger plays up the terminological distinction between *Historie* and *Geschichte*. *Historie* is the science of history.[52] *Geschichte* is existentialistist history, which is the inner meaningfulness of one's own historic existence. It is what gives rise to *Historie*. Heidegger summarizes four popular views of history. First, history is interpreted to mean something that is past and no longer present-at-hand. Second, history means something that is past, but is still having an effect on the present. Here history is a becoming in which events are related through a connection of time—the past, the present, and the future. Third, history means the historical development of cultures. Fourth, history is what is handed down by tradition.[53]

In each of these four interpretations of history, Heidegger noted that they assume one is the "subject" of history. Heidegger stressed the idea that history (*Geschichte*) is primarily the "happening" (*Geschehen*) of *Dasein*, i.e., a person is history in its essence. The secondary meaning of *Geschichte* is called "world-historic."[54] For example, remains, monuments, records have a *historisch* significance because of their world-historic (*welt-*

geschichtlich) character.[55] A battlefield, place of worship, a countryside are world-historic beings, for they have an "essential existent unity with *Dasein*."[56] Thus, whatever *geschichtlich* significance adheres in world beings is only derived from having stood in relationship to *Dasein*'s historicity.[57] In this way, Heidegger stresses that *Geschichte* precedes and is the basis of *Historie*.[58]

The ultimate goal of the historian is to make a study of the possibilities of *Dasein* as opposed to providing a mere chronicle of events of the past.[59] Facts are important only as they arise in connection with the question of human existence.[60] In a nutshell, Heidegger elevates subjectivity at the expense of objectivity, and his notion of historicity as mere meaningfulness which excludes the idea of world events, was to become the basic presupposition in the theology of Rudolf Bultmann, who divorced the Jesus of history (*Historie*) from the Christ of faith (*Geschichte*). Concisely stated, historicity does not mean real history, but existential meaningfulness. Contemporary theology often uses the Heideggerian concept of historicity to argue that the historical Jesus is relatively unimportant. Rather the decisive issue is the historicity of faith in Christ, who is not the historical Jesus but rather Christ is a picture that represents the potentialities of human existence. As I will show in a separate chapter, Bultmann used Heidegger's hermeneutic of existence as the means of demythologizing the New Testament.

Being and Truth: A New Direction

Although his book, *Being and Time*, sought to explain the meaning of Being through an *existenzial* hermeneutic of *Dasein*, Heidegger recognized that a clear and precise definition of Being was not set forth. Rather, what emerged was a hermeneutic of *Dasein*,[61] which he believed was a necessary step "on the way" to an investigation of the meaning of Being.[62] Heidegger changed his hermeneutical approach from an existentialist analysis of *Dasein* to a more direct approach to Being in his subsequent writings.[63] This change is explained in his *An Introduction to Metaphysics*. In the preface to the seventh edition of *Being and Time*, he observed that when it was first published, it was designated as the "First Half." Heidegger acknowledged that the second half that was to follow could no longer be added "unless the first were to be presented anew."[64] He said that one should turn to his *An Introduction to Metaphysics* for an "elucidation of this question" of Being.[65] It is this book that represented the methodological change in the second Heidegger and which was influential among Bultmann's students who began a new search for the historical Jesus based in large part upon Heidegger's new approach..

Heidegger wanted to overcome traditional metaphysics, which basically is nothing more than an inquiry into beings as mere entities rather than into the Being of beings. Such metaphysics is ontical, i.e., a type of physics. What he called for was a *meta*-physics; an investigation into what lies behind beings.[66] This investigation into Being follows from the question, "Why are there beings rather than nothing?" Heidegger noted: "The question aims at the ground of what is insofar as it is."[67] This question is to be taken strictly as ontological as opposed to any particular ontical being. Heidegger wrote: "Accordingly, if our question 'Why are there beings rather than nothing?' is taken in its fullest sense, we must avoid singling out any special, particular being, including man." He asked: "For what indeed is man? Consider the earth within the endless darkness of space in the universe. By way of comparison it is a tiny grain of sand; between it and the next grain of its size there extends a mile or more of emptiness; on the surface of this grain of sand there lives a crawling, bewildered swarm of supposedly intelligent animals, who for a moment have discovered knowledge." If humans are so insignificant in size, there are even more insignificant in terms of their duration: "And what is the temporal extension of a human life amid all the millions of years? Scarcely a move of the second hand, a breath." He concluded: "There is no legitimate ground for singling out this being which is called mankind and to which we ourselves happen to belong."[68] With these belittling remarks about human beings, Heidegger's philosophy made a decisive shift away from *Dasein* in his search of true Being.

In asking the question of Being, Heidegger did not intend to be asking a theological question. Heidegger maintained theology cannot raise the question "why" there are beings, for theology already assumes it knows the answer. To speak of a Christian philosophy is like talking about a "round square."[69] Heidegger said: "Only epochs which no longer fully believe in the true greatness of the task of theology arrive at the disastrous notion that philosophy can help to provide a refurbished theology if not a substitute for theology, which will satisfy the needs and tastes of the time. For the original Christian faith philosophy is foolishness."[70] In thus posing the "why" of beings, the second phase of Heidegger's thinking was not raising the traditional metaphysical questions of God, the soul, and the world. Basically, his question of Being was an epistemological primordial question—how can one know the ground (the Being) of beings?[71] To ask what is Being is thus to ask what is truth.[72] The "second Heidegger" believed the question of the truth of Being is found in language. Heidegger wrote: "It is in words and language that things first come into being and are."[73]

He contended that Being is an empty word today because one has not learned to exist authentically, i.e., one does not stand in an adequate relationship to Being. The conquest of beings in technology has caused the question of Being to be eliminated. It is this "destroyed relation to Being as such" that "is the actual reason for the general misrelation to language."[74] If the possibility is to be opened up for a new relationship of one to Being, then we must look for the meaning of Being, not in the existentialist analysis of *Dasein*, but in the grammatical and etymological question of language. Heidegger explained: "Because the destiny of language is grounded in a nation's *relation* to *Being*, the question of Being will involve us deeply in the question of language. It is more than outward accident that now, as we prepare to set forth, in all its implication, the fact of the evaporation of Being, we find ourselves compelled to take linguistic considerations as our starting point."[75]

This shift of emphasis from "authentic existence" in his *Being and Time* to "authentic language" in his *An Introduction to Metaphysics* does not represent a clean break between the two works. *Being and Time* gives a considerable amount of attention to the question of language,[76] and *An Introduction to Metaphysics* does not ignore *Dasein*. In fact, Heidegger makes it explicit that there is no truth except as *Dasein* stands in a relation to Being.[77]

Just as time and history were interpreted in the primordial sense of *Dasein*'s existence and only secondarily in their external objective sense, even so truth is primarily *existenzial*, i.e., Being discloses itself to *Dasein*. Heidegger did not believe that truth is in the primary sense a correspondence between a thing (*res*) and its idea (*intellectus*). Rather, truth is the appearing of Being much as the sun appears to the inhabitants of the earth. The sun's appearance and relationship to the earth can be scientifically explained, but the primary reality is the historic (*geschichtlich*) manifestation of the sun "grounded in poetry and myth." [78] Heidegger denied that this definition of truth as the appearance of Being is mere subjectivism. Rather, truth is self-disclosure. He insisted: "Only the tired latecomers with their supercilious wit imagine that they can dispose of the historic power of appearance by declaring it to be 'subjective.'"[79]

The historic (as opposed to the historical) experience of Being as appearance shows why "linguistic considerations" are the point of departure for getting at the "why" of beings.[80] Heidegger called language "the

House of Being."[81] "Essence and Being express themselves in language."[82] He stated that his aim was to engage in "an essential clarification of the essence of Being in respect to its essential involvement with the essence of language."[83] In order for language to open up Being, there must be a return to primordial thinking. Primordial thinking is the way the pre-Socratic thinkers expressed in authentic language the meaning of Being as the unity of subject and object.[84]

Heidegger engaged in a detailed grammatical and etymological study in order to unpack the meaning of Being through authentic language. Whether this study was "philological fancies"[85] or whether it was intended to be scientific philology[86] is not of great importance for our purposes. We will not pursue the intricate details in his attempt to open up the primordial and authentic language of Being in early Greek thought. Instead we will use some of the results of these word studies to indicate how Heidegger, in his attempts to resolve the epistemological question of Being, delineated a dualism of language as the "happening of Being" and language as the "statement of correctness," i.e., the primordial significance of language as the coming-into-expression of Being and language as propositional correctitude.

The Concept of Nature in Early Greek Thinking

Heidegger believed that Being for the early Greeks was nature (*physis*)–the emerging, arising, enduring presence of Being. It was an overpowering presence; it was not yet something which had been conquered in thought.[87] The word, nature, comes from the Latin *natura*, which means to be born. Thus, the original meaning of the word is forfeited, for the Greek word, *physis*, originally meant "self-blossoming emergence (e.g the blossoming of a rose), opening up, unfolding, that which manifests itself in such unfolding and perseveres and endures in it; in short, the realm of things that emerge and linger on."[88] Thus, *physis* was the emergence of what we today call "nature" (phenomena), but this emerging was not the same as nature in itself. Heidegger explained: "This opening up and inward-jutting-beyond-itself must not be taken as a process among other processes that we observe in the realm of being." Rather, *physis* "is Being itself, by virtue of which beings become and remain observable."[89] The early Greeks thus learned what Being was, not through natural phenomena, but through Being itself emerging into being. Being is known because it emerges from the hidden.[90]

Physis is the same as *alētheia* (truth as un-concealment). Truth is not an addition to Being; it is not a correspondence of Being and thought. It is not "propositional correctitude."[91] Rather, truth is the very essence of Being. Truth is Being unveiling itself.[92] Truth is freedom in the sense that truth is the "letting-be" of what is.[93] *Physis* entails conflict (*polemos*), as it is seen in Heraclitus, a 6th century B.C. Greek philosopher in Ephesus which is near Miletus, the birthplace of philosophy. Conflict is the original struggle which is prior to beings. It is a struggle between concealment and un-concealment of Being. This conflict is not a split in Being, but is its unity, its binding-together. It is this conflict that causes beings to emerge.[94] When the conflict ceases, beings emerge in the conflict, but Being itself falls into the background. The being which has emerged becomes a ready-made datum. *Physis* consequently degenerates into a mere object; it becomes "nature."[95]

The Concept of Logos in Early Greek Thought

Though *logos* has come to mean speech, Heidegger claimed that it did not originally relate primarily to language. Rather, its primordial meaning was to gather, to collect (in the sense of an orderly collection), even as the primary meaning of the Latin *legere* and the German *lesen* mean to gather, to collect. For example, "*Holz lesen*" means to gather wood. *Lesen* in the sense "to read" is a derived meaning of *lesen* in the strict sense, for reading is the joining of one word with another word in an orderly fashion, i.e., a bringing together and collecting of words.[96]

Heidegger believed that the decline of Western metaphysics began with Plato when "idea" became the name for Being, replacing *physis*.[97] Idea (=Being) became the "whatness" of beings (the visible "thatness"). Being became an extended thing, i.e., reduced to the level of being.[?] This reduction of Being led to the definition of truth as "correctness of vision," as the correlation of a "thatness" and a "whatness."[99] The idea (as true Being) became what-really-is, and being (objects) a mere copy of the idea. [100] Here Heidegger said the distinction between thinking and Being became decisive, and the deterioration of Being to beings began. Heidegger complained that Being as self-disclosure is forgotten.[101]

Logos (=Being) in Aristotle underwent the same misfortune as *physis* (Being) in Plato. Originally, *logos* as Being meant a "collecting-collectedness."[102] It is a "collecting" in the sense that Being is a process of disclosing itself. It is a "collectedness" in the sense that Being (*logos*) is the collectedness of beings. [103] *Logos* in the secondary sense of language meant that speech and hearing were authentically oriented towards Being. In this way, a "phonetic sound"[104] is an authentic word. Language thus became "the custodian of the disclosed being."[105] What comes to expression in language is Being (as the *logos,* the collecting-collectedness). Just as Being as *physis* is "what-is-as-such-in-totality"[106] even so Being as *logos* is the orderly collection of being in its totality. When *logos* finally became misunderstood primarily in terms of language, the truth that was passed on was not freshly appropriated by the hearers with the result that language was corrupted as an objectively true statement rather than self-disclosure.[107]

Despite his protest against the disconnection between subject and object that developed in the history of philosophy, Heidegger has bifurcated nature and history, *Vorhandenheit* and *Geschichte.*[108] This is ironic considering that Heidegger's goal was to overcome the subject-object split, which he believed Western philosophy had developed. However, what is primordially significant for *Dasein* is not the world as an object (*Vorhandenheit*), but *Dasein* in the ontological sense of Being-in-the-world (historicity); not history as facts, but history as the historic (*geschichtlich*) structure of *Dasein;* not time as the moving succession of "nows," but time as the temporal structure of *Dasein;* not death as an ontical possibility, but death as the ontological possibility which opens up *Dasein's* "ownmost Potentiality-of-Being" (authentic existence); not thought as the arbiter of truth, but thought as the means of truth coming to expression in language; not language as statement, but language as the happening (self-disclosure) of Being; and finally, not truth as the correspondence of subject and object, but truth as the primordial self-disclosure of Being.

The question arises whether or not the truth of Being is adequately defined so long as things-present-at-hand (*Vorhandenheit*) and *Existenz* are split into two parts. To be sure, Heidegger intended to view the structure of *Dasein* in its primordial wholeness, but this unity can hardly be achieved so long as the ontology of human existence does not take into sufficient consideration the ontical aspects as well, including what-is-present-at-hand (*Vorhandenheit*). Though Heidegger cogently pointed out the inauthenticity of mere things, does not his exclusive preoccupation with Being on the other hand undermine the significance of beings

In some of his latest writings, Heidegger seemed to have despaired of trying to achieve a synthesis of being and Being. Laszlo Versényi has pointed out that in his final quest for Being he resorted to mystical overtones, especially in two of his works, *Gelassenheit* and *Nothing is without Ground.* Even speech fell into the background, and what became methodologically decisive was a passive waiting for the disclosure of the

Wholly Other, the absolute, transcendent Being, although not understood in a theistic sense.[109]

A Critique

Heidegger's existentialism was a needed protest against rationalism with
its concept of irrefutable and self-evident truth (foundationalism). His
idea of historicity helped to restore a focus on the meaning of human
existence. However, existentialism was not able to replace the presuppositions of rationalism with a convincing alternative. Heidegger swung the
pendulum away from the modern idea of rational certainty to ambiguity, skepticism and a virtual nihilism.[110] Instead of backtracking to the
original unity of subject and object, he set the stage for the fact-value
dichotomy of Bultmann's existentialist theology, which divorced the real
Jesus of history from the symbol of Christ of faith.

Notes

1. Because of the difficulties involved in the translation of Heidegger's work,
I will in all cases give reference both to the English editions and the German
editions. The German editions will be enclosed in parentheses.

2. Thomas Sheehan, "Heidegger's Early Years," in *Heidegger: The Man the
Thinker*, ed. Thomas Sheehan (Chicago: Precedent, 1981), 4. David D. Roberts,
Nothing but History, Reconstruction and Extremity after Metaphysics (Berkeley:
University of California Press, 1995), 111-113.

3. Cf. Thomas Sheehan, "Heidegger and the Nazis," *New York Review of
Books*, 16 (June 1988): 38-47.

4. The word "Sein" will be translated throughout this section as "Being, while
"Das Seiende" (that-which-is) will be tanslated as "being."

5. Heidegger, *Being and Time*, trans. John Macquarrie and Edward Robinson
(London: SCM Press Ltd., 1962), cited hereafter as BT, 41-49 (*Sein und Zeit*
[Tubingen: Max Niemeyer Verlag, 1953], 19-27, cited hereafter as SZ).

6. BT, 22, 26 (SZ, 3, 6).

7. Heidegger, *Essays in Metaphysics: Identity and Difference*, trans. Kurt F.
Leidecker (New York: Philosophical Library Inc. 1960), 44-45, cited hereafter as
Essays in Metaphysics (Identität und Differenz [Pfullingen: Verlag Gunther Neske,
1957], 47-48, cited hereafter as *Identitat*).

8. Heidegger, "On the Essence of Truth," *Existence and Being*, trans. R. F. C.
Hull and Alan Crick, with an intro. By Werner Brock (London: Vision Press Ltd.,
1949), 335, cited hereafter as *Existence and Being*. ("Vom Wesen der Wahrheit,"
Wegmarken [Frankfurt Am Main: Vittorio Klostermann, 1967], 84-85, cited
hereafter as *Wegmarken*).

9. BT, 67ff. (SZ, 41ff).

10. Because of the technical distinction that Heidegger made of these two terms and because of the difficulty of conveying this distinction in English, *existenzial* and *existenziell* will be left untranslated in this chapter.

11. BT, 32-33 (SZ, 12-13).

12. BT, 31 (SZ, 11).

13. *Essays in Metaphysics*, 44 (*Identität*, 48).

14. William J. Richardson, *Heidegger* (The Hague: Martinus Nijhoff, 1962), 259. Marjorie Grene, *Martin Heidegger* (London: Bowes and Bowes, 1957), 12. John Macquarrie, *An Existentialist Theology* (London: SCM Press Ltd., 1955), 29-30.

15. BT, 50 (SZ, 27).

16. BT, 62 (SZ, 38).

17. BT, 61 (SZ, 37).

18. BT, 61 (SZ, 36).

19. BT, 61-62 (SZ, 37).

20. BT, 62 (SZ, 38).

21. Ibid.

22. BT, 70 (SZ, 44).

23. BT, 235-236 (SZ, 191).

24. BT, 33 (SZ, 13).

25. BT, 236 (SZ, 191).

26. BT, 186 (SZ 145-146).

27. BT, 236 (SZ, 192).

28. Ibid.

29. BT, 174 (SZ, 135).

30 BT, 174 (SZ, 135).

31. BT, 220, 236, 237 (SZ, 175, 176, 191-192).

32. BT, 231 (SZ, 186).

33. BT, 318 (SZ, 273).

34. Ibid.

35. BT, 349, 354 (SZ, 302, 307).

36. BT, 237 (SZ, 192).

37. BT, 370 (SZ, 323).

38. BT, 376-377 (SZ, 328).

39. BT, 377, 425 (SZ, 328-329, 373).

40. BT, 378, 401, 373 (SZ, 329, 350, 325-326).

41. BT, 293, 373 (SZ, 249-250).

42. BT, 293, 373 (SZ 250, 325-326).

43. BT, 236-237 (SZ, 192).

44. BT, 374 (SZ, 326-327).

45. BT, 428 (SZ, 376).

46. BT, 427 (SZ, 374-375).

47. BT, 427 (SZ, 374-375).

48. BT, 427 (SZ, 375).

49. BT, 426 (SZ, 374).
50. BT, 427 (SZ, 375).
51. BT, 437 (SZ, 385).
52. BT, 430 (SZ, 378).
53. BT, 430-431 (SZ, 378-379).
54. BT, 433 (SZ, 381).
55. BT, 446 (SZ, 394).
56. BT, 440 (SZ, 389).
57. BT, 432-433 (SZ, 380-381).
58. BT, 433 (SZ, 381).
59. BT, 447 (SZ, 395).
60. BT, 447 (SZ, 395).
61. BT, 486 (SZ, 436).
62. BT, 487-488 (SZ, 437).
63. William Richardson, *Heidegger*, 623-628.
64. BT, 17 (SZ, V).
65. Ibid.
66. Heidegger, *An Introduction to Metaphysics*, trans. Ralph Manheim (London: Oxford University Press, 1959), 17, cited hereafter as *IM*. [*Einführung in Die Metaphysik* (Tübingen: Max Niemeyer Verlag, 1953), 13-14, cited hereafter as *EM*.]
67. *IM*, 3. (*EM*, 2).
68. IM, 4 (EM, 3).
69. IM, 7 (EM, 6).
70. Ibid.
71. IM, 3, 22, 27 (EM, 2, 17, 21).
72. BT, 196 (SZ, 154).
73. IM, 13 (EM 11).
74. IM, 51. (EM, 39).
75. IM, 51 (EM, 39).
76. BT, 203-214 (SZ, 160-170).
77. BT, 269-270 (SZ, 227).
78. IM, 105 (EM, 80).
79. Ibid.
80. IM, 51 (EM, 39).
81. William Richardson, *Heidegger*, 528.
82. IM, 53 (EM, 41).
83. IM, 54 (EM, 41).
84. BT, 44, 122-134 (SZ, 22, 89-101); IM, 195 (EM, 149).
85. Marjorie Grene, 100.
86. William Richardson, *Heidegger*, 296.
87. IM, 61 (EM, 47).
88. IM, 14 (EM, 11).
89. IM, 14 (EM, 11).

90. IM, 14-15 (EM, 11-12).

91. *Being and Existence*, 334. (*Wegmarken*, 84).

92. IM, 102 (EM, 77-78).

93. *Being and Existence*, 333 (*Wegmarken*, 83).

94. IM, 61-62 (EM, 47-48).

95. IM, 63 (EM 48).

96. IM, 124 (EM, 95).

97. IM, 180 (EM, 137).

98. IM, 181 (EM, 138).

99. IM, 185 (EM, 141).

100. IM, 181 (EM, 140).

101. Cf. William Richardson, *Heidegger*, 321. BT, 46 (SZ, 24).

102. IM, 128 (EM, 98).

103. IM, 130 (EM, 100).

104. IM, 185 (EM, 141).

105. IM, 185 (EM 141).

106. *Existence and Being*, 335 (*Wegmarken*, 85).

107. IM, 185 (EM, 141-142).

108. Cf. Macquarrie, *An Existentialist Theology*, 85ff.

109. Laszlo Versényi: *Heidegger, Being and Truth* (London: Yale University Press, 1965), 159-198.

110. Ibid., 196-197

Part Three

Modern Theology and
The Rise of Critical History

As a result of Kant's epistemology, Karl Barth (1886-1968) delineated three options for modern theology.[1] First, he suggested that theology can adopt Kant's philosophy, assuming the validity of its presuppositions. This approach is seen in the rationalistic theologians at the end of the eighteenth century and the first half of the nineteenth century who tried to rewrite the life of Jesus based on a non-miraculous and positivistic interpretation of biblical history.[2] Their interpretation united historical criticism with Kant's critical philosophy, reducing Christian faith to the status of an ethical religion.

This first option also includes the "Back to Kant" movement in the second half of the nineteenth century as represented in the liberal theology of the German theologians, Albrecht Ritschl and Wilhelm Herrmann. This movement also led to the history-of-religions theology of Troeltsch in Germany and to "liberal theology" in America.[3] Liberal theology noticed that Kant left one door open for seeing beyond the finite realm—the moral imperative. According to Kant, the one thing we know for sure is the moral demand placed upon us in our conscience, and this can be accounted for only on the basis that God is the moral legislator who placed that demand within us. Liberal theology adapted this idea and interpreted Jesus as the preeminent representative of one who was morally well-pleasing to God. The liberal use of historical criticism relativized everything in the gospels except Jesus' inner moral life, which was assumed to be untouchable. Through Jesus' perfect example we are inspired to believe in God as our Father and to accept each other as brothers and sisters who must live together in love.[4] This method eliminated the idea of salvation history and substituted in its place a non-mystical and non-miraculous religion of morality.

Charles Sheldon's classic novel, *In His Steps*, written in 1897 and still published today, represents this liberal, moralistic theology.[5] Sheldon's novel was a sentimental story about following in the footsteps of Jesus, and his basic assumption was that one's rational ability empowered one to be a moral person without the miraculous aid of supernatural grace. Sheldon's work says nothing about the power of the Holy Spirit as the third person of the divine Trinity. Sheldon's work was a non-mystical emphasis on living a good moral life by following Jesus' moral example. As was typical of the "back to Kant" movement, this novel reduced the message of Jesus to love and forgiveness.[6]

One of the greatest preachers in American history was Harry Emerson Fosdick (1878-1969), pastor of the famous Riverside Baptist Church in New York City. His theologically liberal sermons highlighted the moral excellence of Jesus as a person to be imitated. He interpreted "the greatness of Jesus" as one who inspires a sense of respect for God as a personal, loving being, but there is nothing about the incarnation, or the doctrine of the Trinity, or the resurrection of Jesus in his sermons and writings. The essence of Christianity is its moral teaching, which serves as the guide to interpreting the Bible.[7]

Paul Tillich (1886–1965) said this moralistic, non-mystical element in effect was denying the power of God and was the weakest point in liberal theology,[8] but on the other hand, classical liberal theology was steeply embedded in the text of Scripture and warmly affirmed the moral presence of a personal God in Jesus—unlike much of subsequent modern theology, including Tillich's systematic theology. If classical liberal theology died an early death in the middle 1930's,[9] its spirit unfortunately did not live on in some of its theological offspring, which often turned away from the idea of a transcendent and personal God. Although classical liberal theology is no longer an option in contemporary theology, it opened the door to an even more radical interpretation of Christian faith, which denied the decisiveness of history for faith.

In addition to the first option of merely pursuing theology within the bounds prescribed by Kant, Barth suggested that one can modify the basic Kantian premise by adding another capacity for knowing God that is part of human reason, but distinct from Kant's theoretical and practical ideas of reason. Schleiermacher called this additional capacity "feeling."[10] Tillich defined Schleiermacher's method this way: "The methodologically decisive thing is that theological propositions about God or the world of man are derived from man's existential participation in the ultimate, that is, from man's religious consciousness."[11] This is likewise the method of Tillich who substituted "ultimate concern" for "feeling."[12] This is largely a modification of the view of Kant who said that matters of faith are based "on a certain (though not a demonstrable or explicable) feeling of divinity."[13] So instead of knowledge being limited to what is derived from (1) the senses, (2) the concepts of understanding, and (3) the ideas of practical reason as Kant proposed, there is a fourth capacity called feeling. But this "feeling" is more than an emotional feeling; it is cognitive feeling; it is an intuitive participation in the divine.

Tillich explained that this method also includes what he called "the method of correlation."[14] Philosophy and theology work together as allies in the task of constructing a systematic view of theology. Philosophy has its unique role to play that is distinct from the task of theology, and theology must not interfere with philosophy's uninhibited intellectual exploration of truth. Philosophy focuses on the "situation" of truth as it is understood in the context of contemporary culture. Tillich meant by "situation" the scientific, artistic, economic, political, and ethical forms through which human existence is interpreted.[15] Philosophy thus sorts through the variety of data about the world that is scientifically and critically established by the various disciplines across the university curriculum.

The task of theology is not to compete with philosophy as it makes judgments about what is objective knowledge of the world and human history. Philosophy asks questions about this information once it has been understood, but theology provides the answers. However, the answers provided by theology do not entail any factual information. Theology, for example, cannot affirm the virgin birth of Jesus or his resurrection from the dead because science has ruled out the possibility of miracles. However, theology can talk about the moral and existential significance of life and death because these judgments do not entail facts about the world. It can discern in the story about Jesus' resurrection how one ought to live courageously in the face of human despair about the finality of death. It can develop an understanding of God as denoting the larger meaning of the world, but it cannot develop a notion of God as a personal being who created the world out of nothing. If theology begins to import factual statements into its notions about God and the world, then it has transgressed into the field of philosophy and overrides the contemporary situation. When theology does this, it becomes obscurantist.

Here then is allegedly the significance of Schleiermacher's readjustment of Kant's theory of knowledge. Critical knowledge derived from the situation is preserved, while theology is able to reinterpret the symbols of faith in ways that are intellectually responsible and consistent

with one's mystical participation in the divine. Hence for Tillich, Jesus as
the Christ can be affirmed without speaking of the real Jesus of history.
"Jesus as the Christ" is a way of speaking about the fullness of human
potentiality. One can talk about God, but God is not a personal being
who is "above" the world, but is rather the "abysmal depth" and the all
inclusive reality that is "within" the world and "within" human life. Tillich
called his theology panentheism (everything is in God) or process theology because he defined God as the basis of the process, which the world
continuously is undergoing. God is the center of this change and is being
shaped by it.[16] Process theology is espoused in a variety of forms in contemporary theology, and its basic method is that theology is a rational
interpretation of the world through understanding the religious implications of the disciplines of critical thought of academia. It is a basic denial
of the history of salvation.

We now come to the third method that Barth suggested one may
choose as an alternative to Kant's philosophy. This is the possibility of
theology insisting to stand on its own feet in relation to philosophy. This
would mean that theology would take as its point of departure the
method of revelation just as philosophy takes reason as its point of
departure. Theology would engage in "a dialogue with philosophy, and
not, wrapping itself up in the mantle of philosophy, a quasi-philosophi-
cal monologue."[17] This third option assumes that theology is more than
merely repeating Bible verses, for it involves explaining in a thoughtful
way the message of the Bible. Barth pointed out that this third option is
characteristic of the "right wing" Hegelian school of theology
(Marheineke and I. A. Dorner), as well as other conservative schools of
thought.[18]

This third option is likewise Barth's method—that theology finds its
justification solely within the context of the Bible.[19] This means that theology will not intrude into the philosopher's domain of deriving truth
through reason. Nor will the theologian be concerned with the philosopher's speculations. Barth explained: "Philosophy, however, is in itself a
strict study concerning a vast field, and it is not for the theologian to conduct himself as if he were in a position to propound a philosophy, as if
this were some subsidiary part of his office, and to pull a philosopher's
work to pieces, especially if that philosopher happens to be Kant."[20]
Rather, the theologian must be content with the Bible as the source of
religious knowledge.[21]

Barth believed that one of the enduring insights of Kant was to maintain the separation of theology and philosophy. Kant contended that

philosophy and theology form two distinct kinds of professions. Since each possesses its own unique characteristics, one should not invade the other's restricted domain, which in turn possesses its own unique features.[22] Since theology takes its teaching from the Bible and not from reason, Kant said it should not attempt to refute philosophy, but neither should philosophy infringe on the rights of theology.[23] Further, since there is no one individual or institution that is authorized by God to interpret Scripture, Kant believed theologians must rely on their understanding by means of the Spirit who guides into all truth. Kant said this means reason cannot be the source of biblical theology.[24]

However, Kant did not mean to suggest that the biblical theologian can dispense with reason: "Were Biblical theology to determine, wherever possible, to have nothing to do with reason in things religious, we can easily foresee on which side would be the loss; for a religion which rashly declares war on reason will not be able to hold out in the long run against it."[25]

Nevertheless, Kant maintained that the biblical theologian can prove that God exists *only* because God has spoken in the Bible. This means that the biblical theologian establishes God's existence as a fact of faith based "on a certain...feeling" (*auf ein gwisses Gefühl*).[26] While "this certain feeling of divinity" may be valid, it cannot be objectively demonstrated, for the biblical theologian as such cannot prove that God has spoken through the Bible as a historical fact. Neither can the theologian prove that the Bible itself contains historical facts as such, for it is the sole prerogative of the philosopher to deal with such matter as objective proof.[27] Kant thus renounced any attempt of the biblical theologian to validate the authority of the Bible through historical or philosophical proofs. Rather, the reliability of the historical faith of the Church must come from the Bible itself as a fact of faith.[28] Here in his separation of theology and philosophy, Kant represented the view of Pietism, which was his spiritual background in his childhood days.

Barth suggested that in this segregation of theology and philosophy "an *insight* lies hidden, which had, and still has, a right to be heard, an insight which, it is true, was of no direct usefulness within the framework of Kant's undertaking, but one in which that determination of the place of theology might well have its deep and justified reason."[29] Barth pointed out that some of Kant's apparent concessions to theology may have been made in view of the Wöllner edict, issued on July 9, 1788, which threatened with civil punishment and dismissal from all offices under King Frederick William II's jurisdiction those who failed to adhere to biblical teachings.[30] In spite of whether or not these concessions were made in the lights of this edict, Barth asks: "Is it not the case that the philosopher of pure reason has said something very significant to the theologian in telling him in all succinctness that '*The biblical theologian proves that God exists by means of the fact that he has spoken in the Bible'?*"[31]

What Barth overlooked is that Kant's separation of philosophy and theology was simply repeating what he had heard from the Pietism of his childhood. I do not believe it had anything directly to do with the Wöllner edict. As I noted in Chapter 7, Kant considered Pietism to be the valid interpretation of Christian theology, and he considered his Enlightened interpretation of religion to be a secularized version of Pietism.

Barth was not friendly to Pietism and rejected its method of personal experience. Barth's own theological method reflected this third option—that the only proper prolegomenon to theology is the doctrine of the Word of God. Barth was thus influenced by the restriction which Kant placed upon reason and affirmed that faith cannot look for support in either philosophy or objective critical study. Unwittingly, Barth himself was influenced by Pietistic thinking when he embraced Kant's verdict that the Bible alone is the source of Christian belief. As Kant said, faith is effected through "the reading of the Bible," or, as Barth said, faith comes from the Word of God, the truth of which is self-authenticating. [32] Following the lead of Kant, Barth renounced any objective proofs of faith, for the truth of the Word of God "is based purely upon itself."[33] Theology precedes anthropology, God-certainty precedes self-certainty. This means no historical or philosophical question can be considered prior to hearing the Word of God, for "men can know the Word of God because and so far as God wills that they should know it, because and so far as over against the will of God there is only the weakness of disobedience, and because and so far as there is a revelation of the will of God, in His Word, in which this weakness of disobedience is removed."[34]

While Kant in principle segregated theology and philosophy, in practice he showed that theology must come to terms with the questions raised by philosophy. In this connection, he suggested that it would be beneficial for a candidate of biblical theology to include in his curriculum a course in the philosophical theory of religion. After having taken this course, the theological candidate should either adopt the theories of the philosopher, or else he must refute the philosopher.[35] Barth would disagree, for the theologian is not concerned with philosophical theories.[36] Theology's sole responsibility is to examine the language of the

Church in the light of the Bible.[37] There is no need of any objective demonstration of faith, for the certainty of faith comes from the unmediated self-revelation of God. "Faith as faith in God stands on its own feet, and is the basis of knowledge."[38] Ironically, because of his emphasis upon the subjectivity of truth, Barth himself is considered to be a "modern theologian," though his intent was to overcome the human-centered subjectivity of modern philosophy.[39]

These three options reflect how modern theology responded to the subject-object distinction—how can God and the world, faith and history, certainty and probability be reconciled? Part Three will examine four modern theologians who tried to reconcile this duality.

Notes

1. *Protestant Thought*, 190-196.

2. Strauss, *The Life of Jesus Critically Examined*, 47ff. Albert Schweitzer, *The Quest of the Historical Jesus* (New York: The Macmillan Company, 1954), 103.

3. Tillich, *A History of Christian Thought*, 215.

4. Ibid., 216-217.

5.Cf. Timothy Miller, *Following In His Steps* (Knoxville: The University of Tennessee Press, 1987), xiii.

6. Ibid., 230.

7. Harry Emerson Fosdick, *A Guide to Understanding the Bible* (New York: Harper & Brothers, 1938). Cf. Fosdick, *As I See Religion* (New York: Harper & Brothers, 1932).

8. Ibid., 219.

9. William E. Hordern, *A Layman's Guide to Protestant Theology* (New York; Macmillan Company, 1973), 93.

10. Barth, *Protestant Thought*, 190.

11. Tillich, *A History of Christian Thought*, 111.

12. Ibid., 98.

13. Immanuel Kant, "Der Streit der Facultaten in drei Abschnitten," *Sämmtliche Werke*, ed. G. Hartenstein (Leipzig: Leopold Voss, 1868), 7:339-340. Translation Mine.

14. Tillich, *Systematic Theology*, 1:59-66.

15. Ibid.

16. Ibid.

17. Barth, *Protestant Thought*, 191.

18. Ibid. Hegel believed the Bible is the authoritative source of truth, but he noted that it still must be interpreted for each age. He wrote: "But here the opposing thesis perhaps comes in, for the theologians say that we ought to hold exclusively to the Bible. In one respect, this is an entirely valid principle. For there are in fact many people who are very religious and hold exclusively to the

Bible, who do nothing but read the Bible, cite passages from it, and in this way lead a very pious, religious life. Theologians, however, they are not; such an attitude has nothing of a scientific, theological character. But just as soon as religion is no longer simply the reading and repetition of passages, as soon as what is called explanation or interpretation begins, as soon as an attempt is made by inference and exegesis to find out the meaning of the words in the Bible, then we embark upon the process of reasoning, reflection, thinking; and the question then becomes how we should exercise this process of thinking, and whether our thinking is correct or not. It helps not at all to say that one's thoughts are based on the Bible. As soon as these thoughts are no longer simply the words of the Bible, their content is given a form, more specifically, a logical form. Or certain presuppositions are made with regard to this content, and with these one enters into the process of interpretation. These presuppositions are the permanent element in interpretation; one brings along representations and principles, which guide the interpretation." *Lectures on The Philosophy of Religion*, 400-401.

19. Barth, *Protestant Thought*, 191-196.

20. Ibid., 192.

21. Ibid., 196.

22. Sämmtliche *Werke*, 7:340. Cf. *Protestant Thought*, 191-196.

23. *Sämmtliche Werke*, 7:339. Cf. *Religion within the Limits of Reason Alone*, 8.

24. *Sämmtliche Werke*, 7:340.

25. *Religion within the Limits of Reason Alone*, 9.

26. *Sämmtliche Werke*, 7:339-340.

27. Ibid.

28. Ibid., 378. Translation mine.

29. Barth, *Protestant Thought*, 196.

30. Ibid., 195. Cf. *Religion within the Limits of Reason Alone*, xxxii; *Sämmtliche Werke*, 7:324ff.

31. *Protestant Thought*, 196.

32. *Church Dogmatics: The Doctrine of the Word of God*, trans. G. T. Thomson (Edinburgh: T. and T. Clark, 1963), 1.1.260-261.

33. Ibid., 223. Paul Althaus pointed out that the attempt to place revelation beyond the necessity of historical proof is the direct result of Kant's critical philosophy, which thus led to the inflation of the idea of revelation ("Die Inflation des Befriggs der Offenbarung in der gegenwärtigen Theologie," *Zeitschrift für Systematische Theologie*, 18 [1947], 134-135, 148f.).

34. *Church Dogmatics*, 1.1.223-224.

35. *Religion within the Limits of Reason Alone*, 10.

36. *Church Dogmatics*, 1.1.223; *Protestant Thought*, 192.

37. *Church Dogmatics*, 1.1.11.

38. Ibid., 15.

39. Cf. Jürgen Moltmann, *History and the Triune God* (New York: Crossroad Publishing Company, 1991), 140.

11

Martin Kähler: the Historical Jesus and the Historic, Biblical Christ

Martin Kähler (1835-1912) was a Pietist who was Professor of Systematic Theology and New Testament Exegesis at the University of Halle. He is known as a mediating theologian because he attempted to bridge the new ways of thinking in the modern world and orthodox Christianity.[1] Paul Tillich was one of his students whom Kähler counseled to stay in the church despite his doubts about traditional Christian belief during his seminary days.[2] One of the tenets of Pietism is that sincerity of heart is more important than doctrinal purity. To be sure, Kähler affirmed the importance of a right theological understanding, but he believed that one needed to be regenerated in order to be a theologian because one's thinking is decisively influenced by experience.[3] This dialectic between reason and personal experience is a hallmark of theological method in Pietism.

The emphasis on personal experience in Pietism was Tillich's basis for reconstructing theology. However, he used the criterion of ultimate concern as the primary category of doing theology rather than a regenerated experience.[4] So long as one was sincerely motivated by pursuit of the divine he believed that was an adequate experiential basis for doing theology. The Pietistic distinction between doctrine and experience served as the basis for his method of correlation—i.e., factual questions that philosophy asks should be carefully distinguished from the valuational answers given by theology.[5] Tillich's method of correlation assumed a divorce between the factuality of the Jesus of history and the religious value of the symbol of the Christ of faith. If Tillich became a prominent representative of this dualistic motif, he first learned it from the tendency in Kähler's theology, which distinguished between the historical Jesus and the Biblical Christ.

Ironically, one of Tillich's students is Carl Braaten, a nationally known systematic theologian of the Lutheran School of Theology at Chicago (emeritus), whose doctoral dissertation was on the theology of Martin Kähler.[6] He has become a contemporary promoter of Kähler's thought and performed a real service to the contemporary discussion by translating Kähler's *The So-Called Historical Jesus and the Historic, Biblical Christ*. Braaten has written extensively on the theme of the historical Jesus, and he faithfully represents the theological concerns of Kähler.[7] I say this is ironic because Tillich took Kähler's thought in a direction that he would not have approved of, but then Tillich's own student has restored and defended Kähler's original intent. It is like saying the son departed from the orthodox way of the father, but the grandson returned.

The Failure of the Search for the Historical Jesus

Kähler felt compelled to defend the New Testament history of Jesus during the time of "the quest for the historical Jesus" in the second half of the 19th century. These "questers" attempted to write a biography of the historical Jesus on the basis of a positivistic historiography. Positivism, as I already noted, assumed that history was made up of isolated, uninterpreted, brute facts. It also assumed that there could be no absolutely unique occurrence in history.[8] Albert Schweitzer's *The Quest of the Historical Jesus* provided detailed research into the "life of Jesus" movement,[9] and it signaled the end of the movement. Carl Braaten writes: "In retrospect we can see that Albert Schweitzer's *The Quest of the Historical Jesus*, 1906, served as an impressive scientific obituary to a movement which fourteen years earlier had been mortally wounded by Kähler's prophetic pen."[10]

Barth listed the following presuppositions of these liberal, rationalistic biographies of Jesus.[11] (1) They were composed mainly under the influence of Kant's dualistic epistemology. (2) Just as faith comes from one's inner consciousness, so it developed in Christ in the same way as it had in any other historical personality. (3) The gospels are the only existing sources for our knowledge of Christ, and they must be used in the same way as any other source material for historical study. (4) The historical Jesus is the object of our source material. It is both possible and necessary to discover his true personality behind the sources. (5) Jesus was immersed in the relativities of history as much as any other historical personality. The miracles ascribed to him can thus be explained away by interpreting them as misunderstandings, hidden forces of nature, or myth. In any case, Jesus was a religious genius who had a spectacular form of God-consciousness. (6) Insofar as we are able to comprehend

Jesus historically, the nineteenth century biographers believed that he was the chief revealer of God.

Kähler maintained that the historical Jesus presented by the "modern biographies" (Reimarus, Eichhorn, Paulus, Strauss, Renan, etc.)[12] only hid the real Christ from the believers. Their so-called historical Jesus was no better than the dogmatic Christ of Byzantine Christology, which they attacked because he was supposedly not defined in a historical manner but in a philosophical way. Kähler observed: "In this respect historicism is just as arbitrary, just as humanly arrogant, just as impertinent and 'faithlessly gnostic' as that dogmatism which in its day was also considered modern."[13]

The Distinction between the Historical and the Historic Jesus

Kähler draws a sharp distinction between *"der sogenannte historische Jesus"* (the so-called historical Jesus) and *"der geschichtliche, biblische Christus"* (the historic, biblical Christ). In this way, he "mortally wounds" (as Braaten puts it) the "life of Jesus" movement and provides a theological alternative to the problem of faith and history with his emphasis upon the historic, biblical Christ as opposed to the so-called historical Jesus. This theological alternative to the "life of Jesus" movement makes him important for contemporary theology. Heinrich Ott believed that Kähler's *So-called Historical Jesus and the Historic, Biblical Christ* "still speaks with astonishing pertinence."[14] Tillich concurred, noting that Kähler "was a prophetic forerunner of what developed more fully only in the twentieth century. The heritage of Martin Kähler has been rediscovered only in the present day discussion in view of the radical [New Testament] criticism."[15]

Kähler's terminological distinction between *historisch* (historical) and *geschichtlich* (historic) seems to be the origin of the modern theological distinction between *Historie* and *Geschichte* as used by Bultmann.[16] This is not to suggest that Kähler intended to bifurcate faith and history, but that is what happened in subsequent modern theology. Tillich said: "One emphasis in Kähler's answer is decisive for our present situation, namely, the necessity to make the certainty of faith independent of the unavoidable incertitudes of historical research."[17]

Kähler's first concern in his work, *The So-called Historical Jesus and the Historic Biblical Christ,* was "to criticize and reject the wrong aspects" of the methodology of the "life of Jesus" movement.[18] He believed this movement failed to make the Bible the source of belief. If one is going to criticize the abstract dogmatism of Church doctrine, one should go back to the Scriptures as the primary source of theology. The life of Jesus biographers failed to understand the nature of Scripture, which is why their methodology was wrong. He maintained: "We have no sources for a biography of Jesus of Nazareth which measure up to the standards of contemporary historical science."[19] This is why Kähler charged the "modern biographers" were heading up a blind alley—they did not understand the nature of their source material. He noted: "Our sources, that is, the Gospels exist in such isolation that without them we would know nothing at all about Jesus, although the time and setting of his life are otherwise entirely clear to historians. He could be taken for a product of the church's fantasy around the year A.D. 100. Furthermore, these sources cannot be traced with certainty to eyewitnesses." Kähler concluded that because we only have fragments of various traditions that circulated among the earliest Christians and that these oral traditions shaped the New Testament, this situation must "awaken serious doubts about the faithfulness of the recollections."[20]

The Christological Authority of the Bible

Though Kähler was quite skeptical about the possibility of writing a scientific biography of Jesus, he was quick to point out the reliability of the kerygma's presentation of Jesus as the Savior.[21] He pointed out that the "perfection" of the Bible must be understood from the standpoint of its purpose, which was not to present a "scientifically reconstructed biography of Jesus." Rather, the gospels have a theological intention: "To awaken faith in Jesus through a clear proclamation of his saving activity."[22] The perfection of the Bible is thus a theological one. It contains recollections that are also confessional. The gospels intend to witness to a reality that is beyond any mere historical fact. The Scriptures "have a reliability which lies completely beyond proof and which would preclude the necessity of submitting them to a scientific test."[23]

Because the "life of Jesus" biographers were concerned with the scientific discovery of the real historical Jesus, they discarded all confessional statements. Kähler believed this was destructive of Christian faith. "Portrayals likes those of a Renan or a Strauss...are for believers in Christ an offense which cuts to the quick."[24] If their portrayals are correct, then the generations who have humbled themselves before the Christ of the Bible are in conflict with the First Commandment. He wrote: "All of us who want to remain—and out of innermost conviction must remain—

within the churchly tradition of the Reformers and thus in continuity with the theologians who have held to the divinity of Christ are united in our concern for the 'biblical' Christ." He maintained that belief in the "biblical Christ" necessarily entailed belief in "the divinity of Christ." The problem with the modern biographers of Jesus was that in their attempt to give us a merely historical and factual record of Jesus that they made it impossible to see him as the Christ. However, faith requires that he " become the object of faith" without "coming into conflict with the First Commandment and without its leading to deification of the creature."[25]

The failure of the modern biographers to understand the nature of the Gospels was the basis of their misunderstanding of the person of the biblical Christ. They seemed to think that he was only a man who possessed larger dimensions than our own human nature. However, Kähler noted: "The distinction between Jesus Christ and ourselves is not one of degree but of kind."[26]

This means any attempt to write a biography of Jesus according to the standards of modern historical criticism cannot be successful. This is so, for the principle of analogy would have to be used. Kähler asks: "Is this method justified in writing about Jesus? Will anyone who has had the impression of being encountered by that unique sinless person...still venture to use the principle of analogy?"[27] If he is the incarnate God, does this not rule out the principle of analogy?

The meaning of history for Christian faith is brought into clear focus at this point. If it is impossible to assert that God came into the world at a definite moment in time, then Kähler correctly pointed out that the New Testament is wrong and the historical continuity within church tradition is broken. This is the reason why he rejected the "life of Jesus" movement: "The historical approach is no longer concerned with safeguarding and interpreting a solid core of the content of faith. Only an extremely fluctuating picture of Jesus' personality is approximately certain."[28] Therefore, faith cannot afford to put itself at the mercy of the "modern biographers."

As opposed to the quest of the historical Jesus, faith is only concerned with the biblical presentation of Jesus. Kähler put it this way: "It is clear that the historical Jesus, as we see him in his earthly ministry, did not win from his disciples a faith with power to witness to him, but only a very shaky loyalty susceptible to panic and betrayal." If the historical Jesus did not produce faith within the disciples, what did? "It is clear that they were all reborn, with Peter, unto a living hope only through the resurrection of Jesus from the dead (1 Pet. 1:3) and that they needed the gift of the Spirit to 'bring to their remembrance' what Jesus had said, before they were able to understand what he had already given them and to grasp what they had been unable to bear (John 14:26, 16:12, 13)."[29]

Kähler believed it was a mistake to try to go behind the New Testament picture of Jesus in order to get at a "historical Jesus" without taking into account the perspective of the resurrection and the Pentecostal gift of the Spirit. Kähler further pointed out that the disciples did not think of Jesus as the founder of some new school of religious belief. Nor did they envisage their task as merely spreading his teachings. Rather, they went forth into the world to witness to his person. They went forth to call everyone everywhere to faith in Christ.[30] They understood him to be "the offer of God's grace" with "universal and lasting significance" and this meant "the *end* of the historical Jesus. Even though we once knew the Messiah according to the flesh, now we regard him thus no longer (2 Cor. 5:16)."[31] The real Jesus is thus the preached Christ, who was not seen for what he really was until after the resurrection. Any picture of Jesus that bypasses the resurrection kerygma is not a true picture of Jesus Christ.

In contrast to the rationalistic theologians, Kähler argued that faith in Christ does not mean "an assent of our conscience to Jesus' religious ethic."[32] Faith cannot be reduced to such a moralism. Neither is this historic Christ an "ideal to be realized in the remote future by scientific investigation."[33] Rather, this faith is now "directly accessible" through the biblical tradition which "possesses the inherent power to convince us of its divine authenticity...That makes it impossible for me even to differentiate the 'historic' from the 'biblical' Christ."[34]

Kähler thus did not allow for a bifurcation between faith and history. Rather, he was calling into question the dualistic thinking of positivistic historiography with its fact-value split. In this respect, he asked: "How can Jesus Christ be the authentic object of the faith of all Christians if the questions what and who he really was can be established only by ingenious investigation and if it is solely the scholarship of our time which proves itself equal to this task?"[35] Kähler also did not reject historical criticism. He believed the New Testament could be read historically as other documents, but he said: "For me the more important question is whether we can do justice to the Bible when we view it from the historical perspective alone."[36] Kähler thus affirmed the Christological authority of the Bible, and he was not willing, on theological grounds, to surrender the authority of the Bible and replace it with the authority of the alleged results of a scientific investigation, which prides itself with an alleged presuppositionless approach to history.

The Relevance of Historical Criticism for Faith

Kähler maintained that theology and historical studies must converge in appreciating and understanding the real Jesus. Theology is the mediator between the past and the present. It takes what is a past reality and puts it at the service of the present.[37] "This task of mediation, then, belongs to dogmatics, after it has made a thorough and serious study of what historical study can accomplish and has learned from history what is important enough to warrant consideration by dogmatics. The task of dogmatics is to provide an inventory of our assets."[38] The convergence of theology and historical studies shows that faith is interested in the Jesus who is at the same time the risen Christ and that this picture of the whole biblical Christ is the true basis for understanding the "real" Jesus. This means faith cannot endure a divorce between the "Christ of faith" and the "Jesus of history," because the Christ of faith is "a tangible human life,"[39] and not a mere symbol of morality.

Although the Bible contains "historical accounts," they do not "have the value of historical documents in the strict sense of the term. Nor do they themselves make such a claim."[40] Neither is the Bible primarily a book of doctrinal propositions nor a book of devotion and edification.[41] Rather, *the Bible is kerygma* (proclamation). Because the central theme of the Bible is the proclamation of Jesus as the Christ, the authority of the Bible is derived from the authority of Christ, i.e., "the passionately held dogma about the Savior vouches for the reliability of the picture transmitted to us by the biblical proclamation of Jesus as the Christ."[42] Whatever view one holds of Jesus as the Christ predetermines his view of the authority of the Bible.[43] It would be wrong to conclude from this that Kähler depreciates the historical quality of faith. To be sure, historical criticism cannot construct a modern biography of Jesus because "from the sources we know his personality for a period of only about thirty months, at the most, of his public ministry."[44] Yet, we know enough of the historical facts as such that are "sufficient for preaching and dogmatics."[45]

If the authority and truth of the Bible (including historical events) are authenticated in faith, is there any necessity for a critical historical validation of faith? The answer seems to be YES and NO. The answer is NO, insofar as the necessity of historical science is concerned. The picture of

Jesus as the Christ in the Bible is as easily accessible to the layman as to the trained historian. "For in relation to the Christ in whom we may and should believe the most learned theologian must be in no better or worse a position than the simplest Christian."[46] On the other hand, the historical "validation" of faith may have an apologetic use. For example, those who are predisposed against the idea of revelation and the authority of the Bible would be encouraged to abandon their prejudices against the Bible when they realize it has a historical basis. Kähler contended that "we must go to the content of the earliest preaching and, starting with a 'minimum' of what can be historically ascertained, introduce them to problems which serious research cannot easily dismiss."[47] In this way, one may be led to faith in Jesus as the Christ. In the final analysis, it is not the historically-ascertained 'minimum' that brings one to faith in Christ, though it may be the apologetic occasion for causing one to listen with openness to the message of Christ. Rather, faith comes from the preaching of the Word of Christ.[48]

Kähler used the idea of "suprahistory" to differentiate the history of the Bible from the modern notion of history.[49] Pannenberg believes the concept of suprahistory is misleading and unwittingly undermines the meaning of revelation. This terminology implies that the historical-critical method with its emphasis upon a scientific examination leaves no room for redemptive event. Pannenberg believes that Kähler should have instead challenged the historicist split between bare facts and interpretation.[50] Consequently, because Kähler allowed the historicist split between fact and interpretation, he conceded too much by making faith independent of the probabilities of historical knowledge. Although Kähler did not intend to divorce faith and history, he did contribute to the bifurcation between *historisch* and *geschichtlich* that has come into technical usage for differentiating the Jesus of history and the Christ of faith.[51]

A Summary of Kähler's Contributions

Here is a list of Kähler's contributions to the discussion of the problem of history and faith. (1) The gospels have primarily a theological intention and only secondarily are they to be used as scientific historical sources. (2) The gospels were written by authors, not by objective reporters.[52] (3) The "life of Jesus" historians, despite their claim of neutrality and objectivity, were motivated by preconceived ideas with the results that the true image of Jesus was distorted. Kähler wrote of this distortion: "What is usually happening is that the image of Jesus is being refracted through the spirit of these gentlemen themselves."[53] (4) Faith has its *sole condition* in the preaching of the Word of God, although this preaching has a historical frame of reference. The trained historian thus does not have any "corner" on the truth of faith. (5) The Christ of faith is not divorced from the Jesus of history; he is "a tangible human life."[54] (6) What Jesus did and who Jesus was cannot be separated, for Jesus' "work is his person in its historic-suprahistoric effect."[55] (7) The authority of the Bible has its validation in the authority of Jesus whom the primitive church proclaimed as the living Christ. Even as the principle of analogy is without force in considering Jesus as the Christ, even so the Bible cannot be merely treated as one book among books, despite Lessing's advice that "if you simply place the Bible alongside of all other books, it will prove itself to be a very reliable and excellent book." Kähler responded to Lessing a century later: "Yes, indeed—but it will no longer be the Book of books."[56] Kähler thus argued for the Christological authority of the Bible. (8) Finally, the real Jesus is none other than *der geschichtliche Christus der Bibel*, and not *der historische Jesus* of the "life of Jesus" movement. This biblical, historic Christ is not an importation of the primitive community upon the historical Jesus, but rather, the primitive community proclaimed Jesus as the living Christ because "*Christ himself is the originator of the biblical picture of the Christ.*"[57]

In whatever way Kähler may have been the forerunner of form criticism in New Testament studies, he did not share the skeptical conclusion, for example, of Bultmann who maintained that there is no continuity between the Jesus of history and the Christ of faith. Nor did Kähler contend that the preaching of the primitive church was mere confession as opposed to what is historically factual. Rather, the kerygmatic Christ is none other than the Jesus who died and rose again and whom the church confesses as Savior. If Leibniz's distinction between the truths of experience and the truths of reason was misconstrued by Lessing into a divorce between the accidental truths of history and the necessary truths of reason, so Kähler's distinction between the historical Jesus and the historic, biblical Christ was misconstrued by Tillich and other contemporary theologians into a divorce between them.

Notes

1. Carl E. Braaten, "Introduction," in Martin Kähler, *The So-called Historical Jesus and the Historic, Biblical Christ,* trans. with an introduction by Carl Braaten (Philadelphia: Fortress Press, 1964), 6ff.

2. Paul Tillich, "Foreword," in Martin Kähler, *The So-called Historical Jesus and the Historic, Biblical Christ*, xii; Tillich, *A History of Christian Thought*, 510.

3. Tillich, *A History of Christian Thought*, 312-313; Braaten, "Introduction," in Martin Kähler, *The So-called Historical Jesus and the Historic, Biblical Christ*, 4ff.

4. Tillich, *Systematic Theology*, 1:10-11.

5. Ibid., 1:60ff.

6. Braaten, "Acknowledgements," in Martin Kähler, *The So-called Historical Jesus and the Historic, Biblical Christ*, xiii.

7. Cf. Braaten, *History and Hermeneutics* (Philadelphia: Westminster Press, 1966).

8. Cf. Collingwood, *The Idea of History*, 136.

9. *The Quest of the Historical Jesus* (New York: The Macmillan Company, 1954).

10. Carl Braaten, "Martin Kähler on the Historic Biblical Christ," *The Historical Jesus and the Kerygmatic Christ* (New York: Abingdon Press, 1964), selected essays trans. and ed. Carl Braaten and Roy Harrisville, 79.

11. Barth, *Protestant Thought*, 378-379.

12. Cf. David Strauss, *The Life of Jesus Critically Examined*, 45ff. Cf. Schweitzer, *The Quest of the Historical Jesus*.

13. Martin Kähler, *The So-called Historical Jesus and the Historic, Biblical Christ*, 43.

14. Heinrich Ott, "The Historical Jesus and the Ontology of History," *The Historical Jesus and the Kerygmatic Christ*, 148.

15. Paul Tillich, *Perspective on 19th and 20th Century Protestant Theology*, edited Carl Braaten (New York: Harper & Row, 1967), 215.

16. Cf. Julius Schniewind, "A Reply to Bultmann," *Kerygma and Myth*, 1:82; Braaten's introduction in Kähler *The So-called Historical Jesus and the Historic, Biblical Christ*, 20; Ott, *The Historical Jesus and the Kerygmatic Christ*, 143ff.; Bartsch, "The Present State of the Debate," *Kerygma and Myth*, ed. Hans Werner Bartsch, trans. R. H. Fuller (London: S.C.K., 1962), 2:51; Michalson, *Worldly Theology*, 9.

17. Tillich, "Foreword," *The So-called Historical Jesus and the Historic, Biblical Christ*, xii.

18. Kähler, *The So-called Historical Jesus and the Historic, Biblical Christ*, 45.

19. Ibid., 48.

20. Ibid., 48-49.

21. Ibid., 48.

22. Ibid., 127.

23. Ibid., 126.

24. Ibid., 45n.

25. Ibid., 103-104.

26. Ibid., 53.

27. Ibid.

28. Ibid., 103.

29. Ibid., 65-66.
30. Ibid., 66.
31. Ibid.
32. Ibid., 121.
33. Ibid., 121-122.
34. Ibid., 122.
35. Ibid., 102.
36. Ibid., 124.
37. Ibid., 67.
38. Ibid., 67-68.
39. Ibid., 95.
40. Ibid., 125-126.
41. Ibid., 129.
42. Ibid., 95.
43. Ibid., 95, 104, 112, 119, 123, 148.
44. Ibid., 92.
45. Ibid., 95.
46. Ibid., 73.
47. Ibid., 144.
48. Ibid., 104-105.
49. Ibid., 47, 65, 95.
50. Pannenberg, "Redemptive Event and History," *Essays on Old Testament Interpretation*, trans. Shirley Guthrie, 314f.
51. Braaten, *The Historical Jesus and the Kerygmatic Christ*, 96n.
52. Kähler, *The So-called Historical Jesus and the Historic, Biblical Christ*, 44.
53. Ibid. 57.
54. Ibid., 95.
55. Ibid.
56. Ibid., 117-118.
57. Ibid., 87.

12

Karl Barth
The Word of God and History

Karl Barth (1886-1968) was the most significant theologian of the 20th Century. His father was a Swiss reformed New Testament scholar who stood against the emerging liberalism, but despite his father's conservative views Karl Barth embraced liberalism during his days as a theological student when he came under the powerful influence of the premier liberal theologians, Adolf Harnack and Wilhelm Hermann, at the Universities of Marburg and Berlin. However, shortly after he became a pastor, he rejected liberal theology. He did so in part because of the outbreak of World War I. The message of theological liberalism minimized the sinfulness of human life, but WWI unveiled human sinfulness at its worst level of depravity.[1]

Barth had become disillusioned with the theology of neo-Protestantism (liberalism) even before the outbreak of World War I.[2] He had already come to realize the inadequacy of the liberal message, which highlighted "the inner life of the Jesus of history," as opposed to the traditional view of Jesus as God and man. By the inner life of Jesus, liberalism meant that Jesus' uniqueness was his heightened sense of morality and personal sense of God-consciousness. The moralism of liberal theology thus did not take seriously enough human sin and the human need for transformation. Jesus as a moral teacher and example was not enough to transform a person, unless Jesus was also God. This awareness of the difference between what he had learned from Herrmann and what he discovered was the actual message of the Bible came as the result of the practical need of communicating Christian faith to people in a desperate situation. The practical task of preaching had occupied Barth's time since the second year following his graduation.[3] Because preaching lies at the basis of his theology of the Word of God, it will be helpful to indicate some events in his early life as a preacher and theologian which helped to shape his theology.

Two year after Barth had begun his pastorate in Safenwil, Switzerland (1911-1921), he became intimately acquainted with Eduard Thurneysen, who had come to serve a pastorate in a neighboring valley. They frequently met together to discuss their sermons, theological studies, and the problems of the church and the world at large.[4] Thurneysen introduced Barth to new points of view, including the ideas of the Blumhardts (father and son) whose emphasis upon the sovereignty of God revealed to Barth how anthropocentric his own sermons had been.[5] There was also the influence of Dostoevsky whose writing exposed the contradictions between Christianity and Western culture.[6]

The greatest influence upon Barth during this time was his own intensive study of the Bible. Thurneysen described how Barth took seriously the task of the preacher: "He sat down before the Bible each day of the week and in his own new way ploughed it like a farmer who goes out into his fields in the early morning and makes furrow after furrow." He further noted: "Karl Barth stands before us already in this early period as a reader and expositor of Scripture. The tablets of Holy Scripture are erected before him and the books of the expositors from Calvin through the biblicists and all the way to the modern critical biblical interpretation lie open in his hands. Both then and now this has been the source from which his theology has come." Thurneysen believed "that the springs of the Bible should flow afresh in our time" is due to Barth reinstating the Bible as the "sole concern" of theology as opposed to the method of liberalism.[7]

On September 4, 1914, the change that had already taken place in Barth's theology became quite evident. On this day he had written a letter to Thurneysen expressing his regret and amazement at the manifesto that appeared in Rade's *Die christliche Welt* in which many German theologians (including some of Barth's most respected teachers) had given approval of the Kaiser's war.[8] This manifesto indicated to Barth the impoverishment of liberal theology. Smart writes: "A failure in ethics revealed to him a bankruptcy in theology. But he was able to see it only because already for him forces had been at work shaking the theological structure in which he had been living and laying bare ominous cracks in its foundations."[9]

The Barth of *The Epistle to the Romans*

In 1919, Barth published his commentary on Romans, which he subsequently revised in 1921.[10] In Barth's preface to the English translation, he pointed out that his only purpose for producing the commentary was to interpret the Scripture. He writes: "I felt myself bound to the actual words of the text, and did not in any way propose to engage myself in free theologizing."[11] He further specified his purpose: "The purpose of this book neither was nor is to delight or to annoy its readers by setting out a New Theology. The purpose was and is to direct them to Holy Scripture, to the Epistle of Paul to the Romans, in order that, whether they be delighted or annoyed, whether they are 'accepted' or 'rejected', they may at least be brought face to face with the subject-matter of the Scriptures."[12]

The priority of Scripture from then on characterized all of Barth's writings. He rejected the liberalism of Schleiermacher-Ritschl-Herrmann "because in any thinkable continuation of this line I can only see the plain destruction of Protestant theology and the Protestant church."[13] In his *Church Dogmatics* the first volume is entitled "The Doctrine of the Word of God." He believes the "Word of God" in Holy Scripture is the only valid prolegomenon to theology, that there is no other method of theology apart from God's Word, which is God's self-revelation.[14] In the preface to the English translation of his *Epistle to the Romans*, Barth said: "Theology is *ministerium verbi divini*. It is nothing more nor less."[15]

Barth believed this priority of Scripture had been subordinated to an interest in historical criticism in theological liberalism. He felt a preoccupation with historical criticism over against an exegesis of Scripture was incompatible with the preacher's task. He put it this way: "I myself know what it means year in year out to mount the steps of the pulpit, conscious of the responsibility to understand and to interpret, and longing to fulfill it; and yet, utterly incapable, because at the University I had never been brought beyond that well-known "Awe in the presence of [critical] History.'"[16] Barth maintained that historical criticism must not usurp the primary task of theology. Otherwise, there can be no "Protestant theology" or "Protestant church."[17] Surely this is the greatness of Barth's contribution to theology—the Word of God in Scripture. However, this emphasis upon the Word of God in Scripture points to what was his greatest weakness—he did not adequately integrate historical criticism and faith.

This dualism of faith and history was in part derived from the influence of Kierkegaard's philosophy, particularly his emphasis upon "the infinite qualitative difference" between God and human beings.[18] Reflecting on this influence in his later years, here is what Barth said of

Kierkegaard: "What attracted us particularly to him, what we rejoiced in, and what we learned, was the criticism, so unrelenting in its incisiveness, with which he attached so much." He noted that Kierkegaard rejected "all the speculation which blurred the infinite qualitative difference between God and man, all the aesthetic forgetfulness of the absolute claims of the Gospel and the necessity to do it justice by personal decision." He further appreciated Kierkegaard's attack on the contemporary theology in his day because of its "attempts to make the scriptural message innocuous" with its "too pretentious and at the same time too cheap christianism and churchiness . . . from which we ourselves were not as yet quite free."[19]

The later Barth spoke of Kierkegaard's influence on his earlier thought: "The second edition of my *Commentary on Romans* is the very telling document of my participation in what has been named 'the Kierkegaard Renaissance.'"[20] In the early years of his developing theology, Barth found in Kierkegaard "new dawns with New Questions and answers."[21] We noted earlier that Barth's contemporary, Paul Tillich, likewise had been greatly influenced by Kierkegaard during his student days as well. Like Tillich, the early Barth used Kierkegaard's divorce between the method of faith and the method of history as a basis for distinguishing between the historical Jesus and the Christ of faith.

Kierkegaard's influence on Barth's *Epistle to the Romans* can be seen in the way that God and history are absolutely contrasted. History is understood to be the relative, the profane, the materialistic. History under the judgement of God means the end of history. It is "separated absolutely" from God.[22] This means that God cannot be "concreted and humanized in a particular department of history," for God would then cease to be God.[23] God cannot share in the relativities of history. This means that the promises and faithfulness of God "is a matter neither of historical nor of psychological experience, and because it is neither a cosmic happening within the natural order, nor even the most supreme event of our imaginings."[24] The only point of contact between God and human beings is faith in Jesus Christ. But this means faith is a miracle. It is the establishing of a relationship with God, which takes place freely by God's grace alone.[25] But, this salvation is not a part of history, nor does it arise out of one's experience. Rather, it comes solely from the mercy of God; it is a "miracle—'vertical from above.'"[26] Salvation is the possibility "where the history of the relation between God and man begins; where there is no history to record, because it only occurs, and occurs eternally...And this occurrence IS—in Jesus Christ."[27]

This "occurrence" is thus not a recordable fact of past history because it has no structural relationship to objective historical events. This is so because God cannot be domesticated within the historical process. Barth believed this is the fallacy of all religions, for they look for the evidences of God in history or in themselves. [28] On the other hand, faith is the "occurrence" of Jesus Christ, the "Moment." It is the point of eternity inserted vertically from above.[29] Therefore, it is the moment that is decisive for faith. It is "the eternal 'Moment' when before God we are unrighteous and humiliated, in order that by God we may be justified and exalted."[30]

In this early work, Barth even said the "life of Jesus" is a non-historical event. Paul said that Jesus is "declared to be the Son of God with power according to the Spirit of holiness by his resurrection from the dead" (Romans 1:4). Barth understands this "declaration" not to mean some kind of historical assertion. The period of time in the life of Jesus from his birth to his death/resurrection is not historical.[31] By historical, Barth meant events which can be observed and recorded by human beings and which critical historians can reconstruct. Barth offered this explanation: "In so far as our world is touched in Jesus by the other world, it ceases to be capable of direct observation as history, time, or thing."[32] What Barth is doing is to bifurcate the Jesus of history from the Christ of faith: "Within history, Jesus as the Christ can be understood only as a Problem or Myth. As the Christ, He brings the world of the Father."[33]

Barth was trying to do at least two things in his *Epistle to the Romans.* First, he was seeking to overcome Neo-Protestantism (liberal theology), which emphasized the immanence of God over against divine transcendence. Second, he was re-asserting the priority of Scripture. He overreacted to liberalism with his bifurcation of revelation and history, but this can be partly explained on the basis of his acceptance of the presuppositions of the historical-critical method, which left no room for redemptive events. Rather than offering a critique of the positivistic presuppositions of historicism, he accepted without question Troeltsch's historiographical principle of causality which ruled out the possibility of anything absolutely unique occurring in history. Barth's acquiescence to Troeltsch's is obvious when he said: "There is under this heaven and this earth no existence or occurrence, no transformation, be it never so striking, no experience, be it never so unique, no miracle, be it never so unheard of, which is not caught up by a relativity in which great and small are inextricably woven together. Therefore, if the Resurrection be brought within the context of history, it must share in its obscurity and error and essential questionableness."[34]

The Barth of *Church Dogmatics*

If Barth's theology divorced God and history in this early stage of his thought, it was to undergo a significant shift in his later thinking. If Kierkegaard played a decisive influence in his early dualistic thinking about faith and history, it was to be modified in his later thinking. In his later years, Barth said that he had "remained faithful to Kierkegaard's *reveille*, as we heard it then, throughout my theological life, and that I am so today still."[35] He further noted: "I consider him to be a teacher into whose school every theologian must go once. Woe to him who has missed it! So long as he does not remain in or return to it! His teaching is, as he himself once said, "a pinch of spice" for the food, not the food itself."[36] The writings of Kierkegaard thus made it impossible for Barth to return to the objectivist thinking of Orthodoxy, which assumed that history "proved" the truth of revelation. Like liberalism, Barth believed Orthodoxy obscured the difference between God and humanity with its objectivistic thinking. Yet Barth acknowledged that Kierkegaard's attack could not be theologically normative. That is why Barth warned against anyone remaining in Kierkegaard's school of thinking.

Barth thus revised his theology of history in his *Church Dogmatics* (1932-1967). In it he called attention to his previous over-reaction to liberalism, which had placed God and humanity virtually on the same level. He conceded: "I should like at this stage to utter an express warning against certain passages and contexts in my commentary on Romans, where play was made and even work occasionally done with the idea of a revelation permanently transcending time, merely bounding time and determining it from without." He admitted this was done in reaction to "the prevailing historism and psychologism which had ceased to be aware at all of any revelation other than an inner mundane one within common time." In this regard, he allowed that "the book had a definite, antiseptic task and significance.[37]

In *Church Dogmatics*, revelation is no longer understood as permanently transcending time. Neither is God the Wholly Other. Revelation is now given an objective basis in temporal reality. "God's freedom for us men is a fact in Jesus Christ, according to the witness of Holy Scripture. The first and the last thing to be said about the bearer of this name is that He is very God and very Man."[38] This means the life of Jesus is no longer understood as a non-historical occurrence. Rather, Jesus Christ, as very God and very Man, is the objective reality of divine revelation.

Although Barth placed revelation within history, revelation is not subject to historical examination. Here Barth is much closer to Kierkegaard who emphasized that faith has a historical point of departure, but its sole condition comes from God alone. Barth likewise emphasized that the Word of God is God's act. Revelation is attested in the Bible; it proceeds from the Father; it is objectively fulfilled in the Son; and subjectively made possible by the Holy Spirit.[39] But revelation "has nothing to do with the general problem of historical understanding."[40] Barth disallowed the idea of revelation as being part of the relative sphere of history, as we ordinarily know it. This is crucial to Barth's theology of the Word of God, for he wanted to guard against the idea of revelation being something one could "have." Revelation is always a matter of God's free grace. "To say 'the Word of God' is to say the work of God. It is not to contemplate a state or fact but to watch an event, and an event which is relevant to us, an event which is an act of God, an act of God which rests on a free decision. That God's Word is from eternity to eternity does not allow us to evade it…But it happens, and happens as nothing else happens."[41] Here the Word of God is identified as an "event" or an "act" that "happens," but not as a fact of history which could be critically examined and scientifically documented.

The Word of God is thus never subjected to the relativities of history. Revelation "comes" through the Bible, the written Word of God,[42] and yet there is a distinction between *"God speaks"* and *"Paul speaks."* However, when the Word of God becomes an event in the moment of faith, the Bible and the Word of God are one and the same in a dialectical sense.[43] Barth makes a distinction between the Bible and revelation because he defined revelation as the Word of God. "God's Word is God Himself in His revelation."[44] Revelation thus means the Self-revelation of God. What is revealed is God's very Self, not information about God. The Bible "becomes" revelation in the moment of God's Self-revelation through the Bible, but the Bible as such is not revelation.[45] As a result of his new definition of revelation, to say the Bible is the revelation of God is to turn God into a book. God inspired the words of the Bible, but God is only known through those words when they become the Word of God in the moment of God's Self-revelation. Divine revelation can thus not be controlled by human effort. God's Word is known when God the Father makes Himself known in Jesus Christ through the power of the

Holy Spirit.

The Barth of *Church Dogmatics* still defined revelation as the "Moment" of the pure presence of God as he did in his commentary on Romans. This is why Barth said revelation is not concerned with the general understanding of history as such.[46] Barth thus retained a radical distinction between revelation and history, although not as radical as in his earlier thought. I have heard it jokingly said that the difference between the Barth of *The Epistle to the Romans* and the Barth of *The Church Dogmatics* is that the later Barth simply dropped his footnote references to Kierkegaard. To be sure, the later Barth did integrate faith and history more decisively by insisting that Jesus Christ is the Word of God in real history—that the virgin birth really happened and that Jesus' resurrection included the historical reality of the empty tomb. Barth affirmed these doctrines on the basis of faith alone, but this faith has nothing to do with the science of historical understanding. This means that the question of the knowability of the Word of God is answered by the Word of God alone and is totally self-authenticating.[47]

Barth saw the modern discussion on the problem of revelation and history to be "a portentous failure to appreciate the nature of revelation."[48] He delineated what he considered to be three persistent errors. First, the question of revelation cannot be answered from the standpoint of history, for "it may well be said it is the historical as such in its universality and relativity which is the necessary 'offence' to revelation."[49] This "questionableness and uncertainty of history"[50] stand in sharp distinction to revelation. Barth believed that "there has been a failure to see that in answering this question we cannot start with the general phenomenon of time, or, as it is preferably called, history." He argued that " we cannot assume that we know its normal structure on the basis of comparative observation, and then go on to ask whether and how far the phenomenon of revelation discloses itself, perhaps, to the said comparative observation at a specific point." Historical critical studies "is certainly not the text in perusing which we will ever come directly or indirectly upon the phenomenon of revelation."[51]

Second, revelation can be "seen" only when it has already been "found." We seek God only to discover that God has sought us and found us. Revelation entails "no problems" of an intellectual or scholarly nature.[52] The Word of God does not depend upon our ability to see it before we believe and receive it. God's Word is self-authenticating; it does not depend on empirical verification; and historical criticism cannot disturb or undermine God's Word. Barth argued strongly for the independence of God's Self-revelation over against all critical thinking. He recognized that the revelational method of theology "apparently—but really only apparently—grossly contradicts all honest investigation of truth," but he argued that it "is the inevitable result of the nature of the question before us here. God's revelation in Christ, in the way in which Holy Scripture declares that it has taken place, is not something problematic."[53]

Third, revelation precedes history. Revelation is always the subject and history is the predicate. Revelation becomes history, but history never becomes revelation. "*Revelation is not a predicate of history, but history is a predicate of revelation.*"[54] This means that revelation cannot be discovered by human means: "There has been a failure to see that if revelation is revelation, we cannot speak of it as though it can be discovered, dug up, worked out as the deeper ground and content of human history." Barth contended that if the sentence, "God reveals Himself," means anything, it has nothing "even remotely in common with interpretation, hypothesis, assertion, with appraising and valuing, with an arbitrary fixing, extracting, or excising of a definite bit of human history." Any human effort intended to help authenticate the idea of divine revelation through "historical intuition" is irrelevant.[55] If one attempts to determine historically the reality of revelation and to locate revelation through historical investigation, Barth believes then one shows in this human endeavor that he or she is in fact not obedient to revelation.[56]

One of Barth's many contributions to theology was his emphasis upon the rationality of faith. Reason, however, was used only as a means of understanding the revelation of God in Holy Scripture and not as aid to demonstrate its historical reliability. Barth's focus on the importance of reason for understanding faith shows that he is right to disclaim that his theology has any connection with Pietism, which he believed opened the door to the "irrationalist" trend in liberal theology with its denial that the mind could have any objective knowledge of God.[57] Whereas Pietism only elevated personal experience as more important than doctrinal understanding without minimizing the need for orthodoxy, liberal theology dropped significant doctrines of Christianity, such as the Trinity, the Virgin Birth, the Incarnation, and the Resurrection because these doctrines were allegedly not based on critical rationality. The most that liberal theology believed reason could know was a moral knowledge of God—that God is and that the principles of moral behavior have been exemplified uniquely in Jesus.

Barth exposed the doctrinal superficiality of liberalism and the weakness of its "extraordinary polemic...against the so-called "intellect" of man"[58] In a classical assessment of the weakness of liberalism, Barth argued: "We might very well be of the private opinion that it would be better and nicer if God had not spoken and did not speak with such deliberate 'intellectualism' and that it would be more appropriate for God if 'God's Word' meant all sorts of different things, apart from the meaning 'God speaks.' But is this private opinion of ours so important, resting as it does upon some sort of philosophy?"[59]

Barth may be excused for his narrow definition of the Word of God as the *direct* Self-revelation of God considering that he in no way minimized the importance of doctrinal propositions based on a proper exegesis of Scripture. Yet it must be asked if it is exegetically sound to limit the meaning of the Word of God to the moment of the pure presence of God. Neither does it seem appropriate to limit revelation to Jesus Christ. To be sure, he is the final revelation and the only redeemer, but not the only revelation.[60] If revelation is identical with the unmediated and pure presence of God, does this do justice to the Scriptures where the Word of God is identified with the words of God as propositions to be believed? (Mark 13:31; Luke 11:28; John 6:63; John 14:23-24; Rev. 1:1-2). This is the question that Pannenberg has addressed to the Barthian theology of the Word of God.[61]

Pannenberg has suggested a modification of Barth's idea of a *direct* Self-revelation. He has proposed the idea of an *indirect* Self-revelation of God. Recognizing that the purpose of revelation is that God wants to be known, Pannenberg agrees with Barth's basic idea of revelation as the Self-revelation of God. However, the Selfhood of God is indirectly revealed in the events of salvation history. History is thus a reflex of who God is. In this sense, God's Self-revelation is indirect. We know that God is Father, Son, and Holy Spirit only because that is the way that God has been revealed in the course of events in history. The *direct* Self-revelation will occur only in the eschaton when Jesus will finally usher in the kingdom of God. This will be a direct Self-revelation because Who God Is will fully correspond with our knowledge of God in eternity.

By *indirect* Self-revelation, Pannenberg is not at all suggesting that we do not have a personal and saving knowledge of Christ now. Indeed through the Holy Spirit one has salvation through trusting in Christ.[62] Pannenberg is using the concept of revelation in Barth's sense of an objective knowledge of Who God Is in God's very essence. The problem with Barth's concept of a *direct Self-revelation* is that it is similar to Gnosticism in which revelation was disconnected from the real events of real history in a real world.[63] To be sure, Barth believed in the real history of salvation and in the inspiration of the Holy Scriptures, but this history and the Scriptures are not revelation; they only attest to revelation. Of course this is not to say that Barth's theology was Gnostic; it is only to say that his definition of revelation is Gnostic-like. So this is only a criticism of his revelational method that was disconnected from historical criticism and not a criticism of his theology. Barth's *Church Dogmatics* is the most extensive explanation of the doctrines of Christian faith that has ever been produced.

Finally, unless the concept of the Word of God entails the idea of what has really happened in history and is not merely a knowledge of the unmediated pure presence of God, then Barth's concept of Self-revelation too easily leads to Bultmann's existentialist theology in which the self of Self-revelation is the human self, not God's Self, and revelation is altogether disconnected from the real history of salvation.[64]

Notes

1. James Smart, *The Divided Mind of Modern Theology*, (Philadelphia: The Westminster Press, 1967), 57f.

2. Ibid..

3. Ibid., 44.

4. Ibid., 58.

5. Ibid., 60.

6. Ibid., 65.

7. *Revolutionary Theology in the Making; Barth-Thurneysen Correspondence, 1914-1925*, trans. James D. Smart (Richmond: John Knox Press, 1964), 12-13, cited by Smart, *The Divided Man...*, 66.

8. Ibid., 67.

9. Ibid.

10. Karl Barth, *The Epistle to the Romans*, trans. from the sixth edition by Edwyn C. Hoskyns (London: Humphrey Milford, 1932), vi.

11. Ibid., ix.

12. Ibid., x.

13. Barth, *Church Dogmatics*, I, I, x.

14. *Church Dogmatics*, I, I, 304.

15. *The Epistle to the Romans*, x.

16. Ibid., 9.

17. *Church Dogmatics*, I, I, x.

18. Karl Barth, "A Thank You and a Bow: Kierkegaard's Reveille," *Christian Journal of Theology*, trans. H. Martin Rumscheidt, XI, (January, 1965), 5.

19. Ibid.

20. Ibid.

21. Ibid.
22 *Epistle to the Romans,* 77.
23. Ibid., 79.
24. Ibid., 98.
25. Ibid., 102.
26. Ibid.
27. Ibid., 76.
28. Ibid., 111.
29. Ibid.
30. Ibid., 440.
31. Ibid., 29.
32. Ibid.
33. Ibid., 30.
34. *Ibid.,* 204.
35. Ibid.
36. Ibid., 7.
37. *Church Dogmatics,* I.2.50.
38. Ibid., I. 2. 25.
39. Ibid., I..2.1.
40 Ibid. I. 1.168.
41 Ibid., I. 2.527.
42. Ibid., I, 1, 136.
43. Ibid., I.1.127.
44. Ibid., I.1.339.
45. Ibid., I.1.134.
46. Ibid., I.1.168.
47. Ibid., I.1.350.
48. Ibid., I. 2.56.
49. Ibid., I.2.57.
50. Ibid.
51. Ibid., I..2.56.
52. Ibid., I..2.57.
53. Ibid.
54. Ibid., I.2.58.
55. Ibid.
56. Ibid.
57. Karl Barth, *The Theology of Schleiermacher,* ed. Dietrich Ritschl, trans. Geoffrey W. Bromiley (Grand Rapids: Wm. B. Eerdmans, 1982), 276-279.
58. Ibid., 231.
59. Ibid., 150.
60. Cf. Carl Braaten, *History and Hermeneutics* (Philadelphia: The Westminster Press, 1966), 14.
61. *Revelation As History,* trans. David Granskou (London: The Macmillan Publishing Co., 1969), 12.

62. Pannenberg, *Theology As History*, ed. James M. Robinson and John B. Cobb, Jr. (New York: Harper and Row, 1967), 238, 251-255. Cf. Pannenberg, *Systematic Theology*, 3:122-135.

63. Pannenberg, "Dogmatic Theses on the Doctrine of Revelation," *Revelation As History*, 136.

64. Moltmann, *Theology of Hope*, trans. James W. Leitch (New York: Harper & Row, 1965), 61.

13

Rudolf Bultmann
The Divorce of *Historie* and *Geschichte*

Rudolf Bultmann (1884-1976) was the son of a German Lutheran pastor who was sympathetic to the emerging theological liberalism in his day. His paternal grandfather was a missionary to Africa, and his maternal grandfather was a pastor in the Pietist tradition. Bultmann received his education at the universities of Tübingen, Berlin, and Marburg, which were committed to liberal theology. He was professor of New Testament Studies at the University of Marburg from 1921 to 1950. If Barth was the most significant theologian in the 20th century, Rudolf Bultmann became the most influential New Testament scholar. Early in their academic careers both were aligned together in their opposition to liberal theology, and yet these two scholars came to represent diametrically opposed theological viewpoints. James Smart referred to their differences as representing the divided mind of modern theology.[1] Both were influenced by the philosophy of Kierkegaard, but Barth sought to free himself from some of the extremes of Kierkegaard's existentialist method, while Bultmann went beyond Kierkegaard toward a radicalization of his thought.

Hans Werner Bartsch remarked that "no single work which has appeared in the field of New Testament scholarship during the war years has evoked such a lively discussion as Bultmann's original manifesto, *New Testament and Mythology*."[2] In 1941, when this essay was first published, it produced an explosion in theological circles and opened up again the historical question, which Barth had largely silenced with his theology of the Word of God.[3] Tillich noted: "Bultmann saved the historical question from being banished from theology."[4] That is because Bultmann insisted that theology must respect the conclusions of historical criticism.

Existentialism as the "Only Solution"

In his commentary on the Book of Romans, the early Barth had refused to base revelation in history. In so doing he was over-reacting to historicism. For Barth, God alone proved God's Self through God's Self, not through history. Barth added objectifying elements to his later theology, although he continued to define revelation as a direct encounter with God and exempted theology from having to deal with the general understanding of history. On the other hand, Bultmann took seriously the question of history in biblical criticism as it is seen in his *History of the Synoptic Tradition*. This work summarized his research in form criticism.[5] Form criticism is one of the disciplines of higher Biblical criticism and assumes that unwritten, oral traditions served as sources for the writing of the Gospels. These oral traditions are believed to have been widely circulated among the earliest Christians in stylized format, which were memorized and passed on within the community before they were written down and became part of the Gospels. The method of form criticism arose after the demise of the quest for the historical Jesus when younger scholars like Bultmann began to examine the idea of unwritten sources as the basis of the written Gospels.[6]

Using the form critical method, Bultmann tried to show that the Gospels reflected the beliefs of the primitive church rather than that of Jesus of Nazareth. He thus adopted an extreme historical skepticism about the reliability of the Gospels. Oscar Cullmann (1902 – 1999), an internationally respected New Testament scholar from Basel Reformed Seminary and a contemporary of Bultmann, pointed out that Bultmann's historical skepticism is not due to the discipline of form criticism, but rather it was because Bultmann imported his existentialist philosophy into form criticism.[7] Hence Bultmann was philosophically predisposed to discount the historical accuracy of much of the material in the Gospels. Bultmann was also philosophically predisposed not to accept the idea of miracles in the New Testament. To do so would be to sacrifice one's intellect, for the modern scientific worldview made it impossible to revive an alleged obsolete worldview.[8]

As an alternative to Barth's realistic reading of the New Testament, Bultmann proposed that the New Testament be demythologized through using existentialist categories as the means of reinterpreting the event of salvation.[9] He contended that "an existentialist interpretation" was the "only solution" for understanding the New Testament.[10] He saw the categories of Heidegger's philosophy of existence to be "saying the same thing as the New Testament and saying it quite independently."[11] Bultmann noted that secular existentialism largely transposed Christian concepts into its philosophy: "Heidegger's existentialist analysis of the ontological structure of being would seem to be no more than a secularized, philosophical version of the New Testament view of human life."[12]

Barth did not seriously engage in historical criticism, but Bultmann did. Tillich believed that Bultmann's use of form criticism underscored his importance for theology because he forged again to the surface the question of history, which Barth had suppressed.[13] On the other hand, Barth could only see the current existentialist takeover in theology to mean the destruction of theology. He said: "To the best of my ability I have cut out in this second issue of the book [*Church Dogmatics*] everything that in the first issue might give the slightest appearance of giving to theology a basis, support, or even a mere justification in the way of existential philosophy."[14] As we noted in the previous chapter, Barth insisted upon the priority of the Word of God over against any other criterion, but he embraced a bifurcation of history and theology by defining revelation as encounter rather than history, thus bypassing the critical problem of history. In so doing, Barth implicitly agreed with historical skepticism and then tried to overcome it by insisting that faith is based merely in the Self-authenticating revelation of God.

Like Barth, Bultmann did not want to make faith insecure by equating revelation and history. So they both spoke of revelation as a non-historical, divine "event," which is not open to historical investigation. However, there is a profound difference in their understanding of what the "self" of the *self-revelation* of God refers to. While Barth interpreted *self*-revelation to mean the transcendental selfhood of God, Bultmann defined *self*-revelation as a correspondence between God and the human self.[15] Bultmann's basic thesis is that revelation is personal encounter with the Word of God here and now.[16] As with Barth, the Word of God is not a set of doctrines or objective facts. Nor can faith be proved in any way: "True faith is not demonstrable in relation to its object."[17] The revelation of God instead comes in the moment of faith and cannot be understood prior to its relation to faith. However, there is a profound difference in their understanding of the concept of God, despite their similar ways of defining revelation. For Barth, the Self-revealing God confirms the historical frame of reference of faith. Hence Barth affirmed the real history of salvation and believed that God was Trinitarian. Not so with Bultmann. If God can be known independent of the facts of history, then why retain the importance of historical facts for faith? If the Word of God is self-authenticating and does not involve a report of what God has said and done in the world, why is it necessary to add on speculative doctrines, such as the Trinity and the historical resurrection of Jesus.

God's Being as an Unknown Quality

If the Word of God does not refer to the transcendental selfhood of God, what then does it mean? Bultmann drew from existentialist philosophy to provide an answer to this question: "To speak of the act of God means to speak at the same time of my existence."[18] Bultmann denied that he was turning the reality of God into a mere subjective experience when he said that to speak of God means to speak of human existence. One's encounter with God is no mere psychic phenomenon just as to experience the love of another is no mere psychic phenomenon.[19] Bultmann argued that the proof for God is existential, i.e., it is only in the "moment" of faith's decision that God is to be known at all. He maintained that "real belief in God always grows out of the realization that being is an *unknown quantity*, which cannot be learned and retained in the form of a proposition, but of which one is always becoming conscious in the 'moment' of living."[20] Bultmann thus argued that the true being of God is unknowable by humans. In this sense, Bultmann was agnostic about having an objective knowledge about God, and yet he insisted that in the "moment" of faith's decision to believe in God one comes to a new and authentic understanding of oneself that would not have been possible except as an "act" of God in the kerygmatic Christ.[21] This act of God in Christ is not a historical (*historisch*) act, which happened in some datable event of the past. Rather, it is an historic (*geschichtlich*) occurrence which happens existentially, but happens *now* and happens only through the proclamation of Christ as the *word*. The preached Christ, however, is not the Jesus of history. Jesus is thus not the "bearer" of the word[22] as tradition had imagined, but the idea of Christ as a symbol of the best in human existence is what is meant by the Word of God. Bultmann explained: "It is clear that *Christ* is revelation and that revelation is the *word*; for these two are one and the same."[23] The word of proclamation is also not about doctrines or propositions. What is also not revealed is the objective reality of God. Bultmann asked: "What, then, has been revealed?" He answered: "Nothing at all, so far as the question concerning revelation asks for doctrines—doctrines, say, that no man could have discovered for himself—or for mysteries that become known once and for all as soon as they are communicated." On the other hand, Bultmann said that *"everything has been revealed, insofar as man's eyes are opened concerning his own existence and he is once again able to understand himself."*[24] In essence, Bultmann says that one's own self-understanding has been revealed, but nothing about God, and yet it is only through faith in the kerygmatic Christ that one comes to this self-knowledge and authentic existence.

This anthropocentric definition of faith (i.e., theology is about human existence) that places Bultmann in the line of nineteenth century modernism. as Barth pointed out.[25] On the other hand, his existentialist definition of faith distinguishes him from liberalism. Bultmann observed that for liberal theologians as Adolf Harnack "the great truths of religion and ethics are timeless and eternal, though it is only within human history that they are realized, and only in concrete historical processes that they are given clear expression."[26] On the other hand, what is important for Bultmann is not timeless truths being exemplified in history. He said that "history may be of academic interest, but never of paramount importance for religion."[27] What is important is to see the way that the understanding of human existence comes to expression in New Testament mythology. Instead of Jesus of Nazareth fulfilling the goal of salvation history, Bultmann believed that the history of the Old Testament resulted in a "miscarriage"[28] and that the Gospels must not be taken as real history about Jesus of Nazareth, except in a very limited sense. Rather the Gospels used first century mythological categories to express their newly-understood possibilities of human existence. The New Testament is thus not primarily a report of real history, but rather its imagery must be demythologized and interpreted existentially.[29]

The Historical Jesus and The Kerygmatic Christ

We noted earlier that Martin Kähler introduced the terminological distinction between *Historie* and *Geschichte* in order to show that the real Jesus is the historic, biblical Christ instead of the abstract idea of the so-called historical Jesus. We noted that the early Barth in his commentary on *The Epistle to the Romans* had radicalized this distinction and turned it into a divorce between the Jesus of history and the non-historical occurrence of the Christ of faith, but the later Barth of *The Church Dogmatics* abandoned this way of thinking in favor of a new orthodoxy. Younger German scholars were attracted to the early Barth following the publication of his commentary on *The Epistle to the Romans,* including Bultmann.[30] The early Barth used Kierkeggard's paradox of faith and history to interpret the Gospels as portraying a non-historical, faith-based theology. His distinction between the Jesus of history and the Christ of faith paved the way for Bultmann, but when the later Barth of *The Church Dogmatics* rejected this divorce, many of the younger scholars who had been drawn into his theology of *The Epistle to the Romans* did not follow him in his later phase of neo-Orthodoxy. Bultmann in particular continued on with the assumption of a divorce between the Jesus of history and the Christ of faith, and this view was reinforced as he drank deeply at the well of Heidegger's philosophy of existence.

In a critique of Bultmann's existentialist theology, Julius Schniewind suggested that Bultmann had not done justice to the relationship between *Historie* and *Geschichte* and between the Jesus of history and the Christ of faith.[31] Schniewind said that "it is impossible to run away from *Historie* to *Geschichte*. We cannot reject *Historie* because it is not vitally present for us and accept *Geschichte* because it is. It is impossible to escape from the relativity of past history."[32] Bultmann replied by saying he is "not running away from *Historie* and taking refuge in *Geschichte*." Instead, he said: "I am *deliberately renouncing* [italics mine] any form of encounter with a phenomenon of past history, including an encounter with the Christ after the flesh, in order to encounter the Christ proclaimed in the kerygma, which confronts me in my historic situation."[33] In very plain speech, Bultmann said the idea "that God has acted in Jesus Christ is, however, not a fact of past history open to historical verification."[34] Bultmann thus made a decisive substantive break between *geschichtlich* and *historisch*. *Historie*, in Bultmann's usage, refers to the datable past, i.e., to the actual event of past history. *Geschichte* refers to what is meaningful existentially regardless of what the past fact might or might not have been.[35]

Bultmann's immediate source for using these two words as technical terms is Heidegger's philosophy. Bultmann used this distinction to show that faith is concerned only with *Geschichte* (i.e., history as human existence), not *Historie* (i.e., history as the scientific study of objective facts of the datable past). Bultmann argued that "the Jesus of history is not kerygma....For in the kerygma Jesus encounters us as the Christ—that is, as the eschatological phenomenon *par excellence*."[36]

In calling Jesus Christ the eschatological phenomenon, Bultmann borrowed from Heidegger who used the concept of the future to mean the possibilities of human existence. We earlier showed that Heidegger defined time in existentialist terms—the *past* refers to the feeling of "thrownness" into the world, the *present* refers to a sense of fallenness and inauthenticity, and the *future* refers to the possibilities of authentic human existence. Authentic existence entails the idea of living from the perspective of the future instead of being overpowered by the failures of the past. For Bultmann, the concept of eschatology does not refer to a real objective future, such as the real coming of the risen Lord at the end of salvation history. Bultmann meant that Jesus Christ (and not the Jesus of Nazareth) is only a symbol that expresses the idea of openness to the possibilities of human existence. Those who respond to the Word of God in Jesus Christ are said to exist eschatologically.[37]

A Critique of Bultmann's Existentialist Theology

Does the existentialist reinterpretation of the gospel mean that Bultmann completely compromised the gospel and turned it into a humanistic philosophy? I think the answer to this question is a mixed one. Although Bultmann demythologized and de-historicized the gospel, in one sense he did not de-kerymatize it because he insisted that eschatological existence comes *only* through the message of Jesus Christ. Bultmann maintained that "the question is not whether the nature of man can be *discovered* apart from the New Testament. As a matter of fact it has not been discovered without the aid of the New Testament, for modern philosophy is indebted both to it and to Luther and to Kierkegaard."[38] Bultmann strongly affirmed the importance of preaching the gospel if authentic existence is to be realized, and he criticized Heidegger because existentialist philosophy is only able to offer an analysis of human existence derived from Christian categories. Without the preaching of the gospel, Bultmann maintained that Heidegger's existentialist call to "become what you are" cannot be attained.[39] Bultmann devoted his professional career to explaining the New Testament, and his *Theology of the New Testament* is one of the most brilliant expositions of its kind. In fairness to Bultmann, it should be recognized that he sincerely sought to reconcile modern thought with the enduring meaning of the gospel, although his intent was thwarted because his starting point assumed a dualistic split between fact and value, *Historie* and *Geschichte*.

In spite of all that Bultmann said about the independence of faith and historical criticism, he did at least recognize that there is a limited connection between them. He argued that the kerygmatic tradition must not be questioned because this would make the eschatological event insecure and would make it part of the relativity of all historical knowledge.[40] Bultmann also argued there are two historical fact necessary for faith—the mere "thatness" of the historical Jesus and that he died on the cross.[41] Bultmann explained that these two facts are necessary in order to protect the kerygmatic Christ from being reduced to a mythological Christ.[42] Nothing else, however, other than these two facts of history is needed.

Did Bultmann succeed in preserving faith from the incertitude of historical research? I think the answer to this is No. Although Bultmann said the historical Jesus *has no continuity* with the Christ of faith, he did insist that the historical Jesus serves as the basis of the kerygma.[43] If so, how else other than through historical judgments can one decide if Jesus actually existed. Further, if the validity of the kerygma requires that we believe Jesus actually died on the cross, then in spite of all that Bultmann has said, faith is not independent of the results of historical research. Further, why should faith be divorced from historical research? If the Gospels claim to have a historical basis, then is it not incumbent upon the theologian to examine this claim. One of Bultmann's internationally known students is Gerhard Ebeling who has argued that to have a Christology without the historical Jesus is a mere illusion.[44]

Heinrich Ott argued that Bultmann was unable to integrate faith and history because his historiography was positivistic in the sense that he believed there are bare facts independent of interpretations.[45] This dualistic thinking has been the bane of modernist theology, making it virtually impossible to embrace the Trinitarian faith of the Church. Bultmann's positivistic historiography is also connected with his acceptance of the modern scientific worldview, which assumes all events are the result of an unbroken chain of cause and effect. Bultmann believed the modern scientific worldview implied the need for theology to accommodate itself to its presupposition. Hence he said: "The only way to preserve the unworldly, transcendental character of the divine activity is to regard it not as an interference in worldly happenings, but something accomplished *in* them in such a way that the closed weft of history as it presents itself to objective observation is left undisturbed."[46]

If this modernist presupposition is allowed, then it is impossible to speak "christianly" of faith and history.[47] Although John Macquarrie does not embrace Trinitarian orthodoxy, he has noted that Bultmann's rejection of miracles is based on an outdated view of modern science, as if the law of cause-effect is absolute. He notes that Bultmann was laboring under "the hangover of a somewhat old-fashioned liberal modernism.

He is still obsessed with the pseudo-scientific view of a closed universe that was popular half a century ago, and anything which does not fit into that tacitly assumed world-picture is, in his view, not acceptable to the modern mind and assigned to the realm of myth."[48] Postmodern science has certainly destroyed our commonsense assumptions about the nature of space-time, and quantum mechanics in particular has replaced the Newtonian view of a mechanistic universe. Whether or not miracles can occur is not so much a scientific question as it is a historical and theological one.

Another positivistic notion that Bultmann borrowed from existentialist philosophy was his excessive historical skepticism. The modern critical historian demands irrefutable certainty and because the New Testament cannot measure up to this standard, Bultmann retreated inwardly looking for moral and spiritual values that cannot be damaged by the uncertain results of historical study. Positivism and existentialism are like two sides of the same coin. Positivism looks for facts and existentialism looks for meaning. Unable to unify them, he disconnected the kerygmatic Christ from the historical Jesus, unwilling to risk the value of human existence at the hands of the critical historian. So he made the most of historical skepticism, turning a vice into a virtue by creating a cleavage between faith and history. He extended his historical skepticism to the limit by saying: "We must frankly confess that the character of Jesus as a human personality cannot be recovered by us."[49] To be sure, Bultmann believed that historical research could recover something of his preaching.[50] He further believed that we can know that he appeared as a teacher of wisdom, a lawgiver, and as a prophet.[51] However, Bultmann said: "I do indeed think we can know almost nothing concerning the *life* and *personality* of Jesus" [italics mine].[52]

Bultmann believed this was not a fact to be regretted, but a liberating truth that helps us to understand that the gospels are not about history. So he celebrated the idea that historical research can never "encounter any traces of the epiphany of God in Christ"[53] because "what God says to us through the Bible is in the form of *address*. It can only be listened to, not examined."[54] Clearly Bultmann's excessive historical skepticism has much in common with Gnosticism and its world-denying and anti-historical attitude. Further, his historical skepticism was derived from the presuppositions of Heidegger's philosophy of existence rather than from a critical investigation of the facts of history. If the schizoid split between the historical Jesus and the kerygmatic Christ is allowed to stand, it would put an end to Christology. Significantly enough in a book entitled, *The Vindication of Liberal Theology*, Henry P. Van Dusen, a promi-nent liberal theologian and President of Union Theological Seminary in New York City from 1945 to 1963, rejected Bultmann's divorce between the Jesus of history and Christ of faith, noting if such a divorce is true that "both intellectual honesty and ethical integrity would compel me not merely to renounce the Christian ministry and resign from member-ship in the Church, but to surrender adherence to Christian faith."[55]

Bultmann's existentialist theology was intended to make the Christian message relevant for modern people. He assumed no one today can interpret the Bible literally, especially its three-storied uni-verse—a local heaven above and hell located in the center of the earth.[56] Any one who plays a radio cannot believe in miracles.[57] He believed the liberal method of picking and choosing from the Bible those parts which are compatible with the modern scientific worldview was not success-ful.[58] The only viable method is to recognize that the New Testament is steeped in mythical imagery. Hence his demythologizing exegesis of the New Testament was an attempt to preserve the enduring message of the Bible for today; namely, its offer to experience authentic existence.

Bultmann's description of the so-called New Testament worldview is a terrible caricature. It is fair to say that the New Testament writers sim-ply used the language available to them out of their Hebrew heritage and Greco-Roman background without trying to develop a systematic worldview. Since the time of the early Christian Apologists in the sec-ond century, theology has never assumed the extreme literalism that Bultmann has superimposed upon the New Testament. They well under-stood that God created the universe and that God transcended it. The concept of *creation out of nothing* was well developed by the time of Ireneaus and the Early Church Fathers, who developed systematically the implicit New Testament understanding by using categories derived from Greco-Roman philosophy. The idea that God was literally up in the material sky somewhere and hell literally located in the center of the earth contradicts the very notion of God's cosmological transcendence and the eschatological expectation that this world would be destroyed. The problem is that modern thinkers are much more literalistic than the premodern world. For modern philosophers, something must be clear, distinct, and literal, if it is true. Part of the difficulty with modern unbe-lief is that its scientific literalism has interfered with its ability to appreci-ate the religious and metaphorical significance of language.

Bultmann assumed that language must be either literally true or merely symbolic. Since the imagery of the Bible cannot be taken as literal language, he placed it in the category of myth. He overlooked the history of theology in which much discussion and debate focused on how literally the Bible should be interpreted. Thomas Aquinas in the 12th century proposed that between univocal (literal) language and equivocal language there is analogical language. Words that refer to transcendent realities, such as God as Father, contain only a small measure of literal content, but enough to help the mind to understand that it is comprehending a truth that transcends the natural world. Hence God as Father does not mean that God is a human being with male features, but rather it suggests God is the source of all things. The prophet asked, is God's "hand shortened, that it cannot redeem?" (Isaiah 50:2). Such anthropomorphisms are common, and certainly the prophet was not suggesting that God literally had a hand. When the Bible speaks about heaven, it does not necessarily assume literally that heaven is a local place out in the universe somewhere. Solomon recognized this in his prayer of dedication for the Temple in Jerusalem, after it had been built. He invited God to take up his abode in the Temple, but then immediately shrank back from that idea, recognizing that "heaven and the highest heaven cannot contain thee; how much less this house which I have built" (2 Chronicles 6:18).

Cullmann has noted that Bultmann's demythologizing method is after all not really demythologizing, but a de-historicizing and thus a re-mythologizing in existentialist categories. Over against Bultmann, Cullmann argued that the New Testament writers had already demythologized by historicizing the gospel story.[59] Tillich too criticized Bultmann for using the category of demythologizing and said he should have called his method a process of de-literalization.[60] There is surely nothing wrong about Bultmann theologizing existentialist categories, but it is problematic to allow any philosophy to dictate the terms of belief. Philosophy is a useful tool for communicating and providing clarity to thought, but as the Early Church Fathers showed, one can use philosophical categories to do this without destroying the content of faith

Finally, Bultmann's existentialist interpretation of eschatology restricts meaning only to this life and sees no goal in the process of history itself.[61] His concept of "eschatological existence" only refers to existential possibilities without any reference to an objectively real future. This contradicts the human need to hope. It has been said that an eschatology without a future is an "eschatology without hope."[62] Paul put it this way: "If for this life only we have hoped in Christ, we are of all men most to be pitied" (Romans 15:19).

Notes

1. James Smart, *The Divided Mind of Modern Theology*, (Philadelphia: The Westminster Press, 1967).
2. "Foreword," *Kerygma and Myth*, vii.
3. Tillich, 242.
4. Ibid.
5. Cf. James Smart, *The Divided Mind of Modern Theology*, 191.
6. Rudolf Bultmann, *The History of the Synoptic Tradition*, trans. John Marsh (Oxford: Blackwell, 1963).
7. Oscar Cullmann, *Salvation in History*, 1, 49-50, 120, 170; *The Christology of the New Testament*, 7.
8. *Kerygma and Myth*, 3.
9. Ibid., 10.
10. Ibid., 15.
11. Ibid., 25.
12. Ibid., 24.
13. Tillich, 242.
14. Barth, *Church Dogmatics*, I, 1, ix.
15. Moltmann, *Theology of Hope*, 61.
16. *Kerygma and Myth*, 201.
17. Ibid.
18. Ibid., 196.
19. Bultmann, *Kerygma and Myth*, 199-200.
20. *Essays, Philosophical and Theological*, trans. James C. G. Greig (London: SCM Press, Ltd., 1955), 7.
21. *Kerygma and Myth*, 202.
22. *Essays, Philosophical and Theological*, 18; Bultmann, *Jesus and the Word*, 14, 215-219.
23. *Existence and Faith*, shorter writings of Rudolf Bultmann, selected, translated, and introduced by Schubert M. Ogden (London: Hodder and Stoughton, 1961), 87.
24. Ibid., 85.
25. *Church Dogmatics*, I. 1. 39.
26. *Kerygma and Myth*, 13.
27. Ibid., 13.
28. Rudolf Bultmann, "Prophecy and Fufillment," *Essays on Old Testament Hermeneu-tics* (Richmond, VA: John Knox Press, 1969), 72.
29. Ibid., 16.
30. Helmut Gollwitzer, "Introduction," in Karl Barth, *Church Dogmatics, A Selection*, trans. and ed. G. W. Bromiley (New York: Harper and Row, Publishers, 1961), 16.
31. *Kerygma and Myth*, 37, 82-85, 117.
32. Ibid., 83.

33. Ibid., 117.

34. Ibid., 207.

35. *Kerygma and Myth*, 37. Cf. Carl Braaten, *History and Hermeneutics*, 38. Cf. Cisbert Greshake, *Historie Wird Geschichte* (Essen: Ludgerus-Verlag Hubert Wingen KG., 1963), especially 1f., 36-42. Macquarrie, *An Existentialist Theology*, 158-160.

36. *Kerygma and Myth*, 117.

37. Ibid.., 208.

38. Ibid., 26.

39. Ibid., 28.

40. Ibid., 116.

41. Bultmann, "The Primitive Christian Kerygma and the Historical Jesus," *The Historical Jesus and the Kerygmatic Christ*, 20.

42. Bultmann, "Reply," *The Theology of Rudolf Bultmann*, trans. H. C. Kee, ed. C. W. Kegley (New York: Harper and Row, 1966), 260.

43. Bultmann, "The Primitive Christian Kerygma and the Historical Jesus," *The Historical Jesus and the Kerygmatic Christ*, 18._

44. *Word and Faith*, 292.

45. *The Historical Jesus and the Kerygmatic Christ*, 151; cf. Ott, *Geschichte und Heilsgeschichte in der Theologie Rudolf Bultmanns*, 210f., cited by James Robinson, "The German Discussion of the Later Heidegger," *The Later Heidegger and Theology*, 31.

46. *Kerygma and Myth*, 197.

47. Moltmann, *The Theology of Hope*, 180.

48. John Macquarrie, *An Existentialist Theology*, 168.

49. *Existence and Faith*, 52.

50. *Jesus and the Word*, 12.

51. *Existence and Faith*, 52-53.

52. *Jesus and the Word*, 8.

53. Ibid.

54. Ibid., 166.

55. Henry Van Dusen, *The Vindication of Liberal Theology* (New York: Charles Scribner's Sons, 1963), 128.

56. *Kerygma and Myth*, 1ff.

57. Ibid., 5.

58. Ibid., 12ff.

59. Cullmann, "Die Verbindung von Ur- and Endgeschehen mit der neutestamentlischen Heilsgeschichte," *Vorträge und Aufsätze 1925-1962* (Tübingen: J.C.B. Mohr, 1966), 163.

60. Tillich, *Perspectives in 19th and 20th Century Protestant Theology*, 228.

61. Bultmann, *History and Eschatology*, 155.

62. H. Grass, "Das eschatologische Problem in der Gegenwart," *Dank an Althaus*, 1958, 64, cited by Oscar Cullmann,

14

Gerhard Ebeling
"Pure Word" and "Mere Fact"

In 1953, Ernst Käsemann delivered a lecture to a group of Bultmann's former students entitled, "The Problem of the Historical Jesus." He cautioned that unless some aspects of the historical Jesus could be discovered through historical critical research, then Jesus would be largely meaningless for faith.[1] This lecture initiated what came to be known as "the New Quest for the historical Jesus."

The Call for a New Quest

One of Bultmann's students, Gerhard Ebeling (1912 - 2001) of Zurich University, became a prominent participant in this New Quest. He called into question the validity of Bultmann's exclusive preoccupation with the kerygma as opening up a new self-understanding. He pointed out that the kerygma is not merely concerned with one's existence, but that also it is "a testimony to that which has happened."[2] If Jesus had no material relationship with the kerygma, then the kerygma is nothing more than mere myth.[3]

Ebeling argued that kerygmatic statements such as "Jesus is risen" and "Jesus is Christ" cannot be interpreted on the basis of their *predicates*, but they must take into full consideration the *person* of Jesus.[4] The necessary connection between Jesus and the kerygma is why Ebeling said theology must renew the quest for the historical Jesus.[5] We noted earlier that the *old quest for the historical Jesus* was an attempt to write a non-miraculous, rationalistic biography of Jesus in the 19th Century. We also noted that Martin Kähler criticized this movement in his book *The So-Called Historical Jesus and the Historic, Biblical Christ* on the grounds that the New Testament does not offer the kinds of source material that these biographers were looking for. The rationale for the *new quest* is not the discovery of new source materials, but it is based on the necessity for finding a "hermeneutic key to Christology."[6] This new quest does not mean that the New Testament scholar thinks one can get behind the kerygma in order to prove it; rather, it is based on the assumption that the historical Jesus is the criterion of the kerygma and thus he is necessary for interpreting the kerygma.[7]

Ebeling was not interested in establishing a basis for faith "behind" the Word. Faith comes only in response to the Word. If faith were based on some fact behind the Word, this "would thus sully the purity of faith."[8] Ebeling agreed with Bultmann's existential interpretation of the kerygma as moving in the right direction for overcoming a positivistic idea of history, and he believed Bultmann rightly saw the kerygma was not interested in objective facts of the past. The use of the historical-critical method often assumed that its purpose was to lay bare the facts.[9] However, Ebeling called for the use of the historical-critical method to do more than discover isolated facts. He wanted to use it as tool to find out what Jesus understood about his relationship to God. Ebeling explained: "If one only has objective facts in mind when one talks about getting back behind the kerygma, then one will hardly do justice to the questions we are dealing with here. For if one has to do with Jesus, one has to do not with *mere facts* [italics mine] but with *pure Word*."[10] Ebeling drew a sharp distinction between "facts which confirm the Word" and "the word-event."[11] His interest in getting "back behind the primitive Christian kerygma" was to discover the words that Jesus used to express his relationship to God.[12]

Going behind the Words to the Word

If the first quest for the historical Jesus by the rationalistic theologians of the 19th century was to discover the *facts* behind the words of the Gospels, the new quest for the historical Jesus wanted to go behind the Gospels to discover the *words* that the historical Jesus used to express his faith in God. If Bultmann drew from the early Heidegger's philosophy of existence, Ebeling drew from the later Heidegger's philosophy of language. One might refer to Ebeling's search for the historical Jesus as a methodological emphasis upon the linguisticality of reality, not upon the historicality of reality. The reality of revelation thus expresses itself in words, not in historical facts. He writes: "Hence the proper question regarding the past is not: What happened? What were the facts? How are they to be explained? or something of that kind, but: What came to expression?"[13] This focus on *word-event* instead of *historical event* is why the new quest of the historical Jesus has been called "the new hermeneutic."[14] It is derived from Heidegger's later philosophy of hermeneutics as the means through which the Being of all beings is revealed.

Jesus as the Witness of Faith

Ebeling explains that the significance of the historical Jesus is thus to see how faith came to expression in him as the word-event: "The quest of the historical Jesus is the quest of this linguistic event which is the ground of the event of faith."[15] What is faith? Is it not a relationship with God? In answer to this question Ebeling would say Yes.[16] If then faith is entering into a relationship with God and if Jesus is the "Son of God," does this not mean that Jesus is the "object" of faith? Ebeling says No. Rather, Jesus is the "witness of faith." He says: "This unity of Jesus with faith comes properly to expression not really in what Jesus says of his own faith, but as a witness to faith in existing for others—in a word, in the communication of faith."[17] So the believer today cannot be expected to accept the objective teachings of Jesus about God, and he cannot be expected to believe that Jesus was the incarnation of the pre-existent Son of God. Objective, historical facts are largely irrelevant to faith— except that the Jesus of history was a witness to faith.

The Easter event is a word-event, not a historical fact involving an empty tomb, Jesus did not rise again from the dead, but rather faith arose. If faith arose after Jesus' death, it was because Jesus was the occasion of faith prior to the Easter event. After the Easter event, faith became "proclaimable."[18] In this way, Ebeling seeks to link the historical Jesus and the kerygmatic Christ. Ebeling argued: "The faith of the days after Easter knows itself to be nothing else but the right understanding of Jesus of the days before Easter. For now Jesus appeared as what he really was, as the witness to faith."[19] In reading the literature on the new quest for the historical Jesus, one must get used to the idea that the traditional understanding of biblical words is no longer intended. For example, when Ebeling asserts that "Jesus appeared as what he really was," this does not refer to an objective fact of history. It does not mean that Jesus was historically resurrected and continued to have communication with his disciples. Rather, the words, "Jesus appeared," only means that the disciples came to the same experience of faith that Jesus had prior to his death so that the rise of faith and the appearances of Jesus are the same thing.[20] When the Gospels thus report that only believers saw the risen

Lord, this was a mythical way of expressing their understanding that they too had come to experience the rise of faith even as Jesus had been a witness of faith prior to his death. Ebeling argued in this way for the continuity between the historical Jesus and the Christ of faith as opposed to Bultmann's disjunction between them. The historical Jesus thus gives the kerygma its legitimacy, but this is not to say that the kerygma is *proven* by ascertaining the facts of Jesus' life. Rather, Jesus is the hermeneutical key (as a word-event) for Christology. Jesus is constitutive for Christology in so far as what came to expression in his person is the occasion of faith for others.

Ebeling sees the importance of putting *faith* into a proper relationship with *history*, arguing that the two cannot be divorced. Bultmann was interested in the Christ of the kerygma because it is "faith in Christ" as an existential moment of encounter with the possibilities of authentic existence that makes eschatological existence possible. Ebeling was thus interested in the historical Jesus as the witness of faith who is the word-event, but he is not the object of faith. Bultmann considered the historical Jesus of little consequence for faith, except that he really existed and served as the inspiring force that gave rise to the kerygma. Thus, "faith in Christ" is not faith in Jesus as a historical person, whereas faith in Christ for Ebeling refers to the idea of Jesus being a witness of the word-event.

Both Bultmann and Ebeling are interested solely in the linguistic elements of the kerygma. Ebeling thus said: "Now of course we would agree completely with Bultmann's resolution to confine speech about God's action strictly within the relationship between Word and faith."[21] In other words, the notions of event and action take place only in the sphere of words, not as events and actions of history. If the later Heidegger's shift to an emphasis on hermeneutics did not exclude his earlier philosophy of existence, so Ebeling's shift to the historical Jesus as the word-event did not exclude Bultmann's idea of faith as eschatological existence. The basic difference is that Ebeling maintained that the form-critical study of the Gospels could be used to show that the historical Jesus actually had faith in God and that his faith inspired the rise of faith in his followers after his death. Whereas Bultmann maintained that the historical critical scholar today cannot know what Jesus really thought of himself, Ebeling insisted that we can know enough to say that he experienced authentic existence. Beyond that bare minimum, faith is not jeopardized by the uncertainties of historical research.

Was Ebeling Successful in Moving beyond Bultmann?

Ebeling said that the kerygma is testimony to something that happened, but why does he limit that happening merely to Jesus' personal appropriation of the world-event? Why is reality otherwise communicated only through linguistics? Why is it impossible for a transcendent God of creation to be revealed in history? The answer is because Ebeling allowed the modern scientific worldview to prescribe the limits of belief. He also used the later Heideggerian philosophy of hermeneutics as the basis of his theological method, which was enmeshed in the dualistic thinking of modern thought. Like Bultmann, Ebeling assumed the positivism of the modern scientific worldview and the existentialism of Heidegger. Ebeling said he appreciated Bultmann's attempt to overcome the positivistic idea of history, but he believed Bultmann did not fully understand the historical problem.[22] Running away from positivism to existentialism, Bultmann failed to connect the historical Jesus and the kerygmatic Christ and was unable to see the real fact of Jesus' faith in God was a necessary basis for understanding how faith could emerge after his death.

If this is true of Bultmann, Ebeling was also not able to get beyond the influence of positivism himself. This is true for two reasons. First, Ebeling, like Bultmann, over-reacted to the positivism of the first quest of the historical Jesus with its search for bare facts of the past. Ebeling's exclusive interest in "pure word" over against "mere facts" illustrates the dualistic split of positivism and existentialism. Like Bultmann, his espousal of existentialist philosophy was largely an over-reaction to positivism. Ebeling believed the meaning of the phrase, "the act of God in Jesus Christ," has nothing to do with historical facts, but with existential meaning only. Hence Ebeling, like Bultmann, intentionally rejected positivistic facts for existential meaning.

Secondly, Ebeling did not get beyond positivism because he permitted the modern scientific worldview to determine what can and cannot be. He spoke of the self-evident presuppositions that must guide the historian in his or her investigation of the past. He believed modern people can no longer accept the idea of miracles or of sacred history, which is exempted from the closed weft of ordinary history. Nor can they subscribe to the idea of sacred scripture.[23] Ebeling argued: "The fact that for the modern age all that is metaphysical and metahistorical has entered the dimension of the problematical is also a thing the modern historian cannot simply put out of his mind when reading sources which presuppose the self-evident character of the metaphysical and metahistorical."[24] As opposed to the unenlightened interpretation of traditional theology, Ebeling maintained that "the modern historian is rightly convinced that he knows certain things better."[25]

Was Ebeling suggesting that only in the modern period has it become "self-evident" that God does not act in history? Cullmann pointed out that the scandal of a historical divine revelation is no "modern" dilemma, for it was a problem for antiquity as well. Cullmann asked: "But is it not immediately suspicious when the very elements in the thinking of the Bible which is foreign to modern thought is excluded from the definition of its essence."[26] Cullmann further asked: "Should we not instead consider whether perhaps the 'offensive' element, the *skandalon*, does not constitute the essence and centre of the New Testament proclamation, so that it simply cannot be removed from it?"[27] Cullmann believed that it is wrong to think the idea of salvation in history first became offensive in modern thought. He argued that the difficulty of believing in a real history of salvation "has nothing to do with a changed world (as Bultmann thinks), but was felt to be just as offensive in the ancient world."[28] The historical claims of the Gospels also constituted a serious intellectual problem for the first century. The claim that Jesus is the real presence of God in history who died and rose again was mocked by Greek philosophers at the Areopagus in Athens (Acts 17:32). For the Greeks, truth is universal and rational and is in no way dependent upon the particular facts of history. This is why the Greeks considered faith in the particularity of Jesus Christ as the basis of knowing God to be foolish and the Jews considered it scandalous. (1 Cor. 1:23). This "scandal of particularity" was also not easy for Jesus' own disciples who were offended at his claim that "unless you eat the flesh of the Son of man and drink his blood, you have no life in you." (John 6:53). They admitted this "was a hard saying; who can listen to it?" (John 6:60). His disciples knew as well as we do in the modern age that dead men do not rise from the dead. This is why the Gospels reported that even when Jesus presented himself to them, "some doubted" (Matt. 28:17). The disciple Thomas had considerable difficulty believing in the risen Lord (John 20:24-29). Karl Jaspers, an existentialist philosopher, has noted Bultmann failed to consider that the first century religious leaders in Palestine were well acquainted with the problems of believing in miracles, for they too lived in the intellectual environment of Greek philosophy. The idea that the disciples were gullible and mythological in their religious views, as if they did not understand the difference between myth and reality, is an inaccurate portrayal of the first century.[29]

Ebeling may have wanted to shift his teacher's existentialist focus more toward the importance of the historical Jesus as a witness of faith, but he uncritically accepted Bultmann's belief that the disciples possessed a mythological worldview. This explains in part why Ebeling's attempt to integrate faith and history was not successful. It may be that Ebeling cannot accept the idea of miracles in history, but it does not follow that his new hermeneutical theology is intellectually superior on the grounds that the disciples were too naïve and were myth-makers. The very fact that the disciples had to be convinced that Jesus was bodily raised from the dead shows that they were not myth makers. They instead possessed a historical understanding of reality, which is why they were not myth-makers. We noted in the beginning of this work that the distinctive feature of the early Hebrew understanding of reality was its historical consciousness and this set them apart from the mythical views of their Ancient Near Eastern neighbors.

In an important sense, Ebeling ironically proposed that the modern Christian community should espouse the "self-evident" assumption of pagan antiquity, as Cullmann has argued: "The metaphysics of antiquity and modern existentialist philosophy, which is so different, both share a hostility to salvation history."[30] The very center of Christian faith is the "scandal of particularity," as Paul put it: "We preach Christ crucified, a scandal to Jews and folly to the Gentiles" (1 Cor. 1:23). To delete this center is to deny "the power of God and the wisdom of God," as Paul maintained (1 Cor. 1:24).

Bultmann's Critique of Ebeling

If the first quest of the historical Jesus failed because it re-created Jesus in the image of each of the rationalist theologians as Kähler argued, the second quest of the historical Jesus also re-created Jesus to reflect their own particular agenda. Bultmann acknowledged this propensity of the new quest of the historical Jesus, accusing Ebeling of making the kerygma say something that in fact it does not say; namely, that Jesus is the witness to faith. Bultmann said the kerygma did not speak of Jesus' own faith. He further noted: "In Heb. 12:2, Jesus is described as the 'pioneer and perfecter of our faith.' But this is not a description of Jesus as a believer, as Ebeling would suppose,[31] for he does not appear in the 'cloud of witnesses' in Heb. 11."[32]

If Ebeling criticized Bultmann's disconnect between the historical

Jesus and the kerygmatic Christ as reflecting an inadequate Christology, Ebeling's own idea of Jesus as the word-event is just as inadequate. David F. Strauss' criticism of the Christology of the 19th century rationalistic quest for the historical Jesus is pertinent to Ebeling's second quest. The rationalistic theologians saw Christ as the greatest man who ever lived and endowed by God with such natural capacities that he became the perfect moral example of humankind. His death served as a motivation for the reformation of the sinner, for it revealed the forgiving love of God. Strauss argued that this Christ was not the Christ who was the *object* of worship, but the one who was the example of pure obedience to God; he was not the Christ whom the church proclaimed as its Lord.[33] As a result, Strauss believed that the rationalistic reconstruction of the life of Jesus inadvertently reinforced the credibility of the tradition-al view because it was so unbelievable.[34] To be sure, Strauss argued the Gospels contained mostly myths and legends and lacked little historical core to them at all, which anticipated Bultmann's views.

Strauss' criticism of the rationalistic lives of Jesus during the first quest is similar to Bultmann's criticism of the new quest. Ebeling's new hermeneutic assumed that the historical Jesus was the preeminent model and witness of faith, but this view cannot be supported from the Gospels. It is rather a desperate attempt to preserve faith without hav-ing to surrender the positivistic and existentialist notion of reality. In this respect, Ebeling has not moved beyond an existentialist bifurcation between *Historie* and *Geschichte*.

One cannot gloss over the death and resurrection of Jesus merely with an existentialist interpretation. The intellectual depth of belief among the disciples and the earliest believers concerning Jesus' resurrec-tion cannot be explained away so easily. Paul described the depth of commitment among the earliest followers of Jesus this way: "Now if Christ is preached as raised from the dead, how can some of you say that there is no resurrection of the dead? But if there is no resurrection from the dead, then Christ has not been raised; if Christ has not been raised, then our preaching is in vain and your faith is in vain" (1 Cor. 15:12-14). Paul here showed that even among some of the earliest Christians there were those who were having difficulty believing in the resurrection of the dead. Paul showed the implications of this doubt: "We are even found to be misrepresenting God, because we testified of God that he raised Christ, whom he did not raise if it is true that the dead are not raised. For if the dead are not raised, then Christ has not been raised. If Christ has not been raised, your faith is futile and you are still in your sins" (1 Cor. 15:15-17). To be sure, Bultmann acknowledged the force of Paul's reasoning, but dismissed it as a being a dangerous argument that threatened the true meaning of faith.[35] Ebeling simply dismissed it as unbelievable.[36]

Because he sought to integrate faith and history through interpreting the historical Jesus as the word-event, Ebeling believed he could avoid the charge of Docetism.[37] However, he connected the historical Jesus and the kerygmatic Christ only by means of a forced transformation of what the kerygma originally meant by "faith in Christ," as Bultmann pointed out. Hence Ebeling's exegesis appears arbitrary. On the other hand, Bultmann retained the "myth" of "faith in Christ," as the essence of Christian faith, and he sought to demythologize it in existentialist categories. Ebeling, however, was right to worry about Bultmann succumbing to the danger of Docetism. Only if the kerygma is justifiably derived from the real historical Jesus can faith and history be integrated.

The Renewal of the Second Quest of the Historical Jesus

The new quest of the historical Jesus eventually lost some of its momentum until it was renewed in America with the emergence of the Jesus Seminar.[38] In March of 1985 Robert W. Funk called together a groups of scholars to update and expand Bultmann's *History of the Synoptic Tradition,* and he presided over their first meeting under the label, "The Jesus Seminar." They voted to meet semiannually.[39] Their continuing purpose has been to determine which of the sayings and deeds of Jesus are authentic by taking a vote among themselves.[40]

Its method is still guided by Bultmann's form-critical presupposition that anything miraculous cannot be historical and hence it is automatically rejected.[41] It retains Bultmann's belief that anyone living in the age of modern science cannot affirm the Trinitarian faith of the Church. In the "Introduction" to *The Five Gospels, The Search For The Authentic Words of Jesus,* which is a report of the results of the Jesus Seminar, it is said: "The Christ of creed and dogma, who had been firmly in place in the Middle Ages, can no longer command the assent of those who have seen the heavens through Galileo's telescope. The old deities and demons were swept from the skies by that remarkable glass. Copernicus, Kepler, and Galileo have dismantled the mythological abodes of the gods and Satan, and bequeathed us secular heavens."[42] Interestingly enough, Copernicus, Kepler, and Galileo were Christians, and did not interpret their new discoveries as incompatible with the Bible. The idea that modern science made it impossible to affirm belief in the biblical worldview confuses the biblical appreciation for metaphor and imagery with modern literalism. The Jesus Seminar further espouses the modern scientific worldview that has been superceded by postmodern science, which offers a new paradigm of openness and novelty in the world as opposed to the modernist idea of determinism and mechanical causality. The Jesus Seminar is further guided by the modernist distrust of the idea of revelation in history, preferring to identify religious values with the sayings of Jesus rather than with his miraculous deeds. This corresponds to the linguistic theory of Ebeling's New Hermeneutic, which equates revelation with "word-event" as opposed to the real history of salvation. Its preoccupation with the Gnostic Gospel of Thomas as the fifth gospel shows its prejudice against history being the decisive ingredient of faith.

Over against the renewal of the new quest by the Jesus Seminar, a third quest for the historical Jesus has been launched that believes Bultmann's form-critical methodology is basically flawed because of its excessive historical criticism about the oral traditions that underlie the Gospels. The third quest assumes that the way to assess the historicity of the Gospels is to examine it in the context of the religious and social world of Second-Temple Judaism rather than focusing on Hellenistic influences. Another key element in evaluating the historicity of the Gospels is a new appreciation of the role of oral traditions in Middle-Eastern cultures, which are noted for their accuracy and reliability.[43] As Kähler noted, the Gospel authors did not intend to write a biography based on modernist notions of scientific precision. The Third Quest also argues that the Gospels must be seen as Jewish-style biographies, and there is no reason to distrust them simply because they do not conform to the criteria of modern critical thought. Drawing critically from the insights of the first and second quests for the historical Jesus, the third quest offers a promising and constructive approach to the life of Jesus that avoids the bifurcated thinking and historical skepticism of modern thought.

Notes

1. Käsemann, Ernst. "The Problem of the Historical Jesus." *Essays on New Testament Themes* (London: SCM Press, 1964), 15-47.

2. Gerhard Ebeling, *Theology and Proclamation: A Discussion with Rudolf Bultmann*, trans. John Riches (London: Collins, 1966), 38.

3. Ibid., 39.

4. Ibid., 51-52.

5. Ibid., 55.

6. Ibid.

7. Ibid., 57.

8. Ibid., 39.

9. Ibid., 58.

10. Ibid.

11. Ibid.

12. Ibid.

13. Gerhard Ebeling, *Word and Faith*, trans. James W. Leitch (Philadelphia: Fortress Press, 1963), 295.

14. Cf. *The New Hermeneutic*, edited by James M. Robinson and John B. Cobb, Jr. (New York: Harper & Row, 1964).

15. Ibid., 304.

16. Ibid., 302.

17. Ibid., 297.

18. Ibid., 301.

19. Ibid., 302.

20. Ibid., 301.

21. *Theology and Proclamation*, 37.

22. Ibid., 58.

23. *Word and Faith*, 47.

24. Ibid.

25. Ibid.

26. Oscar Cullmann, *Salvation in History*, translated by Sidney G. Sowers (London: SCM Press, Ltd., 1967), 22. Cf. Karl Jaspers, "Myth and Religion," *Kerygma and Myth*, 2:134ff.

27. *Salvation in History*, 22.

28. Ibid.22.

29. Karl Jaspers, "Myth and Religion," *Kerygma and Myth*, trans. R. H. Fuller (London: S.C.K, 1962), 2:134ff. Cf. Jaspers, Karl. *Philosophical Faith and Revelation*, trans. E. B. Ashton (New York: Harper and Row, Publishers, 1962).

30. Ibid.

31. *Word and Faith*, 304.

32. Bultmann, *The Historical Jesus and the Kerygmatic Christ*, 34.

33. David Strauss, *The Life of Jesus Critically Examined*, 768.

34. Ibid.

35. Bultmann, "Reply to Theses of J. Schniewind, *Kerygma and Myth*, 112.

36. *Theology and Proclamation*, 56.

37. *Theology and Proclamation*, 35.

38. Cf. Robert W. Funk, *Honest to Jesus: Jesus For A New Millennium* (San Francisco, CA: HarperSanFrancisco, 1996) for an explanation for reviving the new quest; Marcus J. Borg, *Jesus & the Restoration of Israel*, 331.

39. *The Five Gospels, The Search For The Authentic Words of Jesus,* new translation and commentary by Robert W. Funk, Roy W. Hoover, and The Jesus Seminar (San Francisco, CA: HarperSanFrancisco, 1997), 34f, 540.

40. Ibid., 35.

41. Cf. Marcus J. Borg, "An Appreciative Disagreement," *Jesus & The Restoration of Israel, A Critical Assessment of N. T. Wright's Jesus and The Victory of God,* ed. Carey C. Newman (Downers Grove, Illinois: InterVarsity Press, 1999), 232.

42. *The Five Gospels, The Search For The Authentic Words of Jesus,* 2.

43. Cf. Oscar Cullmann, *Salvation in History,* 111, 191; N. T. Wright, *Jesus and the Victory of God* (Minneapolis: Fortress Press, 1996), 134.

44. Cf. N. T. Wright, *Jesus and the Victory of God* (Minneapolis: Fortress Press, 1996); Ben Witherington, *The Jesus Quest: The Third Search for the Jew of Nazareth* (Downers Grove, Illinois: InterVarsity Press, 1995).

Part Four

History And Eschatology: The Dialectical Synthesis of Appearance and Reality

In the previous section, I argued that the distinction between appearance and reality adumbrated in the philosophy of Plato was carried to an extreme dualism in modern philosophy and in modern theology. The theology of Wolfhart Pannenberg is one of the earliest attempts to retain the insights of modern thought while overcoming its dualistic thinking. Modern thought highlighted the principle of criticism by focusing on the need to make an exact analysis of reality, but it came up short on synthesis. Pannenberg offers what can be called a post-critical reconstruction of modern theology by integrating the methods of critical analysis and constructive synthesis. He specifically rejects the modern split between faith and history. He studied under Karl Barth at Basel, and was deeply influenced by his emphasis upon the sovereignty of God, but he came to believe that Barth's extreme supernaturalism unnecessarily divided God and the world.[1]

In a programmatic work in 1961, entitled *Revelation As History*, Pannenberg, along with a group of other scholars who formed what was called "the Pannenberg circle," proposed a theology of history as a correction to Barth's theology of the Word of God and Bultmann's existentialism,[2] which they believed did not give adequate attention to history. Since then, Pannenberg has developed a systematic theology that focuses on eschatology and the doctrine of the Trinity.[3] He believes eschatology is the key to integrating faith and history and for relating the Triune God and the world. Based on Jesus' preaching on the coming Kingdom of God, Pannenberg transposes the Platonic distinction between *appearance* and *reality* into a distinction between the *present* and the *future*. The present is identified with the appearance of the future reality of all things in God. I will argue in this section that Pannenberg's eschatological ontology is a constructive way of reconciling the transcendence of God with the history of salvation. It is also a key for understanding the distinction between the historical Jesus and the Christ of faith.

Notes

1. Pannenberg, "God's Presence in History," *The Christian Century* (March 11, 1981): 260-263.

2. Wolfhart Pannenberg, *Revelation as History*, coauthored with Rolf Rendtorff, Trutz Rendtorff, and Ulrich Wilkens, trans. David Granskow (New York: Macmillan, 1969).

3. Pannenberg, *Systematic Theology*, trans. Geoffrey W. Bromiley. 3 volumes (Grand Rapids: Eerdmans, 1991).

15

Eschatology and Transcendence: An Alternative to the Nature-Supernature Dichotomy

Supernaturalism as a Paradigm of Transcendence

Supernaturalism became the dominant worldview of Christian theology during the thirteenth century A.D. The term supernatural was widely used by Thomas Aquinas and the Scholastics as a technical term to describe God as eternally, self-subsistent, and hence God was different in essence from the created, natural order because God stood above (*super*) it. The term lost its technical meaning as it was more generally used outside the classroom and it eventually became popularly understood to designate something beyond the normal.[1] Because of this secondary meaning, some prefer to use the term supra-natural since supra conveys the original technical meaning of "above."[2]

The Latin term *supernaturalis* first appeared in the ninth century when John Scotus Erigena used it in his translation of the works of pseudo-Dionysius from Greek into Latin. He coined this Latin term as a translation for the Greek adjective *hyperphyes*. The prefix *hyper* (beyond) was used in inference to *physis* (nature or essence of reality) to denote something as transcending the ordinary, visible world.[3] Thomas Aquinas featured this term prominently and is largely responsible for its widespread technical use in Christian theology.[4] The distinction between the natural and the supernatural worlds became the fundamental categories for describing the relation of God and the world.

Supernatural ontology is a hierarchical/monarchical model derived in part from feudalism. Even before Thomas Aquinas featured supernaturalism, classical theology tended toward monarchianism in spite of its rejection of this heresy.[5] For example, Augustine articulated the three persons of God, but for all practical purposes he (as well as the Western Church in general) tended toward monarchianism because his primary interest was in the unity of God rather than in the three divine persons.[6] With the subsequent development of a supernatural ontology in Latin Scholasticism, the oneness of God became even more so interpreted in a hierarchical, monarchical, feudalistic manner. For God's oneness as a feudal-like lord over subjects was featured rather than the Three Persons. Yet, theology in the Middle Ages did not define God as a person. That would have been considered what we call today "a Unitarian heresy."[7]

Although the term *supernatural* is not found in the Septuagint, nor in the New Testament, nor in the early Church Fathers,[8] the term is standard currency in Roman Catholic, Anglican and Protestant theology. Even those theologies, which reject supernaturalism, depended upon its terminology for expressing an alternative form of Christian naturalism. For example, Paul Tillich proposed "ecstatic naturalism" as an alternative to the supernaturalism of Protestant Orthodoxy.[9] In his last public lecture, Tillich said his own theology was heavily dominated by an attempt to provide an alternative to supernaturalism.[10] One could argue that all modern theological movements are unintelligible without supernaturalism, which they attempted to refute or rehabilitate.[11]

Has Supernaturalism Outlived Its Usefulness?

The question is whether or not the paradigm of *supernaturalism* has outlived its usefulness and should now be abandoned in spite of its venerable history. The two basic models for defining God's whereabouts have been "above" or "within." The "above" model led to supernaturalistic deism and finally to a secularistic naturalism, which dropped "the aboveness" of God, believing the world "below" was adequate within itself. The supernatural hypothesis was thus declared irrelevant for modern thought. Tillich's critique largely focused on the artificiality, as well as the logical incoherence, of two separate realms. To postulate the idea of a God above the world who *interferes* with, and breaks into, the lower realm involves the destruction of the created order itself.[12] He proposed a naturalism in which God is located "within" the world as the ground of being. The "within" model tends toward pantheistic mysticism in which the distinction between God and the world is blurred. Since Schleiermacher, all forms of modern theology which rejected supernaturalism in favor of naturalism have been hard-pressed to defend themselves against the charge of blurring the difference between God and creation.

On the other hand, forms of modern theology that defended supernaturalism have tended to turn God into a super-individual who stands over against the world. Tillich traced the origin of this modern idea back to an extreme view of the principle of distance, which emerged in the 14th century in the philosophy of nominalism of William of Ockham.[13] The principle of distance affirms God's difference from the world, while the principle of identity affirms God's unity with the world. God is the power present in all things, although God is also different from the world. The interrelated principles of identity and distance are assumptions of what was called philosophical realism in the premodern world.

The major tenet of realism was that the categories of thought are universal and identify the very essence of reality. As such, they transcend particular things because they inhere in things. Some extreme forms of realism asserted that universals were the only realities and that particular things in the world were merely copies. This view represented Platonism and tended toward pantheism. The prevailing form of realism in the premodern world was fairly moderate, which asserted that particular things are real and that categories also define a real state of affairs that exist among them. For example, moderate realism believed that the category of humanity is a real designation of what is objectively true about all people. According to the principle of distance, each person has their own particular individuality, but according to the principle of identity, there is something common among all people that justifies talking about humanity. The particular and the general are thus interrelated and interdependent.

Nominalism was another philosophical viewpoint that was developed in opposition to realism. It believed that terms (universals, categories) exist only in the mind and do not reflect a real state of affairs in the world. This is why nominalism was also called terminism because categories are mere terms.[14] Hence the category of humanity for nominalism does not define an objective state of affairs—except as a mere convenient term of the mind for classifying people.

The rise of nominalism with William of Ockham (ca. 1285-1349) undermined the principle of identity, while accentuating the principle of distance. The result was that God became separated from other individuals and was no longer the underlying center of all beings. Ockham called God *ens singularissimum*, the most single being.[15] God as the most single being was like a monarch who existed on the outskirts of a feudal society instead of being the personal focus of community life. If the implications of nominalism were followed through consistently, it would destroy the meaning of community because there can be no unity if society is merely an aggregate of individuals. Nominalism presupposes that society is made up of individuals working together for common goals or working against each other, but the idea of community presupposes more than this. It also entails the idea of real participation and intimacy in the life of others.[16] When nominalism prevailed in modern thought under the label of positivism, individualism tended to dominate the idea of personhood, and God came to be thought of as the highest individual who stood at a distance on the outside looking in. We noted earlier that Kant's deism espoused such an extreme supernaturalism.

Barth attempted to rehabilitate supernaturalism in the modern period, but his tendency was to make God a "wholly other" individual, "permanently transcending time,"[17] and hence rationally inaccessible. The further dilemma of his supernaturalism was its excessive revelationism, and consequently the relation of reason and faith was seriously damaged. In effect, Barth conceded the atheistic critique (expressed by Feuerbach and Nietzsche), which had declared the world devoid of any rational justification for belief in God. Feuerbach argued that the idea of God was a projection of ourselves on to the screen of reality. In other words, we have created God instead of God having created us. Barth sidestepped the atheistic criticism by declaring that God is unknowable except in the divine moment of revelation. Barth further said that human words are inherently unable to express the reality of God, noting that language is "an unsuitable means for the self-presentation of God" because language "contradicts it."[18] God thus commandeers human language to say what it is really incapable of saying. Hence rational arguments are without merit in speaking of God and without the self-revelation of God in the moment of faith the world is devoid of any knowledge of God. There is no general revelation and any rational attempt to provide probabilities and arguments for God's existence is idolatry.[19] This extreme difference between God and the world is why Barth's theology is also called dialectical theology—i.e., God cannot be talked about except in a roundabout and broken manner.[20] Dialectical thinking in Barth does not mean what it did in Hegel for whom dialectics was the synthesis of opposites. It rather highlights contrasting and irreconcilable differences. Pannenberg called Barth's theology of the Word of God a "revelational positivism."[21] Reason is unable to discuss the merits of believing or disbelieving in God. One simply believes because God is self-revealed in the moment of faith. As Barth put it, "Truth of revelation is the freely acting God, Himself and quite alone."[22]

To be sure, Barth's emphasis upon the sovereignty of God who is in control of the truth of divine revelation is a basic conviction of the Christian faith, but is it not overdone when Barth brushes aside all questions about the reasonableness of faith? Pannenberg asks: "But is Feuerbach really overcome in this way?" Pannenberg believes that Barth's revelational method cannot resolve the issue of atheism so easily: "Is it not instead merely a case of withdrawing from controversy with Feuerbach and his disciples if theology, unperturbed, begins to speak about God as if nothing had happened; without establishing any basis, or offering any justification for this concept except by referring to the fact that Christian preaching about God actually goes on?" To divorce reason and revelation is in effect a "senseless renunciation of all critical discussion, and thus an act of spiritual capitulation to Feuerbach?"[23]

Pannenberg thinks theology must take seriously the modern atheistic critique of supernaturalism. He believes Barth's approach of pursuing theology "from above" is like "a blind alley" and endangers "the truth of the Christian faith itself and its speech about God."[24] What is now needed is "a philosophical anthropology worked out within the framework of a general ontology" in order to address the legitimate concerns of secularistic naturalism.[25]

Anglo-Catholic theologian-philosopher, E. L. Mascall, impressively attempted to rehabilitate supernaturalism. His brilliant exposition of the classical doctrine of God is found in *He Who Is.*[26] Yet he admits that the tendency of the supernatural/natural distinction is to make the two realms only artificially related. He specifically recognized that the "imagery of levels...is quite inadequate, for it fails to do justice to the intimacy of the relation" between the supernatural and natural. He especially criticized the Catholic textbooks for fostering this misunderstanding.[27]

With the help of all the intricacies and sophistication of modern symbolic logic, many contemporary philosophers in the Anglo-American analytic tradition have impressively attempted to resolve the ambiguities and alleged contradictions of the traditional, supernatural view of a personal God.[28] However, whether or not the logical tools of analytical philosophy can repair the damage done by the atheistic critique is problematic. It may be that the atheistic critique too *simplistically* dismissed and distorted a supernatural view of God. However, the *complicated* arguments of analytical philosophy used to defend supernaturalism may indirectly serve to reinforce the atheistic charge that belief in a personal God is only contrived.

The Meaning of Personhood

The monarchical tendency of Western Christianity finally led to a redefinition of God as a Person rather than three Persons in the modern period. Tillich pointed out that this happened explicitly "only in the nineteenth century" with Kant's deistic supernaturalism.[29] Pannenberg also points out that in *Critique of Pure Reason* (1781) Kant's redefinition of person as an independent being with a radically individualized self-consciousness became determinative for the modern concept of personhood. This absolute understanding of personhood was implied in the sixth century in Boethius' definition of person as rational individuality.[30] It was more decisively developed in the nominalism of William of Ockham with the idea of God as the most single being. With Kant the ideas of self-consciousness, individuality and autonomy became the constitutive element in the meaning of being a person.[31]

The pre-modern view assumed that the decisive component of personhood was one's capacity to experience community and to develop intimate relationships with others. This relational understanding of person was decisive for the theological development of a Christian understanding of God as three Persons in the fourth and fifth centuries. As a result of absolutizing individual self-consciousness as the meaning of personhood in the modern world, Tillich said that "ordinary theism has made God a heavenly, completely perfect person who resides above the world and mankind." Tillich agreed with "the protest of atheism against such a highest person."[32]

The development of the modern understanding of personhood can be traced back to the Christological and Trinitarian doctrines of the third and fourth centuries to its culmination in Hegel's philosophy in the 19th century.[33] Of course, the ultimate source lies in the history of Ancient Israel where God's very self was disclosed to Abraham as the personal Lord of history.[34] The Old Testament idea of God's spiritual transcendence and difference from nature was a necessary prerequisite for understanding human self-transcendence and the meaning of personhood, as secularist philosophers and psychologists generally recognize as well.[35]

Pannenberg has shown how modern atheism was the logical conclusion of Kant's concept of absolute subjectivity. He further shows that Kant, not Descartes, was the real father of modern subjectivity. This is because Kant was the first thinker to make individual *self*-consciousness the actual creator and source of the world that we know, as well as the basis of sure knowledge.[36] Kant's deistic supernaturalism allowed for both God and humans to be autonomous persons and creators. Instead of a relational understanding of persons as classically expressed in the doctrine of the Trinity, Kant introduced a new element into the concept of personhood which made self-consciousness the basis of reality itself. The consequence was that the practical monarchianism of Western theology became actual Monarchianism in the deistic supernaturalism of Kant's concept of God. God was now defined as an infinite Person.

Hegel continued and deepened this new idea of God as the Supreme Person, and he replaced the classical terminology of *one divine substance* with *one divine subject.*[37] God is the Absolute Subject. Whereas Kant deistically polarized God and the world, Hegel attempted to reconcile God and the world through his philosophy of history. Unlike Kant, Hegel would not accept the idea of a lifeless Supreme Being who dwells outside the sphere of the world. He believed those modern theologians who accused Spinoza of atheism because he did not believe in a Supreme Being had embraced a worse kind of atheism because they affirmed the existence of the Supreme Being but denied that human beings could really know God. Hegel rejected Spinoza's pantheism also, and he did so precisely because Spinoza's concept of the divine substance did not include the idea of God as "the absolute Person."[38] His emphasis, then, was that God is a personal Subject, not an impersonal Substance.

Hegel also sought to include the Trinity within his doctrine of God's personality. So he combined the absolute and the relational understanding of personhood. Hegel's philosophy represented the culmination of the modern idea of personhood, showing that the modern emphasis on personhood is a extension of the Christian doctrine of the Trinity.[39] However, Hegel primarily applied the concept of person to the *unity* of God instead of the *trinity*, and that is where the difficulty lies. This is why the modern notion of personhood tends toward individualism.[40]

Moltmann has shown that Barth's concept of God as the divine Subject is largely borrowed from Hegel's modern redefinition of God as Absolute Personality.[41] Pannenberg has also shown that Barth's idea of God's revelation as a *self*-revelation is borrowed from Hegel's philosophy of religion where this idea first appeared.[42] As we have already seen, the idea of revelation had traditionally distinguished between natural and special revelation. Natural revelation entailed the idea that God's existence could be proved by rational considerations, and special revelation was defined as propositions and information about God that were revealed in the history of salvation and that were reliably recorded in the Bible. Now with Hegel the decisive thing about revelation was the revelation of God's very *self* rather than information about God. This was an important insight, except the selfhood of God was highlighted in terms of God's oneness instead of the Three Persons.

Moltmann argues that monotheism in the West was an abstract theory that fundamentally contradicted the doctrine of the Trinity, and it culminated in the idea of God as a personal Subject in Hegel, although it can be traced back to the monarchical tendencies of Western theology. Deistic supranaturalism was the penultimate culmination of this trend, with modern atheism as the final product. Barth's theology restored an emphasis upon the doctrine of the Trinity, but he so strongly emphasized the oneness of God's being that he undermined his otherwise proper restoration of the Trinity to its rightful place in theology. Barth preferred to speak of God's oneness as a Person and downgraded the Trinity as impersonal modes of being. Moltmann calls Barth's abstract monotheism "a late triumph for the Sabellian modalism, which the early church condemned."[43]

To summarize, classical theology since Tertullian defined God's unity as a substance, not as a person. The concept of person was reserved for the three persons of God. Yet, the subsequent development of Western theology tended, for all practical purposes, to treat the oneness of God as a person instead of the Trinity as persons. With the rise of Kant's rationalistic philosophy of religion, God was specifically defined as a supermundane Person. If Spinoza held to an extreme view of the principle of identity (pantheism), Kant held to an extreme view of the principle of distance (supra-naturalistic deism). How to reconstruct the supernaturalistic, monarchical interpretation has been the preoccupation of modern theology from Schleiermacher to Barth.

Modern Atheism as the Errant Child of Supernaturalism

The atheism of the left-wing Hegelian philosopher, Ludwig Feuerbach (1804-1872), is based on a critique of the alleged arbitrariness of God who alone possesses all the qualities which humans desire but are destined to do without. Beginning with Kant's and Hegel's new definition of personhood as the creative, autonomous self, Feuerbach's projection theory explained that human beings created God in their own image rather than God creating human beings in the divine image.[44] In his critique of supernaturalism, he argued that God as "the highest being" is set over against the natural world as if God dwells above us in a supernatural world with an air of superiority, while human beings are totally bereft of any goodness or worth. Supposedly our only hope for a meaningful life comes as a gift when this angry God is appeased. This condescending attitude of a supernatural God whose superiority is placed above us destroys the foundation of human happiness, according to Feuerbach.[45]

Previous to Feuerbach, modern atheism was largely an assumption which grew out of the development of modern natural science and its mechanistic picture of the world, as seen in eighteenth century France. For example, the mathematician Pierre-Simon Laplace (1749-1827) developed a mechanistic system of finite causes, which were said to be self-sufficient. The mechanistic worldview of classical physics discarded the idea of a creator and, as such, the supernatural world was eliminated. Now, with Feuerbach's critique, modern atheism was provided with a philosophical rationale.[46]

A further critique made by the proponents of secularistic naturalism, first advanced by German philosopher, Johann Fichte (1762-1814), and subsequently reinforced by Feuerbach, was that the idea of a God above the world means God is simply another person who coexists alongside (or above) us.[47] If God is a person who co-exists with us, then God is necessarily finite, which is a contradiction to the doctrine of divine perfection. For personhood means having a specific self-consciousness, and whatever is *specific* is necessarily finite and limited as *a thing.* Another criticism is that the idea of a supernatural Person who coexists above us in another world entails the elimination of human freedom. If God is *totally present* in this moment as the one who coexists above us, then there is no room for human action based on free choice.[48]

Pannenberg takes seriously the critique of modern atheism. He believes it would be "premature" simply to dismiss modern atheism as "hatred of God."[49] Its criticisms are acute and must be addressed thoughtfully. He admits that a supernatural Being who exists alongside the natural world "would destroy such freedom by virtue of his overpowering might.[50] The way out of modern atheism is not "to retreat into a supranaturalistic wildlife sanctuary,"[51] as Barthian theology does with its divorce between faith and reason. Pannenberg believes Barth's theological subjectivism largely surrenders to the nihilistic criticism of Nietzsche (1844-1900).

Modern atheism is the outcome of the philosophy of human subjectivity.[52] Modern subjectivity and atheism are unwitting implications of the idea of a supernaturalistic Absolute Subject (Person) who coexists "above" us. The atheistic critique developed by Fichte, Feuerbach and Nietzsche is based particularly on this concept of a supramundane Person.[53] Secularistic naturalism refuted the idea of this supernaturalistic Subject (a divine Person) and replaced it with the autonomous subject (a human being). Not God but humans choose what is the truth. It can be argued that Nietzsche's atheistic emphasis on self-affirmation and subjectivity is the consequence of *a metaphysic of the will*, which Barth's subjectivism presupposes[54] and which is presupposed in modern thought generally. By a metaphysic of the will is meant that the nature of reality is determined by the subjective decision of the will rather than a rational consideration of evidence. That is, truth is what is willed rather than what is seen to be true based on an fair and open consideration of facts.

Subjectivism associated with Descartes' rationalism, Locke's empiricism, and Kant's deistic supernaturalism can be credited with contributing to the rise of modern atheism. The seeds were also sown in Medieval scholastic theology with the development of a contrived compartmentalization of God above the world whose *will* was superimposed upon the world below. Pannenberg writes: "It is just supranaturalistic thought which turns out in the last analysis to have already presupposed Nietzsche's grounding of the truth upon the will."[55] "The only way to overcome" modern atheism, Pannenberg observes, "is by means of a more radical inquiry into being."[56]

The Impasse of the Greek and the Biblical Ideas of True Being

Pannenberg believes it is understandable that Christian theology combined the *true being* of Greek thought with the God of the Bible because God is unchanging, reliable, and the all-embracing truth. Yet there are significant differences. First, the Greek divorce between true being and changing sense-appearances was "superseded in the biblical understanding of truth" where "true being is thought of, not as timeless but instead as, historical, and it proves its stability through a history whose future is always open."[60] A second significant difference is that God as true being is personal in contrast to the Greek idea of true being as an abstract principle.

The combined Greek-Hebrew idea of truth dominated Christian theology until modern thought recognized the impasse between them[61] If all truth is historically conditioned, how can it also be timeless? Secular thought concluded there is no transcendent, universal, or timeless Being because everything is embedded in historical contingency. It is ironic that the definition of a supernatural Being who stands above or behind the world is an extension of the Greek idea of true being and timelessness rather than from the biblical understanding of God as the Lord of history and the power of the unbounded future. It is also ironic that secularistic naturalism borrowed the biblical notion that all truth is historically conditioned to criticize and refute the Greek-inspired doctrine of Christian supernaturalism. Hence, as Ernst Cassirer demonstrated, the rise of the secular, modern historical consciousness is the product of Christian faith itself.[62]

Pannenberg argues that Hegel offered a way out of this impasse with his concept that truth is not a finished product existing behind or within the world, but rather truth is historically developed and only at the *end* of history does the unity of truth become known.[63] Hegel's point is that the meaning of each event is determined, not by the present or past, but by its relationship to the future goal of history.[64] He derived his philosophy of history from the biblical idea that God is progressively revealed in history. However, in a shocking way Hegel identified the future goal of world history with his own present situation. Hence Hegel had no open future.[65] However, Pannenberg believes Hegel should be commended for the idea that all reality is history and that it receives unity and meaning from its future goal. Pannenberg thinks it is regrettable that no one since Hegel has posed the question of the unity of truth "with a comparable depth."[66]

Eschatology as a Paradigm of Transcendence

Pannenberg argues that Jesus' preaching on the priority of the future provides the solution to the problem of the unity of truth raised by the Greeks. Unlike classical theology that defined God's true being according to the Greek notion of the timeless *present*, Pannenberg defines God as the power of the unbounded *future*. Jesus' eschatological message assumes that true being and the unity of all things is based in the future of God's kingdom,[67] which already made its appearance in the history of Jesus.

Pannenberg proposes that instead of God being "above" or "within" the world, God stands "ahead of" us as the power of the unbounded future. The "above" and "within" models are flawed because they picture God as timeless, whereas the "ahead of" model includes the reality of space-time in God. Divine transcendence is thus identified with futurity. Pannenberg regrets that "the idea of the future as a mode of God's being is still undeveloped in theology despite the intimate connection between God and the coming reign of God in the eschatological message of Jesus."[68]

Pannenberg proposes this eschatological paradigm as a replacement for supernaturalism.[69] This is not an attempt to reconstruct Christian theology according to a non-miraculous interpretation, which eliminates the activity of a personal God in history. Rather, Pannenberg's eschatological ontology is an attempt to overcome the dualism of the supernatural/natural way of thinking. He explains that his "approach to the ontological question takes into account the concerns of supernaturalism (in contrast to a self-sufficient secularist concept of nature), while not yielding to the temptation of dualism that is not very well reconcilable to the biblical faith in creation."[70] Pannenberg thus proposes a new way of thinking about the relation between God and the world without identifying God as being dependent upon the world. Indeed he says that any use of the word God, which eliminates the idea of a personal, independent being, is meaningless.[71]

Pantheism dissolves divine personality into a timeless space as an impersonal power "within." Supernaturalism elevates God into a space far "above" the finite world and thus depersonalizes human life because it is separated from an intimate relationship with God. Because of the unnaturalness of God's presence in the world "below" which the supernatural model entails, the divine-human relationship seems forced and unnatural as well. An eschatological doctrine of transcendence locates God "ahead of" us. Pannenberg writes: "Man participates in God not by flight from the world but by active transformation of the world which is the expression of the divine love, the power of the future over the present by which it is transformed in the direction of the glory of God."[72] God is really present in our world through the events of salvation history. God is not an absentee landlord. An eschatological ontology thus avoids the schizoid split of two worlds, while at the same time it avoids the emotionally flat and impersonal one-storied world of naturalism.

The eschatological model also preserves the idea of human freedom because it assumes an open future where reality is not yet decided and formed. If God is "ahead of" us as the unlimited future, this means time is real for God as well as for finite persons, and we are partners with God in shaping the undecided and unformed future.

The eschatological model also avoids the condescending attitude of the monarchical/supernatural model in which human beings feel the *ultimate put-down* of reality, as if human beings are totally depraved and worthless because of their finite humanity. It was this misperception which led to Nietzsche's ethical refutation of God—that such a dehumanizing God ought to be killed.[73] Contemporary theologians, such as Paul Tillich, Thomas Altizer and John Cobb, Jr., embraced Nietzsche's idea of the death of a supernatural/monarchical God,[74] but their alternative to supernaturalism is naturalism which obscures and confuses God's relation with creation.

I believe the atheistic criticism is effectively met in Pannenberg's eschatological ontology. The idea of God is not based on logical inferences and philosophical speculation, but on the self-revelation of God in history. God is not the projection of one's self-image onto the screen of reality, but rather God is revealed as the unbounded future of all reality. The paradigm of futurity emphasizes that the Trinitarian persons invite believers to share in the fellowship of the *coming* kingdom of God. *This world is God's world,* not something inherently alien to God's true being, and history is the field of God's action.[75] This is more than merely the idea that God does something for us or gives us some information about ultimately reality, but rather we are offered a personal relationship with God. As Pannenberg says, "The salvation that God promises is himself."[76] The idea that God's very self is revealed was the significant contribution of Karl Barth to contemporary theology, as Pannenberg acknowledges.[77] It is knowledge of God, of being personally acquainted with God in Jesus through the indwelling Spirit. Feuerbach's projection theory is thus not applicable to the theology of God's self-revelation because it is based in the realism of history.

Barth's emphasis on God's Self-disclosure is weakened by the notion of a supernatural Being who stands over against this godless world. For Barth, this finite, natural world is so different from God that not even human language is fit to speak of God's reality. Barth says God has to commandeer human speech to say what it is totally unprepared and inadequate to say.[78] Hence Barth's theology undermines the relation of reason and faith and labels any type of analogy between God and the world as unchristian.[79]

The Distinction Between Appearance and Reality

Pannenberg wants to reassert the priority of Jesus' own teaching as the basis for thinking about the being of God. This does not mean that he discards the Greek concept of being (ontology). Indeed Pannenberg believes it is important to give Jesus' teaching an ontological structure. However, the essence of that ontology is that the meaning of history eventuates out of the future goal of all things in God. Pannenberg thus identifies the Greek idea of true being, not with "a mere beyond contrasting with man's present," but with "the pure futurity of God."[80]

Pannenberg's eschatological ontology is exegetically based in Jesus' message on the imminent kingdom of God, which is the key to Christian theology.[81] Jesus began his public ministry by preaching that the time was fulfilled and that the kingdom of God was at hand (Mark 1:15). Pannenberg takes seriously the tension in the Gospels between the "already" and "not yet" aspects of the kingdom of God. On the one hand, Jesus said that the kingdom of God had already come in his life and preaching, and yet he announced that the Kingdom of God was yet to come in the future. Pannenberg sees this tension to mean both future and present are "inextricably interwoven."[82] God's kingdom is not merely some future cosmic event that human beings simply endure while waiting for its arrival. Rather, the present is filled with meaning because God's rule has already arrived. Hence the past action of God in Jesus of Nazareth is available in the present because the past and present eventuate out of the eschatological future.

Plato was the first thinker to make a clear distinction between appearance and reality, which we earlier noted became the primary problem for all subsequent philosophy to try to resolve. In modern theology, this appearance-reality distinction (or subject-object distinction) was expanded into a full-blown divorce between the external *appearance* of Jesus as a historical fact and the inner *reality* of the Christ of faith as an existential symbol. Pannenberg's eschatological ontology reinterprets this distinction between appearance and reality as a distinction between the present and the future.[83] Jesus of Nazareth announced that the Kingdom of God had already made its appearance in himself in the present, and yet he declared he would emerge as the Lord and Sovereign over all to establish the future reality of the kingdom in its perfection. He *appeared* as the Son of God through his resurrection from the dead (Romans 1:4), but he will emerge as the sovereign *reality* over all in the eschaton.

The key thus to understanding the significance of Jesus is not through a critical analysis of his life based on an epistemological dualism of appearance and reality. Although critical analysis is important, the decisive means for understanding the life of Jesus is to see him as the one who appears to us out of the unbounded future. In an important sense, our own personal biographies cannot be written at our death, but rather the history and the meaning of our lives must be composed in the light of what we will be like in the eschatological future. For our true identity will be given to us in the eschaton, and this will illuminate and refocus all the events of our earthly existence. Likewise with the earthly life of Jesus. Who Jesus was in his historicity cannot be determined apart from the resurrection narrative. Any attempt to write a biography of Jesus based solely on his pre-Easter activity is an inadequate method for properly explaining his life. This is why the Gospels interpreted the historical Jesus from the perspective of his resurrection. His future destiny as the resurrected Lord and Christ (Romans 1:4) possessed retroactive power for re-defining his earthly life. This epistemological priority of the future for interpreting the life of Jesus is what is overlooked in the modern debate on the difference between the Jesus of history and the Christ of faith. So long as the appearance-reality distinction is used to locate a hidden meaning to the earthly Jesus that would distinguish him from the way he appeared to his disciples, the life of Jesus cannot be properly composed. Only if the appearance of his earthly existence is seen against the background of his future destiny as the risen Lord can the real Jesus be known.[84]

Jesus' preaching on the coming kingdom thus has cosmic implications. It cannot be simply narrowed down existentially to mean that one should appropriate the possibilities of human existence, as Bultmann does. Nor must it be reduced to the idea of a mere ethical attainment on the part of human beings as though they could bring about the kingdom of God on earth by means of their own initiative, as classical liberal theology maintained.[85] Jesus' teaching on the imminent kingdom of God means "this future is expected to come in a marvelous way from God himself; it is not simply the development of human history or the achievement of Godfearing men," Pannenberg writes.[86] Further, the uniqueness of Jesus' eschatological message did not consist in his mere preaching on the coming of God's kingdom on earth. The decisive significance of Jesus' preaching was that this coming kingdom was now already happening in him, thus showing that the present is to be seen in the light of the future and that Jesus himself as God's Son is the pre-actualization of the future. What appeared in Jesus will be fully revealed as the reality of the very essence of God in the eschatological future.

Does this reduce the infinite to the finite? Does this identify God with the process of history itself? Pannenberg answers No. He explains that "history is not the field of a finitude which is enclosed within itself, an 'immanence' to which once could and indeed would have to oppose a 'transcendence.'" As opposed to this, history is "the ongoing collapse of the existing reality which is enclosed in its own 'immanence' (because centered on itself). The power of the infinite is active and present in this collapse of the finite."[87] History is not merely the sum total of what human beings have done and suffered. Neither is history merely the creation of human beings. What human beings are and what they create is finite, but history in this sense is not finite. "Rather, it accomplishes the crisis of the finite throughout time. Hence man shows himself to be finite in his history."[88]

Pannenberg further points out that history is not itself self-explanatory apart from the transcendent reality of God who chooses to be made known in history. If history were thought of as being "wholly other" from the reality of God and fully comprehensible, then there would be no purpose in speaking of God. "Only because the infinite reality, which as personal can be called God, is present and active in the history of the finite, can one speak of a revelation of God in history. For it is thereby concretely shown that the finite is not left to itself."[89]

An Appreciation of Pannenberg's Eschatological Ontology

Many who hold to the historic Trinitarian faith of the Church have appreciated Pannenberg's theology of Jesus' resurrection, but some have also been skeptical of his historical-critical methodology because of its supposedly anti-supernaturalism. Daniel Fuller was one of the earliest American Evangelicals to embrace Pannenberg's theology, but he disagreed with its non-supernatural worldview.[90] What some fail to appreciate is that Pannenberg is not an anti-supernaturalist in the sense that many theologians are (like Paul Tillich), but rather he wants to preserve the essential truth of supernaturalism with its emphasis on God's transcendence and divine otherness. Further, Pannenberg's replacement of supernaturalism with an eschatological ontology is not linked to any hesitancy to embrace miracles. Rather, he objects to the idea that miracles are interruptions from *above* and superimposed on the created, natural order below. For Pannenberg every event is a miracle because of God's personal and intimate involvement with creation.[91] He thus believes a supernatural/natural dichotomy is the wrong paradigm for theology.

Some theologians describe themselves as Protestant in their theology, but Thomistic in their metaphysic.[92] Some find little in Thomistic theology or Thomistic metaphysics which they like,[93] but continue to use the supernatural/natural categories of Thomism. Almost no one who embraces historic Christianity would question the validity of supernaturalism—a situation for which they really have Thomas Aquinas largely to thank. The most influential defense and creative use of supernaturalism in the contemporary period is C. S. Lewis (1898–1963). His classic work, *Miracles*, has influenced countless thousands of students, ministers, and philosophers over many years since it was first published in 1958 and it continues to be published and bought in large numbers to this very day, and it certainly deserves to be read.[94]

I find myself thankful for the clarifying function of the supernatural model, which I first learned from reading Lewis' book on *Miracles*, especially during my seminary student days. With no alternate model available that could help put the biblical doctrines into a metaphysical framework, supernaturalism was an important intellectual tool for enabling me to appreciate the mystery and reality of a transcendent, self-sustaining God who created the world *ex nihilo*. And I have found supernaturalism helpful as a teaching aid for enabling my students to grasp the difference between a biblical understanding of God and the various sub-biblical views which obscure God's difference from creation. It also provided for a more sophisticated way of interpreting the figurative language in the Bible of a three-storied universe of heaven above us with God in the "highest heaven" (2 Chron. 6:18) and hell beneath us.

However, the insurmountable difficulty of supernaturalism is this—how can we speak of God's revelation if God is really separated from the world in another world above us? To speak of God's "aboveness" seems to vertically locate God in an artificial way and it leaves unanswered the question of what is meant by the relatedness of God to the world. Of course God is ultimately mystery and incomprehensible, and our explicit knowledge of God's reality is limited. That is why in worship our language becomes doxological. Our tacit knowledge of God exceeds our explicit knowledge. But the supernatural model obscures our understanding of how God can be known as a real presence in our world, if God dwells cosmologically above us. Supernaturalism speaks of God on the analogy of the natural world, but analogical language is too embedded in the artificiality of two levels of reality to show how God and the world can be distinguished without a split between them.

Pannenberg's early research into the history of religious language convinced him of the essentially religious nature of human speech in general and that it is unnecessary to think in dualistic terms of the natural-supernatural dichotomy.[95] Instead of the Thomistic doctrine of analogical language, Pannenberg believes that Michael Polanyi's distinction between *tacit* and *explicit* knowledge, along with his emphasis on the personal/religious nature of human language in general, is a more fruitful way of explaining the nature of theological language.[96] This avoids the logical difficulty associated with the doctrine of the analogy of being—that our words are *forced* to speak of two separate realms at the same time. Analogical language is vulnerable to the charge that its speech is equivocal and artificial, whereas Polanyi's analysis of the tacit dimension suggests a model, which maintains that human words are user-friendly for religion. The theological task of developing a more *explicit* understanding of our *tacit* knowledge of God does not require an artificial linkage between the supernatural and the natural. Human speech is first and foremost religious in its essence and can be further refined by philosophers and theologians to accommodate a more precise and explicit understanding of the religious dimension. On the other hand, the Thomistic concept of analogical language, with its assumption that human words must be lifted beyond their natural meanings and given a supernatural denotation, resulted in the secularistic rationalization of language—as if words are inherently secular.

The reason for the virtual demise of classical orthodox belief in major centers of learning today is often attributed to the rationalistic presuppositions of Enlightenment thinking, but it can be argued that the logic of supernaturalism, which its proponents and opponents have defended and assailed, may in part be the cause. Cardinal Henri De Lubac (1896-1991) believed that secularism is a consequence of the dualistic tendency of supernaturalism itself.[97]

As a creative response to Kant's rationalism, Schleiermacher's theology has been blamed for charting the future course of theology down the road toward self-destruction,[98] but clearly he was seeking to find a way of interpreting the doctrines of Christian faith, which did not succumb to the inherent logical conundrums of supernaturalism.[99] To be sure, his reformulation of Christian doctrine seriously wounded orthodoxy, and it has never recovered. Perhaps if Schleiermacher had worked from a different model than his "pantheistic" one, and if he had focused his attention on the need to revise an ontological model, which was more in accord with the biblical understanding of God, then the subsequent course of modern and contemporary theology might have been quite different.

Is it right for us to blame the rationalistic presuppositions of Kant and

Enlightenment thought in general for the demise of orthodoxy? To be sure, theology since Kant cannot be understood except as an attempt to come to terms with his bifurcated metaphysic. But perhaps the blame for the demise of orthodox Christian doctrines in modern thought may in part be related to the supernaturalism in which orthodoxy was *enmeshed* and less to the actual assaults of Enlightenment rationalism. Kant was only attempting to work out more consistently the philosophical implications of his own pietistic/orthodox training, and in the process of doing so he sought to replace the logical incoherence of orthodox supernaturalism itself with his deistic supernaturalism.

Unfortunately, the orthodox doctrines of classical Christianity and the supernaturalism, which eventually came to surround those doctrines, have not been sufficiently distinguished with the consequence that orthodox doctrines have often been thrown out along with supernaturalism. What has emerged, as a result of confusing a supernaturalistic ontology as the necessary presupposition for understanding the major doctrines of the Christian faith, has been largely ineffective or unduly complex rehabilitations of supernaturalism, or various forms of so-called Christian naturalism, which eliminate the essential doctrines that make Christianity truly Christian.

So long as supernaturalism is still the inherent intellectual framework of Christian doctrines, the secularistic and atheistic critique of Christian faith will likely continue to hold. But the collapse of supernaturalism into secularistic naturalism may not prove itself to be the final word. While the secular critique of supernaturalism has validity, secular naturalism may inevitably collapse under the weight of its own critique of supernaturalism. For secular naturalism may not be able to survive except in reference to the supernaturalism, which it critiques. Paul Tillich pointed out that modern atheism is not paganism; rather, it is "anti-Christian in Christian terms."[100] In short, modern atheism is a Christian heresy.

Perhaps the next step beyond secularistic naturalism (if supernaturalism were simply wiped out) is a revitalized paganism. For the humanistic values that secular naturalism wants to preserve cannot be intellectually substantiated apart from the values of the Christian tradition from which it learned them. It can also be argued that secularistic values are a mere illusion and based on mere psychological need without the metaphysical framework of Christian theology. Supernaturalism is not an essential component of the orthodox doctrines of Christian faith, but rather the history of salvation is the foundation of Christian theology. Perhaps the secularistic critique of supernaturalism has performed a useful service for Christian faith by exposing the logical-theological incoherence of a bifurcated worldview.

There may be some truth then to the Death of God theology of the 1960s, as well as process theology which has praised Nietzsche for his bold declaration that the God of supernaturalistic theism is dead. Nietzsche's insight was his perception that a personal God who is so totally other from the world cannot be taken seriously by human beings whose daily concerns are related to personal survival and existential meaning. Such interference by an alien authority only stifles human happiness and leads to a negation of the importance of this world. In defense of human dignity and worth, Nietzsche opposed an unethical concept of a tyrannical God who arbitrarily superimposed an arbitrary will on frail human beings who are dominated by fear and guilt.

Of course, supernaturalism did not intend to imply such a truncated and bifurcated view of God and the world. Yet, inadvertently, it perhaps did lead to such an extreme dualism. The doctrine of the Trinity with its emphasis on the temporal development of a historical revelation of God as Father, Son and Holy Spirit who are intimately involved in a loving and redeeming way in the affairs of this world stands in contradiction to a supernaturalistic distancing of God from the world.

What creates spiritual distance from God? Is it God's spatial transcendence above us in another, alien world? Is this natural world to be despised and downgraded because it is totally depraved and devoid of any inherent goodness? Is it God's spatial distance from us that defines holiness and our sinfulness? This misconception of God's relation to the world, which supernaturalism fosters in spite of itself, is why Schubert Ogden says that "supernaturalism . . . is in principle an inconsistent and self-stultifying position."[101]

It is significant that the concept of a supernatural distancing of God from the world emerged in the feudalistic society of the Middle Ages where landowners (lords) lived in isolated and well-protected castles, separated from the rest of the human community. In contrast to the self-serving, tyrannical power of a feudal lord is the shepherding concept of the Lord in the Old Testament (Ps. 23:1). Also, the Medieval development of a supernatural *ontology* which implies tyrannical loftiness over the world is essentially contradictory to its own *theology* of the God of history whose lordship entails friendship with subjects ("I will dwell among the people of Israel, and will be their God" Exod. 29:45). The biblical imagery of God being high and lifted up (Isa. 6:12) expresses God's moral, qualitative difference from sinful humanity, rather than a literal, spatial separation of God above the natural world. The history of salvation was the overcoming of this distance in Jesus of Nazareth.

The spatial imagery in Scripture is largely relational in meaning. For example, Jesus' ascension to his Father is a figure of speech to indicate that Jesus would take up a new relationship with his people through the Pentecostal outpouring of His Holy Spirit. The interpretation of Jesus' ascension as implying that God resides above or outside the natural universe in a supernatural realm contradicts the relational intent of the biblical spatial imagery. The essential meaning of the ascension is not God's removal from us, but rather that a deeper and closer relationship to God is now possible because God dwells "within" God's people through the Spirit (John 14:17, Acts 1 and 2). The spatial imagery of the "descent" of the Holy Spirit is a corollary to the imagery of Jesus' "ascent" to heaven. Of course, this spatial imagery implies divine transcendence, but a supernatural ontology is not the only way to interpret it.

This concept of God dwelling "within" us through the giving of the Spirit to the Church is, of course, not a pantheistic mysticism, for God is other than the world. God transcends us as the power of the unbounded future, but God is immanent because God, as the future, determines the present course of history. God is infinite; we are finite. We are not distant from God because God is too lofty for us and is separated from us on a higher plane. Rather, what creates spiritual distance from God whose presence (space) no one can escape (not even in hell, Ps. 139:8) is sinfulness and rebellion against the only possible source of our being and meaningfulness. It is spiritual distance, not spatial distance, which creates fear and makes us sinners.

That we "feel" distance from God proves that our problem with estrangement from God is a spiritual separation, not a spatial absence of God. If God's absence were spatial, we would not feel it as such. We would simply be ignorant of divine reality. This is the problem with Barth's supernaturalism: that the natural world is so spatially empty of God that any religious feeling is tinged with human arrogance and is the product of an anthropocentric attempt to create God in our own image.[102] Hence Barth's capitulation to Feuerbach.

To be sure, God' triune being is ontologically different from humans. God alone is self-existent. This is the insight which supernaturalism rightly seeks to capture, but as a model of what is true being, supernaturalism fosters an inherent, self-deprecating attitude as if we are unworthy humans because we are spatially isolated from God in a lower level of (un)reality. An eschatological paradigm assumes that God is the power of the unbounded future whose reality includes the past and present. God is not above us in a deistic sense, nor within us in a pantheistic sense, but ahead of us as the transcendent and sovereign one who is also with us as we share together in the ongoing history of salvation.

Summary

The eschatological concept of God in which the future interfaces with the past and present preserves the unity of truth, which Greek philosophy eagerly but unsuccessfully attempted to achieve with its distinction between the visible and invisible worlds. It offers a way of overcoming the fact-value dualism of modern thought with the divorce between the Jesus of history and the Christ of faith. It affirms divine transcendence in terms of God as the power of the unbounded future, which is consistent with the Ancient Hebrew way of understanding that God is personal and is cosmologically transcendent. It avoids falling into the deistic and atheistic implications of extreme supernaturalism. Finally, it is an implication of Jesus' eschatological preaching, which looked to the future for the restoration of all things in God in the coming kingdom of God

Notes

1. Michel Despland, "The Supernatural," *The Encyclopedia of Religion*, ed. Mircea Eliade (New York: Macmillan Publishing Co. 1987), 14:159-163; Ian Knox, *Above or Within?* Foreword by Richard McBrien (Mishawaka, Indiana: Religious Education Press, 1976), 16-37.

2. Paul Tillich everywhere used *supra*naturalism, as seen in the index of his *Systematic Theology*, three volumes in one (Chicago: University of Chicago Press, 1971).

3. Knox, *Above or Within?*, 24.

4. Ibid.

5. Tillich, *A History of Christian Thought*, 116.

6. Ibid. Cf. Jürgen Moltmann, *The Trinity and the Kingdom* (New York: Harper and Row, 1981), 16-20

7. Tillich, *A History of Christian Thought*, 190.

8. Knox, *Above or Within?*, 23.

9. *The Theology of Paul Tillich*, ed. Charles W. Kegley and Robert W. Bertall (New York: The Macmillan Co., 1964), 341.

10. Tillich, "The Significance of the History of Religions for Systematic Theology," in *The Future of Religions*, ed. Jerald C. Brauer (Chicago: University of Chicago Press, 1966), 80-94, cited by Pannenberg in *Basic Questions in Theology*, trans. George H. Kehm (Philadelphia: Westminster Press, 1971), 2:65.

11. Tillich defines the various options for doing theology as oscillating

between supernaturalism and naturalism. His proposal for an "ecstatic natural-ism" is still under the sway of the supernatural/natural metaphysics which he rejects. *Systematic Theology,* 1:64-66; *A History of Christian Thought,* 332. Cf. Schubert Ogden, *The Reality of God* (New York: Harper, 1966), 52.

12. Tillich, *A History of Christian Thought,* 332.

13. Ibid., 198ff.

14. Ibid.

15. Ibid.

16. Ibid.

17. Barth thus criticizes his earlier *Epistle to the Romans* in *Church Dogmatics,* trans. G. T. Thompson (Edinburgh: T. and T. Clark, 1963), 1:2, 50.

18. Barth, *Church Dogmatics,* 1.1.188-189.

19. Ibid., 3.3.177ff; ibid., 2.1.443. Cf. Herbert Hartwell, *The Theology Karl Barth* (Philadelphia: Westminster Press, 1964), 48-53.

20. Cf. Helmut Gollwitzer, "Introduction," to Karl Barth, *Church Dogmatics, A Selection* trans. and ed. G. W. Bromiley (New York: Harper and Row, Publishers, 1961), 8.

21. Pannenberg, "God's Presence in History," *The Christian Century* (March 11, 1981): 260-263.

22. Barth, *Church Dogmatics,* 1.1.16.

23. Pannenberg, *Basic Questions in Theology,* 2:189.

24. Ibid., 2:189-190.

25. Ibid., 2:190.

26. Cf. E. L. Mascall, *He Who Is* (London: Longmans, Green, & Co., Ltd., 1966).

27. Mascall, *The Importance of Being Human* (New York: Columbia University Press, 1958), 59, 61.

28. Cf. Thomas Flint and Alfred J. Freddoso, "Maximal Power," *The Existence and Nature of God,* ed. Alfred J. Freddoso (Notre Dame: University of Notre Dame Press, 1983), 81-113.

29. Tillich, *Systematic Theology,* 1:245. Pannenberg has shown how from Kant to Fichte to Hegel and finally to Feuerbach this radical emphasis on self-con-sciousness as the basis of all forms of knowledge became the model of think-ing of personhood and resulted in the atheistic critique (*Metaphysics and the Idea of God,* trans. Philip Clayton (Grand Rapids: Wm. B. Eerdmans Publishing Co., 1990), 43-46, 56. Cf. Moltmann, *Trinity and the Kingdom,* 13-16. Pannenberg says Leibniz inaugurated the modern idea of a personal God. *Basic Questions in Theology,* 2:227; Theodore M. Green and Hoyt Hudson, "Introduction" to Kant's *Religion within the Limits of Reason Alone,* trans Greene and Hudson (New York: Harper and Row, 1960), xxxvii-xxxviii. However, in fairness to Leibniz, it must said that he strongly affirmed the Trinitarian nature of God.

30. Pannenberg, *Anthropology in Theological Perspective,* trans. Matthew J. O'Connell (Philadelphia: Westminster Press, 1985), 201, 235, 236, 240; *Metaphysics and the Idea of God,* 44-46.

31. Pannenberg, *Anthropology in Theological Perspective*, 201, 235, 236, 240; *Metaphysics and the Idea of God*, 44-46.

32. Tillich, *Systematic Theology*, 1:245. Pannenberg, *Basic Questions in Theology*, 2:202.

33. Pannenberg, *Basic Questions in Theology*, 2:227-233; Pannenberg, *Metaphysics and the Idea of God*, 66.

34. Gerhard von Rad, *The Problem of the Hexateuch and Other Essays*, trans. E. Dicken (New York: McGraw-Hill, 1966), 153, 157.

35. Vitezslav Gardavsky, *God Is Not Yet Dead*, trans. Vivenne Menkes (Baltimore: Penguin, 1973), 28; Erich Fromm, *The Art of Loving* (New York: Harper, 1963), 53-69. Cf. E. L. Mascall, *The Importance of Being Human*, 38-39, who writes: "The concept of personality is not, of course, confined to Christianity or even to the Judaeo-Christian revelation, but it is very significant that it was only when it entered into theology, through the controversies in the early Church about the nature of God, that its full content and implications became manifest . . . . The idea of personality was present in Greek thought only in embryo, and to this day it is practically absent from Hinduism and Buddhism."

36. Pannenberg, *Metaphysics and the Idea of God*, 44-46. Cf. Kant, *Critique of Pure Reason*, trans. Normal Kemp Smith (London: Macmillan and Co., Ltd. 1929), 147, where he says: "The order and regularity in the appearances, which we entitle *nature*, we ourselves introduce. We could never find them in appearances, had not we ourselves, or the nature of our mind, originally set them there."

37. Eberhard Jüngel, *God as the Mystery of the World*, trans. Darrell L. Guder (Grand Rapids, MI: Wm. B. Eerdmans Publishing Co. 1983), 80-85. Cf. Jüngel, *The Doctrine of the Trinity* (Grand Rapids, MI: Wm. B. Eerdmans, 1976), 32.

38. Hegel, *The Encyclopaedia Logic*, 226-227. Cf. Quentin Lauer, *Hegel's Concept of God*, 155.

39. Pannenberg, *Metaphysic and the Idea of God*, 40.

40. Pannenberg, *Systematic Theology*, 1:295.

41. Moltmann, *Trinity and the Kingdom*, 139.

42. Wolfhart Pannenberg, "Introduction," in *Revelation As History*, 3-5.

43. Moltmann, *The Trinity and the Kingdom*, 139; cf. Pannenberg, *Jesus—God and Man*, trans. Ulrich Wilkens (Philadelphia: Westminster Press, 1977), 181.

44. Ludwig Feuerbach, *The Essence of Christianity*, trans. George Eliot (New York: Harper & Row, 1957), 29-30.

45. Ludwig Feuerbach, *The Essence of Faith According to Luther*, trans. Melvin Cherno (New York: Harper and Row, 1967), 31-39, 126-127. Feuerbach, *The Essence of Christianity*, 26-32.

46. Pannenberg, *Basic Questions in Theology*, 2:184-185.

47. Ibid., 2:197, 202, 227, 241; Pannenberg, *Metaphysics and Idea of God*, 34-35, 44-45. Pannenberg, *Systematic Theology* 1:374.

48. Feuerbach, *The Essence of Faith According to Luther*, 33.

49. Pannenberg, *Basic Questions in Theology*, 2:193.

50. Ibid., 2:242.

51. Ibid., 2:191-192.

52. Ibid., 2:193.

53. Ibid., 2:202.

54. Ibid., 2:194-195.

55. Ibid.

56. Ibid., 2:195.

57. Ibid., 2:241.

58. Ibid., 2:11

59. Hans von Soden, *Was ist Wahrheit? Vom geschichtlichen Begriff der Wahrheit, Marburger akademische Reden* 46 (Marburg, 1927), cited by Pannenberg, *Basic Questions in Theology*, 2:3.

60. Ibid., 2:9-10.

61. Ibid., 2:3, 10-11.

62. Ernst Cassirer, *The Philosophy of the Enlightenment*, 182-196.

63. Pannenberg, *Basic Questions in Theology*, 2:21.

64. Ibid., 2:22.

65. Ibid.

66. Ibid., 2:23. Pannenberg denies he is a Hegelian. Cf. *The Theology of Wolfhart Pannenberg*, ed. Carl E. Braaten and Philip Clayton (Minneapolis: Augsburg Publishing House, 1988), 16. Cf. Timothy Bradshaw, *Trinity and Ontology A Comparative Study of the Theologies of Karl Barth and Wolfhart Pannenberg* (Lewiston, New York: The Edward Mullen Press, 1988) for a study of the influence of Hegel upon the theologies of Pannenberg and Barth.

67. Pannenberg, *Basic Questions in Theology*, 2:27.

68. Ibid., 2:242.

69. Pannenberg, *Theology As History*, 262 n72.

70. This is a quotation from a personal letter from Pannenberg to the author, May 6, 1991.

71. Pannenberg, *Basic Questions in Theology*, 2:236.

72. Ibid., 2:248.

73. Friedrich Nietzsche, *The Joyful Wisdom*, trans.Thomas Common (New York: Frederick Ungar Publishing Co, 1960), p167-168.

74. Tillich, *Courage To Be* (New Haven, CT: Yale University Press, 1952), 185; John Cobb, Jr., *God and the World* (Philadelphia: Westminster Press, 1976), 22-33; Thomas J. J. Altizer and William Hamilton, *Radical Theology and the Death of God* (Indianapolis, IN: The Bobbs-Merrill Company, 1966).

75. Pannenberg, *Theology As History*, 133.

76. Pannenberg, *Basic Questions in Theology*, 2:248.

77. Pannenberg, *Jesus–God and Man*, 130.

78. Eberhard Jüngel, *The Doctrine of the Trinity*, 15.

79. Barth, *Church Dogmatics*, 1:1.x.

80. Pannenberg, *Basic Questions in Theology*, 2:249.

81. Pannenberg, *Theology and the Kingdom of God* (Philadelphia: Westminster Press, 1969), 53.

82. Ibid.

83. Ibid., 127-143

84. Ibid.

85. Ibid., 52.

86. Ibid.

87. Ibid.

88. Ibid.

89. Ibid., 253.

90. Daniel Fuller, *Easter Faith and History* (Grand Rapids: Wm. B. Eerdmans, 1965), 186-187.

91. Pannenberg once said to me that he liked Schleiermacher's insight that all events are miracles. To be sure, he does not agree with Schleiermacher's overall theology, which failed to incorporate the history of salvation as the essential component of faith. Pannenberg's point is that it is theologically inappropriate to cordon off reality into secular and sacred domains as if God is active in one but not the other.

92. Norman L. Geisler, "A New Look at the Relevance of Thomism for Evangelical Apologetics," *Christian Scholar's Review,* 4.3 (1975): 189-200.

93. Colin Brown, *Philosophy and the Christian Faith* (Downers Grove, Illinois: InterVarsity Press, 1968), 26ff.

94. Cf. Scott Burson and Jerry Walls, *C. S. Lewis & Francis Schaeffer* (Downers Grove, Illinois: InterVarsity Press, 1998), 178.. .

95. Cf. *The Theology of Wolfhart Pannenberg,* 14-15.

96. Pannenberg expressed his preference for Michael Polanyi's notion of tacit knowledge when he visited and lectured on his first visit to the campus of Asbury Theological Seminary in 1991. Michael Polanyi, *Personal Knowledge* (Chicago: University of Chicago Press, 1958) and Polanyi, *The Tacit Dimension* (New York: Doubleday, 1967), 3-25. For a superb interpretation of the theological implications of Polanyi's epistemology, cf. Jerry Gill, *The Possibility of Religious Knowledge* (Grand Rapids, MI: Wm. B. Eerdmans Publishing Company, 1975), 128-137.

97. Henri de Lubac, *The Mystery of the Supernatural,* trans. Rosemary Sheed (New York: Herder and Herder, 1967), xi. Pannenberg frankly says supranaturalism inevitably leads to Nietzsche's atheism. *Basic Questions in Theology,* 2:195.

98. Barth, *Church Dogmatics,* 1:x.

99. Friedrich Schleiermacher, *The Christian Faith,* ed. H. R. Mackintosh and J. S. Steward (New York: Harper and Row, 1963, 1:66-68.

100. Tillich, *Systematic Theology,* 1:27.

101. Schubert Ogden, *The Reality of God,* 46.

102. Barth, *Church Dogmatics,* 1:x.

16

Space-Time And Eternity

The previous chapter developed the idea that God is the power of the unbounded future. This means the future of space-time already exists in God. This is why God has been considered in the history of theology as eternal, omnipresent, and omniscient—all times and places are instantly present and known to God. By space-time is meant creation from the moment of the Big Bang to its final reconstitution in the eschatological future. By eschatological future is meant the final triumph of God's kingdom in human history.

This final chapter will explore the relationship between creation as space-time and eternity, which Boethius (c.480-525 AD) classically defined as the fullness of all things existing all at once in God.[1] I will draw from postmodern science and cosmologists to show how the relation between space-time and eternity can be explained in an intelligible manner without falling into a dualism of God and the world. The tension between human freedom and omniscience will be considered as a test case for understanding the relationship between space-time and eternity.

Salvation History Connects Space-time and Eternity

We earlier showed that the problem of relating faith and history in modern thought developed out of the Kantian dualism of appearance and reality, of the finite and the infinite. For Kant, time is the realm of the finite, while eternity is the realm of the infinite. He believed time and eternity never connect with each other, and because time is only a subjective human perception, God cannot be revealed in history. Modern theology often assumed the validity of this Kantian premise with the result that the realism of salvation history was denied, the doctrine of creation was weakened, and the eschatological future were discarded.

Pannenberg offers a more constructive way of relating space-time and eternity. He refutes the Kantian dualism of the finite and the infinite and argues against the notion that temporal events are necessitated by mechanical causality as if the present is the inevitable outcome of the past. He has shown that one of the implications of salvation history is that the present moment is not determined simply by the past. Rather the present eventuates out of the future, and the past which influences our present is itself the product of the future goal of all things in God. Hence creation is not simply a past event, but rather it is moving forward toward the eschatological future.[2]

His suggestion concerning the priority of the future and its openness to unpredictable things happening has remarkable similarities to postmodern science. In a meeting of the American Physical Society in New York in 1966, Hilary Putnam who is the Professor Emeritus of Mathematical Logic of Harvard University said that relativity physics had resolved the problem about the future of time by showing that the future events in one's slower moving time-frame actually exists for someone else in a faster-moving time-frame.[3] Heisenberg has shown that quantum physics is a repudiation of the materialism of the modern scientific worldview with its mechanistic concept of causality, thus leaving the future open.[4] Determinism has thus been superseded in postmodern science with an openness to new and unexpected things happening in the world. However, Roger Penrose observes that biologists tend toward a more mechanistic view of the world than do the physicists "who are the more directly familiar with the puzzling and mysterious ways in which matter *actually* behaves."[5] Both relativity and quantum physics contain the notion that the future is open to new possibilities and is not deterministic and yet the future can exist in a faster moving time-frame. The relativity of time and quantum physics reinforce the views of the Early Greek Fathers and Boethius, who defined eternity as including the future of time while affirming the reality of human freedom.

If the Early Church Fathers used Greek categories for explaining the history of salvation, I think it is appropriate for contemporary theology to utilize the insights of postmodern physics to explain the relationship of space-time and eternity. Just as the Early Church Fathers did not imagine that they were proving faith simply because they used Greek philosophy, so it is not imagined here that science proves Christian faith. Although contemporary physics may be used to illustrate a variety of philosophical points of view, it will be argued here that contemporary physics can also be used to illustrate how the theology of eternity in the Early Church Fathers is an intelligible and coherent doctrine.[6]

Time as Objectively Real

The Bible assumes that time entails more than measuring temporal happenings according to a wrist watch; it is an objectively real sequence of things and not just a mental perception. If the realism of salvation history is not to be relinquished, then the contingency of time is to be affirmed. This means the future is open to new and unexpected things and that there are free and surprising developments that will take place in time. Eternity, on the other hand, is the fullness of life because the undivided wholeness of everything exists instantly in God, including the contingent events and real developments in time.

Time derives its meaning from its relationship to eternity; otherwise, there would be no transcendent unity of temporal events and no direction to the flow of history. As Pannenberg has shown, this is the point that Plotinus argued in his philosophy—that unless there is a wholeness of everything in the unconditioned unity of God, then there can be no real meaning and unity in life.[7] On the other hand, if eternity is merely the unending extension of time toward an indefinite future, then God is a prisoner of time like finite beings and is still waiting to see what the future holds. To put it rather humorously, if God has a future, then God may worry that there may be a greater God in the unknown future who has not yet been discovered. Just maybe there is something out there that God does not know about. Like the Athenians, perhaps God should erect an altar to an "unknown God" of the future just in case there is a shocking surprise out there. It could of course be argued that God already knows that there is nothing in the future to fear, but how would God know that? Perhaps God puts faith in deductive logic, but this places abstract principles of logic in a higher bracket than God's own personal being. To be sure, all of this sounds absurd, but the purpose of this humor is to underscore that what is at stake in this discussion is the being of the Creator God.

Eternity as Simultaneous Duration

A basic biblical assumption is that God is a living, personal God who has duration, not a timeless Being hidden in the background of the world as in Greek philosophy. There is a "before" and "after" in God, although they exist in the transcendent unity of God's instant moment. God exists "before" the creation of space-time, and God exists "after" space-time will cease to exist. To be sure, it is odd to say that something existed before time and will continue to exist after time has ceased. It is like saying that there was a time before creation when there was no time. To speak of duration in eternity thus seems like an oxymoron, but that is because in our earthly environment time moves slowly and we are misled to think that time moves slowly everywhere else in the universe. Contemporary physics now tells us this is wrong because time is relative to one's own time-frame of reference. The tick of the clock moves slower in a faster moving environment. In the consciousness of God who transcends all time-references, our earthly sequence of time moves with infinite speed and occurs instantly. We nonetheless must use our time-bound words in a figurative way to speak of what lies beyond earthly time, and "duration" is one of those words.

Barth has argued that it is appropriate to think of God as "pure duration"[8] as distinct from finite duration in the sense that God is not a lifeless or abstract entity. Eleonore Stump and Norman Kretzmann have also shown Boethius conceived of eternity as "fully realized duration" as compared to finite duration where things persists through time. As analytical philosophers, they argue that just because the idea of infinite duration contradicts ordinary usage does not disqualify it as a valid term.[9]

John Wesley asked in the 18th century: "And what is eternity? It is boundless duration."[10] He further observed that eternity means "duration which had no beginning" and "which will have no end."[11] Wesley asked, "But what is *time*? It is not easy to say, as frequently as we have had the word in our mouth. We know not what it properly is. We cannot well tell how to define it." Although recognizing the human limitation to define time, Wesley gave this definition: "Is it not in some sense a fragment of eternity, broken off at both ends?—that portion of duration which commenced when the world began, which will continue as long as this world endures, and then expire for ever?"[12] The concept of duration as Wesley used it is a term used in the history of theology to show that eternity is not sheer timelessness, but rather eternity entails the duration of life in its perfection. So it is possible to speak of the duration of "before" and "after" without referring to space-time.

This is not a problem just for theologians. As a result of the Big Bang theory, contemporary physicists are equally confronted with the same paradox in talking about what may have existed "before" the creation of space-time. Yet they do so because they believe time came into existence as a result of the big expansion.[13]

Eternity is More Than Endless Time

In his defense of salvation history as the key category of theology, Oscar Cullmann argued in a highly influential book, *Christ and Time*, that eternity means unending time and that God is only a temporal Being. His concern was to refute Bultmann's notion that faith was a timeless decision that had little to do with real events. At the same time Cullmann also argued that God was "Lord over time" and was able to foresee the future and plan for its development.[14]

Cullmann was not a systematic theologian, and it was not apparent to him that his idea of divine foreknowledge necessarily entailed the idea that everything was present to God, at least in terms of God's knowledge. Hence he did not for all practical purposes exclusively locate God within time. On the other hand, his concept of foreknowledge tended toward the idea of "a timeless God"[15] despite his opposition to it. This is because he believed God predetermined and foreordained the future through divine decrees,[16] thus in effect making the future timeless, immutable, and uninfluenced by human decision.

Cullmann argued aggressively against Bultmann's view of time because Bultmann lacked an appreciation of salvation history and because he demythologized real time into existentialist categories. However, if Bultmann accentuated the timeless and non-historical nature of faith, Cullmann went to the other extreme of interpreting everything as temporal, maintaining that the difference between world-time and eternity is that eternity is unending time. This created a climate of uncertainty about what it means to affirm that God is the Lord of time and the distinction between time and eternity was blurred.

Cullmann's book on *Christ and Time* (1949) helped to set the stage for the contemporary debate on the meaning of time and eternity, but it took a direction that he did not envisage. Little did he realize that his idea of eternity as unending time and of God as only a temporal Being would foreshadow a new theology of limited omniscience.[17]

I will focus the rest of this chapter on the theology of limited omniscience to illustrate what happens when the subject-object distinction is inadequately used to explain the difference between God and the world and between eternity and space-time.

A New Theology of Limited Omniscience

Since the 1970's, there has been a highly publicized debate about the dilemma of God's sovereignty and human freedom in Anglo-American religious philosophy, especially among analytic philosophers. The major concern among some of these scholars is that if God knows the future this eliminates human freedom. Hence they deductively argue that the future is unknown for God.

Richard Swinburne, a British philosopher and one of the leading proponents of this view, says God is "only a temporal being"[18] who "exists at each moment of unending time."[19] He frankly draws the conclusion that this means God could be mistaken: "No one (not even God) can know today (without the possibility of mistake) what I will choose to do tomorrow."[20] This is a fundamental denial of the possibility of biblical prophecy, such as is assumed in Ezekiel 12:27, where the prophet is able to engage in "prophecies of times far off." Swinburne draws God into the sequence of the past, the present, and future of time and thus God has an undeveloped future and is unable to know what tomorrow holds.

Another group of scholars who endorse a similar view of limited omniscience in America are allied together under the label, "the openness of God theism." One of their main leaders is Clark Pinnock with a Reformed background who came to reject the doctrine of absolute predestination in favor of *libertarian freedom* (i.e., God does not predetermine human actions).[21] He believes that divine foreknowledge necessarily entails a Calvinistic view of predestination, which his writings have intended to refute.[22] Although I agree that the emphasis on libertarian freedom is an essential component of salvation history, there are many philosophical and theological problems with the new theology of limited omniscience.

An Exclusively Temporal God is Finite

First, to imply that God needs a wrist-watch in order to keep time implies that God is finite. If God is an exclusively temporal Being, this entails the presupposition that God is not the Lord over time and not the transcendent Creator of space-time.

Nelson Pike in his book, *God and Time* (1970) wrote a defining work that gave momentum to this view. His work heavily influenced philosophers such as Richard Swinburne.[23] However, Pike's interpretation of Boethius'view of eternity is not reliable.[24] He lists six assumptions that he believed are associated with Boethius.[25] The two main ones are (1) God is infallible and (2) that God knows the outcome of human actions in advance of their performance.[26] Pike misses an important nuance in this second assumption. Pike says Boethius assumed God knows *at a certain point in time* that certain events in the future will happen. Pike explains this assumption with this illustration. If God knows at a certain point in time that Mr. Jones is going to mow his lawn on a certain day eighty years from now, then Mr. Jones is not free to do otherwise than mow his lawn because God's infallible foreknowledge requires that he does so. However, this illustration does not represent Boethius's view because he did not believe that God knows something *at a certain point in time.* Nor did Boethius believe God decided anything *at a certain point in time.* God transcends time, and the divine decisions and knowledge are based in eternity in which the past, present, and future are already and always present.

The thing that Pike missed is this—God knows everything because everything is already present to God, including the past and the future. Pike wrongly interprets Boethius as assuming that God predicts or merely foresees what is a future happening. Quite the contrary, in very clear terms Boethius said that if God foreknow events, then there is no human freedom. He agrees that literal divine foreknowledge entails determinism. Here is what Boethius said: "For if God, who cannot be deceived, *sees everything in advance* [italics mine], then whatever his Providence foresees will occur must of necessity come to pass. If from all eternity he knows not only the deeds of men, but also their deliberations and decisions, there can be no freedom of will. For no other deeds or decisions can exist save those foreseen by God's infallible Providence."[27]

How then does God have omniscience? Boethius believed that God knows the future, not because God has "prevision," but because God is "located far above all lesser things" and "looks down upon them all from on high."[28] Everything is thus present in God because God is not bound by time. Boethius said: "Only that deserves to be called eternal which comprehends and possesses the entire plentitude of endless life all at once with none of the past or future missing."[29] Notice that the past and the future are already present "all at once" in God's eternity. Boethius further explained that God "with a single glance of the mind ...encompasses all future events."[30] He further described God's knowledge as based on his ability of "looking down on all." This is why Boethius said: "The vision looking down on all does not alter the nature of what is present before it, though in terms of time, the events are in the future." Hence God has "knowledge based on truth" and not "mere opinion."[31]

Boethius further argued: "But those future things which result from free will God sees as present."[32]

Contrary to Pike's interpretation, here Boethius believed that God actually saw the future events of our earthly time because they are already present and not because God imagined or predicted them. As Richard Sorabji, Emeritus Professor of Philosophy, King's College, London, shows, Boethius believed God knows our future *but not in advance of it happening*.[33] Hence Boethius maintained that the divine knowledge of our future time in no way compromises the reality of human freedom.[34] Boethius further explained that God "correctly envisions the future quality of our actions, since his eternity is copresent to all time."[35] He further said that God sees "the past and future...as if they were going on now."[36] Thus the past and the future are "copresent" with God. As Boethius explains, this is not foreknowledge, but knowledge. Boethius is thus careful to point out that divine omniscience does not mean that future events cause God to have foreknowledge of them. It only means God is able to see the future events and that is why God knows them.[37] So God's knowledge of the future does not cause events to happen, and neither do future events cause God to have knowledge of them. God simply knows them because God sees them in the eternal present.[38]

If one is free to act, does this mean that one can "frustrate" God's knowledge if one chooses to do something other than what God foresaw. Boethius' shows that this question misses the point of how God knows the future of time: "To this I answer that you may indeed alter your decision, but since the present truth of Providence sees not only that you can, but also whether you will, you can no more frustrate divine foreknowledge than you could escape the eye of one watching you now by freely changing the course of your actions."[39] God thus sees everything "in one unchanging glance" because everything real or possible is already present; it is not because God has to see through a looking glass into the future. Rather, the future is actual to God. Hence God does not see "everything in advance"[40] because that would be a denial of human freedom. Rather, the future of all things in time is already present to God. This carefully nuanced interpretation of omniscience—that God knows everything but not in advance of it happening—is missed by Pike. His arguments, which are offered with many illustrations, all assume that Boethius believed that God knew things in advance of their happening.[41]

The Boethian view of eternity has been ably defended recently by Brian Leftow, who is Richard Swinburne's successor at Oxford as the

Nolloth Professor of the Philosophy of the Christian Religion. Leftow writes: "I think that a defender of God's eternity can assert that (in a strictly limited sense) one and the same event is present and actual in eternity though it is not yet or no longer present or actual in time. That is, it can be true at a time t that an event dated at $t + 1$ has not yet occurred in time, and yet also correct at t to say that very event exists in eternity. That all events occur at once in eternity, I submit, does not entail that they all occur at once in time"[42] Leftow's explanation thus shows that although our future does not exist for us, it already exists in God's eternity.

It is an anthropomorphic projection of the worst kind to locate God merely within our time-frame of reference and to assume that God is an individual who sees things exactly the same way that finite human beings do. Pike repeatedly misrepresents Boethius when he says Boethius assumed that God knows "the outcome of human actions in advance of their performance."[43] Boethius fully agrees that literal foreknowledge entails determinism. Boethius allows that our future is really future to us and to God from within the context of our inertial frame of reference on earth, but from God's eternal and transcendent standpoint these contingent happenings already exist. As I will show below, this paradox is intelligible from the standpoint of Einstein's theory of space-time relativity. The arguments of Pike against Boethius thus collapse because they are based on a misunderstanding.

Wolfhart Pannenberg has argued that Pike's view "makes God into a finite being if it implies that like ourselves God at every moment of his life looks ahead to a future that is distinct from the present and sees the past fading away from him."[44] If the new theology of limited omniscience is worried about Calvinism and its virtual denial of personal freedom, a greater worry ought to be making God into a finite being. The price of preserving human freedom at the cost of God's sovereignty is too great and unnecessary.

Is God an Individual?

Second, the idea that God is a supermundane Being who exists spatially above and temporally along side human beings is an example of the Kantian idea of God as a supernatural Individual. Feuerbach's atheistic critique rightly demolished this notion as an anthropomorphic projection, noting that in effect "*Christianity made man an extramundane, supernatural being*"[45] by defining God as such.

Nelson Pike objects to the idea of total omniscience on the basis of deductive logic, claiming that "a timeless *individual* [italics mine] could not *produce, create, or bring about* an object" because this would have the effect of making such an individual temporal.[46] Hence he argues that God is necessarily a temporal individual: "I assume that God...is *a being*—a single individual."[47] Throughout his book, Pike frequently speaks of God as an "individual" existing in time. To think of God as an individual is an example of creating God in our image and projecting finite human characteristics on to God. Feuerbach noted the unwitting result of modern thought was to transform theology into anthropology: "The reduction of the extrahuman, supernatural, and antirational nature of God to the natural, immanent, inborn nature of man, is the therefore the liberation of Protestantism [and] the necessary, irrepressible, irrefragable result of Christianity."[48] For Pike to speak of God as a single Individual is an example of dressing up God in finite human terms and of turning theology into anthropology.

If God is to be thought of as the God of creation and the Lord of history, then God should be thought of in infinite terms. Although the word *infinite* is not found in the Scriptures, the Early Greek Church Fathers have shown it is a corollary term to eternity.[49] Infinity is not simply a mathematical concept implying that finite time is extended endlessly. Rather, infinity is a theological-metaphysical concept that entails the idea of God's cosmological transcendence—that God transcends space-time finitude, while also embracing it.[50] The infinite is not simply the negation of the finite; it also embraces it. If the infinite were simply the negation of the finite and defined as something over against it, then the infinite would simply be another "finite" thing alongside other finite things, as Hegel has shown in criticism of Kant's deism.[51]

Because there are dialectical polarities inherent in the very nature of reality, I do not believe that truth can be altogether squeezed into literal categories of formal, deductive logic, as Pike apparently assumes. We earlier talked about the principle of identity and the principle of difference in speaking of God's relationship to the world. If the principle of identity alone is emphasized, one tends toward pantheism. If the principle of difference is emphasized, the opposite extreme of a deistic notion of God as a trans-Individual prevails. This is why Feuerbach charged that Kant's deistic notion of a trans-Individual was an illusory human projection onto the screen of reality. This is also why Fichte and Hegel argued that if the infinite is defined as the opposite of the finite it is a relation of one thing to another thing and thus is finite itself.[52]

The new theology of limited omniscience assumes the principle of God's *spatial difference* from the world and thus it is not pantheistic, but it posits the notion of God's *temporal identity* with the world and thus turns God into a finite, trans-Individual. We noted that the early Hebrews were the first to use the subject-object distinction to explain the uniqueness of human life as opposed to the world of nature. Their Near Eastern neighbors saw the world mythically and identified the gods with nature, like the wind, sun, and mountains. Unlike the mythical thinking of the Ancient Near East where the subject-object distinction did not exist in an explicit way, the historical thinking of the early Hebrews led them to an awareness of the element of transcendence—that there is more to the world than natural objects and that God cannot be reduced to nature. Ironically, it seems to me that the new theology of limited omniscience fails to appreciate the Hebrew understanding of transcendence and mystery and tries to explain the reality of God on the analogy of the natural world, human experience, and deductive logic. The result is that the distinction between God and nature (space-time) is obscured.

The Idea of a Merely Temporal God Disrupts the Unity of the Trinity

Third, to fragment the nature of God into a sequence of the past, present, and future destroys the unity of the Trinity, as the Early Church Fathers pointed out. Origen argued that the relationship of the Three Persons of the Trinity must not be considered to be a temporary relationship because this would disrupt the Unity of the Trinity.[53] Likewise Gregory of Nyssa argued to limit God's being to the flow of time disrupts the unity of the Trinity because God would be split into three separated Persons who individually must keep time with what happens with each other.[54] If God knows things sequentially and the future is unknown to God, then the Father and the Son and the Holy Spirit are no longer a triunity of Persons because the Father must relate to the Son through the Holy Spirit as temporally distinct from each other.[55] To offset this implication one must define God in monarchical terms of One Person (albeit a finite Person) with three temporal modes of being, which in effect is what the new theology of limited omniscience does. Hence the new theology of limited omniscience is implicitly a contemporary version of ancient modalism, and I predict that future proponents of limited omniscience will reject Trinitarian orthodoxy for this very reason.

The Early Church Fathers and Full Divine Omniscience

Fourth, the new theology of limited omniscience contradicts the consensus of the Church down through the ages, particularly the theology of the Early Greek Church Fathers who formulated the standard doctrines of Trinitarian orthodoxy.[56] The idea that God lacked perfect omniscience was rejected as an unworthy view of God whom they argued created space and time *ex nihilo*.[57]

Some of the proponents of limited divine omniscience like Swinburne have claimed that the Early Church Fathers affirmed that God existed everlasting in time.[58] Swinburne does not cite any evidence for his claim, and the clear statements of the Early Church Fathers show that Swinburne is mistaken. For example, Ireneaus noted that we say "that a man sometimes is at rest and silent, while at other times he speaks and active." Yet God "always exists one and the same [instant]" and "divisions [of time] cannot fittingly be ascribed to Him."[59] Irenaeus thus concluded that God has the power of "foreknowing all things."[60] Clement of Alexandria defined eternity this way: "Eternity...presents in an instant the future and the present, also the past of time." Like the other Early Greek Church Fathers, Origen rejected determinism, but he insisted that the future is already known to God because God's existence "environs" the past, the present, and the future.[61] Gregory of Nyssa said that "every duration conceivable [past, present, future] is environed by the Divine nature, bounded on all sides by the infinity of Him Who holds the universe in His embrace."[62]

Boethius in the 6th century A. D. summarized the prevailing view of the Early Greek Church Fathers in *De Consolatione Philosophiae* (5.6) with this definition: "Eternity then is endless life possessed all at once its totality and perfection."[63] The Early Church Fathers thus held to a clear distinction between time and eternity. Time had a beginning and will have an end, whereas eternity is the instant whole of all reality.

Richard Sorabji's classical study, *Time, Creation, and The Continuum* (1983), has shown that there were two senses of eternity prior to the third century A.D.—it could mean everlasting or it could mean the instant moment of the past, present, and future.[64] Plotinus created two terms, everlasting (*sempiternus*) and eternity (*aeternus*), so that it was no longer necessary to distinguish between the two senses of the same word. Boethius introduced this terminological distinction into Christian theology.[65] Everlasting refers to perpetual duration in time, whereas eternity means the "total sweep of...infinite life all at once," or "the fullness of . . . life all at once."[66] Divine omniscience thus means "a knowledge of a never fading instant [rather] than as foreknowledge of the future."[67] God thus does not foreknow them, but simply sees them. Hence Boethius argues [through Lady Philosophy] that just as our vision of things happening does not "invest" then with necessity, so God seeing our future events does not entail necessity.[68] The new theology of limited omniscience overlooks this useful terminological distinction and defines eternity as everlasting time, thinking that if God knows our future, then this would imply determinism.

Sorabji noted that Augustine gave the first complete definition of eternity, but he believed Boethius gave a "philosophically superior" definition, which became normative for Christian theology.[69] He noted that Boethius overcame the determinism of Augustine by allowing that the flow of time was as real to God as to human beings. Although Sorabji used the term "timelessness" for a Boethian concept of eternity, he used it in the restricted sense that God transcends time, while allowing that God also includes time.[70] As opposed to the view of Augustine's notion of sheer timelessness, Boethius believed God has "a knowledge of things temporal."[71] This means time is not a negation of eternity, but is real to God, thus permitting human freedom. Sorabji notes that Boethius "enhances it [the divine knowledge of the future], by making the further point . . . that somebody who sees your action, but not in advance, in no way restricts your freedom."[72]

Sorabji notes this concept of eternity was clearly distinct from Augustine's idea of eternity.[73] Helen M. Barrett has also shown that Boethius' concept of eternity goes beyond Augustine's idea of timelessness and that Boethius was indebted largely to the Greek philosophical tradition. She shows that for Boethius eternity is a "quality of life, not mere quantity, something quite different from everlastingness, something infinitely richer and fuller than timelessness or perpetual duration."[74]

Likewise Pannenberg has argued that the view of Boethius is significantly different than the Augustinian view.[75] He draws from *The Church Dogmatics* of Barth who argued that Augustine and Boethius held to two different views of eternity.[76] Barth regretted that Boethius' definition "was never properly exploited"[77] in theology and was often conflated with Augustine's notion.[78] Recent discussions among Anglo-American philosophers often reflect the confusion of these two radically different positions. They assume either God exists in time and thus does not know the future, or else God is merely timeless and knows the future in which case there is no genuine human freedom.[79] Boethius offered a third option, affirming both ideas that God transcends time and yet includes it.

John Wesley specifically embraced the view of Boethius because it preserved both omniscience and human freedom. Wesley said there is neither "foreknowledge or after-knowledge in God." Wesley wrote: "The sum of all is this: the almighty, all-wise God sees and knows from everlasting to everlasting all that is, that was, and that is to come, through one eternal now. With him nothing is either past or future, but all things equally present. He has, therefore, if we speak according to the truth of things, no foreknowledge, no afterknowledge."[80] All time is present to God as a single whole, but this does not erase the reality of temporal developments. It is as if temporal events pass with infinite velocity before God. He sees everything all at once, although we see them in fragments of time. The source of Wesley's view is not from Augustine; rather, Wesley's source is Boethius.[81] He argued that it was pastorally significant[82] to affirm a Boethian interpretation of eternity in his sermon "On Predestination." He is particularly sensitive to the problem of theological determinism because he wants to preserve the integrity of human freedom. Otherwise, God is responsible for acts of sins. In a lucid discussion, Wesley explains the relation of time and eternity, noting that time is a real fragment of eternity:

All time, or rather all eternity (for time is only that small fragment of eternity which is allotted to the children of men) being present to him at once, he does not know one thing before another, or one thing after another, but sees all things in one point of view, from everlasting to everlasting. As all time, with everything that exists therein, is present with him at once, so he sees at once whatever was, is, or will be to the end of time. But observe: we must not think they *are* because he *knows* them. No; he knows them because they are. Just as I (if one may be allowed to compare the things of men with the deep things of God) now know the sun shines. Yet the sun does not shine because I know it: but I know it because it shines. My knowledge *supposes* the sun to shine, but does not in any wise *cause* it. In like manner God knows that man sins; for he knows all things. Yet we do not sin because he knows it; but he knows it because we sin. And his knowledge *supposes* our sin, but does not in any wise *cause* it. In a word, God looking on all ages from the creation to the consummation as a moment, and seeing at once whatever is in the hearts of all the children of men, knows everyone that does or does not believe in every age or nation. Yet what he knows, whether faith or unbelief, is in no wise caused by his knowledge. Men are as free in believing, or not believing, as if he did not know it at all.[83]

Wesley concluded that unless this distinction between time as a real development as opposed to eternity as the comprehensive moment of all time is preserved, then humanity would "not be accountable" for its moral behavior and not "capable either of reward or punishment."[84] Wesley of course rejected the theological determinism of Augustine and Calvin.[85]

Foreknowledge and Biblical Anthropomorphism

Fifth, the recent reinterpretation of omniscience confuses the use of biblical anthropomorphisms with literal language. Anthropomorphisms are figures of speech to express the view that God is a living God who respects and interacts freely with his creatures. God speaks (Gen. 1:3), hears (Ex. 16:12), sees (Gen. 6:12), smells (I Sam 26:19), laughs (Ps. 2:4), whistles (Isa. 7:18), has eyes ((Amos 9:4), hands (Ps. 139:5) arms ((Isa 51:9), ears (Isa. 22:14), feet (Nahum 1:3), and foreknows ((Acts 2:23).[86] God is often described as limited by the unfaithful actions of Israel. On occasions, God is described as "surprised" and thus capable of changing His mind.

Another example of anthropomorphism is when the Lord is described as appearing to Abraham "by the oaks of Mamre" (Gen 18:1), announcing to him that Sodom (where his nephew Lot lived) would be destroyed. On the one hand, God said he will investigate to see if Sodom is as bad as it has been reported so that "I will know"—as if God really did not know! Yet, in this same context, God is said to foreknow that "Abraham shall become a great and mighty nation, and all the nations of the earth shall bless themselves by him" (Gen. 18:17).

Anthropomorphisms thus do not entail a rejection of God's knowledge of future, but rather their intent is to show that God is a living, personal reality who respects human freedom and that God holds human beings responsible for their misuse of freedom. In this respect, Origen spoke of "the stretching of language" when the Bible attempts to speak of God as a personal reality who is involved in time.[87] Clement of Alexandria referred to these anthropomorphism as allegorical.[88] However, recent advocates of limited omniscience assume a literalistic interpretation of these anthropomorphisms. For example, if the Bible says God "changed his mind" and decided not to destroy Nineveh, this is interpreted to mean God did not really know that he would have the opportunity to show compassion in the future.[89] This literal reading of the text misconstrues the intent of biblical anthropomorphism and cannot be reconciled with other portions of Scripture where it is assumed that God knows the future.

Predictive Prophecy and Divine Omniscience

Sixth, limited omniscience cannot be reconciled with the idea of predictive prophesy in the Bible. Gerhard von Rad has shown that Isaiah considered himself to be following in the succession of earlier prophets (Isaiah 44:26; 45:19), and that what they had "prophesied long ago is now beginning to be fulfilled" (Isaiah 443:9ff; 44:7; 45:21).[90] Von Rad further showed that Isaiah believed that the words being put into his mouth by God would also be fulfilled (Isaiah 45:10ff).[91] Von Rad further explained that Isaiah believed that the difference between a true prophet of God and a false prophets of heathenism is that the Lord is "controller of world-history."[92] This distinctive feature of a true prophet is an answer that "almost takes one's breath away—the Lord of history is he who can allow the future to be told in advance."[93] Von Rad shows that "proof from prediction" is an idea that Isaiah "is conspicuously eager to use."[94]

Von Rad shows that one of the features of apocalyptic literature in the Book of Daniel is that the whole scope of world-history is presented as "already present."[95] The events of history have already taken place in "heaven."[96] The Son of Man who comes down from heaven "does not come from the realm of the unformed, but from the divine world on high. All this is described as from a spectator's point of view; the vision is not conceived as projected from its recipient's own historical standpoint, he does not stand within the events he beholds, but outside, and as he looks, all world history passes before his spirit like a film."[97] Von Rad demonstrated that this concept of "foretelling" means that the past and future are present in "heaven." This means "the past and the future ...were alike revealed as a complete course of historical events foretold by God."[98] In the prophetic literature such as in Isaiah, the future was foretold based on its unfolding developments in the course of salvation history, but in Daniel's apocalyptic writings the future was already present in heaven.[99] Pannenberg particularly refers to von Rad's exposition of Ps. 119:8, Ezek. 2:1ff, Isa. 34:4, and Zechariah 1:7-6:8 where the end-time events on earth are already present in heaven.[100] This is offered as a biblical basis for the validity of Boethius' interpretation of eternity as the simultaneous moment of all times.

The idea of predictive prophecy was used among the Early Christian Apologists as proof for the truth of Christianity. In *The Apology* addressed to the Roman emperor Antonius Pius in defense of Christianity, Justin Martyr (ca. 99-165) gave special and extensive attention to predictive prophesy as proof of the truth of Christianity.[101]   His main point is that "the things which He absolutely knows will take place, He predicts as if already they had taken place."[102] Justin Martyr argued that the idea of predictive prophecy did not entail the idea of determinism. He was greatly concerned to show that foreknowledge and human freedom were compatible.[103]

Speaking of the paradox involved in trying to understand difficult spiritual realities, Irenaeus recognized the element of mystery in matters of faith and cited the earthly Jesus as a role model in this regard. He noted that the Scriptures affirm that the Father has foreknowledge of the very day and the very hour when Jesus will return to the earth, but Jesus did not have this knowledge in his earthly existence.[104]   Consequently, he says: "If, then, the Son was not ashamed to ascribe the knowledge of that day to the Father only, but declared what was true regarding the matter, neither let us be ashamed to reserve for God those greater questions which may occur to us."[105]   He thus writes: "We are able by the grace of God to explain some of them, while we must leave others in the hands of God."[106] If we today have trouble with the logic of divine omniscience, the biblical writers did not. They believed God knew the future of all things in detail and not in mere generalities as if God were only some super-intelligent person who might have extraordinary powers of prognostication (cf. Acts 2:23; Romans 11:2; Romans 8:29).[107]

Although openness theism allows that God has some foreknowledge of future events, they argue God does not have exhaustive knowledge of the future. This assumes that the events God foreknows must necessarily happen according to the divine foreknowledge, and the other events that God chooses not to foreknow are to be freely decided in the future.[108] This view is refuted by Von Rad's exegesis of the Book of Daniel in which all the events of human history are completely present "in heaven" as having already happened. It is not that the totality of human events in history are simply foreknown, but they are actually present "in heaven."

This particular version of openness theism is similar to the view of Adam Clarke who is reported to have believed God put on blinders so that God could not see the future choices of human beings in order that it could not be said that human actions are predetermined by God's foreknowledge.[109] Interestingly enough, John Wesley did not agree with Adam Clarke, and Clarke held these ideas fairly privately to himself. As noted above, Wesley embraced the view of Boethius because he believed it was compatible with Scriptures and preserved libertarian freedom.

Time began with Creation

Seventh, proponents of the new theology of limited omniscience do not identify time with creation, although this has been more than an incidental view of the Church throughout its history beginning with the Early Church Fathers. Irenaeus affirmed that time came into being with creation, and then he noted that "no Scripture reveals to us what God was employed about before this event. The answer therefore to that question remains with God, and it is not proper for us to aim at bringing forward foolish, rash, and blasphemous suppositions."[110]

Basil of Caesarea (ca. 330-379) affirmed that time began with creation. He spoke of the "eternal and infinite" as "outstripping the limits of time." He wrote: "Thus was created . . . the succession of time, for ever pressing on and passing away and never stopping in its course. Is not this the nature of time, where the past is no more, the future does not exist, and the present escapes before being recognized? And such also is the nature of the creature which lives in time."[111] He further wrote: "Thus the writer who wisely tells us of the birth of the Universe does not fail to put these words at the head of the narrative. 'In the beginning God created;' that is to say, in the beginning of time."[112] He further says that "the first movement of time" occurred "when the formation of this world began."[113] Creation thus serves as "the training ground where they learn to know God."[114]

Gregory of Nyssa (ca. 331 – ca.396) emphasized that the divine life is exempted from all temporal distinctions unlike created things. He wrote: "The creation . . . comes into existence according to a sequence of order, and is commensurate with the duration of the ages....But the world above creation, being removed from all conception of distance, eludes all sequence of time; it has no commencement of that sort; it has no end in which to cease its advance, according to any discoverable method of order."[115] He was insistent that there is no "time-interval as existing before Creation."[116] Because God is "uncreated," his nature "escapes all distinctions of before and after."[117] He further wrote: "There is nothing by which we can measure the divine and blessed Life. It [the

Trinity] is not in time, but time flows from it; whereas the creation starting from a manifest beginning, journeys onward to its proper end through spaces of time; so that it is possible, as Solomon somewhere says, to detect in it a beginning, an end, and a middle; and mark the sequence of its history by divisions of time. But the supreme and blessed life has no time-extension accompanying its course, and therefore no span nor measure." He further said that the divine preexistent reality has "no reckoning of time."[118] He also argued: "The world's Creator laid time and space as a background to receive what was to be; on this foundation He builds the universe. It is not possible that anything which has come or is now coming into being by way of creation can be independent of space and time. But the existence which is all-sufficient, everlasting, world-enveloping, is not in space, nor in time: it is before these."[119] He concluded that "eternity is characterized by having no beginning and end." Eternity is defined "where time is not."[120] This means "extensions in time find no admittance in the Eternal Life."[121]

The belief that time had a beginning was recently confirmed by two Oxford University mathematicians/physicists, Stephen W. Hawking and Roger Penrose, who demonstrated in 1970 space-time had a beginning with a big bang singularity.[122] That is, the universe began from a single point (a singularity). This means our universe had a finite beginning approximately 15 billion years ago when an infinitesimally small, dense soup of energy (a trillionth the size of a proton in the nucleus of atom)[123] began to expand. Although this "big bang singularity" was virtually nothing in size, it contained all the matter-energy in the universe as we know it today, including all the planets, stars, and galaxies.[124]

It should be carefully noted that the universe did not begin to expand into an already existing space. Rather, the expanding universe was the expansion of space itself. Into what is space expanding if it is not more space? Relativity physics tells us the answer is— nothingness.[125] There is nothing "out there" into which space-time is expanding. Like the paradox of having to use temporal words like "before" to speak of eternity as existing prior to time, so contemporary physics has to use spatial terms like "nothingness" to speak of what space is expanding into, and it speaks of something existing before time came into being.

Space-Time as a Single Entity

Eighth, the new theology of limited omniscience assumes the outdated Newtonian physics with its view that space and time are entirely different entities. In his book, *Space and Time* (1968), Swinburne disregards relativity theory, affirming instead that "time would exist without physical objects"[126] and that "time is absolute." In an astonishing way, Swinburne says that "Newton's claims about time were correct."[127] His notion of the "universe's clock" contradicts relativity theory and his comment about "the cosmic clock ticking away" is a relic of Newtonian physics.[128]

One of the most dramatic paradigm shifts in the history of physics was the discovery that space and time are not two independent entities but a single entity woven together like a piece of fabric. This understanding of space-time was one of the consequences of Einstein's theory of special and general relativity. Special relativity says that energy is equivalent to mass times the speed of light squared ($E=MC^2$). The significance of this formula is that it shows that the tick of the clock depends on how fast things are moving. We usually think of space as having three dimensions. For example, one walks into a room and notices that it has width, length, and height. One can move back and forth in the room or climb stairs allowing us to go up or down. But we experience time quite differently. We cannot go back and forth in time. We only move forward in time. Yet when things are described in terms of very high energy (at the speed of light), space and time are seen as one thing. They appear independent in our daily lives because of our slow motion on planet Earth, but they become one as motion approaches the speed of light so that the distinction between the past, present, and future disappears. So there is no space where there is no time, and there is no time where there is no space.

The law of special relativity destroyed Newton's view of absolute time. Newton interpreted time as being the same everywhere in the universe. Whether in London or in another galaxy, the tick of the clock was the same. This is what he meant by absolute time. Just as atoms were thought to be indivisible and uniformly spread throughout absolute space without change, so time was absolute throughout the universe without any variation. Common sense based on our slow moving environment thus supposed there was no essential connection between space and time. Physical space was held to be a flat, three-dimensional continuum. Time was also imagined to be independent of space—as a separate, one-dimensional continuum, completely homogeneous along its infinite extent. Any point in time could be regarded as an origin from which to take duration past or future to any other time-instant.

Contrary to this view, Einstein showed that while space is three dimensions, time is the fourth dimension. According to special relativity, time beats at different rates, depending on how fast one (or something) moves through space. Time as measured by real clocks actually ticks differently relative to the speed of the observer.[129] Thus one's time-frame of reference depends on how fast one's physical environment is moving. Einstein's prediction about time slowing down with increasing speed has been confirmed repeatedly with atomic clocks orbiting around the earth.[130] We perceive space and time as separate entities only because we move slowly in our earthly relation to them, but the tick of the clock becomes slower with high velocity. So the idea of a universal or cosmic clock has been shown to be wrong because time is relative to one's inertial frame of reference. This means, as Heisenberg put it, "when two events are simultaneous for one observer they may not be simultaneous for another observer, if he is in motion relative to the first observer."[131]

Einstein used the paradox of the twins to explain the implications of the relativity of simultaneity.[132] If a twin name Paul takes a trip in space traveling at near the speed of light and is gone for a period of 30 years according to earth time, when he returns his earth-bound twin Peter will look thirty years older. However, the space-traveler Paul will only be a few minutes older than when he first took his space trip. All the events of thirty years in the life of his twin brother would have occurred instantly for him because his speed and the turn-around back to earth put him in a different inertial frame of reference.[133] Yet the events of thirty years in the life of his twin brother are real and not illusions. Both the instantaneity of events for Paul and the thirty years of time for Peter are equally real. The relativity of simultaneity illustrates that the concept of all times occurring instantly for God in eternity, while the events of our history are spread out in time, is an intelligible idea.

Einstein's theory of general relativity shows that space is also relative just as time is. Unlike Newton's view of absolute space, Einstein showed that matter (=condensed energy) curves space-time. Without the density of matter, there would be no curved space, and without this curvature of space there would be no gravity. Newton defined gravity as the attraction between masses, and the closer masses are to each other the stronger the force of attraction is to each other. However, Einstein showed that gravity was acceleration caused by the curvature of space.

Michio Kaku, Professor of Physics of New York City University, offers a helpful way to visualize space with the following illustration. Stretch out a bed sheet and place a rock in the center. The rock will curve the sheet in its direction. Then imagine rolling marbles around the bed sheet in a circular fashion. This circular movement is caused by the curvature of the bed sheet around the rock.[134] This is the Einsteinian definition of gravity—curved space-time causes acceleration or motion. The reason why planets orbit around the sun is because they are moving in the space curved by the density of the sun. The reason we can stand on the earth is because the earth warps the space around us. Hence we are pulled in the direction of the earth. Space cannot remain flat in the presence of matter.[135]

Motion is not "a motion in space" but rather motion is just "motion"; it is the "displacement of various spatiotemporal regions."[136] Acceleration thus depends upon the curvature of space determined by the amount of matter-energy in that space. This is illustrated in the science fiction movie, *Star Trek*. Captain Kirk uses "dilithium crystals" to power the Enterprise that is able to generate enough energy to warp space-time into pretzels. When the Enterprise travels from the earth to Alpha Centauri at "warp-factor 5," it does not physically move through space to this star; rather, the star comes to the Enterprise.[137]

Just as time is not the same for every frame of reference, so the size of spatial objects is not the same. The relativity of space means that one person may see something as being twelve inches long, but another person traveling at a much faster rate of speed will view the same object as one inch long; and both are right. This is because the faster something moves the denser its space becomes.[138]

I have been surprised to learn that some who insist that God is solely a temporal being refuse to accept Einsteinian relativity, arguing that space and time are entirely different realities. They prefer the theory of Hendrik Lorentz, who was professor of mathematical physics at the University of Leiden from 1878-1912. He was famous for his part in the development of the FitzGerald-Lorentz contraction theory, which maintained that the length of an object is contracted at relativistic speeds. He proposed the theory that as mass is increased, the length of objects is shortened, and time is dilated as the speed of light is approached.

Lorentz offered this theory of contraction in order to explain why the Michelson-Morley experiment in 1887 seemed to disprove the existence of ether.[139] Ether was thought to be a invisible substance that was evenly spread out throughout the universe. It was a notion used in the 19th century in order to explain how electromagnetic waves travel through space because it was believed these waves could not travel through "empty space." Attempts were made to verify the existence of this hypothetical substance, most notably the Michelson-Morley experiment, but this experiment disproved its existence by showing the speed of light was not altered as it moved in opposite directions. Lorentz argued that the reason why no differences were shown in the speed of light moving in opposite directions was because the instruments used by Michelson and Morley were contracted by the speed of the ether. Einstein agreed with the Lorentzian view of contraction of space and time at relativistic speeds. However, he interpreted contraction as a property of space-time, arguing that the Michelson-Morley experiment disproved the existence of ether as well as that the concept of ether was an unnecessary presupposition. Heisenberg also noted "in a conclusive way that the concept of the ether . . . had to be abandoned"[140] because the Michelson-Morley experiment offered "definite proof" that it did not exist.[141] As Čapek put it: "By the discovery of the constant velocity of light the classical mechanistic-visual model of aether was wrecked beyond repair."[142] Consequently, the notion of ether was discarded and Einstein's view that contraction is a property of space-time has been accepted universally and is the only view offered in textbooks on physics. [143]

Although only a very few philosophers and physicists continue to debate this issue, the consensus of the scientific community is that Einstein was right to interpret contraction as a property of space-time relativity.[144] The scattered attempts here and there of a few scholars to reinstate the Lorentzian notion of ether is dismissed by the larger scientific community as mythical and mistaken.[145] Hence the attempt of some religious philosophers to reinstate the notion of ether and of space and time as separate realities can be judged to be motivated by a theological agenda, which is designed to support the view that God is only a temporal being.[146]

The Half-Way Position of Polkinghorne and Peacocke

John Polkinghorne fails to appreciate the connection between contemporary physics and the Boethian view of eternity. Polkinghorne is an Anglican priest and former professor of quantum physics of Cambridge university and is deservedly a well-known author of many books on the interface between theology and science. He notes that time is relative, and he appropriately does not consider God simply a temporal being. He sees in the "divine nature a temporal pole of engagement with creation as well as, of course, an eternal pole."[147] This is consistent with the Boethian interpretation. Polkinghorne also writes: "The strongly temporal character…seems to imply that God, knowing the universe as it actually is, would know it temporally. The future would be brought into being as time evolves and it would appear that God, knowing all that can be known, would nevertheless not yet know the unformed future."[148] In a restricted sense, this is consistent with Boethius who believed that contingency was real to the essence of God. However, Polkinghorne misunderstands Boethius' basic insight that God does not know events in advance of their happening, although all events are already present to God in eternity. God's knowledge of our future thus allows for human freedom because God's sees our future but does not cause it. Polkinghorne thus confuses Boethius' view with Augustine's view of divine timelessness.

Similarly, Arthur Peacocke argues against God's knowledge of the future because he thinks this is deterministic.[149] Peacocke is also a deservedly well-known religious author who writes on the role of science and religion. Peacocke and Polkinghorne cite each other as support of their own views, and they incorporate space-time relativity in their thinking of God's relation to time.[150] In this respect, they recognize time is finite and created, and they affirm that time is fundamentally distinct from eternity. So they do not define eternity as endless time. Instead, Peacocke affirms that time is created by God.[151] Peacocke thus says that "God transcends created time as its Creator" while acknowledging "that created time is 'in God.'"[152] All of this is perfectly consistent with Boethius, but there is a basic incoherence in their thinking about God's relation to space-time relativity. Peacocke affirms that God is the Creator of space-time and that God transcends the past and present of time, but God is unable to transcend our future. The incoherence is that God is supposedly the Creator of all time, but God is unable to transcend future time. Is God then truly transcendent? Peacocke recognizes that space-time belongs together as a single entity, but if God transcends space, God necessarily transcends time; otherwise, space-time do not belong together as a single entity. Peacocke and Polkinghorne unwittingly have fallen back into a Newtonian view of space and time, as if they are independent entities.

They also fail to incorporate fully an important element of space-time relativity in their thinking—the concept of the relativity of simultaneity. On the one hand, they say God "transcends" all created times simultaneously[153]—except that God does not transcend the future. Willem Drees, a Dutch philosopher of science and religion, shows this represents a misunderstanding of relativity theory:

In the special theory of relativity the notion of simultaneity as having a universal meaning with respect to a 'now' is lost. This in turn raises serious issues for statements about God having time, being related in a special way to 'the past' or acting as to influence 'the future.' 'Past' and 'future can be used as concepts relative to a[n] observer located at some position on a specific worldline in spacetime. The problem arises when a definite article is used, speaking about 'the past' and 'the future,' as if these are global concepts. Thus, problems arise in theologies which insist that 'God's future' is open, or make other claims which assume the existence of a universal notion of time. As long as God lacks a specific location and state of motion, it is difficult to understand the meaning of God knowing 'the past' or influencing 'the future.'[154]

Drees rejects the view of Polkinghorne and Peacocke because they assume God is spatially coincident with every space-time point—except the future. Because Polkinghorne excludes God being spatially coincident with the future, Drees notes that Polkinghorne's view "is not in line with relativity theory."[155] If God transcends space as Polkinghorne and Peacocke insist, then God also transcends time—the past, present and the future. One cannot separate space and time in this way—unless one is falling back into the discredited Newtonian view of absolute space and absolute time. As Roger Penrose puts it, "it is not even "space'; it is 'space-time'."[156] Finite persons are bound by space-time, but God transcends it as Creator.

Polkinghorne's view is really a compromise between Newton's and Einstein's theory of time. He holds to the relativity of the past and present, but then falls back on a Newtonian concept of the future. Given the relativity theory of time dilation and the relativity of simultaneity itself which has been confirmed repeatedly by experiments,[157] the concept of God knowing the future is an intelligible idea that is consistent with human freedom.

Boethius' Concept was not a Block Theory of Eternity

A further weakness of the new theology of limited omniscience is that it believes Boethius held to a block view of eternity.[158]

There has been considerable debate in the history of philosophy over whether or not time is real or is like a trick of the imagination and thus a subjective state of mind. A prominent view among philosophers of science is what William James called a block view of time.[159] It considers reality to be one undifferentiated unit, or four-dimensional block, and assumes that time is only our way of measuring the way things appear to happen in space. To be sure, this view allows that there is an arrangement of things in the worldline that we can refer to as having happened sequentially, but everything that is in our future and in our past, as well in our present, depends upon our own perspective and does not have any ontological objectivity. Reality is simply fixed in a deterministic sense and the various time-frames exemplify subjectively the immutability of things.

Einstein's philosophy is an example of this view. When his lifelong friend, Michele Besso died on March 15, 1955 (four weeks before Einstein's own death), he said in a letter to the Besso family: "Now he has departed a little ahead of me from this quaint world. This means nothing. For us faithful physicists, the separation between past, present, and future has only the meaning of an illusion, though a persistent one."[160] Einstein embraced the pantheism of Spinoza and assumed that reality is one larger whole and that the constituent parts in space-time are less than real because things that are real are fixed and immutable.[161]

Relativity theory could certainly imply this subjectivism of time because it maintains there is no place in time where there is a universal present because there is no simultaneity among events in different inertial frames of reference. Rather, simultaneity varies from observer to observer and depends on one's state of motion, and hence there is no universal time-frame. There will be different perceptions of which events are in the future and which are in the past according to different inertial frames of reference, and there is no way to absolutize a particular point in space-time as the present moment. Time thus does not really flow anymore than space flows, but it is rather "*only* the phenomenon of consciousness that requires us to think in terms of a 'flowing' time."[162] This relativity of simultaneity implied to Einstein that time is an illusion and the only enduring and permanent reality is the predetermined Whole, or God.[163] Einstein said the harmony of the physical universe made it possible for him to "believe in Spinoza's God who reveals himself in the orderly harmony of being," but he rejected the personal view of God contained in Christian faith.[164]

As opposed to Einstein, Milič Čapek and Ian Barbour argue that a "block" view is incompatible with relativity theory. Čapek and Barbour point out that though some events are past for one observer in one inertial reference frame and future for another observer in a different inertial reference frame, there is a still real distinction of the past and future of the same event for all observers. This means the future does not have the possibility of causing an event to occur in the past. The relativity of simultaneity and causality are thus compatible with each.[165] This distinction among the past, present, and future is essential to Boethius's view of eternity.[166] God transcends all inertial reference frames, but the causal relation among events in the flow of time in our inertial reference frame is not negated. Hence a Boethian view of eternity assumes the realism of time as opposed to a block view. The Boethian view also explains how the objectivity of the various time-frames can be affirmed because each has its own finite reality within the unity of the divine consciousness. Because God is the infinite being who includes all things, one does not have to fall back on the subjectivizing of time as if it were only a phenomenon of human consciousness. In the final analysis, the block view of time leads to a pantheistic denial of the real world, resulting in what Hegel called acosmism.[167]

Unlike Augustine who viewed the flow of time as a subjective perception,[168] the Early Greek Church Fathers who preceded him, as well as Boethius, assumed the future is real and has not yet been decided, but because God is eternal, the undetermined future of all things is present to God. Hence the flow of time is not an illusion. The various inertial frames of reference are equally real and equally true and God knows them instantly as what they really are in themselves. The realism of time and its future openness means that God is truly "enriched" by the finite developments in the world, as Father W. Norris Clarke has argued. He shows that there is no serious reason why the idea of God as the infinite fullness of life implies "a single motionless block."[169] Although God is the infinite being, finite beings exists as well within the larger life of the Triune God.

One can use the analogy of a sentence to explain the part-whole relation of time and eternity. For example, one can create this sentence: "Eternity is the simultaneous Whole of the past, present, and future divisions of time." The division of a sentence into a subject, verb, and predicate noun are necessary to form a whole sentence with a complete thought. Without the individual words and parts of speech, there is no whole or complete thought. Yet the whole is what makes sense out of the parts. The whole is thus more than the sum of the parts, but it nonetheless depends upon the parts. Likewise, the divisions of time form the basis of one simultaneous whole existing all at once. The divisions of time as fragmented into the future, present, and past are thus incorporated into the idea of eternity, but it is eternity that gives meaning to time. To be sure, all analogies are limited, including this sentence analogy. Eternity entails more than the instant whole of time; it also includes God's boundless duration even before space-time was created and after it has ceased to be.

The Either/Or Thinking of Commonsense Literalism

The new theology of limited omniscience is snared by commonsense literalism. It thinks in terms of either/or—either God knows everything and hence there is no freedom, or else God does not know the future and hence there is freedom. Either God is timeless and thus does not interact with world history, or else God is related to the world and hence is only a temporal being. The bottom-line of this either/or thinking is that foreknowledge necessarily entails determinism. Although openness theism allows that God has some foreknowledge, those foreknown events are said to happen necessarily.

This either/or thinking is too simplistic and fails to appreciate the nature of dialectical thinking. To insist that theological language must be literal and univocal is another instance of anthropomorphism. Who God Is cannot be reduced to literal language without the loss of divine transcendence. Analytical philosophy of religion has rightly insisted on the importance of clear thinking, but it sometimes tends to obfuscate the mystery of God by assuming an anthropocentric definition of language and truth, as if something that is not said with the precision of deductive logic is not a meaningful statement. One of the decisive contributions of Michael Polanyi was his insight that even in the realm of science the idea of literal and purely objectivist language is impossible. All knowing is more tacit than explicit. Hence one knows more than one can literally tell.[170] Herein lies the limits of analytical philosophy and its assumption that reality can be uniformly defined and clearly explained. It is easy enough for such a logician, for example, to discredit the notion of eternity as duration without temporal distinctions, if one assumes a literalistic, deductive way of conceiving reality.[171]

The Early Greek Church Fathers and Boethius offered a third option to this either/or alternative. God transcends time and yet includes it. God knows everything and yet humans are genuinely free. The future is yet to be decided within our temporal frame of reference, but the future is already present in eternity. These polarities are counterintuitive to our earth-bound commonsense, and yet dialectical thinking is required to grasp the deeper significance of reality. These polarities are things that we can think, although we cannot imagine them literally as picture in our minds. To deny dialectical thinking because it is not literal language is being unnecessarily anthropomorphic. There are many truths that are accepted theologically in the Church that defy commonsense. The idea of the Triune God is not something that commonsense could have discovered. The ideas of the incarnation, virgin birth, resurrection, ascension, and return of Jesus are not commonsensical, but they are believed because they were revealed in the history of salvation. To be sure, these ideas are intelligible and thinkable, although they are counterintuitive and cannot be literally pictured. There are many things one can think but cannot picture. One can think of an infinitely sided polygon, but one cannot draw a picture of it. Herein lies the difficulty with the new theology of limited omniscience—it is misled by commonsense literalism and unable to appreciate the deeper levels of reality and its polarities, which can be thought but not literally pictured or put in a Venn diagram.

The philosophical bias in favor of commonsense literalism among the proponents of limited omniscience accounts in part for their inattention to the philosophical and theological implications of relativity physics. A. N. Whitehead noted over sixty years ago the "obvious commonsense notion [of time] has been entirely destroyed" by relativity theory, though it "still reigns supreme in the work-a-day life of mankind." [172] Whitehead notes: "One by one, every item [of the Newtonian scientific worldview] has been de-throned." [173] Likewise Čapek noted that a "Newtonian-Euclidean form of understanding" still prevails even though physicists "explicitly reject the authority of Euclid and Newton." [?] He also points out that even some scientific and philosophical "interpreters failed to draw all the consequences" of contemporary physics. [175]

One of the apparent reasons why the commonsense view of time still prevails is because the ideas of relativity seem so unbelievable. Sartori has noted "relativity is a challenge, but the challenge is in the ideas, not in the mathematics." [176] So radical is the new way of thinking that Čapek has observed that "the contemporary revolution in physics is more far-reaching than the so-called Copernican revolution in the sixteenth century." [177] He points out that one of the most revolutionary features is that time had a real beginning instead of existing before the universe came into existence. [178]

One should certainly hesitate to set aside commonsense, but relativity physics illustrates that the logic of commonsense is not always right. In this respect, Kip S. Thorne speaks of the "weird behavior of space and time" which is not observed in our everyday life because of our "slowness" as compared to the speed of light. [179] In other words, a commonsense view of time is contradicted by the way things really are, but if we could move at the near speed of light we would experience space-time as it really is. This transition to a higher speed environment would thus create a new commonsense, disproving Earth-bound commonsense. Admittedly, the paradoxical ideas of eternity—that God both transcends time and yet time is real to the essence of God—seem to be illogical from the standpoint of deductive logic. Yet if that is the way God is revealed in the history of salvation, then commonsense has to enlarge its understanding of the way things really are.

Interestingly enough, postmodern science and theology have come to recognize the limits of deductive logic because there is a measure of reality that goes beyond rational deduction. Experimental evidence in science has changed the way the world is perceived to be, and it often contradicts the logic of commonsense. This is especially true in quantum theory where experimental results contradict classical physics and forced a new way of perceiving the world.[180] Quantum physics deals with microscopic particles as packets of energy at the atomic and subatomic levels as distinct from relativity theory which deals with larger things that exists in the space-time continuum. The quantum world entails "very tiny differences in energy" among particles, although the smallness of the quantum world does not mean that its effects does not cover large distances in space.[181] It is called "quantum" because it was discovered that energy (particles) can change at this microscopic level of reality only in discrete units (or quanta) rather than in a continuous manner.[182] It is as if particles jump from one unit, or quanta, to the next rather than flowing continuously as things do in space-time.

Although quantum theory is concerned with probabilities and uncertainty, it is the most exact theory in dealing with physical reality,[183] and yet there is so much about it that puzzles scientists and contradicts formal logic. For example, a formal rule of logic is the principle of the excluded middle. This rule states that something must be one thing or another; it cannot be both. For example, a dog cannot be a cat. It is either one or the other. However, this rule does not always apply at the quantum level. For example, it has been discovered that light exhibits both electromagnetic waves and streams of particles. What is further remarkable about this phenomenon is that *"each individual particle behaves in a wavelike way entirely on its own."*[184] This weird behavior of light and particles has shocked physicists and raises the question, why?[185]

Related to this apparent contradiction of wave-particle duality is the behavior of electrons orbiting the nucleus of an atom. It is impossible for the physicist to determine both the position and the speed of an electron at the same time. It is as though the non-disruptive and non-invasive observation of the physicist introduces uncertainty into its behavior, according to Neils Bohr who was a pioneer of modern quantum theory. Bohr thus insisted on a hidden relationship between the scientist and the behavior of electrons.[186] His protégé, Werner Heisenberg, argued that scientists should not introduce philosophical assumptions into what constitutes the nature of reality, as if something exists objectively only because it is subjectively measured. Instead of saying that there exists a hidden relationship between the knower and the behavior of electrons, Heisenberg developed the principle of uncertainty, saying that experimental evidence demonstrated that there is an element of uncertainty and chance at the quantum level of reality.[187] In other words, there is no way to account for this unpredictability other than it is empirically observed.

This shocked Einstein whose pantheistic need for the perfect harmony of the universe would not permit him to believe that God would engage in "dice-playing."[188] In their friendly discussions together, Bohr humorously told Einstein that he should be "cautious" about ascribing to God human ways of thinking and telling God how to do things.[189] Einstein believed the uncertainty was simply epistemological, reflecting the physicist's inability to understand the law of nature underlying its cause.[190] However, as Stephen Hawking has noted, quantum theory has proven to be an "an outstandingly successful theory and underlies nearly all of [post]modern science and technology."[191] Hawking shows that the consensus among physicists is that the building blocks of the universe are composed of unpredictable quanta (or packets) of energy called particles. Without denying the principle of causality, it appears that chance is built right into the very structure of reality at its most elemental level.[192] A shocking fact about these particles is that one particle can occupy two places at the same time as it has been demonstrated in a two-slit experiment in which a beam of electrons was fired through a pair of narrow slits to a screen behind.[193]

Formal logic is thus not very reliable in dealing with the quantum level. Werner Heisenberg said if one insists on "complete logical clarity," then that "would make science impossible."[194] Roger Penrose has argued the human mind exceeds the computational method of mathematics and logic and that science is unable to explain the conscious activity of the brain. He argues that the mind is capable of engaging in non-computational understanding that transcends mathematics and logic.[195] This human trait, he believes, is something that computers or artificial intelligence cannot do, and it underscores the uniqueness of conscious thinking. Mathematics and logic are important tools for explaining things, but they have their limitations because there is a dimension of truth that is derived from the non-mathematical activity of conscious thinking in general.[196]

This non-mathematical and intuitive grasp of things corresponds to the inexplicable nature of reality itself. For example, a logical conundrum in relativity physics is the behavior of the speed of light. The one absolute in relativity physics is the speed of light. Everything else is measured relative to it. No matter how fast different things travels, their comparable speeds have no bearing on their relation to the speed of light. If one vehicle is going 1000 miles an hour and another vehicle is only going 1 mile an hour and if they both are trying to catch up to a beam of light, they would in fact find themselves the same distance from it, and the faster vehicle would show no signs of gaining on the slower moving vehicle relative to the speed of light because both would be 186,000 miles per second behind the light beam. The speed of light is absolutely the same no matter what one's inertial frame of reference is. This was a shocking discovery to Einstein, [197] but it has revolutionized our understanding the way the world really is. Time is thus relative to the speed of light as the one physical absolute. One way to put this is to say that the speed of light has no future time; it is the future. The past, present, and future are instantly the same moment with light.

If one wanted to move into the future, one could do this if one could technologically develop a space machine that would allow us to travel at or near the speed of light. The faster one moves the lesser the time difference among the past, present, and future, until there is no temporal distinctions at all when one reaches the speed of light. Time only emerges as the result of slowing down to speeds less than the speed of light. Like the definition of eternity, one can refer to the speed of light as the instantaneous whole of all time. The whole is the speed of light; its fragmentation (slowing down) is the meaning of time. This may explain in part why Einstein himself held to the idea that actual time was only measurement and the speed of light served as his model of reality where there is only the pantheistic Whole without differentiation.

The difference between the speed of light as an absolute and the relative speeds of time could also serve as a Boethian model of eternity where the speed of light represents the past, present, and future constituting one single whole and the relative speeds of time constituting the reality of temporal distinctions. The difference between Einstein and Boethius is that for Einstein time was only measurement and was not an essential aspect of reality, whereas for Boethius time is an essential part of the meaning of human life and is included within the Triune life of God.

Pannenberg's eschatological ontology is thus consistent with the logic of relativity physics. This of course does not prove that his ontology is correct, but it does show that his ontology is intelligible. The concept of God as the power of the future is thus no more unintelligible than the idea of relativity physics.

Can the Past Really Be Changed?

One of the key notions in relativity theory is the arrow of time. We can move back and forth and up and down in space, but we cannot go back in time. Newton considered time to be like an arrow that moves in a straight path toward its target, but Einstein shows that time is more like a mighty river that often zigzags through valleys and plains. Matter-energy might briefly shift the direction of time, but generally the river of time flows smoothly forward, never reversing itself.[198]

J. Richard Gott, a professor of astrophysical science at Princeton University, shows that travel to the future is a real possibility because as objects approach the speed of light they move into a different time-frame, but an object would have to travel faster than the speed of light to go back in time. Because the speed limit in the universe is the speed of light, travel into the past is not possible,[199] but if there was the right technology available that would also keep one from being flattened like a pancake travel into the future is possible Gott asks: "Do you want to visit Earth 1,000 years from now? Einstein showed how to do it. All you have to do is get into a spaceship, go to a star a bit less than 500 light-years away, and return, traveling both ways at 9.995 percent of the speed of light. When you come back, Earth will be 1,000 years older, but you will be only 10 years older." He explains that "such speed is possible" because "in our largest particle accelerators we bring protons to speeds higher than this (the best so far has been 99.999946 percent of the speed of light, at Fermilab).[200]

Highly reputable astrophysicists embrace a theory of the universe known as the theory of higher-dimensions (superstring theory), which theoretically allows for time travel.[201] Although he does not hold to the superstring theory, Stephen Hawking, universally recognized as the most brilliant mathematician and cosmologist in the world, once believed that travel into the past was theoretically possible. He believed in the possibility of people coming from the future who would meet us in the present. He abandoned this belief when one of his students convinced him that his mathematical equation was mistaken.[202]

Do you remember the movie, *Back to the Future?* Michael J. Fox travels back in time and there he meets his own parents as teenagers before they were married. His own mother falls in love with him and rejects his father. The troubling possibility is that he may never be born if his parents never marry and have children, and he will then evaporate into nothingness.

This movie is of course science fiction, but in 1988 physicist Kip Thorne of the California Institute of Technology and his associates proposed that time travel, which can alter the course of the past as well as propel one in to the future, is a serious theoretical idea. This view was published in a highly respected journal, *Physical Review Letters*, arguing that it is consistent with Einstein theory of relativity and quantum physics.[203] To be sure, it is not expected that such a theoretical possibility would ever become an actuality because there is not enough energy necessary to probe the higher dimensions of space-time.   Supposedly there was only once when enough energy was available to accomplish this task, and that was the moment of the Big Bang.[204]

In 1949 Einstein was disturbed by the thought of time travel proposed by one of his close colleagues and friends, Kurt Gödel, who was a colleague with Einstein at the Institute for Advanced Study at Princeton. Using Einstein's field equations, Gödel showed that time could be bent into a circle if cosmic dust and gas in space are rotating. This would then mean that time travel is physically possible. Einstein dismissed this idea because it was not experimentally shown that cosmic dust and gas were rotating. Scientific instruments have now shown that the universe is expanding instead of rotating.[205] However, if cosmic dust and gas did rotate, time travel would be a possibility.

Although we are not able to move into the past and alter events that have happened because we cannot move faster than the speed of light, a basic biblical belief is that God as Creator is able to redeem the past and free us from its ultimate consequences. Because our temporal past continues to be in God's eternal present,[206] God is able to redeem the past and transform it into a New Creation by virtue of Jesus' life, death, and resurrection. This transformation entails a real transformation of the past and not just an overhaul of the present. In an qualified sense, divine forgiveness means the past is blotted out or erased and one is no longer held accountable for it. This idea of one's sins being erased or blotted out is frequently mentioned in Scripture. "I, I am He who blots out (Heb. *machah*, erase, obliterate, wipe out) your transgressions for my own sake, and I will not remember your sins" (Jer. 43:25). "Repent therefore, and turn again, that you sins may be blotted out (Gr. *exaleipho*, erase, obliterate, wipe out)." (Acts 3:19).

Redemption means that the past is forgiven, changed, and remembered no more (Isaiah 43:25). The hymn writer put it this way: "My sin—not in part, but the whole—is nailed to the cross and I bear it no more." To be sure, there are lingering consequences for sinful past actions even for the redeemed here and now, but the eschatological hope is that the sinful past will be completely wiped clean and the scars and evil consequences of the past will be removed, and in eternity we will live in the perfection and the fullness of God's Trinitarian life. Then there will be no bad memories and no more sorrow and sighing (Rev 21,22). Just as there was a beginning of time, so there will be an end of time (Rev. 10:6),[207] and everything will be made new (Rev. 21:5).

If one of the implications of relativity theory is that the past of one observer is present to an observer in a different time-frame, it is even more so an implication of salvation history that the past can be changed because it is immediately accessible to God. This is one of the implications of the doctrine of justification by faith—that one's past is not only forgiven but it is just as if one had never sinned. The believer's past that has been marred by sin is erased and no longer exists, and its consequences will be completely wiped out in the eschatological future when space-time will cease and a new earth will come into being (Rev. 21:1) A Boethian concept of eternity shows that forgiveness of the past and its rectification in Jesus Christ is not just a legal notion that merely declares the past is blotted out, but it is really and completely erased in the eschatological future. There are other clarifications that a Boethian interpretation of eternity offers as well, especially in regard to the meaning of petitionary prayer and the continuity of salvation history from its beginning to its end.[208]

Limited Omniscience Undermines Confidence in God

Finally, the new theology of limited omniscience introduces uncertainty and incompleteness into the idea of eternal life. If God is fragmented into a past, present, and future, there is no "fullness of life" and the believer has no sure confidence as he or she looks to the future. Pastorally, the implication of a Boethian interpretation of eternity are enormous. Barth has shown that God exists in "pure duration" and we "exist from one time to another." Because God's duration is boundless and not limited by time, "He can be and will be true to Himself, and we can and may put our trust in Him."[209]

"I AM . . . the Omega, . . . the Last, . . . and the End"

I hope it is evident now why I said at the beginning of this book nothing should be claimed for theology that is not also history. To make a divorce between faith and history is to undermine the transcendent unity of the world in God. At the same time, I hope it is clearer why this unity is not a monism. Although transcending space-time, God embraces the world as its Creator. Creation is a fundamental doctrine because it serves as the basis for understanding that God is cosmologically transcendent. Without an adequate doctrine of God as Creator, the history of salvation is aborted, as Bultmann assumed. This is because the creation of space-time served as the setting for the history of salvation, which began with the call of Abraham (Genesis 12). A decisive moment in this history was the revelation of God's name to Moses as "I AM WHO I AM" (Exodus 3:14). Jesus is presented in the Gospel of John in a series of disclosures as "I AM." For example, Jesus said: "Before Abraham was, I am" (John 8:58). Paul Ricoeur believes that Revelation 1:4—"the one who is, and who was, and who is coming"—is a re-translation of Exodus 3:14.[210]

It is fitting that theology should understand the being of God ("I Am") as the eternal present of all times—the past, the present, and the future: "Holy, holy, holy, is the Lord God Almighty, who was and is and is to come!" (Rev. 4:8). John the Revelator specifically said that the past, the present, and the future already exists for God in the present moment: "*I am the Alpha and the Omega, the first and the last, the beginning and the end.*" (Rev. 22:13). At least, the Early Church Fathers understood John to mean that God is the sovereign "I AM" for whom all times exist in God's eternal "now." Because God transcends all temporal distinctions, God can "show to his servants" what will take place in the future (Rev. 22:6).

Omniscience and freedom, God and the world, faith and history, eternity and time, the subjective and objective poles of reality, are mutually inclusive concepts because God as a tri-personal reality is the transcendent power of the unbounded future. Without the personal and transcendent character of God, the world would evaporate into a sub-jective perception of human consciousness or would be explained away in terms of a pantheistic monism. According to Boethius, the world is real because all things exist instantly and perfectly in God. What gives the world its authenticity is that space-time is being drawn toward the eschatological future of all things in God. We are free to participate or not to participate in this eschatological future through faith in Jesus Christ, whose life, death, resurrection, and the outpouring of his Holy Spirit on the day of Pentecost, initiate us into the kingdom of God.

In the eschatological future, all the imperfections and fragmentations of temporal life will be transformed in eternity by the fullness of the divine life. Boethius personally found great comfort in this hope because of the difficulties that he found himself entangled with, which led to his own execution by his political enemies. He wrote *The Consolation of Philosophy* during his trial and imprisonment, which was based on charges that he denied.[211] In eternity, there will be no more buried and hurt memories of the past, no tribulations in the present, and no fears and uncertainties of the future. All will be bliss in the eschaton as mem-bers of the kingdom of God enjoy eternal fellowship with Jesus (Revelation 21:1-7; 22:1-5).

It is important to note that this eternal fellowship will not entail a bodiless existence, but our temporal existence will be transformed into a "spiritual body" as it is raised by the Holy Spirit into the likeness of Jesus' resurrected body (1 Corinthians 15). It can also be argued that the idea of an intermediate state between death and the final resurrection is not necessary because when one dies one already participates in the future glory of the eschatological hope. Eternity thus is real duration in the concreteness of bodily existence as we are incorporated into the Triune life of God. We frankly do not know what eternal life will be like because we can only see through a glass darkly in our temporal exis-tence (1 Cor. 13:12) but we hope for the perfection and fullness of life freed from the fragmentation of time with its often unnerving sequences of the past, present, and an uncertain future. We have good reason for this hope because we have become "new creations" and "the old has passed away, behold, the new has come" (2 Cor. 5:17) After his resurrec-tion, Jesus was no longer constrained by gravitational force produced by the curvature of space and he was not limited by the arrow of time as his resurrection appearances and ascension to his Father demonstrated. We have hope because we expect to be like Jesus Christ when he appears the second time in the eschaton (1 John 3:2).

As opposed to the dualistic thinking of modern thought that made it virtually impossible to talk about God and history, Pannenberg's eschatological ontology integrates faith and history, showing how God is the transcendent unity of all polarities that characterize our space-time environment. "He is before all things, and in him all things hold together" (Co. 1:17). The history of salvation that was begun with Abraham will culminate in the eschatological future when God will be all in all.

Notes

1. Boethius, *The Consolation of Philosophy*, Book V, trans. A. B. Walter from *Boethii Philosophiae consolatio*, V, ed. L. Bieler, *Corpus Christianorum Series Latina*, Vol. 94 (Turnholti: Brepols, 1957) in *Medieval Philosophy*, ed. John F. Wippel and Allan B. Wolter (New York: The Free Press, 1969), 92. Cited hereafter as *The Consolation of Philosophy*.

2. Pannenberg, *Theology and the Kingdom of God*, 127-143

3. Hilary Putnam, "Time and Physical Geometry," *Journal of Philosophy* 64.8 (April 27, 1967): 240-247.

4. Werner Heisenberg, *Physics and Philosophy: The Revolution in Modern Science* (London: George Allen and Unwin, 1959), 88-92, 144-145, 196ff.

5. Roger Penrose, *Shadows of the Mind* (Oxford: Oxford University Press, 1994), 50.

6. Richard Sorabji is one contemporary philosopher among many who acknowledge that relativity theory can be used to support the logical coherence of eternity, although he does not agree with it and does not profess to be an orthodox Christian. Sorabji, *Time, Creation, and the Continuum* (Ithaca, NY: Cornell University Press, 1983), 254.

7. Pannenberg, *Systematic Theology*, 1:403-404.

8. Barth, *Church Dogmatics*, 2.1.609.

9. Cf. Eleonore Stump and Norman Kretzmann, "Eternity," *The Journal of Philosophy* 78.8 (August 1981): 444-447. Richard Sorabji disagrees with the interpretation of Stump and Kretzmann. Sorabji apparently thinks that Stump and Kretzmann were defining "duration" as a temporally "extended duration," which he denies as representative of Boethius. Cf. Sorabji, *Time, Creation, and the Continuum*, 120. However, Stump and Kretzmann show that by "extended duration" they had in mind the idea of extension as an infinite, pastless and futureless duration rather than a temporal one, noting that this idea "entails duration of a special sort." Eleonore Stump and Norman Kretzmann, "Eternity," *The Journal of Philosophy* 78.8 (August 1981): 433. Sorabji missed this important qualifier, and his own rejection of the Boethian view is based on his *a priori* presupposition that the concept of a God who transcends time could not have omniscience because this kind of God would not even know what was happening in time. Cf. *Time, Creation, and Continuum*, 257-260. Paul Fitzgerald criticized the idea of eternity of Stump and Kretzmann on the grounds that "extended

duration" is not an intelligible idea. Cf. Fitzgerald, "Stump and Kretzmann on Time and Eternity," *Journal of Philosophy* 82 (May 1985), 260-269. Stump and Kretzmann responded by showing that Fitzgerald had misunderstood their idea of "infinite duration" by criticizing it "in terms of ordinary temporal connotations." Stump and Kretzmann, "Atemporal Duration," *Journal of Philosophy*, 84 (April 1987): 218. They rejected the idea that infinite duration entails the idea of time being spread out in a finite way. Rather, time is an indivisible whole in eternity. (Ibid., 219). Although infinite, extended duration is not an extension in time, the extensions of time are really present in eternity in a simultaneous moment. Stump and Kretzmann, "Atemporal Duration," *Journal of Philosophy*, 84 (April 1987): 214-219. Brian Leftow offers a thorough analysis of the Boethian meaning of duration. He argues Boethius implies that eternity is duration, but Leftow nuances it differently than Stump and Kretzmann, calling it "partless extension," which entails the notion of quasi-temporal eternity. Cf. Brian Leftow, *Time and Eternity* (Ithaca, NY: Cornell University Press, 1991), 112-146.

10. Wesley, "On Eternity," *The Works of John Wesley, Sermons* (Nashville: Abingdon Press, 1985), 2:358. Cited hereafter as Wesley, *Sermons*.

11. Ibid., 1:359.

12. Ibid., 2:360.

13.Cf. Leo Sartori, *Understanding Relativity, A Simplified Approach to Einstein's Theories* (Berkeley: University of Califiornia Press, 1996), 301; George Smoot and Keay Davidson, *Wrinkles in Time* (New York: William Morrow and Company, Inc., 1993), 57-58, 292.J. R. Gott III, *Time Travel in Einstein's Universe* (New York: Houghton Mifflin Co, 2001), 161.

14. Cullmann, *Christ and Time*, trans. Floyd V. Wilson (London: SCM Press, 1962), 70.

15. Ibid., 62-63.

16. Ibid., 70-71.

17. Richard Swinburne, *The Coherence of Theism*, revised edition (Oxford: Clarendon Press, 1993), 225.

18. Swinburne, *The Coherence of Theism,* 225

19. Swinburne, *Is There A God?* (New York: Oxford University Press, 1995) 9.

20. Ibid., 8.

21. For a more recent discussion of open theism, cf. *Divine Foreknowledge: Four Views*, ed. Paul Eddy and James Beilby (Downers Grove, Illinois: InterVarsity Press, 1991).

22. Clark Pinnock, "Systematic Theology," *The Openness of God* (Downers Grove, Illinois: InterVarsity Press, 1994), 123.

23. Cf. Swinburne, *The Coherence of Theism*, 176n., 225n. Swinburne, *The Christian God* (Oxford: Clarendon Press, 1994), 131n.

24. Eleonore Stump and Norman Kretzmann have also shown that Pike misrepresents Boethius and that his arguments are "confused," particularly with his claim that the idea of a being who transcends time cannot also include time.

Cf. Eleonore Stump and Norman Kretzmann, "Eternity," *The Journal of Philosophy* 78.8 (August 1981):448-458. Pike's arguments only "proves" what he already assumes, namely, that God is necessarily temporal because only a being who is altogether temporal can engage in temporal activities. This is a circular argument. Stump and Kretzmann show that eternity includes both temporality and atemporality and that it does not entail the idea of a "frozen instant." Eleonore Stump and Norman Kretzmann, "Eternity," *The Journal of Philosophy* 78.8 (August 1981): 430. They further argue that the relation between time and eternity is a coherent one. Ibid., 435ff.

25. Nelson Pike, *God and Timelessness* (New York: Schocken Books, 1970), 55-56.

26. Ibid., 83.

27. Boethius, *The Consolation of Philosophy*, 86.

28. Ibid., 94.

29. Ibid., 93.

30. Ibid., 94.

31. Ibid. 94.

32. Ibid. 95.

33. Richard Sorabji, *Time, Creation, and the Continuum*, 256.

34. Ibid. 95.

35. Ibid. 96.

36. Ibid. 93.

37. Boethius, *Consolation of Philosophy*, 96.

38. For a debate of this issue in contemporary philosophy, cf. Brian Leftow, *Time and Eternity* (Ithaca, New York: Cornell University, 1991), 159-182.

39. Ibid., 95.

40. Ibid., 86.

41. Pike, *God and Timelessness*, 78ff.

42. Brian Leftow, "Eternity and Simultaneity," *Faith and Philosophy* 8 (1991): 165. Cf. Brian Leftow, *Time and Eternity* (Ithaca, New York: Cornell University, 1991), 165-168.

43. Pike, *God and Timelessness*, 83.

44. Pannenberg, *Systematic Theology*, 1:405.

45. Feuerbach, *The Essence of Christianity*, trans. George Eliot, 307.

46. Nelson Pike, *God and Timelessness*, 110.

47. Ibid., 1

48. Feuerbach, *The Essence of Christianity*, 339.

49. Basil, "The Hexaemeron," *Nicene and Post-Nicene Fathers*, ed. Philip Schaff and Henry Wace (Peabody, Mass: Hendrickson, 1994), 8:54. Cf. W. Norris Clarke, "Christian Theism and Whiteheadian Process Thought," *Process Theology*, 231-232, who points out that since the first Greek Fathers the concept of the infinite has been a "common doctrine of all Christians." Cf. Pannenberg, *Systematic Theology* 1:342.

50. Ibid., 1:397.

51. This was Hegel's main criticism of Kant's deistic concept of the infinite. Hegel, *Science of Logic*, 1: 150-152.

52. Cf. Pannenberg, *Systematic Theology*, 1:342.

53. "Origen Against Celsus," *Ante-Nicene Fathers*, 4:253

54. Gregory of Nyssa, "Against Eunomius, Book I," *Nicene and Post-Nicene Fathers*, ed. Philip Schaff and Henry Wace (Peabody, Mass: Hendrickson, 1994), 5:97-100.

55. Ibid.

56. In his defense of openness theism, Michael R. Saia in his book (with a foreword by Gregory A. Boyd) *Does God Know the Future?* (Fairfax, VA: Xulon Press, 2002) omits the view of the Early Christian Apologists and the Early Greek Fathers in his history of the doctrine of foreknowledge and eternity. Saia thus fails to see there is another meaning of eternity than the idea of sheer time-lessness or everlasting time.

57. Gerhard May, *Creatio Ex Nihilo, The Doctrine of "Creation out of Nothing" in Early Christian Thought* (T. T. Clark, 1994), 176.

58. Swinburne, *The Christian God*, 137-138.

59. "Irenaeus Against Heresies," *Ante-Nicene Fathers, Justin Martyr, Ireneaus*, ed. Alexander Roberts and James Donaldson (Peabody, Mass: Hendrickson Publishers, 1994), 1:400.

60. Ibid., 1:566.

61. Ibid., 4:440.

62. Gregory of Nyssa, "Answer to Eunomius' Second Book," *Nicene and Post-Nicene Fathers*, 5:296.

63. Boethius, *The Consolation of Philosophy*, 92.

64. Richard Sorabji, *Time, Creation, and the Continuum*, 114f.

65. Ibid., 115-117.

66. Boethius, *The Consolation of Philosophy*, 93.

67. Ibid., 94.

68. Ibid.

69. Sorabji, *Time, Creation, and the Continuum*, 102, 255-156.

70. Brian Leftow argues the claim that "God is timeless" does not entail a verb that is tensed or tenseless. Rather it is "eternal-tensed." He maintains that eternity requires its own special tense as opposed to tensed verbs which have a time reference. *Time and Eternity*, 61-62.

71. Sorabji, *Time, Creation, and the Continuum*, 255-256.

72. Ibid., 256.

73. Ibid.

74. Helen M. Barrett, *Boethius* (Cambridge University Press, 1940), 133.

75. Cf. Wolfhart Pannenberg, *Systematic Theology* 1.404.

76. *Church Dogmatics*, 2.1.610ff; Cf. Pannenberg, *Systematic Theology* 1:404n.

77. *Church Dogmatics*, 2.1.611; Cf. Pannenberg, *Systematic Theology* 1:404n.

78. *Church Dogmatics.*, 2.1.610-611.

79. Swinburne, *The Christian God*, 137.

80. Wesley, *Sermons*, 2:420, "Predestination,"

81. Wesley published an article in *The Arminian Magazine*, 8 (1785): 336, by "a late author," which was entitled, "On the Eternity of God." It was a critique of Locke's view of "duration," defending Boethius's concept of eternity.

82. Some American theologians initiated what they call "the openness of God" theology" as an alternative to "the traditional Christian view" (=Calvinism). Their main concern is pastoral and devotional, and they want to preserve human freedom that has been vitiated by Calvinism. Unfortunately, they did not take their cues from Barth and Pannenberg on divine omniscience and thus they did not consider that Boethius and the Early Greek Church Fathers offered a way to reconcile divine foreknowledge and human freedom. Cf. *The Openness of Being*, ed. by Clark Pinnock, et al. (Downers Grove, Illinois: InterVarsity Press, 1994).

83. Wesley, *Sermons*, 2:417, "On Predestination."

84. Ibid.

85. For a discussion of Wesley's opposition to absolute predestination, see my discussion in *The Meaning of Pentecost in Early Methodism, Rediscovering John Fletcher As Wesley's Vindicator and Designated Successor* (Lanham, MD: Scarecrow Press, 2003).

86. Edmond Jacob, *Theology of the Old Testament*, trans. Arthur W. Heathcote and Philip J. Allcock (New York: Harper and Brothers Publishers, 1958), 39.

87. Origen, "Origen De Principiis," *Ante-Nicene Fathers*, 4:253. The authors of *The Openness of God* (1994) have rightly argued that biblical anthropomorphisms show that God responds to human freedom and that his actions are conditioned by human choices, but then these authors take a big leap in their argument to conclude that therefore God does not know the future. This is a *non sequitor*. Nor did they draw from other resources such as the Early Greek Church Fathers who offered a solution to this problem. Cf. *The Openness of God*, 30,55.

88. "The Stromata, or Miscellanies," *The Ante-Nicene Fathers*, 2:460.

89. Richard Swinburne, *Is There A God?*, 8.

90. Gerhard von Rad, *Old Testament Theology*, trans. D. M. G. Stalker (Edinburgh: Oliver and Boyd, 1962), 2:242.

91. Ibid.

92. Ibid.

93. Ibid.

94. Ibid., 2:248.

95. Ibid., 2:311.

96. Ibid, 2:312.

97. Ibid, 2:313.

98. Ibid., 2:315.

99. Ibid., 2:314.

100. Pannenberg, *Systematic Theology*, 1:402.

101. "The First Apology of Justin," *Ante-Nicene Fathers*, 1:172-3.

102. Ibid., 1:
103. Ibid.. 1:177.
104. "Irenaeus Against Heresies," *Ante-Nicene Fathers,* 1: 401.
105. Ibid., 1:401.
106. Ibid., 1:399.
107. Richard Rice in his essay on "Biblical Support for a New Perspective," in *The Openness of God* (30-55) cites numerous passages that show God has foreknowledge, but he largely sidesteps their meaning and minimizes their predictive element by expounding on the nature of human freedom that is assumed in the Scripture. His basic working assumption is that divine foreknowledge and human freedom are contradictory, and hence he assumes that the biblical texts on foreknowledge do not really mean that God knows the future! The weakness of this view is well expressed in the authors' own terms when they admit: "We do not believe that this view is capable of 'proof' in any hard sense. We know that our arguments are open to question" (9-10). A basic weakness of the "openness of God" movement is that it did not consider the third option of Boethius. It is also merely assumed a commonsense view of time and ignored relativity physics. .
108. Cf. Gregg Boyd, "Open-Theism View," *Divine Foreknowledge: Four Views,* ed. James K. Beilby and Paul R. Eddy (Downers Grove, Illinois: InterVarsity Press, 2001), 14.
109 Cf. S. Hope, "The Truth of God Defended, A Letter to the Editor," *The Methodist Magazine* 42 (April 1819): 257-261.
110. "Irenaeus Against Heresies," *Ante-Nicene Fathers,* 1:400.
111. Basil, "The Hexaemeron," *Nicene and Post-Nicene Fathers,* 8:54.
112. Ibid. 8:55.
113. Ibid. 8:55.
114. Ibid. 8:55.
115. Gregory of Nyssa, "Against Eunomius, Book I," *Nicene and Post-Nicene Fathers,* 5:69.
116. Ibid., 5:69.
117. Ibid., 5:69.
118. Ibid., 5:69.
119. Ibid., 5:69.
120. Ibid., 5:99.
121. Ibid., 5:100.
122. *A Brief History of Time* (London: Bantam Books, 1988), 50.
123. George Smoot and Keay Davidson, *Wrinkles in Time,* 180.
124. For a popular discussion of space-time by the world's leading theoretical physicist, see Stephen Hawking, *A Brief History of Time;* Steve Hawking and Roger Penrose, *The Nature of Space and Time* (Princeton: NJ: Princeton University Press, 1996); Steven Weinberg, *The First Three Minutes: A Modern View of the Origin of the Universe* (New York: Basic Books, 1977). For a more technical but readable explanation, cf. A Shadowitz, *Special Relativity*

(Philadelphia: W. B. Saunders Company, 1968). Also cf. Leo Sartori, *Understanding Relativity, A Simplified Approach to Einstein's Theories* (Berkeley: University of California Press, 1996). For a specifically Christian approach, cf. R. G. Mitchell, *Einstein and Christ, A New Approach to the Defence of the Christian Religion* (Edinburgh: Scottish Academic Press, 1987); David Wilkinson, *God, the Big Bang, and Stephen Hawking* (Crowborough, East Sussex: Monarch, 1996), 88; Willem B. Drees, *Creation From Nothing Until Now* (New York: Routledge, 2002).

125. Cf. Leo Sartori, *Understanding Relativity*, 301; Smoot, *Wrinkles in Time*, 57-58, 292.

126. Swinburne, *Space and Time* (London: Macmillan, 1968), 208.

127. Ibid., 245.

128. Swinburne, *The Christian God*, 143-144. American process theology holds a more credible view of God and time than the "openness of God" movement because it incorporates relativity theory in its view. In this respect, I believe that the "openness of God" theism is an unintended apologetic for process theology because of the inadequacies of its Newtonian perspective.

129. Shadowitz, *Special Relativity*, 2.

130. Michio Kaku, *Hyperspace* (New York: Doubleday, 1994), 85.

131. Heisenberg, *Physics and Philosophy*, 116.

132. S. Shadowitz, *Special Relativity* (Philadelphia: W. B. Saunders Company, 1968), 43.

133. Cf. Sartori, *Understanding Relativity*, 195ff. As Milič Čapek put it, in the special theory of relativity, time dilation is a "quasi-perspective distortion resulting from the relative motion of two inertial systems and perfectly reciprocal in both systems, [but] in the former [the general theory of relativity] it is an actual modification of the proper time itself." Milič Čapek, *The Philosophical Impact of Contemporary Physics* (New York: D. Van Nostrand Company, Inc, 1961), 200. This means time itself is modified and lengthened by the action of the curvature of space-time.   As Sartori shows, the "paradox of the twins" is resolved when it is seen that what makes the space-traveling twin younger than the one who stays on earth is the "turnaround" when the twin shifts from one inertial frame to another. (Sartori, *Understanding Relativity*, 194). It was this recognition of the two theories of special relativity and general relativity being combined, along with experimental evidence, that ended the controversy over time dilation in the 1950's and 1960's. For a larger discussion of special and general relativity in understanding the relativity of simultaneity, cf. Čapek, *The Philosophical Impact of Contemporary Physics*, 199-205.

134. Michio Kaku, *Hyperspace*, 91.

135. Sartori, *Understanding Relativity*, 277.

136. Čapek, *The Philosophical Impact of Contemporary Physics*, 267.

137. Kaku, *Hyperspace*, 227.

138. A. Shadowitz, *Special Relativity*, 48.

139. For a history of the idea of ether and the disproof of its existence, cf.

Abraham Pais, *'Subtle is the Lord . . .' The Science and the Life of Albert Einstein* (New York: Oxford University Press, 1982), 20-21, 111-134.

140. Heisenberg, *Physics and Philosophy*, 96.

141. Ibid., 112.

142. Čapek, *The Philosophical Impact of Contemporary Physics*, 251.

143. Sartori, *Understanding Relativity*, 199n.

144. William Lane Craig is worried that if one takes relativity theory literally one will succumb to positivism, but I do not see this as a problem. Relativity theory and the big bang theory only tell us what is true about the physical universe (space-time). Willem Drees has noted that the patristic idea that time was created (*creatio cum tempore*) is today "a reasonable interpretation of most contemporary cosmologies" *Beyond the Big Bang*, 127. Craig wants to talk about a philosophical concept of time that is not scientific time. However, the only time we know is the time that science has described as existing, revealing that our commonsense explanation is wrong. To talk about a philosophy of time that is not a "philosophy of *physical* time and space" seems Gnostic. The Bible assumes the realism of space and time as the setting for salvation history. To minimize time as we experience it is similar to the theology of Gnosticism that denied the real existence of the concrete world. Much of the ongoing discussion among American analytical philosophers of religion, particularly in the broadly orthodox tradition, seem to prefer Newton to Einstein. Craig specifically defends Lorentzian relativity, which preserves Newton's idea of the separation of space and time. Cf. Craig, "The Special Theory of Relativity and Theories of Divine Eternity," *Faith and Philosophy* 11.1 (January 1994), 19-37, especially 26. Also cf. Craig, *Time and Eternity* (Wheaton, ILL; Crossway Books, 2001), 38-66.

145. William Lane Craig has argued for the existence of ether, which he believes Bell's Theorem supports. Bell's Theorem entails what Einstein referred to as "spooky action at a distance," which is the idea that separated particles of energy at the quantum level can influence each other at extreme distances apart. Cf. Roger Penrose, *Shadows of the Mind* (Oxford: Oxford University Press, 1994), 294. When a electron is split in half and both halves spin off in entirely different directions, they remain entangled with each other and are in immediate contact even though they may be miles apart. Physicists have proved this to be the case by altering the spin of one part of the electron and have observed that the other half immediately responds in the same way. This seems to be in conflict with relativity theory that says that nothing travels faster than the speed of light. How does this happen? William Lane Craig says the concept of the ether is needed to account for this. Cf. Craig, *Time and Eternity*, 54-56. However, Roger Penrose has shown that the embedded electrons are not communicating information. This is known because it is not possible for technology to use the separated parts of the particle for sending information. Hence the strange behavior of the separated parts of an embedded particle do not violate special relativity theory that the speed of light is absolute. By being embedded, the two

halves still function as one particle. Penrose, *Shadows of the Mind*, 246-9, 294. Penrose shows that although quantum physics deals with things with a very small size like molecules, atoms, and subatomic particles, "quantum-level effects can occur across vast separations." The behavior of these very small things cannot be understood on the basis of space-time relativity, but this does not mean that space-time relativity has been violated.. Penrose, *Shadows of the Mind*, 256; Penrose, *The Emperor's New Mind. Concerning Computers, Minds, and The Laws of Physics* (New York: Oxford University Press, 1989), 282ff, 286f.

146. William Lane Craig has argued for the Lorentzian view of relativity in which space and time are separate entities. He uses Lorentzian relativity as a basis for maintaining that God became temporal after creation, while allowing that God transcends space. Before creation, Craig argues that God was timeless. He also argues that there is only one time in the universe. Craig is afraid the Einsteinian relativity of simultaneity turns God into a relativistic being and makes it impossible to talk about God as the eternal Now. Cf. Craig, *Time and Eternity*, 43. I do not understand why he thinks this. God's eternity transcends all times and yet all times are equally and simultaneously present in God. W. Norris Clarke has made this same point in his critique of Whiteheadian process thought. According to relativity theory, there is no single time-framework for the whole cosmos. Instead of one "now" there are many "nows." Which time-framework is God's? If one says that all time-frameworks are in God's unity of consciousness, then God must transcend time. But process theology makes God a wholly temporal being and hence it contains an irreconcilable contradiction. Cf. W. Norris Clarke, "Christian Theism and Whiteheadian Process Philosophy," *Process Theology*, ed. Ronald Nash (Grand Rapids: Baker Book House, 1987), 241-2. Craig and those who propose God is totally temporal try to avoid the relativistic implications of a temporal God by denying the validity of Einsteinian space-time relativity. This does not seem to be a productive argument considering that the concept of the ether was disproved by the Michelson-Morley experiment and is universally discredited in the scientific community. I do not believe one would be able to find a contemporary university textbook that would support Lorentzian relativity over against Einstein. Cf. Craig, "God and the Beginning of Time," *International Philosophical Quarterly* 41 (2001): 17-31. Process theology denies God knows the future, but Craig (unlike others in the openness of God movement) affirms divine foreknowledge. He identifies with the openness of God movement because he wants to affirm God's openness to future events. Craig espouses Molinism, which says that God infallibly foreknows all possible future human choices and thus God plans for the future accordingly. This is known as "middle knowledge" because God foreknows how any rational agent would freely act under any possible circumstances; hence God's decrees are made subsequently to this knowledge. God's actions are thus coordinated with the results of this foreknowledge in order to present the best possible scenario for the human reception of grace. Quite literally, God foreknows everything actual and possible. In this way, Molinism says God's knowl-

edge precedes God's decrees. Cf. William Lane Craig, "Middle Knowledge, Truth-Makers, and the Grounding Objection." *Faith and Philosophy* 18 (2001): 337-52. Cf. also William Lane Craig, *Divine Foreknowledge and Human Freedom* (New York: J. J. Brill, 1991), 237-278. Molinism, which developed within the Society of Jesus in the late 16th and early 17th centuries, is very different from the Boethian view. Boethius said God literally has no foreknowledge, only knowledge. Foreknowledge is an anthropomorphism at best, but if taken literally, Boethius maintained that foreknowledge entails determinism. Cf. Boethius, *The Consolation of Philosophy*, 86. In fairness to Craig, he does not really fit into the category of those who advocate a theology of limited omniscience. However, he assumes with its proponents that God must be totally temporal if temporal events are real to God. Hence he assumes that God became temporal after the event of creation of space and time. In the final analysis, I do not believe that Craig can really escape the charge of determinism because of his literal interpretation of foreknowledge. Cf. William Hasker, "Anti-Molinism Is Undefeated," *Faith and Philosophy* 17.1 (January 2000): 126-131.

147. John Polkinghorne, *Faith, Science & Understanding* (New Haven: Yale University Press, 2000, 151.

148. Ibid., 150.

149. Peacocke, *Theology for a Scientific Age* (Minneapolis: Fortress Press, 1993), 129.

150. John Polkinghorne, *Scientists as Theologians, A Comparison of the Writings of Ian Barbour, Arthur Peacocke & John Polkinghorne* (London: SPCK, 1996).

151. Peacocke, *Theology for a Scientific Age*, 131, 132.

152. Ibid., 132

153. Ibid., 130.

154. Willem B. Drees, "A Case Against Temporal Critical Realism? Consequences of Quantum Cosmology for Theology," *Quantum Cosmology and The Laws of Nature*, ed. R. J. Russell, Nancey Murphy, and C. J. Isham (University of Notre Dame Press, 1996), 331.

155. Ibid., 332.

156. Roger Penrose, *Shadows of the Mind*, 389.

157. Sartori, *Understanding Relativity*, 82.

158. Cf. John Polkinghorne, *Faith, Science & Understanding*, 132ff.

159. Huw Price, *Time's Arrow and Archimedes' Point* (New York: Oxford University Press, 1996) offers a defense of the block view of time.

160. Cited in Max Jammer, *Einstein and Religion* (Princeton, NJ: Princeton University Press, 1999), 161.

161. Cf. *Albert Einstein: Philosopher-Scientist*, ed. Paul Arthur Schilpp (New York: Tudor Publishing Co, 1951, 103. Max Jammer, *Einstein and Religion*, 138-139.

162. Roger Penrose, *Shadows of the Mind*, 384.

163. Roger Penrose, *The Emperor's New Mind*, 303-304.

164. *Albert Einstein: Philosopher-Scientist*, 103.

165. Cf. Ian G. Barbour, "Bohm and Process Philosophy: A Response to Griffin and Cobb," *Physics and the Ultimate Significance of Time,* ed. David. R. Griffin (Albany: State University of New York Press, 1986), 168; cf. Čapek, "Relativity and the Status of Becoming," *Foundations of Physics* 5.4 (December 1975): 607-617.

166. Brian Leftow, "Eternity and Simultaneity," *Faith and Philosophy* 8 (1991): 165. Cf. Brian Leftow, *Time and Eternity,* 165-168.

167. Hegel, *The Encyclopaedia Logic,* 227.

168. Cf. Barth, *Church Dogmatics,* 1.2.45-48. Clark Pinnock is certainly on target to criticize Augustine for his notion of absolute predestination that entails the idea that the future is not open and that God is unaffected by what goes on in the world. However, he merely identifies Augustine with traditional Christian theism, as if there has not been a more mainstream view of things stemming from the Early Greek Fathers who affirmed human freedom. Cf. Pinnock, "Between Classical and Process Theism," *Process Theology,* ed. Ronald H. Nash (Grand Rapids: Baker Book House, 1987), 314.

169. W. Norris Clarke, "Christian Theism and Whiteheadian Process Theology," *Process Theology,* 234-244.

170. Michael Polanyi, *Personal Knowledge* (University of Chicago Press, 1958), 312.

171. Eleonore Stump and Norman Kretzmann have also shown that Boethius' idea of eternity entailed the notion of duration of a different kind than "persistence *through time.*" It is infinite duration. Cf. Eleonore Stump and Norman Kretzmann, "Eternity," *The Journal of Philosophy* 78.8 (August 1981): 446. In response to Nelson Pike's *God and Time,* they offered a convincing defense of a Boethian notion of eternity, showing that relativity theory can be used to illustrate the intelligibility of all times being already present with God without sacrificing the meaning of contingency. Ibid., 437ff. Some of their critics miss the persuasive nature of their arguments because of not accepting Einsteinian space-time relativity. Cf. Padgett, "The Special Theory of Relativity and Theories of Divine Eternity," *International Philosophical Quarterly* 333.2.130 (June 1993): 221

172. Whitehead, *Modes of Thought* (New York: Macmillan Co., 1938) 177-178.

173. *Modes of Thought,* 177.

174. Čapek, *The Philosophical Impact of Contemporary Physics,* xv.

175. Ibid., xiv.

176. Sartori, *Understanding Relativity,* xi.

177. Čapek, *The Philosophical Impact of Contemporary Physics,* 398.

178. Ibid., 40.

179. Kip S. Thorne, *Black Holes and Time Warps, Einstein's Outrageous Legacy* (New York: W. W. Norton, 1994), 78.

180. Penrose, *The Emperor's New Mind,* 228.

181. Roger Penrose, *Shadows of the Mind,* 257; Penrose, *The Emperor's New*

Mind, 237.

182. Heisenberg, *Physics and Philosophy*, 30ff.

183. Penrose, *Shadows of the Mind*, 309; Penrose, *The Emperor's New Mind*, 226-227.

184. Penrose, *The Emperor's Mind*, 235.

185. Ibid., 231ff.

186. Heisenberg, *Physics and Philosophy*, 44-58.

187. Ibid., 42-43. Penrose, *The Emperor's New Mind*, 248-250, 280.

188. Niels Bohr, "Discussion with Einstein on Epistemological Problems in Atomic Physics," *Albert Einstein: Scientist-Philosopher*, 218; cf Heisenberg, *Physics and Philosophy*, 17.

189. Niels Bohr, "Discussion with Einstein on Epistemological Problems in Atomic Physics," *Albert Einstein: Scientist-Philosopher*, 218

190. F. S. C. Northrhop, "Introduction," to Werner Heisenberg, *Physics and Philosophy*, 4ff.

191. Stephen Hawking, *A Brief History of Time*, 56.

192. Heisenberg, *Physics and Philosophy*, 146.

193. Penrose, *The Emperor's New Mind*, 231-57.

194. Heisenberg, *Physics and Philosophy*, 86.

195. Roger Penrose, *Shadows of the Mind*, 51.

196. Ibid., 52.

197. Thorne, *Black Holes and Time Warps*, 78ff.

198. Kaku, *Hyperspace*, 243. Cf. Hawking, *Brief History of Time*, 143-153.

199. Gott, *Time Travel in Einstein's Universe*, 59.

200. Ibid., 33

201. Kaku, *Hyperspace*, vii-viii, 16ff.

202. Cf. Stephen Hawking and Roger Penrose, *The Nature of Space and Time*, 101. Cf. the interview with Hawking in the Errol Morris film documentary,

203. Kaku, Hyperspace, 20.

204. Ibid, 27.

205. Kaku, Hyperspace, 243.

206. For a helpful discussion on the distinction between God's eternal present and the temporal present, cf. Eleonore Stump and Norman Kretzmann, "Eternity," *The Journal of Philosophy* 78.8 (August 1981): 434ff.

207. Some interpret Rev. 10:6 to mean "there will be more delay." Cf. Marvin Vincent, *Word Studies in the New Testament* (New York: Scribner, 1887), 2:516. Others take the literal translation, "Time will be no more," to be its true meaning. Pannenberg, *Systematic Theology* 2:95, 3:529n.12; Karl Barth, *Church Dogmatics* 1.2.49. Certainly the context would favor a literal interpretation: "And the angel whom I saw standing on sea and land lifted up his right hand to heaven and swore by him who lives for ever and ever, who created heaven and what is in it, the earth and what is in it, and the sea and what is in it, that time will be no more." The contrast is between God who is eternal and creation,

which is temporal. Thomas Aquinas interpreted Rev. 10:6 to mean the world will disappear and everything temporal will no longer exists, following the judgment. There will then be a new world that will be created incorruptible just as our bodies will be. Aquinas, *Summa Contra Gentiles* 4:97, cited by Pannenberg, *Systematic Theology* 3:529. Pannenberg shows that the sequences of time are not an essential part of human finitude, and hence in eternity we will still be finite. *Systematic Theology* 2:95.

208. A Boethian idea of eternity implies many interesting clarifications for other Christian beliefs, such as prayer and the sacraments. One of the controversial notions about the Lord's Supper is whether or not Christ is really physically present. Bishop Ole E. Borgen has argued that John Wesley believed that in the sacrament of Holy Communion the believer really participates in the death-resurrection of Jesus through the power of the Holy Spirit who takes us back in time to the original, once-for-all saving event. Borgen explains that this is not a mere memorial or memory, but a real happening. So quite literally, Christ is present at the Lord's Table because the temporal past is always in God's eternal present. Borgen, *John Wesley on the Sacraments* (Grand Rapids: Francis Asbury Press of Zondervan Publishing House, 1985), 92. The interactive relationship between eternity and time also clarifies the nature of Christian devotion. The risen Lord, who is one with the earthly Jesus, was already offering justifying faith to Abraham in the early stages of salvation history (Roman 4:16-25). Today believers have already been "raised with Christ" and participate in the life that "is hid with Christ in God" (Col. 3:1), and yet they look forward to the completion of their journey through time in the eschatological future when Christ "appears" and they "will appear with him in glory" (Col. 3:1-4). This understanding of eternity as the transcendent unity of all times is the basis for affirming the continuity of salvation history throughout the extent of time. Instead of the temporal present being caused by the inevitable force of past events, God's eternal present is identical with the unbounded future of all times and hence is the basis for meaning in the temporal present.

209. Barth, *Church Dogmatics*, 2.1.609.

210. Ándre LaCocque and Paul Ricoueur, *Thinking Biblically* (University of Chicago Press, 1998), 339-40.

211. "Editor's Introduction," in Boethius, *The Consolation of Philosophy*, ed. and trans. William Anderson (Corbondale, Illinois: Southern Illinois University Press, 1963), 10. Cf. Sorabji, Time, Creation, and the Continuum, 256.

212. This point has been persuasively argued by Charles Gutenson, "Time, Eternity, and Personal Identity–The Implications of Trinitarian Theology." *What about the Soul? Neuroscience and Christian Anthropology*, ed. Joel B. Green (Nashville: Abingdon, 2004).

A Selected Bibliography

Barth, Karl. *Church Dogmatics.* Edited by G. W. Bromiley and T. F. Torrance. Translated by G. W. Bromiley. 5 volumes. Edinburgh: T. & T. Clark, 1969.
———. *Protestant Thought: From Rousseau to Ritschl.* Translated by Rian Cozens. New York: Harper and Row Publishers, 1959.
———.*The Theology of Schleiermacher,* edited by Dietrich Ritschl. Translated by Geoffrey W. Bromiley. Grand Rapids: Wm. B. Eerdmans, 1982.
Bartsch, Hans Werner, ed. *Kerygma and Myth.* Translated by R. H. Fuller. London: S.C.K., 1962
Beilby, James K. and Paul R. Eddy. *Divine Foreknowledge: Four Views.* Downers Grove, Ill.: InterVarsity Press, 2001.
Bernstein, Richard J. *Beyond Objectivism and Relativism: Science, Hermeneutics, and Praxis.* Oxford: Basic Blackwell, 1983
Boethius. *The Consolation of Philosophy.* Edited and translated by William Anderson. Carbondale : Southern Illinois University Press, 1963.
Braaten, Carl. *History and Hermeneutics.* Philadelphia: The Westminster Press, 1966.
Braaten, Carl and Philip Clayton, eds. *The Theology of Wolfhart Pannenberg.* Minneapolis: Augsburg Publishing House, 1988.
Bradshaw, Timothy. *Trinity and Ontology A Comparative Study of the Theologies off Karl Barth and Wolfhart Pannenberg.* Lewiston, New York: Edward Mullen Press, 1988.
Bultmann, Rudolf. *History and Eschatology.* Edinburgh: The University Press, 1957.
———. *The History of the Synoptic Tradition.* Trans. John Marsh. Oxford: Blackwell, 1963
Burson, Scott and Jerry Walls. *C. S. Lewis & Francis Schaeffer.* Downers Grove, Ill.: InterVarsity Press, 1998.
Butterfield, Herbert. *The Origins of Modern Science.* New York: Macmillan Company, 1959.
Ĉapek, Miliĉ. *The Philosophical Impact of Contemporary Physics.* New York: D. Van Nostrand Company, Inc, 1961.
Cassirer, Ernst. *The Philosophy of the Enlightenment.* Trans. Fritz C. A. Koelin and

James Pettegrove. Princeton: Princeton University Press, 1951.

Cassirer, H. W. *Kant's First Critique.* London: George Allen and Unwin Ltd., 1954.

Cobb, Jr., John. *God and the World.* Philadelphia: Westminster Press, 1976.

Collingwood, R. G. *The Idea of History.* New York: Oxford University Press, 1976.

Craig, William Lane. *Divine Foreknowledge and Human Freedom.* New York: J. J. Brill, 1991.

Cullmann, Oscar. *Salvation in History.* Translated by Sidney G. Sowers. London: SCM Press, Ltd., 1967.

———. *Christ and Time.* Translated by Floyd V. Wilson. London: SCM Press, 1962.

Drees, Willem B. "A Case Against Temporal Critical Realism? Consequences of Quantum Cosmology for Theology," *Quantum Cosmology and The Laws of Nature.* Edited by R. J. Russell, Nancey Murphy, and C. J. Isham. University of Notre Dame Press, 1996.

———. *Creation From Nothing Until Now* (New York: Routledge, 2002).

Ebeling, Gerhard. *Theology and Proclamation: A Discussion with Rudolf Bultmann.* Translated by. John Riches. London: Collins, 1966.

———. *Word and Faith.* Translated by James W. Leitch. Philadelphia: Fortress Press, 1963.

Fackenheim, Emil. *The Religious Dimension in Hegel's Thought.* Bloomington: Indiana University Press, 1967.

Henri Frankfort, Mrs. H. A. Frankfort, John A. Wilson, and Thorkild Jacobsen, *Before Philosophy.* Baltimore, Md.: Penguin Books, 1964.

Funk, Robert W. *Honest to Jesus: Jesus For A New Millennium.* San Francisco, CA: HarperSanFrancisco, 1996.

———, ed. *The Five Gospels, The Search For The Authentic Words of Jesus.* New translation and commentary by Robert W. Funk, Roy W. Hoover, and the Jesus Seminar. San Francisco, Calif.: HarperSanFrancisco, 1997.

Gardavsky, Vitezslave. *God is Not Yet Dead.* Translated by Vivenne Menkes. Baltimore: Penguin, 1973.

Gardiner, Patrick, ed. *Theories of History.* New York: The Fress Press, 1960.

Gay, Peter. ed. *The Enlightenment, A Comprehensive Anthology.* New York: Simon and Schuster, 1973.

Gazzaniga, Michael S. "The Split Brain in Man," *The Nature of Human Consciousness.* Edited by Robert E. Ornstein. San Francisco: W. H. Freeman and Company, 1973.

Gill, Jerry. *The Possibility of Religious Knowledge.* Grand Rapids, Mich.: Wm. B. Eerdmans Publishing Company, 1975.

———. *The Tacit Mode, Michael Polanyi's Postmodern Philosophy.* Albany: State University of New York Press, 2000.

Gilson, Etienne. *God and Philosophy.* New Haven: Yale University Press, 1941.

———. *History of Christian Philosophy in the Middle Ages.* New York: Random House, 1955.

Gogarten, Friedrich. *Demythologizing and History.* Translated by Neville Horton Smith. New York: Scribner, 1955.

Gott III, J. Richard. *Time Travel in Einstein's Universe.* New York: Houghton Mifflin Co., 2001.

Griffin, David R., ed. *Physics and the Ultimate Significance of Time.* Albany: State University of New York Press, 1986.

Hawking, Stephen and Roger Penrose. *The Nature of Space and Time.* Princeton: Princeton University Press, 1996.

Hegel, *Encyclopaedia Logic.* Translated by T. F. Garets, W. A. Suchting, and H. S. Harris. Indianapolis: Hackett Publishing Company, 1991.

———. *Lectures on the Philosophy of Religion.* One volume edition. Edited by Peter C. Hodgson. Translated by R. F. Brown, C. Hodgson, and J. M. Stewart. Berkeley: University of California Press, 1988.

———. *Reason in History,* Translated with an introduction by Robert S. Hartman. Indianapolis: The Bobbs-Merrill Company, 1953.

———. *Science of Logic.* Translated by W. H. Johnston and L. G. Struthers with an introductory preface by Viscount Haldane. London: George Allen and Unwin Ltd., 1929.

Heidegger, *Being and Time.* Translated by John Macquarrie and Edward Robinson. London: SCM Press Ltd., 1962.

———. *Essays in Metaphysics: Identity and Difference.* Translated by Kurt F. Leidecker. New York: Philosophical Library Inc. 1960.

———. *Introduction to Metaphysics.* Translated by Ralph Manheim. London: Oxford University Press, 1959.

Heisenberg, Werner. *Physics and Philosophy: The Revolution in Modern Science.* London: George Allen and Unwin, 1959.

Herder, Johann Goffried. *Against Pure Reason, Writings on Religion, Language, and History.* Translated and edited with an introduction by Marcia Bunge. Minneapolis: Fortress Press, 1993.

———.*God, Some Conversations.* Translated with a critical introduction and notes by Frederick H. Burkhardt. New York: Hafner Publishing Company, 1949.

Harris, H. S. *Hegel's Development, Toward the Sunlight 1770-1801.* Oxford: Clarendon Press, 1972.

Hume, David. *An Inquiry Concerning Human Understanding.* Edited with an introduction by Charles W. Hendel. Indianapolis: Bobbs-Merrill, Inc., 1955.

Jammer, Max. *Einstein and Religion.* Princeton: Princeton University Press, 1999.

Jeeves, Malcolm. *Mind Fields, Reflections on the Science of Mind and Brain.* Grand Rapids, Mich.: Baker Books. 1993.

Jepsen, Alfred. "The Scientific Study of the Old Testament," *Essays on Old Testament Interpretation.* Edited by Claus Westermann. Translated by John Bright. London: SCM Ltd., 1963.

Jonas, Hans. *The Gnostic Religion.* Second edition, revised, 1967.

Jüngel, Eberhard. *God as the Mystery of the World.* Translated by Darrell L. Guder. Grand Rapids, Mich.: Wm. B. Eerdmans Publishing Co., 1983.

Kähler, Martin. *The So-called Historical Jesus and the Historic, Biblical Christ.* Translated with an introduction by Carl Braaten Philadelphia: Fortress Press, 1964.

Kaku, Michio. *Hyperspace.* New York: Doubleday, 1994.

Kant, Immanuel. *Religion within the Limits of Reason Alone.* Translated by Theodore M. Greene and Hoyt H. Hudson. New York: Harper Torchbooks, 1960.

———. *Prolegomena to any Future Metaphysics.* Translated with an introduction by Lewis White Black. Indianapolis: The Bobbs-Merrill Company, Inc., 1950.

———. *Critique of Pure Reason.* Translated by Norman Kemp Smith. London: Macmillan and Co., Ltd., 1929.

Kaufmann, Walter. *Hegel: A Reinterpretation.* Notre Dame, Indiana: University of Notre Dame Press, 1978.

Kelly, J. N. D. *Early Christian Doctrines.* Second edition. New York: Harper & Row, Publishers, 1960.

Kierkegaard, Søren. *Philosophical Fragments.* Translated by David F. Swenson and Niels Thustrup. Princeton: Princeton University Press, 1962

———. *A Concluding Unscientific Postscript.* Translated by David F. Swenson and Walter Lowrie. Princeton: Princeton University Press, 1941.

———. *Philosophical Fragments,* Translated by David F. Swenson and Niels Thustrup. Princeton: Princeton University Press, 1962.

———. Kierkegaard, *Sickness Unto Death.* Translated by Walter Lowrie. Princeton: Princeton University Press, 1941.

LaCocque, Ándre and Paul Ricoueur, *Thinking Biblically.* University of Chicago Press, 1998.

Leftow, Brian. *Time and Eternity.* Ithaca, New York: Cornell University, 1991.

Lauer, Quentin. *Hegel's Concept of God.* Albany: State University of New York Press, 1982.

Leibniz, G. W. *Theodicy.* Edited with an introduction by Austin Farrer. Translated by E.M. Huggard. London: Routledge & Kegan, Ltd., 1951.

———. *New Essays in Human Understanding.* Translated by Peter Remnant and Jonathan Bennett. Second edition. Cambridge, England: Cambridge University Press, 1996.

Lessing, Ephraim. *Lessing's Theological Writings.* Translated with an introductory essay by Henry Chadwick. London: Adam and Charles Black, 1956.

Lowrie, Walter. *A Short Life of Søren Kierkegaard.* New Jersey: Princeton University Press, 1942.

Mackie, J. L. *The Miracle of Theism.* New York: Oxford University Press, 1982.

Mascall, E. L. *Importance of Being Human.* New York: Columbia University Press, 1958.

———. *He Who Is.* Archon Books, 1970.

May, Gerhard. *Creatio Ex Nihilo, The Doctrine of "Creation out of Nothing" in Early Christian Thought.* Edinburgh: T. T. Clark, 1994.

McIntyre, John. *The Christian Doctrine of History.* Grand Rapids: Wm. B.

Eerdmans, 1957.

———. *The Shape of Christology*. Philadelphia: Westminster Press, 1998.

———. *The Shape of Pneumatology*. Edinburgh: T. & T. Clark, 1997.

———. *The Shape of Soteriology*. Edinburgh: T & T Clark, 1995.

Michalson, Carl. *Worldly Theology*. New York: Charles Scribner's Sons, 1967.

Moltmann, Jürgen. *The Spirit of Life*. Translated by Margaret Kohl. Minneapolis: Fortress Press, 1992.

———. *History and the Triune God*. Translated by John Bowdan. New York: Crossroad Publishing Company, 1991.

———. *Theology of Hope*. Translated by James W. Leitch. New York: Harper & Row, 1965.

———. *Trinity and The Kingdom*. Translated by Margaret Kohl. San Francisco: Harper and Row, 1981.

Momigliano, Arnaldo. "Time in Ancient Historiography," *History and the Concept of Time*. Middletown, Conn: Wesleyan University Press, 1966.

Mostert, Christiaan, *God and the Future. Wolfhart Pannenberg's Eschatological Doctrine of God*. Edinburgh: T & T Clark, 2002.

Nash, Ronald. *Process Theology*. Grand Rapids: Baker Book House, 1987.

Newman, Carey C. *Jesus & The Restoration of Israel, A Critical Assessment of N. T. Wright's Jesus and The Victory of God*. Downers Grove, ILL: InterVarsity Press, 1999.

Niebuhr, Reinhold, *The Nature and Destiny of Man*. 2 volumes. New York: Charles Scribner's Sons, 1964.

Pannenberg, Wolfhart. *Systematic Theology*. Translated by Geoffrey W. Bromiley. 3 volumes. Grand Rapids: Eerdmans, 1991.

———. *Metaphysics and The Idea of God*. Translated by Philip Clayton. Grand Rapids: Wm. B. Eerdmans, 1990.

———. *The Idea of God and Human Freedom*. Translated by R. A. Wilson. Philadelphia: Westminster Press, 1973.

———. *Theology and the Kingdom of God*. Edited by Richard J. Neuhaus. Philadelphia: Westminster Press, 1969.

———. *Jesus–God and Man*. Translated by Lewis L. Wilkins and Duane A. Priebe. Philadelphia: Westminster Press, 1977.

———. ed. *Revelation As History*. Translated by David Granskou. London: The Macmillan Publishing Co., 1969.

———. *What is Man?* Trans Duane A. Priebe. Philadelphia: Fortress Press, 1970.

———. *Anthopology in Theological Perspective*. Translated by Matthew J. O'Connell. Philadelphia: Westminster, 1985.

———. *Basic Questions in Theology: Collected Essays*. Translated by George H. Kehm. 2 volumes. Philadelphia: Fortress Press, 1983.

Peacocke, Arthur. *Theology for a Scientific Age*. Minneapolis: Fortress Press, 1993.

Penrose, Roger. *Emperor's New Mind, Concerning Computers, Minds, and the Laws of Physics*. New York: Oxford University Press, 1989.

———. *Shadows of the Mind*. Oxford: Oxford University Press, 1994.

Pike, Nelson. *God and Timelessness*. New York: Schocken Books, 1970.

Pinnock, Clark, ed. *The Openness of Being*. Downers Grove, Illinois: InterVarsity Press, 1994.

Polanyi, Michael. *Personal Knowledge*. Chicago: University of Chicago Press, 1958.

Polkinghorne, John. *Faith, Science & Understanding*. New Haven: Yale University Press, 2000.

Putnam, Hilary. "Time and Physical Geometry," *Journal of Philosophy* 64, no. 8, (April 27, 1967): 240-47.

Reardon, Bernard M. G. *Hegel's Philosophy of Religion*. London: The MacMillan Press, Ltd., 1977.

Ricoeur, Paul. *Essays on Biblical Interpretation*. Edited by Lewis S. Mudge. Philadelphia: Fortress Press, 1980.

Robinson, James M. and John B. Cobb, Jr., eds. *New Hermeneutic*. New York: Harper & Row, 1964.

Rorty, Richard. *Philosophy and the Mirror of Nature*. Princeton: Princeton University Press, 1979.

Sartori, Leo. *Understanding Relativity, A Simplified Approach to Einstein's Theories*. Berkeley: University of Califiornia Press, 1996.

Schilpp, Paul Arthur, ed. *Albert Einstein: Philosopher-Scientists*. New York: Tudor Publishing Co, 1951

Schleiermacher, Friedrich. *The Christian Faith*. Edited by H. R. Mackintosh and J. S. Stewart. New York: Harper & Row, 1963.

Sheehan, Thomas "Heidegger and the Nazis," *New York Review of Books* 16 (June 1988): 38-47.

Shortt, C. De Lisle. *The Influence of Philosophy on The Mind of Tertullian*. London: Elliot Stock Publisher, 1933.

Smart, James. *The Divided Mind of Modern Theology*. Philadelphia: The Westminster Press, 1967.

Smoot, George and Keay Davidson. *Wrinkles in Time*. New York: William Morrow and Company, Inc., 1993.

Solomon, Robert. *In the Spirit of Hegel*. New York: Oxford University Press, 1983.

Sorabji, Richard. *Time, Creation, and the Continuum*. Ithaca, NY: Cornell University Press, 1983.

Sperry, Roger. "Some Effects of Disconnecting the Central Hemispheres," *Science* 217, no. 24 (September, 1982),1223-1226;

Springer, Sally and George Deutsch, *Left Brain, Right Brain*. Revised edition. New York: W. H. Freeman and Co., 1985.

Strauss, David F. *The Life of Jesus Critically Examined*. Fourth edition. Translated by George Eliot. London: Swan Sonnenschein and Company, 1906.

Stump, Eleonore and Norman Kretzmann, "Eternity," *The Journal of Philosophy* 78, no. 8 (August 1981): 444-447.

Swinburne, Richard *The Coherence of Theism*. Revised edition. Oxford: Clarendon Press, 1993.

Taylor, A. E. *Socrates.* New York: Doubleday, 1953.

Tillich, Paul. *Courage to Be.* New Haven: Yale University Press, 1952.

———. *History of Christian Thought,* ed. Carl E. Braaten. New York: Harper and Row, 1967.

Troeltsch, Ernst. *Die Bedeutung der Geschichtlichkeit Jesu für den Glauben.* Tubingen: J.C.B. Mohr, 1911.

———. "Historiography," *Encyclopedia of Religion and Ethics.* Edited by James Hastings, 1914.

———. "Historische und dogmatische Methode in der Theologie," *Gesammelte Schriften.* Tübingen: J. C. B. Mohr, 1913.

Thorne, Kip S. *Black Holes and Time Warps, Einstein's Outrageous Legacy.* New York: W. W. Norton, 1994.

Toews, John Edward. *Hegelianism, The Path Toward Dialectical Humanism 1805-1841.* New York: Cambridge University Press, 1980.

von Rad, Gerhard. *The Problem of the Hexateuch.* Translated by E. Dickens. New York: McGraw Hill, 1966.

Whitehead, A. N. *Modes of Thought.* New York: Macmillan Co., 1938.

———. *Science and the Modern World.* New York: The Macmillan Company, 1954.

Whittaker, Thomas. *The Neo-Platonists, A Study in the History of Hellenism.* Second edition. Freeport, NY: Books for Libraries Press, 1970.

Wilkinson, David. *God, the Big Bang, and Stephen Hawking.* Crowborough, East Sussex: Monarch, 1996.

Wood, Laurence W. "Recent Brain Research and the Mind-Body Dilemma," *The Best in Theology.* Edited by James I. Packer and Paul Fromer. Carol Stream, Illinois: Christianity Today, Inc, 1987.

Index

Feuerbach, Ludwig 114, 116, 131, 236–7, 240–242, 245, 253, 255–6, 2–8, 298
Fichte, Johann 108, 116, 120, 241–2, 255, 268
Findlay, J. N. 114, 121
FitzGerald-Lorentz contraction theory 280
foreknowledge vi, 263–7, 271–3, 275, 286, 297, 299–300, 301, 304–305
Fosdick, Harry Emerson 172, 177
foundationalism 59, 166
Frankfort, Henri 3, 15
Frankfort, Mrs. H. A. 3, 15

G
Gilson, Etienne 13–14, 18, 30, 58, 67
gnosticism 19, 23, 128, 135, 145, 147, 200, 213, 303
    distrust toward the historical foundation of Christian faith 130
God
    personal reality of God 117
    Creator *ex nihilo* 13, 15, 18, 19, 249, 270, 299
    Self-knowing mind 13, 25, 45
    Unmoved Mover 13, 25, 45
    Power of the unbounded future, 243, 245
    Trinity and personhood 239–240
    Supernatural, 233–237
    an Individual? 267
    gods as immanent in nature 5
Gott, J. Richard 291
gravity 52, 279–280
    curvature of space 279–280, 295, 302
Greek philosophy xi, 1, 3, 5, 8–9, 14–15, 23, 27–29, 31, 33, 35, 40–41, 44, 47, 81, 83, 117, 224, 254, 260, 261
    Greco-Roman philosophy 14, 27, 39, 214
Gregory of Nyssa 28, 40, 101, 269–270, 276, 299, 301

H
Haldane, Viscount 15, 114
Hawking, Stephen 289, 291, 301–302, 307
Hegel iv, 3, 15, 69, 90, 103–158, 177, 236, 238–240, 243
    categories of logic 106
    dialectical 107
    misinterpreted 109
    historical and relational understanding of reality 117
    left-wing 114, 115, 116, 131, 240, 309
    one divine subject as opposed to one divine substance 239
    Reason" governs world history 104
    right-wing 114, 126, 131, 309

Q
quantum mechanics 213

R
rationalism 58, 65, 71–73, 77, 84, 93, 94, 105, 112, 117, 145, 166, 242, 250–1
realism 26, 36, 145, 235, 245, 259, 261, 285, 303, 305
reason and history iv, 63, 82, 110–111, 132
reconciliation 25, 76, 82, 108, 110, 111, 142, 148, 177, 211, 239, 274, 300
redemption 37, 39, 87, 293
revelation ix, xii, 1, 6–8, 10, 14–15, 24, 27, 29, 31, 40–41, 44, 46–48, 51, 53–54,
    58, 61, 64, 73, 75, 78–79, 82–83, 86, 96–98, 110, 113, 118, 129, 132, 138,
    144, 157, 174, 176-8, 186, 193, 195–203, 206–208, 220, 224, 228-9,
    231–2, 236–7, 239–240, 245, 248–9, 252, 256, 294–5
    revelation in history 24, 58, 206, 228
Ricoeur, Paul 118, 123, 294
Ritschl, Albrecht 171

S
salvation history 1, 19, 83–85, 87, 95, 101, 145, 159, 171, 200, 209, 211, 225,
    244, 259–261, 263–264, 274, 293, 303, 308
Sartre, Jean-Paul 133
scandal of particularity 224–5
Schelling 120, 126, 146–147
schizoid position 125–130
    of Modern Thought 125
Schleiermacher 91, 111–114, 121–2, 131, 148, 172–3, 193, 202, 234, 240, 250,
    258
secular naturalism 251
Sheldon, Charles 171
skepticism iv, 57, 59–62, 78, 84–85, 88, 103–105, 134, 138, 166, 206–207, 213,
    228
Socrates 23-5, 30, 45, 50, 55, 58-9, 119, 122, 127, 146, 153, 155-7, 166, 329
Solomon, Robert 114, 122
space vi, 53, 94–95, 101, 146-7, 161, 213, 244, 253, 259–264, 267–270,
    277–88, 290–296, 301–307
Spinoza 77-80, 82-5, 91, 93, 98, 104, 129, 253-4, 298
Stoicism 21–24, 26, 30, 32
subject–object 4, 5, 6, 8, 10, 21 25–27, 29–31, 40, 43, 71, 65, 107, 111, 118, 126,
    132-3, 137, 152-5, 163, 165, 166, 177, 263, 269
substance 22, 32–33, 36–38, 41, 45–47, 66, 76, 80, 85, 95, 106, 115, 239–240,
    280
    primary substance 36–37
    secondary substance 36–37
substantialism 1, 32–33, 41, 45–47, 52, 85

CPSIA information can be obtained at www.ICGtesting.com
Printed in the USA
BVOW05s1608100915

417279BV00001B/22/P